W9-DGT-869

Discard

DISASTER CAPITALISM

DISASTER CAPITALISM

MAKING A KILLING OUT OF CATASTROPHE

ANTONY LOEWENSTEIN

V

VERSO
London • New York

First published by Verso 2015
© Antony Loewenstein 2015

1 3 5 7 9 10 8 6 4 2

Verso
UK: 6 Meard Street, London W1F 0EG
US: 20 Jay Street, Suite 1010, Brooklyn, NY 11201
www.versobooks.com

Verso is the imprint of New Left Books

ISBN-13: 978-1-78478-115-6 (HC)
eISBN-13: 978-1-78478-116-3 (US)
eISBN-13: 978-1-78478-117-0 (UK)

British Library Cataloguing in Publication Data
A catalogue record for this book is available from the British Library

Library of Congress Cataloging-in-Publication Data
A catalog record for this book is available from the Library of Congress

Typeset in Fournier by MJ & N Gavan, Truro, Cornwall
Printed and bound by
CPI Group (UK) Ltd, Croydon, CR0 YY

For the dreamers who imagine a better world

Contents

Introduction

The Mad Max Economy

Sometimes we win the skirmishes, but the war continues.
Rebecca Solnit, 2011

Back in 1972 Jørgen Randers, today the professor of climate strategy at the Norwegian Business School, published a book called *The Limits to Growth*. He warned of the devastating impact of population and economic growth on a world of limited resources. Revisiting that prognosis in a 2004 essay, he found that his predictions were correct and that global leaders had been much remiss in ignoring the urgent need to battle unsustainable development.

Randers' key argument was a challenge to the inherent rules of capitalism. By 2015, he was pessimistic that the current financial order was capable of—or even had any interest in—reducing the devastating effects of climate change. "It is cost-effective to postpone global climate action," he wrote.

It is profitable to let the world go to hell. I believe that the tyranny of the short term will prevail over the decades to come. As a result, a number of long-term problems will not be solved, even if they could have been, and even as they cause gradually increasing difficulties for all voters.[1]

To encourage a country such as Norway to tax every citizen, his suggested solution was for people to pay an extra 250 euros every year for a generation, thereby drastically cutting greenhouse gases and providing an example to other industrialized nations. The idea never got off the ground.

"The capitalist system does not help," Randers explained.

Capitalism is carefully designed to allocate capital to the most profitable projects. And this is exactly what we don't need today. We need investments into more expensive wind and solar power, not into cheap coal and gas. The capitalistic market won't do this on its own. It needs different frame conditions—alternative prices or new regulation.

Although Randers pushed the worrying idea of "enlightened dictatorship"—"for a limited time period in critical policy areas"—his thesis strikes at the heart of why wealth is concentrated in so few hands in today's world: there is little incentive to advocate for a more equitable planet. The market system guarantees unfairness and rewards greed.

Such debates are starting to emerge even among the class who most benefits from such inequality. During the annual conference in Davos, Switzerland, in 2015, where the world's business and political leaders gather to congratulate themselves, some sessions concluded that inequality was a serious problem facing the globe, and participants were pessimistic about solving it.

Such talk was a start, but hardly enough when the dictator Abdel Fattah al-Sisi, the Egyptian president—a man responsible for the death of thousands of his own people—was warmly welcomed in Davos and allowed to pontificate about his vision for "sustainable development." Human rights and economic freedom must not be mutually exclusive concepts.

The figures speak for themselves. The share of wealth in the US owned by its richest 0.01 percent has quadrupled since the eve of the Reagan Revolution.[2] The top 1 percent of the world's population owns 46 percent of all global assets. US cuts in food stamps have left the nation's largest food bank, in New York, struggling to cope with demand. Around 16.5 percent of the state's population requires emergency food assistance. In 2013, roughly 14 percent of the country's population "lacked access to enough food for an active, healthy life for all household members," according to the US Department of Agriculture—a 30 percent increase since 2007.[3] The US middle class, long viewed as the globe's most successful, now suffers growing income inequality. A crucial factor in this decline has been the failure of educational attainment to progress as successfully as in other industrialized states.[4]

The system is rigged. During the global financial crisis, Bank of America nearly crashed. One of the largest financial institutions in the nation, it was nevertheless granted £45 billion by President Barack Obama to prevent its collapse. Since then, *Rolling Stone* writer Matt Taibbi explains,

> the Obama administration has looked the other way as the bank committed an astonishing variety of crimes ... ripp[ing] off almost everyone with whom it has a significant business relationship, cheating investors, insurers, depositors, homeowners, shareholders, pensioners and taxpayers. It brought tens of thousands of Americans to foreclosure court using bogus, 'robo-signed' evidence—a type of mass perjury that it helped pioneer. It hawked worthless mortgages to dozens of unions and state pension funds, draining them of hundreds of millions in value.[5]

This is the modern definition of capitalism. As Taibbi told those attending an Occupy Wall Street day of action in 2012, "this gigantic financial institution is the ultimate symbol of a new kind of corruption at the highest levels of American society: a tendency to marry the near-limitless power of the federal government with increasingly concentrated, increasingly unaccountable private financial interests."[6] Wall Street bankers were happy. The sum of all executive bonuses in 2014, averaging roughly $173,000 each, came to around double the earnings of all Americans working full-time on the minimum wage.[7]

It is an ideology that thrives despite guaranteeing social disharmony. The US model of reducing the role of government while increasing the influence of largely private power has never been so rapacious, though the problem is global. For-profit colleges burden students with huge debts and worthless credentials while receiving federal student aid. Goldman Sachs, a firm with a large measure of responsibility for the economic meltdown in 2008, now invests in social-impact bonds—a system that enriches the company if former prisoners stay out of jail but reduces the accountability of governments and prioritizes private profit. The corporation also makes money from higher education, pressuring underprivileged students to take on debt while giving scant attention to the standard of teaching.[8]

Republicans in Michigan have pushed for the privatization of public school teachers, using a skewed logic that advocates cutting public schools and selling off facilities at the lowest price. Many tolls operating on public roads and highways in the US service the bottom lines of local and multinational companies. Public libraries have been outsourced, reducing employee salaries or eliminating jobs.

In Europe, many corporations and lawyers shamelessly exploit international investment deals to derive profits from suing crisis-ridden nations. Market speculators pressurize fragile nations such as Greece, whose citizens are forced to survive with fewer public services.[9] British citizens living on the margins face eviction or spiraling rent increases because global fund managers, such as Westbrook—based in the United States—purchase homes as assets to be milked for profit.[10]

The International Monetary Fund (IMF) traverses the world

with the backing of Western elites, strong-arming nations into privatizing their resources and opening up their markets to multinationals. Resistance to this bitter medicine is only one reason that large swathes of Latin America have become more independent since the 2000s. The mass privatization that results—a central plank of US foreign policy—guarantees corruption in autocracies. Wikileaks' State Department cables offer countless examples of this, including in Egypt under former president Hosni Mubarak.[11] The World Bank is equally complicit and equally unaccountable. In 2015 it admitted that it had no idea how many people had been forced off their lands around the world due to its resettlement policies. The story barely made the news and no heads rolled.

One Californian town, Maywood, took the privatization memo a bit too seriously. It literally outsourced everything in 2010, sacking all municipal workers, including the police department, due to budgetary pressure. "We will become 100 percent a contracted city," said Angela Spaccia, Maywood's interim city manager.

Decades of anti-government rhetoric claiming that taxpayer money is always wasted have convinced many voters that the corporation knows best, which is why a sustained campaign against predatory capitalism is so hard to keep up—not helped by the fact that 90 percent of Americans rely on information from media outlets owned by only six multinationals, including News Corporation, Comcast, and Viacom. Rupert Murdoch tried to acquire Time Warner in 2014; had he succeeded, the market would have shrunk even further. In this environment, the fact that movements such as Occupy are born and thrive, albeit briefly, is a remarkable achievement. Indian writer Arundhati Roy saluted the power of this movement in a speech at the People's University in New York's Washington Square Park in November 2011: "What you have achieved ... is to introduce a new imagination, a new political language into the heart of empire. You have reintroduced the right to dream into a system that tried to turn everybody into zombies mesmerized into equating mindless consumerism with happiness and fulfillment."

Although Occupy was dismissed as an irritant and irrelevant by many on Wall Street and in the corporate media, police unleashed a sophisticated surveillance operation to disrupt the protestors. They recognized the danger represented by the threat of a good idea. The challenge faced by opponents of rampant capitalism was how to focus their rage coherently against increasingly pervasive forces. The study of capitalism is soaring at universities across America, indicating the desire on the part of tomorrow's graduates to understand the tenuous connection between democracy and the capitalist economy.[12]

The phenomenal success of French economist Thomas Piketty's book *Capital in the Twenty-First Century*—a work arguing that social discord is the likely outcome of surging financial inequality—indicates that the public knows there is a problem and is in search of clear accounts of it. Piketty advocates a global system of taxation on private property. "This is the only civilized solution," he told the *Observer* newspaper.[13]

In 2014, even the world's leading economic think-tank, the Paris-based Organization for Economic Cooperation and Development, urged higher taxes for the rich to help the bottom 40 percent of the population. When establishment magazine *Foreign Policy* publishes an article by the US managing editor of the *Financial Times*, Gillian Tett, which closes expressing a wish for an "honest debate" about "wealth redistribution," it is clear that the world has gone a little mad.[14]

Canadian journalist Naomi Klein coined the term "disaster capitalism" in her best-selling 2007 book, *The Shock Doctrine: The Rise of Disaster Capitalism*, in which she observes that privatization, government deregulation, and deep cuts to social spending are often imposed after megadisasters, man-made or natural, "all before victims of war or natural disaster [are] able to regroup and stake their claims to what [is] theirs."

The aim of privatizing government itself has existed for decades, but the attacks of September 11, 2001, accelerated the process in the United States because the Bush administration saw its "war on terror" as a boon for the private sector. "Now wars and disaster responses are so fully privatized," Klein argues, "that they are themselves the new market: there is no need to wait until after the war for the boom—the medium is the message."[15]

These ideological changes are implemented by force, despite the routine opposition to them expressed by populations across the world—if they know about the policies at all. Resistance occurs because inefficiency, abuse, corruption, and death cloud the sunny rhetoric offered by privatization's loudest defenders.[16] Still, all too often, corporate power wins. The social and environmental costs of this phenomenon are what I document in these pages.

Predatory capitalism goes way beyond exploiting disaster. Many ongoing crises seem to have been sustained by businesses to fuel industries in which they have a financial stake. These corporations are like vultures feeding on the body of a weakened government that must increasingly rely on the private sector to provide public services. It is surely arguable that the corporation is now fundamentally more powerful than the nation-state, and that it is often the former that dictates terms to the latter. This represents a profound shift in authority that has taken place over the last half-century. A competing position is that the state and the multinationals rely on each other equally, and that companies are only allowed to grow so big by the self-interested largesse of politicians. State oversight is now so weak—often, indeed, nonexistent—in both the Western world and developing countries that corporate power can be said to have won.

I have been reading Klein since her 1999 breakthrough book *No Logo*, which challenged the idea of uncontrolled global capitalism and documented the growing resistance to it. Klein spoke in Australia in the early 2000s, and her arguments resonated with me. She exposed global injustices, but instead of just attacking the individual or group at fault, she took her critique far deeper, into the economic system itself. Follow the money, she argued.

In the aftermath of Hurricane Sandy, which wreaked havoc in New York state in 2012, Klein wrote how the rich would "protect themselves from the less savory effects of the economic model that made them so wealthy."[17] The "shock doctors," she lamented, "are readying to exploit the climate crisis." After Sandy ground its way up America's east coast, the *New York Times* referred to the "Mad Max Economy, a multibillion-dollar a year collection of industries that thrived when things got really, really bad."[18]

In her 2014 book, *This Changes Everything: Capitalism vs. the Climate*, Klein argues that, without serious action to reduce global emissions, the world we know and love will no longer exist. There are massive forces pushing to maintain the status quo—those making money from energy investments. Dangerous hydraulic fracking is sold as the answer, despite the clear evidence of the risks it poses to the land, water, and air. Hillary Clinton's State Department strong-armed nations to embrace shale gas and employ US companies in exploiting it.[19] The growing success of campaigns of divestment from holdings in fossil fuels is a sure sign that business-as-usual is frightening disaster capitalists.

"At its core," Klein writes, "it is a crisis born of overconsumption by the comparatively wealthy, which means the world's most manic consumers are going to have to consume less."[20] The pages that follow in this book are filled with stories of Western greed taking a devastating toll on countries and people rendered invisible by the mainstream media.

It is vital that the corporations that are causing global environmental damage be called out, as is accepting leading US environmentalist Bill McKibben's assertion that "we need to view the fossil fuel industry in a new light. It has become a rogue industry, reckless like no other force on Earth."[21] However, I have expanded Klein's thesis to focus not just on environmental catastrophe, war, and the hidden costs of foreign aid, but also on what happens when the resources sector and detention centers are privatized. These two industries are thriving in the twenty-first century, operating with an alarming disregard for human rights. Nothing less is required, in the words of *Guardian* columnist George Monbiot, than a "democratic mobilization against plutocracy."[22]

Of course, there is money to be made from environmental vandalism. As US journalist McKenzie Funk details in his 2014 book, *Windfall*, insurers, businesspeople, Arctic oil prospectors, private firefighters, and entrepreneurs are all finding business models—for now. The author is savvy enough to recognize that "when you're on the high ground—wealthy enough, northerly enough, far enough above the sea—global warming isn't yet the existential threat that it is for an Egyptian or a Marshall or Staten Islander."[23]

My definition of "disaster" has deepened to include companies that entrench a crisis and then sell themselves as the only ones who can resolve it. Resources and detention centers are just the latest in a long line of assets and institutions that have been made the instruments of unaccountable private power. Whether we call this disaster capitalism or just a product of the unavoidable excesses and inequalities of capitalism itself, the end result is still a world ruled by unaccountable markets.

It is not too fanciful to imagine the end-point of this process being the privatization of the natural world itself.

During the last ten years I have found myself in some of the more challenging places on earth, and the evidence before my eyes convinced me to undertake this project—to visit a range of countries that have been sites of rampant privatization and discrimination. As a journalist and activist, I believe that bearing witness to what I see, and giving unequal players the right of reply, contributes some balance to the privatization debate, rather than the false construct of "balance" that permeates the corporate press, which merely pits one powerful interest against another. A recurring preoccupation of my previous books—*My Israel Question*, *The Blogging Revolution*, and *Profits of Doom*—has been to uncover the untold stories behind the twenty-four-hour news agenda. In this book, I scrutinize an economic system that thrives on ordered chaos and autocracy.

Far too few reporters demand transparency or challenge capitalism, preferring instead to operate comfortably within it. But so-called embedded journalism makes seeing beyond its narrow parameters close to impossible, and I have always opposed the practice. Heavily pushed by governments and the military after 9/11, it has cultivated a media that views business and political leaders as far more important than the individuals and societies affected by them. This work is an antidote to such thinking. It is my contribution to the ongoing fight against silence and complicity in our post-9/11 world. For beyond the shocking stories of torture, rendition, war, drone attacks, and disappearances that occasionally preoccupy the mainstream media, before disappearing to make room for news about the latest reality TV show, lie narratives that are routinely ignored. The effects of policies crafted in Western capitals have clear ramifications for citizens all around the world, but only if we care to look. This book considers the view from below, the experiences of people who are all too often invisible in the daily news cycle.

In the introduction to his book *Heroes*, John Pilger writes that citizens in the developing world are mostly framed in the West as "demons or victims"—a characterization that automatically excludes perhaps the dirtiest word in modern English: imperialism. There is not a country I visited for this book in which the legacy of imperialism does not scar the landscape and people— an injury to which the insult of omission from Western media reportage is routinely added. It is comforting to imagine that this ideology disappeared with the sepia-tinged age of the Edwardians, but that is not the case. The propaganda has simply become more sophisticated, and its proponents more brazen.

Besides, there has never been more money to make. The Pulitzer Prize–winning *New York Times* journalist James Risen, author of the 2014 book *Pay Any Price: Greed, Power and Endless War*, says that "four trillion dollars is the best estimate for the total price tag of the war on terror, including the wars in Iraq and Afghanistan, and much of it has gone to shadowy contractors. It is one of the largest transfers of wealth in American history and yet it has gone largely unnoticed."[24] This book aims to rectify this omission.

Predatory capitalism does not just afflict the developing world. Far too often, policies that have been tried and failed in poor nations are applied in wealthier nations in a time of profound weakness. In the wake of the 2011 earthquake and tsunami in Japan, it did not take long for commentators to start calling for "reform"—code for mass privatization that would allow big business a free hand in redeveloping the devastated areas with the help of generous tax breaks. Murray McLean, Australia's former ambassador to Japan, argued that trade liberalization was one viable solution, but he was worried that leaders would remain "bogged down in policymaking malaise."[25]

His suggestions sounded benign, but they were remarkably similar to the prescriptions described by Klein in *The Shock Doctrine* in relation to the tsunami that bore down on Sri Lanka, among other countries, on December 26, 2004. These included "public-private partnerships," "flexible labor laws," and the opening up of the economy to privatization.[26]

For this book, I visited places that provide unique insights into the cashed-up world of disaster profiteers, resource hunters, war contractors, and aid leeches. The narrative of supposed progress is seemingly unstoppable, and beyond the reach of critique. After all, who would not want to help the people of Papua

New Guinea become independent through mining if this is their path to nirvana? But the facts on the ground tell a different story.

The book is divided into two parts. Part I features the most egregious examples of exploitation: Pakistan and Afghanistan, Greece, Haiti, and Papua New Guinea. These nations have endured hardships because of the determination of particular factions to impose policies that enrich only a local elite and foreign entities.

Since the attacks of 9/11, the geographical heart of the West's "war on terror" has been in Pakistan and Afghanistan. The role in those countries of privatized militaries and intelligence gatherers, both foreign and domestic, prompted me to visit them. This is a murky world, far away from the slick rhetoric deployed in London, Washington, and Canberra, where I met muscled contractors making a packet in the pursuit of a profit motive that has nothing to do with democracy or freedom. These forces partly explain the successful insurgencies against Westerners in these states and Iraq.

Greece has suffered under harsh economic policies more than most Western countries. The rise of the neo-Nazi party Golden Dawn is a logical outcome of this failed economic model. The poor and refugees are especially suffering, and I report here on their plight. This leads me to a discovery of European Union complicity in the crisis, and the success of anti-austerity party Syriza.

Haiti, the poorest country in the Western hemisphere, is still recovering from the devastating earthquake of January 2010. I observed there the collusion between multinationals, NGOs, government officials, armed UN troops, aid groups, and donors, all of whom regard the outsourcing of essential tasks to for-profit companies as progress. On two trips to Haiti, I witnessed what this meant for the local community. Africa should be a warning to Haiti, with the billions of dollars of aid money pouring into the continent more than cancelled by the billions more leaving through tax evasion and multinational profits.[27]

In Papua New Guinea, one of the largest recipients of Australian aid, I investigated whether the mining boom has helped or hindered the country, particularly in the province of Bougainville. Like so many other poor nations blessed with abundant resources, Papua New Guinea is plagued by multinationals that have operated there for decades, investing billions of dollars in exploiting what lies beneath the ground while residents recoup few tangible benefits and see little improvement in their standard of living. Meanwhile, the environmental costs have been massive, and corruption is rampant. In short, the so-called resource curse turns out to be alive and well.

Part II focuses on the United States, Britain, and Australia. These three wealthy Western states dictate economic conditions of their own creation to the world, and punish the most vulnerable in their societies who dare to seek a piece of the action and those who oppose their economic regime.

The United States and Britain have become global leaders in the privatized prisons and detention industries, through which millions of people have passed without any deterrent effect on criminality. Needless to say, this system has enriched favored companies such as Serco, G4S, and Corrections Corporation of America. I investigate in both countries how lobbying, ideology, and a punishment ethos have colluded to produce one of the most destructive experiments in modern times: mass incarceration.

Australia has privatized all of its detention centers for asylum seekers, which are now run by multinational companies. Few other countries have so comprehensively outsourced such facilities to such a small group of companies, and with so little government oversight or media scrutiny. In its remote facilities, I investigated the reality of this privatized world and its effects on refugees and staff, and what they say about a supposedly civilized nation.

These are stark examples of a capitalism that has gone off the rails, though sadly they are not unrepresentative. Some argue that capitalism is inherently predatory, and this book is the case for that proposition. I could have visited Equatorial Guinea, an oil-rich African country beset by corruption and violence; or South Sudan, the world's newest nation, beset with resource conflict, ethnic strife and Western and Chinese corporate interests. In Iraq, I could have researched the Western firms that made a fortune after signing resource deals with the brutal US- and Iranian-backed Baghdad regime. Or I could have investigated the growing Chinese appetite for Burmese jade, causing drug addiction and hardship for locals in Kachin State. China's rise to superpower status places its actions in the spotlight, and it has no shortage of government and private enterprises desperate to make an unethical fortune. Meanwhile, the Western food and drink multinationals forging new markets in developing countries are driving increased rates of diabetes, obesity, and heart disease.[28]

When, in 2000, I was in Mongolia—the fastest-growing state in the world, due to its copper and gold deposits—the boom had not yet begun, and all I saw was a resilient people desperate to emerge from decades of oppressive policies dictated by Beijing and Moscow. Today, US lobbyists see Mongolia as experiencing a resource rush, but really it is just open season for vulture capitalists who can once again plunder a new frontier while leaving the vast majority of the locals with nothing to show for the bonanza.[29] Even in Syria—an apocalyptic war zone—critics argue that some aid organizations and contractors are prolonging the conflict by working too closely with war criminals on all sides.[30]

Each place I investigate here is culturally, politically, and socially distinctive. But what connects them all together is that they are subject to the destructive ideology of corporations aiming to make money on a global scale. An understanding of why this is happening in the twenty-first century entails a challenge to cherished beliefs concerning aid and development, war and democracy, and in particular the modern, borderless nature of capitalism. The most dedicated followers of capitalism and privatization feverishly apply logical market principles in disaster zones, impoverished nations, and developed countries with large inflows of refugees. Yet, time and time again, they fail to enrich anyone other than the handful of individuals clever enough to jump on board the well-stocked gravy train.

This book is a product of the post-9/11 environment. The mass expansion of the privatized surveillance state was confined to the realm of science fiction before that fateful September day in 2001. Today, there are 4 million US citizens who hold Top Secret security clearance, of whom 500,000 are contractors.[31] Robert Greiner, who was the CIA station chief in Islamabad, Pakistan, at the time of the 9/11 attacks, said in 2010 that he believed at least half of the staff working at the CIA's counterterrorism center were private contractors.[32] Former NSA employee Edward Snowden exposed the dangers of mass surveillance being managed by private enterprise when he leaked documents in 2013 proving how easy it was for firms such as Booz Allen Hamilton to view and store information on citizens. It is nothing less than a privatized, modern-day Stasi.

The claim that "the world is a battlefield" reflects a military ideology pursued by both Democrat and Republican administrations, as has been detailed by investigative journalist Jeremy Scahill. This view is only bolstered by WikiLeaks documents, released in 2010, that uncovered a large number of previously unreported murders committed by privatized security and intelligence forces in the Afghan and Iraq conflict zones.[33] These ghost-figures operate in the shadows in dozens of countries, kidnapping, interrogating, and killing suspects without oversight.[34] Modern-day mercenary companies, justified by the state as essential in fighting terrorism, have been completely integrated into America's endless war.

The war on terror has brought untold riches to corporations keen to profit from fear: the US firm CACI, provider of interrogators to Iraq's Abu Ghraib prison, was complicit in torturing Iraqis; the world's largest aerospace company, Boeing, was implicated in "extraordinary rendition" flights, delivering suspects for torture;[35] Lloyds Banking Group was found to have invested in a company that flew individuals to "black sites" around the world.[36] Often, the corporate state is brazen about such exploitation, as are its government associates. British Defence Secretary Philip Hammond told companies to "pack their suitcases" to gain construction contracts at the tail-end of the NATO campaign against Libya's Muammar Gaddafi, in 2011.[37] The country is now engulfed by civil war. Western advocates of intervention have moved on to the next conflict.

It is hard to escape the conclusion that wars are often fought for the key reason of liberating new and willing markets—and with the war on terror likely to continue for decades, there will be no shortage of new business to secure. Even the United Nations is increasingly relying on unaccountable mercenary firms such as DynCorp and G4S, two companies with dubious records.[38] In Afghanistan, the Department of Defense employs nearly 40,000 contractors.[39] The war there is far from over.

Indeed, the battle never ends. When Washington declared war against the Islamic State in 2014, private interests emerged as the big, if largely ignored, winner. Contractors were "looking for the next big meal ticket and this could be it," said Sean McFate, a former Dyncorp employee.[40] Blackwater founder Erik Prince, now running Frontier Services Group to help China in Africa, urged the United States to "let the private sector finish the job" against Islamist militants—presumably hoping that no one would remember how disastrous the effects of Western mercenaries' activities had been since 9/11.[41]

Meanwhile, the erosion of democracy is met with barely a whimper from the political and media establishments. The selling of valuable assets and outsourcing of vital state services occurs because public resistance to it is so minimal—though it is far stronger in countries where people's lives are literally at risk. This book aims to shock, provoke, and reveal a world that has developed by stealth—but also to insist that alternatives are possible.

Part I

1

Pakistan and Afghanistan: "Looking for the new war"

Frankly, I'd like to see the government get out of war altogether and leave the whole feud to private industry.
Major Milo Minderbinder, in *Catch-22* (Joseph Heller)

The rain pelted the car's windshield as we sped through Kabul's streets, which resembled a sea of mud. Women in burqas appeared, faceless and shapeless, and disappeared just as quickly. Young boys put out begging hands when the traffic stopped us, desperate for coins or food. I saw some children pushing wheelbarrows full of bricks, while others played alongside the road. Large trucks roared past, pumping their horns.

I was half an hour from the center of Afghanistan's capital, on Jalalabad Road, which was lined with large compounds owned by logistics companies and protected by guards. Behind one of the nondescript fences were the premises of a private security firm. Speaking to senior players in the private security industry in Afghanistan was notoriously difficult because it was an inherently secretive business, but I had been promised time with a senior manager.

My driver and I pulled up near a concrete barrier. It only took a few seconds before two local armed guards appeared to ask what we were doing here. The men each carried an AK-47 and wore a cap emblazoned with the security company's logo. They took me to a small office near the main gate and offered me a seat and tea. Rain dripped through a small crack in the wooden ceiling, splattering on the dirt below. One of the guards talked to me as he searched my bag. He had spent a number of years in Karachi, the financial capital of Pakistan, but had been with this company in Kabul for two years, and said, "They're a good employer." He liked the job because it provided a steady income.

I was invited into the compound. There was a large courtyard where four-wheel-drive vehicles were parked, and this was surrounded by multi-story, transportable buildings. Around twenty Gurkhas, recent recruits, milled about in one corner. The company's managing director approached and introduced himself. Jack was an affable man in his sixties who wore beige chinos, a blue shirt and a navy fleece jacket. He told me that he had fought as a British soldier in some of the toughest wars of the last few decades, including those in Iraq, Afghanistan, and Central America, but said he made far more money in his current job. "Western militaries should pay their soldiers more money, otherwise they'll continue moving to PMCs," said Jack, referring to private military companies. ("We don't call ourselves mercenaries," he later told me. His company thought the word had a bad connotation.)

Jack lead me into his office, a small, dimly lit room with a window, a desk, and a black leather couch, and on the walls, a map of Kabul outlining where his company operated, a map of Afghanistan, and a photo of the Hindu Kush mountain range. As we entered, he calmly told me that his corporation "survives off chaos."

Jack's company had come to Afghanistan in 2002, the first PMC to arrive after the October 2001 US-led invasion. Now there were more PMCs, about 75 percent of which were Afghan-run. Up until serious resistance against the invaders had begun, in 2004, the violence was relatively low-level. The company offered "assistance to anyone"—journalists, NGOs, and UN employees—for a hefty fee, with its personnel earning at least $1,000 per day. But from 2002 onwards, the company worked with the Afghan government because of a correct perception that its Ministry of Interior could not properly secure businesses and people.

This was the birth of the apparent necessity for private security in Afghanistan. The thinking was that a tough war required hiring the best security, which mostly meant former soldiers looking to make a quick buck. Cultural or social sensitivity and knowledge of a country were not prerequisites.

Kabul's view of PMCs had changed over the years, however, from initially welcoming them to now viewing them with suspicion. The Americans and foreigners still used them to protect their bases, around 3,000 of them, utilizing employees from the "Five Eyes" intelligence sharing nations (the United States, Britain, Canada, New Zealand, and Australia) and NATO.[1] "It's chaos," Jack said, explaining that the Afghan laws against PMCs were applied unevenly. He equated this with injustice, telling me that "in a civilized country, people are not guilty before appearing in a court. Here, you're guilty and arrested first."

With a hint of regret, Jack said: "With constantly changing regulations here, life is difficult." In 2002, he recalled, there had been an abundance of ammunition and guns, and "it was easy to operate." The United States and the United Kingdom were focused on chasing Osama bin Laden and the Taliban, so PMCs could purchase weapons easily and "get the job done" without having to worry about any pesky official oversight. But now, Jack said, the Afghan government had tried to dismantle the foreign PMCs and replace them with locally run outfits and the state-controlled Afghan Public Protection Force (disbanded in 2014 and folded into the Ministry of Interior). He said these groups were incapable of performing their duties competently, yet his company was losing commercial contracts to them.

Nevertheless, in Kabul, Jack's company still managed four embassy buildings, the UN headquarters, and a few banks—what he called "static work." They avoided shadowing convoys, a risky enterprise that required transporting foreign troops' goods through often hostile tribal territory. Jack said such areas were only accessible upon handing over "brown envelopes" (bribes)—as he put it, "the dollar works here." Of course, foreign companies were not allowed to pay bribes; in theory, these firms could be prosecuted at home. But Jack merely smirked when I asked if any companies were doing this.

Jack could not understand why so many activists in the West were "obsessed" with imposing tighter regulations on PMCs. He took pride in the way his company delivered its service. He had an apolitical though patronizing mindset—he had no regard for the exploitation occurring in this privatized war zone, instead seeing it as a job that involved taking some risks. When I challenged him over his lack of curiosity about the problems of outsourcing security during a conflict, he responded that there was nothing inherently unethical about providing a safe service on time. He was also extremely arrogant, believing that he should be able to do business anywhere he wanted.

Jack's company employed six international staff, a number of Gurkhas, and 1,200 Afghans. He spoke proudly of hiring so many locals, saying that many of them were sent to "night school to learn computer skills to use in our HR office and visa section." He said it was one way for a foreign company to contribute some-thing tangible to Afghan society. "My young men and women are the people who could be leading the country," he said. "My 1,200 pay packets feed 12,000 people in their families. If I didn't employ them, where would they work?"

Responding to the idea that Afghan sovereignty was under-mined when PMCs were at work, Jack said, "The US is not capable of running empires." He pointed out that Washington's occupa-tion of the country was done so badly that it was inevitable that outside forces would enter the fray to make money. Besides which, Jack said, it was ultimately cheaper for states to employ PMCs than to put their own "boots on the ground," because the military companies took care of their own insurance, provided vehicles, and managed all the administration. As for anything else a PMC needed, after being in the country for years, Jack understood how the system worked and who in Kabul you had to approach for such things as permission to register weapons. "I'm my own government," he said.

Jack continued his justifications: "America, Britain, and [other] foreign forces, in both Iraq and Afghanistan, are not big enough to rebuild nations. PMCs are needed to fill the void, protecting contractors, building prisons and schools. They're now an essential part of war."[2] (He admitted that this might not have been the case in Afghanistan if the United States had used more troops in the first place.)

Not that Jack saw a long-term future for his company in Afghanistan. He believed that when most Western forces finally departed the country, he and his staff would follow them. "We'll stash some weapons in caves," he told me cryptically, "[but] I don't see any PMCs here then."[3] His company did, however, already operate in several other places around the world, and he expected more wars—in Iran, the Korean Peninsula, and Africa. "If we can make money, we'll go there," he said.

In his mind, the PMC business had no negatives. It was purely "jobs for boys leaving the army who can continue their trade." He expanded on how positively he felt about the work: "Money is not the sole motivator for me, I just want to have a job … I would be bored staying at home. I feel secure. I don't have an operational role and we have good intelligence around the country. It's better than the British military, actually, direct from the provinces and local Afghans, and we inform the UK military if it's relevant to them. We talk with [British security company] G4S, who'll pass intelligence on to us, and vice versa. We're all mates, [we] trained together and fought together globally over the years. We really just compete over contracts." It sounded like a very cosy PMC club.

Jack mentioned an issue I constantly heard about during my stay in the country: a potential Afghan mining boom. "There are massive mineral resources here," he explained, adding that "unless corruption is resolved," greed would win out. "Western corporations won't come here to invest," he said, "but already India and China are buying up land with resources and waiting until security improves." He said his company had been approached by mining multinationals but that they would "need diplomatic permission to operate legally here."

By 2014, Afghan ministers were touting the nation's resources as the best way to bring stability and revenue after the Americans departed. The China Metallurgical Group Corporation (MCC) bought rights to a massive copper mine at Mes Aynak in Logar province in 2008, and after finding rare and ancient Buddhist relics in the region the new owners said they would extract the artifacts or destroy them. At the time of writing there was no news of the mine even opening, though the Afghan government claimed to have increased security around the site in 2014 in a push to get mining started. Claims of 75,000 jobs being created, along with a quarter of a billion dollars in annual revenue, should be viewed with skepticism. In 2015 I visited a local community near Aynak mine and found village elders angry over being displaced from their homes, caught between a raging Taliban and Islamic State insurgency in the area and a trigger-happy Afghan military who are paid to defend the mine's interests.

Integrity Watch Afghanistan had accused local actors of illegally shipping hundreds of millions of dollars of minerals, oil, and gas annually to Iran and Pakistan.[4] The Afghan government had promoted other sites across Afghanistan as perfect opportunities for foreign investors, but security, corruption, and meager tax or royalties, upset villagers moved for botched mines and failed contracts, and instability continued to impede progress. US geologists estimated in 2010 that the country was sitting on at least $1 trillion worth of lithium, iron, and copper.

After nearly one and a half hours, the friendly, fast-flowing conversation ended. As Jack and I exchanged farewells, I could hear the Gurkhas training outside in the drizzling rain. Before I left, I looked out Jack's window—first to the horizon, where dark, menacing clouds hovered, then at the countless similarly appointed compounds around me that lined the main road. It was clear that many PMCs benefited from the war. They didn't ever want the conflict to end.

Before the US-led invasion of Afghanistan, the country was ruled by the Taliban: people were executed in football stadiums, music was officially outlawed, and young girls were banned from schools. It was a barbaric regime, though not so barbaric that it could not negotiate with the US energy company Unocal over running a Turkmenistan-Pakistan pipeline through the country; extremism was rarely a barrier to disaster capitalism. After the invasion, Afghanistan became the perfect place for a war economy to thrive. The Trans-Afghanistan pipeline (also known as the Turkmenistan-Afghanistan-Pakistan-India pipe, or TAPI), scheduled to open in 2018, was intended to transport Caspian Sea gas in a modern continuation of the Silk Road.

The battle that surrounded Iraq's invasion of Kuwait in August 1990 provided a solid model for post-9/11 war propaganda. The US public relations firm Hill+Knowlton was employed to demonize the Saddam Hussein regime—a campaign paid for by a group of Kuwaiti oil sheiks who named themselves Citizens for a Free Kuwait. One of its stunts involved a young woman, calling herself Nayirah, who told a meeting of the United States Congressional Human Rights Caucus that she had seen Iraqi soldiers take babies from incubators and place them on the floor to die. It was a lie—the woman was actually the fifteen-year-old daughter of the Kuwaiti ambassador to the United States.

Nonetheless, it succeeded in encouraging the support of military action against Iraq.

The enlistment of PR personnel continued when the George W. Bush administration declared its "war on terror" in 2001. Countless Hill+Knowlton staff became government staffers to assist in selling the fight, initially against the Taliban. Victoria Clarke, director of the firm's Washington office, left the company to become defense secretary Donald Rumsfeld's press spokesperson, leading the charge to embed journalists in US military units, which helped ensure military-friendly coverage. One of the sharpest critics of this process was the late journalist Michael Hastings, who challenged the close relationship between the press and military in his 2011 book, *The Operators*.[5] Many colleagues damned him for daring to reveal the conceit of the embedding process.

Another Hill+Knowlton staffer, Jeff Raleigh, became a member of the Afghanistan Reconstruction Group, helping the US ambassador in Kabul to encourage public support for the corrupt Afghan government.[6] He worked for the Rendon Group, a company paid tens of millions of dollars by the US government to push war propaganda in Iraq and Afghanistan in the wake of 9/11, and to prepare "a counternarcotics information campaign" in Kabul. This was despite the central government caring little for the anti-drug campaign experience that company founder John Rendon said he had gained while he had been a state official in Massachusetts.[7] In 2006, the company was paid $4 million to persuade Afghans not to grow opium poppies, and so stop fuelling the global heroin trade. The campaign was a spectacular failure.[8]

Hill+Knowlton was just one example of a company that straddled the worlds of big business and high-level government, and in doing so benefited financially from war.[9] Another was DynCorp, one of the firms the United States relied on to conduct the training of its military forces across the world. Its résumé included providing bodyguards to protect Haitian president Jean-Bertrand

Aristide in the 1990s, services for the US military in Somalia, Kosovo, and Bolivia, and assistance in the post–Hurricane Katrina clean-up. But demand for the company's work surged after 9/11, when the US government began outsourcing its war on terror.

The State Department had handed out contracts to DynCorp worth over $1 billion, for "police advisers" to assist US efforts to build up the Afghan security forces. But the results had been disappointing, to say the least. Serious allegations of waste, mismanagement, and overcharging were rampant, and the effectiveness and trustworthiness of the Afghan police force remained in doubt. A 2009 UN report found that at least half of the Afghan police who had been trained by the Americans were corrupt, while a particularly disturbing statistic was the growing number of so-called "green-on-blue" attacks, in which Afghan recruits turned on their trainers.[10] Yet in 2012, after years of consistent failure by DynCorp in Afghanistan, and barely one week after the US special inspector general for reconstruction labeled as "unsatisfactory" the company's work at the Kunduz army base, it secured a $72.8 million contract to train US Air Force pilots.[11] The US State Department gave nearly $4 billion to support reconstruction in Afghanistan from 2002 to 2013—and $2.7 billion of that went to Dyncorp.[12]

DynCorp had a major presence in both Afghanistan and Iraq, earning 96 percent of its $3 billion annual revenue from the US government. This had occurred despite the company's failure to implement any serious mechanisms to consult with the locals with whom they worked, instead relying on ad hoc relationships that almost guaranteed cronyism.[13] Privatization had become so entrenched in the aforementioned countries that placing the affected services back in public hands was rarely even discussed by Western governments.

"[DynCorp] were brought in during the heyday of our innocence," said Ashraf Ghani, Afghanistan's current president, former minister of finance and adviser to President Hamid Karzai, in 2012.[14] A year earlier, journalist Charles Glass reported from Kabul that DynCorp "paid the least and hired people other companies would not touch,"[15] which was also what I heard during my visit.

Another player in the war economy was KBR, a former subsidiary of Halliburton, the company once run by former US vice president Dick Cheney. From the beginning of the Afghan war in 2001, KBR/Halliburton were winning contracts to prepare bases for incoming US troops. The figures were staggering—the companies received hundreds of millions of dollars to provide basic services such as food, laundry, camp maintenance, and airfield services. By 2008, KBR said that it had served more than 720 million meals, driven more than 643 million kilometers in convoy jobs, treated 45 billion liters of water, and created more than 242 million tons of ice in the war on terror.[16]

Many other companies had taken their place in the armed-conflict outsourcing queue. An army reporter for the US Department of Defense wrote a story in 2003 that featured representatives of three contractors talking about how they imported into Afghanistan vegetables and fruits from Germany, soft drinks from Bahrain and Saudi Arabia, and meat from the United States. "A lot of the guys working here are prior military," said one employee. "We've been there and done that too, so this is like we're giving back. I remember what [the soldiers are] going through."[17] The message was clear: no expense was spared to provide the comforts of home, and contractors were enriched in the process.

There were often more contractors than soldiers in Afghanistan, a trend that was likely to continue for years to come, as it had in Iraq and Guantánamo Bay. In the last quarter of 2012, there were over 109,000 contractors in Afghanistan, nearly double the number of US troops.[18] Also in 2012, the US company Mission Essential Personnel received a $2.3 billion contract to provide more than 8,000 translators at 200 bases in Afghanistan.[19] Countless companies, such as the Christian-inspired International Relief and

Development (IRD), received more than $2 billion in support from USAID between 2007 and 2013, and yet its record was desultory.[20] USAID suspended work with IRD in 2015, citing "serious misconduct" in its activities.

Supreme Foodservice AG, based in Switzerland, massively overcharged when providing food and water to American troops. The US government's Defence Logistics Agency accused the company of overbilling by $757 million. In late 2014, Supreme pleaded guilty in a US court for overcharging the US military for food and water; they agreed to pay a $389 million fine—a tiny portion of the $8.8 billion contract secured for a 2005–13 contract.

This was occurring despite the problems being common knowledge for years. There existed, for example, in Afghanistan and other US theaters of war, a two-tier system of privatized employment: one that benefited Westerners and the other that exploited locals. In journalist Sarah Stillman's 2011 investigation of this trend, she wrote of an

> invisible army … primarily from South Asia and Africa [who] often live in barbed-wire compounds on US bases, eat at meagre chow halls, and host dance parties featuring Nepalese romance ballads and Ugandan church songs. A large number are employed by fly-by-night subcontractors who are financed by the American taxpayer but who often operate outside the law.[21]

An Al Jazeera America investigation in 2014 found that the problem still existed, with labor abuses "rampant" on US bases in Afghanistan. The company Ecolog International was even accused of human trafficking.[22]

Of course, the official line was that outsourcing had largely accelerated after the 2001 attacks on New York and Washington as a way for the Bush administration to continue reducing waste and increase efficiency. The day before the attacks took place, Defense

Secretary Donald Rumsfeld gave a speech that set the scene for what was to come. "The topic today is an adversary that poses a threat, a serious threat, to the security of the United States of America," he began. This turned out not to be terrorism, but "Pentagon bureaucracy." Rumsfeld claimed the Pentagon was wasting at least $3 billion annually, and that the logical answer to this was privatization. "When an entire industry exists to run warehouses efficiently," Rumsfeld continued, "why do we own and operate so many of our own? At bases around the world, why do we pick up our own garbage and mop our own floors, rather than contracting services out, as many businesses do?"[23] Events unfolded the following day that gave Rumsfeld the perfect excuse to fast-track his plan, emblemized by the privatization of various war-support services that led to huge job cuts in the US Department of Defense. Cutting a massively bloated budget would undoubtedly contribute to a fairer society if the money was spent on public services, but outsourcing did nothing to address the problem.

Rumsfeld and Cheney's joint legacy cast a long shadow. The favoring of corporations that profited from conflict was now the way that the United States fought its wars. The overthrow of Libya's Muammar Gaddafi in 2012 saw an explosion of private contractors thrust into a dangerous mix, with the State Department relying on little-known British company Blue Mountain Group to protect its mission in Benghazi in 2012. Reuters found that employees had little or no experience in security.[24]

Washington increasingly viewed outsourced private security as the way to protect its assets in the Middle East, Africa, and beyond. The State Department's Bureau of Diplomatic Security protected 275 embassies and consulates, and employed more than 36,000 people, 90 percent of whom were private contractors, according to a 2013 Congressional Research Service report.

And this was not just how Republicans thought. Democrats like Hillary Clinton and John Kerry also argued in favor of this system, saying it was more efficient. The same disease infected the two main arms of American politics. As a result, not enough accountability had been demanded, such as oversight mechanisms to follow the money trail or measure efficiency, and so billions of dollars had been wasted.

There was almost universal support for the US-led invasion of Afghanistan after the 9/11 attacks (although some in the left, myself included, opposed the war because they argued that America's aim was not to create a democratic state that would respect all its citizens, as it claimed, but to seek revenge). The Taliban regime, which had hosted al-Qaeda and its leader, Osama bin Laden, was quickly overthrown by Operation Enduring Freedom, but many of its senior leaders fled to neighboring Pakistan, and the group maintained control over vast swathes of Afghanistan.

The conflict became America's longest-running war. In 2014 the bulk of Western troops were removed, though President Barack Obama reversed a previous decision to massively reduce US troop numbers and military trainers, and continued Washington's involvement in war fighting into 2015 and beyond. In December 2014 Obama closed Bagram prison, the site of torture and indefinite detention without trial, transferring prisoners to the Afghan government.

But the occupation was not over. The large presence of contractors would continue for many years to come. A leaked document in 2013 from leading US contractor company SAIC showed a comprehensive plan in Afghanistan, with hundreds of employed subcontractors, including Lockheed Martin and drone manufacturer General Atomics.[25] The US mission was intimately tied to these unaccountable forces.

The Western occupation of Afghanistan profoundly changed the country, mostly for the worse. In Kandahar today, an Afghan elite enriched by the US occupation fears for the future. Unreliable power generators, supported by US-funded diesel, were a public face of dysfunction.[26]

The bigger picture was that Hamid Karzai had been installed as president in 2004 through undemocratic elections, and then re-elected in a sham vote in 2009 compromised by voter fraud, of which there was widespread evidence. The election of Karzai's replacement in 2014 was a tortuous process leading to uncertainty, despite the victory of pro-American leader Ashraf Ghani arranged by America.

An insurgency against Western forces did not occur immediately, as many Afghans, though opposed to a foreign occupation, initially welcomed the fall of the Taliban. But, in 2003, militants initiated attacks against Kabul and the NATO-run International Security Assistance Force (ISAF). Tens of thousands of Afghan civilians were killed over the last decade—the UN only started publishing estimates in 2009, and by 2014 the total figure of dead and injured had reached at least 47,000. The year 2014 was the deadliest ever, according to the UN, with over 10,500 fatalities and injuries. Over 3,350 foreign soldiers, including at least 2,200 US troops, also died in the conflict. It was estimated that there had been thousands of US contractor deaths since 2001, although many went unreported; in 2011, at least 430 employees of American contractors were reported killed in Afghanistan.[27]

Shockingly, a 2010 US government report, *Warlord, Inc.*, found that a large number of US-paid contractors were actually assisting the insurgency the West was fighting, by paying local warlord-controlled security companies to protect the cargo needed by ISAF forces. This empowered "warlords with money, legitimacy and a raison d'être for their private armies."[28] US officials in Kabul estimated in 2009 that at least 10 percent of the Pentagon's logistics budget was used to pay off insurgents.[29] In 2012, the Afghan Independent Human Rights Commission released an 800-page report titled *Conflict Mapping in Afghanistan since 1978*, which documented scores of atrocities that had taken place in the country in the past decades, many of them committed by the very warlords supported by the West today.[30]

The best account of this sordid agreement appeared in reporter Anand Gopal's stunning 2014 book, *No Good Men Among the Living*. He recounts the myriad of ways Washington after 9/11 was used by Afghans to fight local battles, extinguish enemies while creating new ones, and guarantee a resurgence of the defeated Taliban. "The state became criminalized, one of the most corrupt in the world," Gopal writes, "as thoroughly depraved as the warlords it sought to outflank."

Afghanistan was susceptible to privatized security from the beginning of the post-9/11 war. The country was a veritable blank slate on which a new society could be drawn purely to benefit the bottom lines of corporations that sold themselves as essential to the war effort. And such companies wasted little time in doing so.

But the process has deeper historical roots. The end of the Cold War resulted in an explosion in demobilized labor looking for work, from which PMCs quickly developed. The founder of Aegis Defence Services, Colonel Tim Spicer, said that in the years after the fall of the Soviet Union, PMCs "fill[ed] the gap" where governments were reluctant to engage.[31]

Then 9/11 happened, and America saw an opportunity to reshape the Middle East with overwhelming force. It was a goldmine for PMCs. In his seminal book *Corporate Warriors*, P. W. Singer writes:

> Warfare is no longer an exclusive affair of men in uniform fighting for their state's political causes. Rather, warfare, as it was often in the past, has become a multi-faceted affair, involving men and women, inside and outside the public military, fighting for a variety of causes—political, economic, religious, social and cultural—that often have little to do with the state.[32]

A US Defense Department official, James Des Roches, did not mince words about the PMC world either: "The war on terrorism is the full employment act for these guys ... A lot of people have said, 'Ding, ding, ding, gravy train.'"[33]

It is this environment, combined with minimal media scrutiny and limited public knowledge of PMCs, that allowed this aspect of disaster capitalism to flourish in US war zones over the past years. Compounding the situation was the fact that global legal regulations concerning private security were limited and murky. In 2000, a commentator in the PMC community told Singer that anyone who was taken to court under the Geneva laws deserved to "be shot and their lawyer beside them"—he was referring to the fact that the laws were so weak that it was easy to circumvent them.[34] The security corporations were often based in Western nations, but their operations took place worldwide, and therefore contracts were drawn up in countless jurisdictions.

Operating outside effective state control was the ideal for these firms. It was not just PMCs making a fortune. Take the private airline companies quietly transporting military, CIA, and intelligence forces in and out of Afghanistan and around the world. Corporations such as World Airlines, Evergreen Aviation, and Tepper Aviation serviced the endless rendition needs of the US government.[35]

Singer articulated the post-9/11 environment as "the lax and haphazard way in which governments have privatized their own military services over the last decade. The simple fact that one can outsource does not always mean one should."[36] Perhaps the most remarkable aspect of the recent outsourcing of war was that many US government reports had found the practice to be irresponsible, yet this had had no effect on the granting of massive contracts to the profiteers. The US bipartisan Commission on Wartime Contracting released a report in 2011 that found between $31 billion and $61 billion worth of Pentagon projects in Iraq and Afghanistan had amounted to nothing due to fraud and waste. In the same year, the Center for Public Integrity concluded that the Pentagon's no-bid contract system had exploded from $50 billion in 2003 to $140 billion in 2011.[37]

Soon after taking office in 2009, President Barack Obama announced that he would fight a war against bloated Pentagon spending:

> Last year, the Government Accountability Office, GAO, looked into 95 major defense projects and found cost overruns that totaled $295 billion. Let me repeat. That's $295 billion in wasteful spending. And this wasteful spending has many sources. It comes from investments in unproven technologies. It comes from a lack of oversight. It comes from influence peddling and indefensible no-bid contracts that have cost American taxpayers billions of dollars.
>
> We will stop outsourcing services that should be performed by the government and open up the contracting process to small businesses. We will end unnecessary no-bid and cost-plus contracts that run up a bill that is paid by the American people. And we will strengthen oversight to maximize transparency and accountability.[38]

These were empty words. A member of the Commission on Wartime Contracting, Charles Tiefer, told *Democracy Now!* in 2011 that many US projects in Afghanistan, Iraq, and elsewhere, such as dining services and construction, were never finished, or the work was shoddy. He also said the Pentagon awarded contracts to a subsidiary company of the controversial Blackwater without realizing it, and that corporate lobbying of members of Congress was the key reason disaster capitalism was unstoppable.[39] A 2015 report by the Special Inspector General for Afghanistan Reconstruction (SIGAR) found that Blackwater/Academi was the second largest recipient of Pentagon funding from 2002 to 2014 for its training of Afghan security forces program. Defense manufacturer Northrop Grumman was the largest. Both organizations received hundreds of millions of dollars.

*   *   *

My flight into Kabul was a spectacularly scenic way of entering the country. Most of the trip from Dubai was spent sitting just above the clouds, but twenty minutes before landing, the Hindu Kush appeared and the pilot threaded the plane between these mountains and the Kabul River. Snow sat on the range's uninhabited peaks, seemingly almost touching the bottom of the plane. As the capital approached, I saw small mud-home villages dotting the landscape.

But on the ground in Afghanistan, I found a nation destroyed by brutal occupation, fierce Taliban resistance, and numerous companies making a fortune amid the misery. It was immediately clear to me that the country had suffered extraordinary carnage, visited on it by various outside forces, and that the pain had been reciprocated. Afghanistan was called the "graveyard of empires" for good reason—no nation had ever completely successfully occupied or controlled the country. When I visited the British cemetery in Kabul, I saw countless graves that testified to various British attempts to tame the place from the nineteenth century onwards. The quiet, well-tended space also had signs detailing the fatalities among NATO and ISAF forces since 2001, including the deaths of soldiers from Germany, Spain, and the Netherlands.

One of these failed attempts at British imperialism, between 1839 and 1842, was graphically depicted in William Dalrymple's fine 2013 book, *Return of a King*. Dalrymple recounted the war between the British East India Company and Afghanistan and the near-complete destruction of the invading forces. It remained one of the worst defeats of the Victorian era. Its resonance in the modern age was revealing the same imperial arrogance against local forces displayed by Britain in the 1800s, continued in the twenty-first century. Nothing had changed.

The futility of all these past conflicts hit me: so many states had come here with supposedly noble aims, only to find that the country could not be won. The world's most powerful nations over the last century had all been defeated here, and yet they kept on returning.

It was depressing to think that the United States would inevitably be followed by other powers in the decades to come. China was the new, rising global power intent on exercising influence over Kabul, training Afghan diplomats, opening up a line of communication with the Taliban, and sharing Washington's fear of Pakistani and Uighur militants.[40] Beijing, with not a single soldier in the country, pledged billions of dollars of economic support to Afghanistan.

There had also been terrible social costs. I often heard in the field that pervasive drug use had gradually worsened since the 2001 US invasion. Afghans had used opium for medicinal purposes for centuries, but since the Soviet Union had invaded in 1979, opium production had become a key source of income for warlords fighting the country's various occupiers. Even the Taliban, except for a brief ban it imposed in 2000, had profited from the trade. Today, large-scale opium trading was ubiquitous across the country, with barely any serious effort being made by foreign troops or Kabul to eradicate it.

There had been reports of many thousands of US soldiers abusing drugs in Afghanistan, including the use and dealing of heroin and opium, not unlike the rampant drug problem that occurred during the Vietnam War, but it was the Afghans who were principally suffering.[41] Exact figures were impossible to find, but the United Nations Office on Drugs and Crime alleged that at least 8 percent of the population aged between fifteen and sixty-four were hooked on opium, with few government programs to help manage the epidemic.[42] That was around 1 million users out of a population of 35 million people. Up to 40 percent of the addicts were women and children.

The ISAF-led war prompted a resurgence in the drug trade.[43] The drug economy in Afghanistan was thriving, and only worsened after most Western troops left in 2014. Up to 90 percent of the world's heroin originated there, and countless US and British counternarcotics campaigns staged since 2001 had failed to dent the trade. A poppy farmer in the province of Tarin Kowt told the

New York Times in 2012 that it was worth taking the risk. "The poppy is always good, you can sell it any time," he said. "It is like gold."[44]

Drugs were a central aspect of the war economy, enforced by the devastating effects of the Western occupation. National Public Radio reported in 2014 on the Afghan city of Herat and its more than 70,000 addicts, including a four-year-old child. The US Office on Drugs and Crime found in 2014 that opium poppy cultivation had hit an all-time high despite years of futile attempts to curtail it. Washington acquiesced, with Afghan officials, after 2001, benefiting financially from the drug trade. "Narco corruption went to the top of the Afghan government," wrote Thomas Schweich, a senior US counternarcotics official in Afghanistan from 2006 to 2008.[45]

I decided to see the extent of the crisis for myself by visiting Pul-e-Sokhta, a densely populated and rubbish-strewn area of Kabul that was notorious for drug use. The only relatively safe way of doing this was to have an armed policeman accompany me. So, on the day in question, my fixer, Zubair, approached a handful of young policemen sitting on metal chairs arrayed in the dust near a roundabout. He did not offer a direct bribe but, rather, said that we wanted someone's help to walk under an infamous bridge; $20 was the asking price for being a "guide"— a bribe by another name.

A friendly officer in his early twenties, who carried an AK-47 and wore a mask to shield his face from the dust, obligingly took us under an overpass newly built by USAID. "It's the best in Kabul," Zubair said.[46] The smell was putrid; the Kabul River flowed nearby, and there were discarded plastic bags everywhere. Hundreds of addicts have been known to gather there, but the site was partly underwater, and relatively few users were around. Fifteen men huddled together under shawls while they smoked heroin. A few scattered as soon as we arrived, scared off by my camera and the policeman; the armed cop's presence was serving its purpose.

It was a sorry sight. Discarded bottles, torn clothes, and rotten food lay under the bridge. The men were in a collective drugged stupor, their eyes bloodshot, crouching in the filth to get a fix. One man, who had a bushy brown goatee, said that he had lost his job and was then thrown in jail in Iran, where he became addicted to heroin—many Afghans had become addicts in neighboring Iran and Pakistan and then returned home, swelling the number of local drug users. The policeman, despite being surrounded by illegal drug use, did not attempt to arrest anyone.

Later, we left Kabul and drove east along a winding road towards Jalalabad and Sarobi, swapping the pollution of the capital for the fresh air of the countryside in order to see the opium crops up close. I saw countless poppy fields that remained unmolested by Afghan or foreign forces. Local security forces had erected checkpoints alongside rusted Soviet tanks covered in colorful graffiti, and they simply waved us on with a smile. Narrow mountains soon gave way to a wider expanse, which included some of the most spectacular scenery I had ever seen. Lush green poppy fields and lakes were interspersed with mud-home villages and memorials with colorful flags that commemorated fighters who had fallen against the Soviets or the Taliban. White painted rocks indicated areas that had been cleared of landmines. Overflowing trucks passed us on the road, moving entire families from one part of the country to the other, some of them nomads who shifted with the seasons.

Zubair and I had lunch—freshly cooked fish—in a small, decrepit hotel perched precariously above a valley. The cook was a young man who, along with his two younger cousins, earned a living for his family by selling the fish that were caught in a lake a few kilometers away. The Taliban used to terrorize the area, but today it had the illusion of calm, with clouds floating serenely in the sky and only the whirring sound of NATO helicopters in the distance.

*   *   *

In Kabul, I initially avoided speaking to NATO or government officials, because I knew they would offer little worthwhile information aside from PR spin. But I eventually decided I wanted to hear firsthand why the influence of PMCs in Afghanistan was being limited by the powers-that-be, so I arranged an interview with a senior official at the Ministry of Interior.

I arrived at the Ministry compound on foot, because cars were mostly blocked from using the access road due to the high incidence of suicide attacks and other bombings. Knowing this made me nervous as Zubair and I waited at the first visitors' checkpoint, while armed Afghan security officials radioed their superiors to confirm our presence. We waited and waited, and I tried to remain calm. There were no other Westerners around. After about fifteen minutes, we were waved through, whereupon my backpack was checked and I was frisked. When we reached the next checkpoint, the process was repeated.

A suicide bomber had breached security and killed six policemen nearby in April 2014, and Westerners came to be directly targeted by the Taliban and militants from 2013. One of the most deadly assaults was a brazen attack on a popular Kabul Lebanese restaurant in January 2014 in which Taliban gunmen sprayed diners with bullets, killing twenty-one people. Attacking foreigners was a key Taliban plan, a spokesman told *Rolling Stone* in August 2014. "They are part of our plan and we will target and kill them."[47]

We finally arrived at the Ministry's main building, where a guard asked me to switch on both my camera and video camera to ensure they were not explosive devices. Inside, the atmosphere was chaotic. I showed another guard my press pass while countless armed men walked in and out of the building. Insurgents had previously breached the department's outer defenses and made it to this point to cause mayhem, so all the security seemed somewhat illusory.

We pushed through a pair of large, cushioned doors and walked several flights up a staircase. Sitting on the landing between each pair of floors was a man armed with a large weapon. I smiled at one of them as we passed. He did not return the courtesy. We then waited in a room while a Ministry employee printed and stapled documents and a television showed the pro-US TOLO News channel, which had been launched by an Australian Afghan and was partly funded by Rupert Murdoch. Finally, we were called into the interview.

Sediq Sediqqi was the Ministry's "spokesperson and director of communication/public relations," and remained in the same position in 2015. He was clean-shaven and dressed in a sharp gray suit. He spoke fluent English, but was even more fluent when speaking to a visiting journalist. He told me that the government was committed to eradicating private security companies in the country. "Years ago we needed them, before the Afghan ... forces were built up, but not anymore," he said. With 350,000 Afghan security personnel, Sediqqi claimed the country would soon be standing on its own feet and would not need unaccountable firms running the place. He did not fear a collapse of the national army, as had occurred in Iraq in 2014 against the terror group ISIS. He also said that the Karzai regime had decided to remove the PMCs because it "had intelligence" they were "causing trouble" with locals, and were not helping the state to grow.

What he did not discuss was these companies being run by relatives of Hamid Karzai himself, including his brothers. One of the former Afghan president's siblings, Ahmed Wali Karzai, who had been murdered in Kandahar in 2011, was a notorious drug-dealing warlord. WikiLeaks documents released in 2010 hinted that one of his main activities had been controlling trucking on Highway 1, Afghanistan's national ring road, by demanding bribes.

Sediqqi fretted about the destabilizing conduct of the militants who had taken refuge in Pakistan, including the Taliban, and who launched attacks on Afghanistan from there. He did not sound overly optimistic that this would change in the near future. He also acknowledged the human rights and corruption problems in his country, though he believed these were slowly being addressed.[48] But when I asked him if he imagined leaving Kabul before all Western troops had left, he did not flinch, offering a robust defense of a brighter Afghan future. I did not believe him. Like many elite Afghans, he was sure to have a second passport, and might be tempted to use it when Western forces pulled out.

I also wanted to hear the official line on the Western occupation of the country, so I visited another Kabul compound to speak to M. Ashraf Haidari, who was Afghanistan's deputy assistant national security adviser and the senior policy and oversight adviser to President Karzai (he later went on to work in India as the Afghanistan deputy chief of mission). The suave Haidari studied at Georgetown University in Washington, then worked for seven years at the Afghan embassy in the US capital. When I met him, he was dressed in a Western suit, and his black hair was slicked back.

Haidari gave me the standard line on a range of issues: he said that PMCs were a problem and the government was trying to remove them, as most of them operated illegally, without a license; he wanted me to know that he "appreciates Australian support and troops in the war" (though he wished Canberra had treated Afghan refugee boat arrivals better); he told me that there had been "big progress in Afghanistan since 2001, as there was no real state when war began after 9/11." He was particularly keen to point out that the presence of Western forces in the country would be required, in some capacity, for the foreseeable future.[49] He said that ongoing Western involvement was essential because "terrorists" still resided in the country and must be defeated, "even if Osama bin Laden is dead."

I tried a number of times to challenge his statements, but without success—he knew the media game well. He did acknowledge that Afghanistan was a work in progress and that corruption still existed, but he insisted the nation was on the right track. He also refused to admit to any of the major corruption allegations that had been made against members of the Karzai family.

Perhaps the most troubling part of the interview, however, was when he asserted that the US-led night raids—a counterinsurgency tactic that simply created more enemies by arresting or killing suspected "militants" in the middle of a night—were "effective."[50] He briefly conceded the concern that US forces bursting into Afghan homes might convince people that the Americans were "occupiers, not liberators." (Many already believed the United States could not be otherwise; even the former US ambassador to Afghanistan and Iraq, Ryan C. Crocker, argued that Washington could only ever be a stranger on foreign soil.)[51]

But not to worry, Haidari said, new rules that allowed Afghans to lead the night raids would address the problems. Sovereignty had been restored, he claimed, though the United States still conducted these actions. The lack of legal accountability for US crimes in the country since 2001, including torture, could change with the International Criminal Court (ICC) finally announcing in 2014 that US soldiers should be held accountable for their actions. It seemed like a no-brainer, but Washington refused to recognize the ICC's jurisdiction.[52]

Occupation apologists like Haidari, willing participants in the Washington-led process, were easy to find in Afghanistan. Without them, the project would have been doomed to failure right from the beginning. Instead, a sham political process had lasted more than a decade—one that had armed and empowered the very warlords whom former US president George W. Bush had labeled "evildoers."

My next stop was the privately run, not-for-profit American University of Afghanistan, which had opened in 2006 and was housed behind high concrete, anti-blast walls. It was a tranquil space that seemed a million miles away from the chaos that plagued the nation. I had come to speak to an eloquent supporter of Hamid Karzai and hear why, for him, the former president and his worldview had been the only worthwhile game in town. Davood Moradian was educated in Britain, but returned to the capital of his homeland to teach political science at its new university at the urging of Karzai, whom he had met a few years earlier. He had been a senior adviser to the country's foreign minister and was now the director of the Afghan Institute for Strategic Studies. Our conversation took place on the green grass of the university's grounds, where men and women mixed freely, though the women all wore hijabs.

Having spent many years in the West, Moradian generally looked favorably on the US presence in his country; in many ways, he was the ideal face for the United States there because he was Afghan, wore modern clothing, and talked positively about the need for ongoing Western assistance. However, Moradian did fault America for not understanding Afghanistan, though he believed it had the "right intentions" in helping the place, and he also blamed Washington for empowering local warlords. He had few bad words to say about Karzai and his rule, dismissing the persistent corruption allegations. (He told me after we finished the interview that it was his "responsibility to not talk down Afghanistan when it's in need of much help.")

Moradian was more forthcoming when I asked him about the presence of PMCs and intelligence-gathering companies in the country. He said that when the "profit motive is supreme," there would inevitably be negative outcomes. He blamed people in Washington for allowing this system to thrive after 9/11, and said the companies that benefited from it should not be operating in Afghanistan. Again, he steadfastly refused to blame Karzai or his relatives for this trend.

I asked Moradian if he could see a future for himself in Afghanistan if the Taliban once again took over. He answered indirectly by saying he believed that the people would "never accept that," and that "it's essential Western partners continue to support the country and train and fund its army." If they did not, he believed, there would be a regional war that engulfed many nations.

Such fears about what would happen to Afghanistan after the United States finally departed remained common among the country's urban elite, who returned after the fall of the Taliban in 2001 and helped to swell Kabul's population from 1.2 million to over 5 million within a dozen years. Those who currently lived in relative safety behind high-security walls had the most to lose when the US-backed largesse petered out. Many had second homes in Dubai.[53]

It was hard to take Moradian's thin optimism about the country entirely seriously, and I wondered how many Afghans shared his desire to maintain a strong Western presence indefinitely. As recently as October 2012, he had written in *Foreign Policy* that the "United States and Afghans can still win—together."[54] Win what, exactly? Rejecting true independence seemed to me to be exactly the wrong way to go about weaning a humiliated nation off the Western teat. Such dependence had lasted for over a decade on hundreds of millions of dollars that had been packed into suitcases and shopping bags and given to the Karzai government by the CIA. Money bought influence, and corruption deepened.[55] President Ashraf Ghani pledged in late 2014 to fight corruption so long as the West continued financial and military support. He acknowledged in 2015 that "America's aid will not help our economy and infrastructure," and conceded the need for domestic industries.

Washington made backing its war increasingly impossible. In 2015, after years of detailing how US taxpayers' dollars had been spent in the country—at least $65 billion on the army and police alone—the Obama administration declared this information "classified," refusing even to explain the cost of teaching Afghan forces how to read and write. Security was the spuriously cited reason, though the decision was reversed after a public outcry.[56]

I did, however, agree wholeheartedly with Moradian's thinking on private security, which he compared to a leech that fed on war, "the dark side of globalization." During my visit, I heard the raw anger of locals who had experienced the deadly reality of privatized security.

On one such occasion, I was sitting among colorful cushions in a quiet room above a central Kabul restaurant, chatting to two Afghan men in their thirties, both of whom were from Wardak province. They told stories of Afghan security thugs causing mayhem in their areas, in the past and today.[57]

Habib-Ur-Rahman was a journalist with a long beard who wore traditional garb: a light-blue salwar kameez. Fahim, an unemployed engineer, also had a long beard and wore an army-green waistcoat. The men explained that before moving to Kabul they had both faced threats, not just from the Taliban and US forces—night raids were common, with innocent men from their villages often killed, or captured and held for months without charge before being released—but also from private security companies. The job of PMCs, Fahim told me, was to guard the convoys, but they regularly established so-called security perimeters around the army personnel and, in the process, often engaged in firefights with the Taliban. He said that innocent civilians were regularly caught in the crossfire. Watan Risk Management, a company prominent in this line of work, seemed to be particularly notorious.[58]

Fahim said that his cousin, a shopkeeper, had been shot dead by a private security guard a few years ago for no other reason than being in the wrong place at the wrong time. The PMC that employed the guard admitted fault and offered $20,000 in compensation, but Fahim said the family was still waiting for the money and the dead man's wife and children were now struggling financially despite family assistance. He said that such killings by PMCs were routine across the country, inflaming the resistance to the foreign occupation forces that used them. Journalist Anand Gopal cites in his book *No Good Men Among the Living* that in 2013 there were 60,000 to 80,000 armed private security employees, the vast bulk of whom worked for Afghan warlords. There were also tens of thousands of private militiamen employed by the Afghan government. A 2015 Human Rights Watch report cited Western-backed Afghan officials killing, abducting, and raping across the country.

As tea was brought in, followed by a large bowl of meat and a plate of bread, tomato, onion, and cucumber, Fahim and Habib-Ur-Rahman continued to speak lucidly about their country's situation, without resorting to hyperbole. Fahim reiterated his view that PMCs had "only brought misery and violence." It was also clear that the fact that men in the Afghan army were getting paid much less than private military company men had increased the resentment.

Neither man had ever believed Karzai when he pledged to completely disband the companies, asserting that they were controlled by "powerful" people close to the government. "They have too much to lose if the companies shut down," Habib-Ur-Rahman told me. But Fahim also believed that PMCs, whose employees "never face justice for killing and maiming civilians, will become unnecessary from 2014 because there [will] no longer be any convoys to protect; the US will have left." This never happened. Tellingly, he then said he was not overly concerned about the withdrawal of Western troops, because the Taliban, who he expected to take over, would "hopefully bring some stability and peace to the country, as happened before the 2001 invasion."

This last view is one that may not be shared by many women in Afghanistan. The country's female population endured many severe restrictions under Taliban rule.[59] Change had been slow in coming since the US-led invasion. There had been improvements for women, particularly in some areas of Kabul. While being driven around the city, I saw shops selling all forms of women's clothing, including Western-style garments, and girls in white hijabs, rather than burqas, walking to school. But, as has regularly been detailed by Human Rights Watch, the vast majority of the country's women remains mired in repression when it comes to education, birth control, freedom of movement, and justice.[60]

I had an opportunity to raise some of these issues when I visited a suburb of Kabul that was crowded with Soviet-style concrete apartment blocks. The buildings were enlivened by few colors, except for washing hanging from the windows and children playing around their entrances. I imagined the soulless structures had remained largely unchanged in the decades since the Russians had built them. I knocked on the graffiti-daubed door of one apartment, and a woman dressed in a black hijab answered.

Afghan MP Saima Khogyani, who hailed from Nangarhar province, welcomed me, and I took off my shoes to enter the apartment, which had no security. The hallway floor was concrete, and cold under my feet. I was led into a small living room, which had green couches and a few photos of children on the peeling walls. It was dank and lit by a solitary light on the ceiling. There were two other women there who remained mostly silent during the conversation that followed.

Khogyani did not support the ongoing presence of foreign troops in Afghanistan, though she worried about what would happen when the bulk of them left.[61] She was pragmatic about the PMCs, telling me that they provided jobs for many Afghan men, and that this in turn helped the men's wives, daughters, and sisters. She knew about the human rights abuses that the firms committed, but stressed that "in a poor country such as Afghanistan, employment opportunities are vital."

Khogyani's pragmatism ran deep. She had to be very cautious about what she said because making a comment that could be interpreted as criticism of PMCs or their warlord or political backers might get her killed. It was as simple as that.

On the issue of what confronts Afghanistan's women, Khogyani said that Afghan men tended to see women as needing to be protected and respected. "They react if women are mistreated or disrespected," she said. But she was not afraid to explain the reality of life for a woman, even one who was an MP: "Being a woman in Afghanistan is tough. I'm often unable to speak in the parliament because I'm a woman … [I'm] not given appropriate protection because I'm a woman. I fear for the future of the country because I'm a woman." At the end of Karzai's term in 2014, Khogyani said that one of his "greatest legacies" was to allow women to speak in public. "We are here, and we can say whatever we want, and we can say it to him. Whether he does what we ask is something else, but he listens."

Our talk shifted to the development of the country's mining industry, in which Khogyani was involved. She had been invited by Canberra to visit Australia, where she expected to see how "you've well managed the mineral wealth."[62] I asked Khogyani if she was aware of the exploitation of resources in other poor countries (I was thinking of Papua New Guinea and Haiti) by multinationals and corrupt officials who were uninterested in planning for long-term sustainability. She responded that the contracts that had so far been signed in Afghanistan protected its resources, and that local people would reap the benefits.

Afghanistan had massive untapped mineral reserves. The investor website Money Morning ("Only the news you can profit from") blurted this out in 2011: "Think of Australia, Canada and Latin America. They pale in comparison to the goldmine Afghanistan could be sitting on."[63] The US Geological Society confirmed this wealth prediction by mapping the country's minerals in 2010— the state had trillions of dollars' worth of natural resources—and since then the scramble to claim them had been well underway. The countless foreign companies that had so far struggled to secure mineral-rich areas welcomed new laws, approved by the Afghan Cabinet in 2013, to assist them in doing so.

Other states had joined the feeding frenzy. China had already invested heavily in Afghan mines, while Iran was also spending big in the country, seeking influence through aid projects.[64] Britain announced funding of £10 million to support the Afghan Ministry of Mines when Prime Minister David Cameron hosted UK investors and mining contractors in March 2013. Many individuals had their eyes on the future, too. In 2012, a former US ambassador to Afghanistan, Zalmay Khalilzad, joined the board of Tethys Petroleum, a company dedicated to oil and gas exploitation in Central Asia.

Few Western politicians were urging any caution in this environment, but one who did was Australian Greens Senator Lee Rhiannon, who said in 2012 that the Australian government should not prioritize aid money for "opening up Afghanistan to overseas mining interests." She added that "Afghanistan has little capacity to negotiate the best deal for local interests."[65] I admired Khogyani's bravery. In a country that practiced such blatant misogyny, it took guts to stand up publicly and demand better things for all citizens, including women.

That afternoon I met Maryam Koofi, another female MP, from Takhar province. Her home office had security cameras and armed guards. During our interview, her three mobile phones rang constantly—she said that constituents from her district always needed advice and assistance. There was an unsuccessful attempt on her life in Kabul in 2014. Koofi consolidated what I learned from Khogyani. Like her fellow MP, she was not overly critical of PMCs, citing the positive factor of Afghan men getting employment and supporting their families financially. She also acknowledged her hesitation in saying too much publicly about the companies, especially the ones connected to powerful families, because if she did, she would suffer even more threats than usual. "I face severe threats as a female MP," Koofi told me, "but I try to do good in my province to rehabilitate former Taliban fighters [helping them find] peaceful ways to earn a living and turn away from the gun."

After the interview, she showed me the day's issue of the local paper. Her photo accompanied an article that said she was one of the most influential women in the country, which brought the threats against her into sharp relief.

In Kabul, a large hydrogen balloon sat idly inside a compound, a gift from the United States to the Afghan government, to monitor insurgent activity. It was often seen hovering in the sky above the city and had reportedly been very helpful in catching militants after an attack—an eye in the sky. But in terms of outsourcing in this country, nothing was off-limits. Even intelligence gathering had been privatized.

"They either make it up or exaggerate threats because they don't have reliable intel themselves, and tell clients everywhere is dangerous and they should stay secure in a compound"—so said the head of a private intelligence company in Kabul, explaining how most of his competitors serviced their foreign clients, by lying.[66]

Clive, not his real name, who requested anonymity, was Swedish and in his mid-thirties, with closely cropped hair, and we were talking in a Kabul café. His organization described itself as an "information management consultancy" that provided "ground truth" to enable companies to "operate effectively" in Afghanistan. The group was just one of many such businesses that had sprung up in the country in the last decade, offering the kind of information that the military supposedly could not access itself and had to pay a corporation to source.

Clive was deliberate in his use of the word "information." He said his organization did not gather "intelligence," arguing that that word had been abused and misunderstood over the last decade. He said intelligence had come to mean information that was used for military purposes, something his company, to the best of his knowledge, had never sourced. His major clients were actually Kabul-based embassies and foreign companies that wanted up-to-date, reliable information about the country's various provinces, and how volatile they were at any given time. "They're naturally risk-averse," Clive told me, "and have never ignored our advice and visited an area, as they need to get permission from [their] superiors back home, though I was once asked to rewrite a few lines [of advice] for a client … [who] said he simply had to visit an area, and his superiors relied on my advice."

The company employed a handful of expats to analyze the rough information sent in by twenty Afghan contacts around the country. I asked if there was a risk that these Afghans would send false information as payback against local enemies; this had happened to the Americans, who were regularly given untruthful intelligence that then lead to night raids or the bombing of innocent civilians, all because a tribal elder or another aggrieved individual wanted to use the US military to settle a score. "It's possible," Clive said, "but I don't think [it happens] very often." He admitted, however, that the vast majority of the information his company received was not independently verified. I said the work sounded mundane, but Clive said it did not simply involve reading local publications and sending reports to information-hungry clients in faraway places. Rather, he said, it entailed discovering the lay of the land in various provinces, daily if need be.

Clive argued that such work was increasingly being done by private companies rather than government agencies because "today's wars aren't between two equal sides. Armies don't fight like they used to." He said it constantly struck him how clueless the US and other Western forces were when it came to understanding local cultures, something he put down to the excessive time such personnel spent in a "military-enforced bubble … barely speaking to locals. An insurgency is complex and doesn't allow simplistic explanations of good versus evil."

This cluelessness was evident in how Western forces did not seem to understand why resistance to the Afghanistan occupation was deepening, and how they enhanced their ignorance by paying millions of dollars to corporations to tell them why they were hated. Washington's counterinsurgency strategy involved trying to understand Afghan lives, hence General David Petraeus's directive to soldiers in 2010 to "spend time" with locals, to "listen, consult, and drink lots of tea," and the development of approaches like the Human Terrain System that wielded anthropology and sociology to try to understand the local population better.[67] The director of the counterinsurgency center in Kabul wrote in an email in late 2011 that he hoped to teach his students about "tribal/ village structure" and "what to do to establish mutually respectful relationships." But this was a futile plan, because it presumed that the US could bomb people and romance them at the same time. It was why the ubiquitous David Kilcullen, an Australian counter-insurgency figure who worked with Petraeus on these strategies, should never be taken seriously after being the public face of a failed strategy tried in Iraq, Afghanistan, and elsewhere.

I gained access to some of the intelligence gathered to this end by the US consultancy firm AECOM, which was hired by NATO in 2011 to spy on mosques, universities, and the general community throughout Afghanistan.[68] The company's reports were delivered as spreadsheets with columns titled "Atmospheric Value," "District," and "Province," and they mostly comprised uninteresting conversations between people who were complaining about the Taliban or foreign forces, or corruption in the Kabul government. Take this entry, from March 12, 2012:

ASC-504 overheard a conversation between two Uzbek males between the ages of 40–45 at market in the city of Shibirghan:

One man said, "The other day I was riding on a bus when it became very windy. It seemed as if it was raining dust. People were saying that this could be a sign [of] God's wrath. This is happening to us because the Americans have burned the Quran, but we are calmly sitting idle. We should be rising up against the Americans for what they have done. We are being punished for doing nothing."

The other resident stated, "I do not know, but it might be possible."

And, from March 16, 2012:

> ASC ATE10-003 overheard a 50-year-old Hazara male and a 65-year-old Tajik male in Kandahar province:
>
> The 50-year-old said, "If ISAF continues making mistakes, I promise you that the Afghan people will no longer accept apologies. Every other week, they kill innocent people and insult our religion. I want the entire Afghan community to be united …"
>
> The 65-year-old said, "I believe the Americans are becoming like the Soviets. The Americans killed thousands of innocent people in Iraq and now they are doing the same thing in Afghanistan. They are killing innocent people so they can get revenge for their military personnel that were killed in Afghanistan."

The problem was that these statements could be enough to prompt elements within the US army to capture and interrogate the people involved, because of a perceived sympathy for the insurgency.[69] It was very difficult to make a definitive link between such intelligence and actual NATO actions. But when I met a senior analyst, Carol, at one of Afghanistan's most respected think-tanks, the Afghanistan Analysts Network, she told me there was ample evidence that Western troops regularly actioned night raids on the barest of suspicions.

Carol said it was now rare for a foreign government not to use privatized intelligence-gathering services. Before 2006, she explained, intelligence had mainly been acquired to meet counter-terrorism objectives. But Washington soon realized that broader knowledge was needed, such as an understanding of the tribal system, or even who was marrying whom in strategic areas. Carol said that the war on terror had resulted in the blending of what she called "peace building" with military tactics: "It's the militarization of development that leaves space for privatized intelligence to fill the void, because Western donors ... are desperate to understand the country." This was a short-term strategy, which ignored certain realities, such as the fact that many Afghans had ongoing contact with the Taliban. In NATO's eyes, this was grounds for suspicion, but the Taliban would inevitably be part of any future peace settlement.

Carol told me how she had recently met an Afghan man who had been arrested by US special forces in a night raid: "He never knew why he was arrested and he told of clueless US questioning, suggesting they had no real idea about the area or culture." Apparently, the Americans had been tracking the man's mobile phone and had determined that "suspicious people [were] speaking to each other." Carol said that privatized intelligence simply "adds one more level of confusion."

I had already heard about how deep this confusion ran when I met an Afghan translator who had recently returned from working with the Americans in Kandahar during night raids. He hated the work and said the United States rarely knew what it was doing. "They only understood force," he said. He also explained that the intelligence being relied upon was often wrong, and that during the raids he struggled to make sense of the chaos unleashed in Afghan homes when the US soldiers burst in on sleeping men, women, and children.

Carol slammed the presence of US special forces, calling them mere "Taliban hunters." She argued that "being Taliban or related to Taliban members is not necessarily against the country's positive future, but [the] US seems to see all Taliban as enemy." This did not bode well for future peace in Afghanistan. Documents released by former NSA whistle-blower Edward Snowden revealed that NATO killed not just Taliban leaders but countless low-level and mid-level Afghans, as well as drug dealers. Little evidence was needed to kill these individuals. The head of ISAF intelligence in Afghanistan, Michael T. Flynn, explained the mindset: "The only good Talib is a dead Talib."[70]

Another consequence of intelligence privatization was that local security entrepreneurs had become the new Afghan elite—the inevitable rise of locals out to exploit the naivety of the country's occupiers. A small class of Afghan entrepreneurs grew, often flaunting their wealth in cars and houses, and making a fortune through American contracts, patronage, influence, and corruption.[71] Carol said this exemplified profiteering that she had noticed since first arriving in the country. "If you have a contract with the US as a local, you create [an] imbalance between haves and have-nots," she says. It was the same economic disparity I had witnessed in Papua New Guinea and Haiti.

Disaster capitalism had also thrived in Afghanistan's neighbor, Pakistan, where I traveled to the capital, Islamabad, as well as to Peshawar and Karachi. Here, too, the private security and intelligence business had expanded dramatically since 9/11, with violent internal conflict feeding the PMC beast. This was aided by the now familiar crossover between the government, military establishments, and the profiteers—a leading journalist in Karachi passed me a list of sixty-two former senior figures in the Pakistan army who now worked for PMCs but maintained close ties with their old colleagues.

The civilian government did not control Pakistan. Rather, it was the country's national security organization, Inter-Services Intelligence, which had the power and wielded it ruthlessly, including backing militancy and terrorism while claiming to be a US ally. A leading Pakistani journalist with close ties to the country's military took me to the suburb of Sohrab Goth, on the outskirts of Karachi. There, I saw the run-down concrete apartment blocks sitting far back from the road in swirls of dust, where many key al-Qaeda and Taliban members had lived since 9/11, with the protection of the state and the support of local sympathizers.

I had never been to a country where the state itself was so often absent, incompetent, or criminal. Nor had I ever been to one where conspiracy theories were so rampant. The daily newspapers were filled with wild accusations. During my visit, a columnist for the *Nation* wrote that there were "15,000 [US] marines in the capital," although it was a fact that no one I spoke to took seriously.[72] Sometimes, however, vague suspicions had some foundation. In 2011, Raymond Davis, a former US soldier, killed two Pakistani men in Lahore while working for a PMC, assisting the CIA in tracking militants. Despite calls for him to face justice in Pakistan, he was flown back to protection in America.[73]

PMCs had been able to grow in Pakistan because they were barely regulated. "Private security companies operate under 'law of the jungle,'" boomed a headline in the *Express Tribune*, alleging that at least 500 PMCs were at work in Pakistan[74]—it had also been estimated that there were up to 300,000 private security personnel there.[75] The security companies themselves, however, had a very different view of their existence in the region.

In Islamabad, I met a senior manager of the multinational security firm G4S (the company was bought out in late 2012 by Pakistani company Security and Management Services, though the influence of its former owners remained), Muhammad Alamgir Khan, who had once worked for the Pakistani air force. He told me that the company guarded the offices of the National Bank of Pakistan, UN agencies, Motorola, BP Pakistan, Chevron, Caltex, and the US embassy. He then explained the importance of PMCs in Pakistan: "If direct foreign investment doesn't come to Pakistan, the economy fails. Private security helps protect these investments." Later, in Karachi, in the office of another G4S head, where I was surrounded by photos of him standing alongside famous figures such as former president Pervez Musharraf, I was told that the company's work was a "natural fit" in modern Pakistan, "protecting NGOs and the UN."

I also visited Peshawar, an edgy, dusty town near the Afghan border that had seen countless bombings and other violence in recent years. In the late 1980s, this place had been heaving

with foreign contractors who were involved in the war against
the Soviets in Afghanistan—the American Club was a favorite
hangout of journalists, spies, and mercenaries—but today there
were few non-Afghans here.[76] All the women wore burqas, while
all the men had long, bushy beards. I wore a salwar kameez, like
a traditional Pashtun man, and blended in with the locals. I was
advised not to spend much time walking the town's streets, due to
the risk of kidnapping or assault—though sitting in a car in grid-
locked traffic, where there was the possibility of a suicide attack,
did not exactly calm my nerves.

In Peshawar I met a senior manager in the provincial government, Mohammed, who told me about the relationships between
the US military, USAID, and private companies.[77] He said that
corporations had mapped local communities in the Federally
Administrated Tribal Areas, and this information was used by
the US army in planning action against suspected militants.
"Villagers are asked personal questions about their children," he
explained, "including ID numbers, families, and how many people
sleep in the house. There are local Pakistanis employed by contractors to do the interviews, due to language fluency, but locals
aren't told where the information may go or for what it may be
used." Mohammed gave the example of the consultancy firm Gulf
Associates, which had surveyed the citizens of Peshawar on "water
supply and drainage." Every household was asked questions about
their family size and "told they needed to provide these details to
get water."

Unfortunately, the focus of such community mapping appeared
to be military dominance, with civilians being an afterthought.
Certainly the residents I spoke to believed this mapping was not
being done to help them, but rather to pressure the Pakistani military to crack down on militants who operated against Western
interests there and in Afghanistan.

I also visited the sprawling compound of the Khyber News
Bureau, a local media company, whose journalists confirmed my

suspicion that military and humanitarian work were all too often fused in the post-9/11 world. The journalists told me that foreign NGOs, especially American organizations, often acted as fronts for Washington's ever-deepening spying activities. The bureau's compound had allegedly once been used by Blackwater as a base for its mercenaries. Blackwater had gathered intelligence that had fed directly into the US military drone program. The firm has worked for the CIA, JSOC (America's leading counter-terrorism force), and the Pakistani state.[78]

Everyone I spoke to said they felt as if their country was occupied by outside forces.

One of my aims in Afghanistan was to understand the thinking of the private security contractors who worked there—to know what made someone join a company that was literally in the firing line.

Soon after I arrived in Kabul, I went to one of the city's few quasi-legal drinking holes, the Gandamack (shut down in 2014). It was an airless bar whose walls were covered with images of the British Empire, such as ships sailing off on the high seas to liberate natives. It was full of Americans, Asians, Russians, and South Africans drinking to The Doors' "The End" and Tone Loc's "Funky Cold Medina." Cigarette smoke swirled in the air.

I talked to three South African men in their fifties who had all been in Afghanistan for about seven years, assisting the US forces with logistics and security. One of them wore a bomber jacket, on the back of which was inscribed: "Operation Iraqi Freedom," along with countless world flags arranged in a circle. The most talkative of the trio, Peter, said, "I'm only here for the money, and it's big." He added that the security situation had only worsened since he had first arrived, when things were already wild.[79] The other men agreed.

There was no desire among the group to return to South Africa. Peter said he imagined that before most Western forces left, he would depart himself, going "somewhere else like here, maybe Sudan." They would follow the money.

On another night, I found myself entering a seedy Afghan bar, at the entrance to which a security man demanded that all patrons remove their knives and guns and place them in lockers. Inside, I was surrounded by muscle-bound men in tight T-shirts, their bare arms often covered in tattoos; the few women in the crowd seemed to revel in their attention. Some of the men later told me they were on steroids, and I was reminded of a comment made by a human rights advocate in Kabul, that if you go to a party in the city, "a quarter of the men will have no necks."

I met Josh, a large, gentle, tattooed man in his late twenties, from Townsville, Australia. He had previously been in the Australian army in Iraq, but had now been in Afghanistan for six months. "It's for the money," he said in a matter-of-fact way, confirming a now-familiar trend.

Australian contractors played a significant role in Afghanistan's privatization boom, as they did in Iraq; but the experience was not always a happy one.[80] At least a dozen Australian contractors had been killed there over the past decade, though their names were rarely recorded.[81] Former Australian soldier Robert Langdon, whom I unsuccessfully tried to visit in the notorious Policharki prison, had been found guilty of killing an Afghan colleague in 2008 while working for the PMC Four Horseman International, and was serving a twenty-year sentence, escaping the death penalty.[82]

After talking to Josh, I had a lengthy conversation with Greg, a former British soldier in his thirties who now worked for a PMC. It was a friendly chat, although we disagreed about most things ("You're a liberal," he said). He fought in Iraq in 2003, and while he did not question the rationale for the war at the time, he now referred to former British prime minister Tony Blair as "a cunt," because of the lies he had told over weapons of mass destruction. Today, he coordinated security at US bases around Afghanistan.

Greg was honest. "We're looking for the new war," he said, referring to what PMCs were doing as the conflicts in Iraq and Afghanistan wound down for the West. But, he added, "we aren't baby killers"—apparently assuming I thought PMCs were filled with reckless men on a collective adrenaline rush. He explained that companies such as Academi had previously hired former soldiers who "only knew how to kill," and that that was where the PMC reputation for firing first and asking questions later came from. Today, Greg said, the system was far more regulated, and the hiring practices in PMCs much tighter. The "rogue elements" were now largely absent, he claimed.

"I'm only doing this for the money," Greg said, adding that he dismissed the mental health concerns associated with the work.[83] He had a wife and three kids back in Ireland, and spent nine weeks in Afghanistan then three weeks back home. "My wife knew what she was getting into when we married. I'm from a military family. I was sent to boarding school at eleven," he said. Greg imagined doing this work for as long as he physically could: "I would never earn this kind of money back in Ireland."

The bar became increasingly rowdy as the night progressed. The handful of women, some wearing sleeveless dresses— impossible outside this smoke-filled room—danced with men of various ages to bad techno. Burly men started pushing each other around, and heated words were exchanged—the typical drunken antics of people who had little opportunity to socialize.[84]

This fantasy world started unraveling in 2014, with many drinking establishments shut down over security concerns, foreigners leaving, aid reducing, and the economic bubble bursting. Afghan companies had become too reliant on international support and now struggled to survive. "It's an artificial economy," said Khan Afzal Hadawal, the first deputy governor of the country's central bank, Da Afghanistan Bank, to the *Wall Street Journal* in 2014.[85] This was one of the US legacies here—a short boom that enriched a few in Afghanistan but left the majority of the population poor and enraged.

Pakistan and Afghanistan were not truly independent nations before September 11, 2001, but since the attacks on New York and Washington they were pushed even further from sovereignty, and transformed into entities that sustained corporations overseas.

The bulk of Western forces in Afghanistan left in 2014.[86] But the country's financial situation would be perilous without ongoing international support, not least because PMCs employed over 100,000 people in 2011, the majority of them Afghan. A December 2014 conference in London, attended by Afghan president Ashraf Ghani, UK prime minister David Cameron, and US secretary of state John Kerry, pledged not to walk away from the nation in its "transformation decade." Afghanistan was broke, and without foreign aid it would collapse. It was a fake state.

John Sopko, special inspector general for Afghanistan recon-struction, outlined the challenges in a 2014 speech in Washington. After reminding his audience that US investment in the nation was "more money than we've spent on construction for any one country in our nation's entire history"—over $104 billion—he announced that there was still around $16 billion unspent "in the pipeline."[87]

The departure of foreign troops would leave a huge vacuum that would have to be filled by Afghan politicians and other power-brokers determined to rely mainly on their own people rather than on incoming aid. In 2010, Afghanistan received around $15.7 billion in "development" support, about equal to the state's gross domestic product. This would inevitably decrease as Western forces withdrew.[88] The International Monetary Fund warned that Afghanistan faced a $7.7 billion annual shortfall until 2018. The tragic irony of the failed Western project in the country was that foreign nations had spent years propping up a corrupt government, leaving Kabul unable to survive if this tap was switched off.[89]

The sheer scale of the foreign troop presence, and its equipment, in Afghanistan was overwhelming. NATO estimated that removing all ISAF equipment by the end of 2014 would require a shipping container to leave the country every seven minutes.[90] But the war economy would not end. Instead, as NATO tried but failed to achieve in Iraq, a mentoring and training program for Afghan forces would continue. The occupation was rebranded with a kinder face, but the hated counterinsurgency battle, which often targeted civilians, was ongoing.[91] Still, Afghan forces, after receiving US mentoring despite committing abuses indulged or ignored by the Americans, would be largely on their own. By 2015, the Taliban, far more fractured than its 1990s incarnation, had become in many districts far less ideological. Negotiating with one central leader was no longer possible.

A different future for Afghanistan must be forged—one in which aid is not coupled to sovereignty. Trophy projects must be abandoned, and the will of the Afghan people respected.[92] The building of civil and political institutions, without foreign for-profit corporations being intimately involved in the process, is vital. After more than three decades of conflict, the population deserves freedom from outside intervention. The West was not, as it has claimed, Afghanistan's savior or its liberating force. We created chaos, and the Afghan people now need support, time, and space to recover from the resulting turmoil.

2

Greece: "We are just numbers, not human lives"

Greeks are stupid. They put barbed wire on their sun.
Algerian refugee housed in Corinth detention center, 2013

I was traveling with a blind Afghan refugee, Chaman. It was a searingly hot day when we arrived in the Greek city of Corinth by train from Athens. The detention center was near the station, and as we talked on a quiet Sunday afternoon along empty streets I couldn't help but think how unusual we must have looked—an Australian journalist holding and guiding the arm of a young, talkative man with aviator sunglasses. It was an industrial town with countless businesses competing to survive grim economic times. We passed an electrical power station and walked the short distance to the facility imprisoning refugees.

Chaman had the names of some detainees. We hoped to visit them and understand their plight. We arrived outside the facility with bags of tea and sugar—a gift (or bribe, depending on your point of view) that Chaman knew was required to sweeten the Greek guards who could allow us access. A number of Bengali, Tamil, and Pakistani men were hovering around the main entrance, and they also had bags of food and drink for both the guards and detainees.

Securing formal permission to visit Greek detention centers had proved impossible. A few months before I arrived, I applied through official channels and received a polite but firm rejection; journalists were rarely, if ever, accepted. I wanted to hear the stories of those imprisoned at a time when a wave of racist violence continued against new arrivals.

Chaman and I entered the facility just after visiting hours began, at 4 p.m., and were asked by the guards to hand over our identification. I offered my Australian driver's license and Chaman showed his Greek identity card. The guards were curious as to why an Australian was there. I explained I was visiting my Afghan friend Mohammadi as one of the police said, in halting English, that he had once visited Melbourne.

Apart from demanding some ID, the police asked us no questions and did not check our bags or ask how I knew Mohammadi. Despite being told by every NGO and reporter that it was difficult to gain access to detention facilites (the inside of the center itself—the rooms where men slept, ate, and showered—was inaccessible), I was surprised how relatively straightforward it was once we arrived.

I saw high fences in the distance topped with barbed wire and buildings painted in white. A police van arrived and a few guards appeared, dressed all in blue, each with a gun holstered by his side. They enquired with us in Greek where the detainees we wanted to visit were located—in which part of the camp. Chaman had called before we arrived to ask one of the men the number of the compound. All the visitors piled into a sweltering van and were driven 200 meters through a series of high fences, opened for us one at a time. I saw a number of detainees gathering behind one of the fences. Most men were clad in white T-shirts and pants, though some were also in shorts and shirts.

The van came to a halt, and the guards put on gloves. We stepped out of the vehicle and walked the short distance to stand in front of a high fence with barbed wire at the top. A number of police surrounded us, watching our every move, asking again what was inside the plastic bags—just tea and sugar; they continually directed the refugees to stand back from the fence so that we could not pass them anything. I was holding Chaman's hand so he knew where to stand.

The detainees were all desperate to speak to us. They were all Afghan men under thirty, mostly from the Hazara ethnic group, though I saw a few older men with gray beards standing behind the others. The police had picked them all up in Athens, after they had lived free in the community for different periods of time. Some told me that they had been inside detention centers for more than eighteen months—the maximum time allowed, until the law changed in 2014, that the Greek state could indefinitely detain a refugee. Some had been detained for more than two years.

The Greek Council for Refugees argued that this new directive was in breach of Greek, European, and international law.[1] In such a toxic political climate, it was left to this group to manage the huge load on the Greek system. Spokesperson Elina Sarantou was angry about her country's attitude towards refugees. The European Refugee Fund, as well as national and international foundations, supported her group. With around sixty staff and little public trust in NGOs after some high-profile scandals, its profile was small and funds were limited. As a consequence, the council was overwhelmed by the demand. It had only twelve lawyers and twelve social workers in a country that needed thousands more— they saw over 8,000 refugees annually. "We are running programs of legal support for victims of racist violence, by police, far-right thugs, and others," Sarantou said, "though 80 percent of these victims don't have legal papers so are scared of taking the cases to court."

The sheer number of asylum seekers arriving on Greek shores has given Greece an opportunity to use both its head and its heart. Sarantou explained how the government started an Asylum Service in 2013—a small and positive step towards addressing the abuses in arbitrary detention. The UNHCR praised the move. Despite this, she said, police still saw asylum seekers as "clandestines"; the police still had an "Aliens Department." The service was mostly funded by the UN and remained in need of more backing. The EU's border management agency, Frontex—condemned by Human Rights Watch in 2011 for "exposing migrants to inhuman and degrading conditions"[2]—said that eight out of ten refugees coming to Europe were entering through Greece.

The Greek infrastructure of control for asylum seekers included a first-reception center in Evros, on the land border with Turkey, which was funded by the UNHCR and the EU. It had a maximum stay of twenty-five days, and claims were assessed in that time if possible. "It's a decent place," Sarantou said, "though still like a prison, and you can't leave. We oppose these facilities, as there are few rights. The state has laws that put Greeks first for employment and asylum seekers last. They should provide protection for those in need—especially minors, single-parent families, and those with health and psychological problems."

Instead, Athens announced in 2012 that it had opened thirty new camps for immigrants on disused army sites. With countless refugees living in squalor in and around Athens—I saw many sleeping rough and in need of a good meal and a wash—it was unsurprising that the government announced the decision as a response to rising levels of violent crime. With unemployment soaring and the youth jobless rate reaching well above 50 percent, the state reacted according to a tradition of impulsiveness, lacking any long-term plan.

"Hundreds of thousands of people are wandering aimlessly through the streets," said the former citizens' protection minister, Michalis Chrysohoidis, "being forced to break the law, being exploited by criminal networks and deterring legitimate immigrants from staying in the country." Authorities announced that migrants would be moved into shabby "closed hospitality centers," to keep them off the streets and out of sight of angry Greek voters.[3]

In mid 2014, Global Detention Project released a comprehensive list of Greek facilities that itemized over thirty central and remote locations that were mostly staffed by police—a group with a long history in Greece of assaulting refugees.[4]

It was a strange and sad experience, standing on one side of the Corinth fence, under the glaring sun, unable to get inside the center, and exchanging halting words with caged men. Everyone wanted to talk to us—to share their stories, explain their pain, and protest their detention. "We are suffering in here," they said. A mass hunger strike by detainees occurred in June 2014 to protest a new ministerial order allowing indefinite detention, unofficially supported by harsh European Union directives.[5] The facility was hit with riots in 2013. A statement released by the migrants read in part: "With the systematic and open-ended detention, the Greek government is massacring us. They are wasting our lives and killing our dreams and hopes inside the prisons. All of that while none of us has committed a crime."[6]

Chaman translated for me. None of the men wanted to return to Afghanistan because they feared persecution or worse. They all hated Greece for the way it treated refugees. They wished to get to Germany, or other European nations with better conditions. One man showed me a bullet lodged in his foot since he had been shot by guards while trying to escape. He had asked for surgery to remove it but was refused. All the men stated that the police regularly beat them, and that conditions inside were awful. The European Court of Human Rights had condemned conditions inside Greek detention centers eleven times, as had many Greek courts when considering excessive periods of detention. The UN opposed extended periods of administrative detention as "standard practice aimed at discouraging irregular entry or stay in the country."[7]

After one minute, the guards wanted us to leave. We refused and said we needed more time. I passed the tea and sugar to the detainees, and after ten minutes we were directed to leave. The fence was firmly shut. The smell of sweat hung in the air from men cooped up in the searing heat. Chaman told me that he felt obliged to help his fellow Afghans and visit them in detention, taking them to lawyers and doctors in Athens when they were released. "It's part of my mission," he said.

Afghan refugees like Chaman experienced anxiety every day. During our time together, he offered countless anecdotes detailing the practical effects of extreme austerity on his life. This was not just economic harshness, but a culture that tolerated and celebrated exclusion. His own story was a helpful reminder of why Greece made a fundamental mistake by shunning and imprisoning such people out of fear and political expediency. He was willing to be a productive member of society, but felt jaded and skeptical.

Chaman was twenty-four. His family had moved to Iran from Afghanistan, where he was born, when he was six, because the Taliban threatened his Hazara father. Near Tehran, Chaman said that life as a child was fine, not too tough; it was only when he became a teenager that he started getting into trouble. When he was sixteen he asked his local imam at the mosque about the supremacy of Islam and questioned its infallibility. He was sent to prison for fourteen days, interrogated about his views, and asked where he was getting such "insulting" perspectives. Why didn't he support the chants of "Death to America!" and "Death to Israel!"? Soon enough, he was imprisoned again, for one month, and again asked to explain why he had such controversial views on Islam, as authorities feared he might inspire other citizens to challenge the state.

Chaman had only had four years of schooling, and at sixteen he started working for no pay with a mechanic in order to learn new skills. He was soon very proficient and started his own business, at his family home, repairing motorbikes. But within a few years his eyesight started to fail. He went to doctors and the hospital, and he was diagnosed with cataracts. Subsequent surgery was botched, rendering his sight even worse. By his late teens, he could barely see anything at all.

Life became increasingly difficult for him in Iran. With the aid of a people-smuggler and borrowed money, he made the journey to Europe, leaving his parents and four siblings behind. He arrived in Greece and entered the community, but he was soon taken by police into detention. He escaped and applied for asylum, claiming that his life would be in danger if he lived in Afghanistan or Iran as a Hazara man.

One of his brothers, also in Greece seeking asylum, had his case rejected by the Greek authorities and was sent back to Afghanistan—a country he did not know. He had disappeared, and his family had no idea where he was or what had happened to him. "I lie awake at night worrying about him," Chaman told me.

Today, Chaman lived in a small apartment with other Afghan men. His room, shared with another Hazara man, had one mattress on the floor and a bed in the corner. It was a cozy place, barely furnished, and the living room had a TV tuned to BBC Persian. One night when I visited, he played on his homemade guitar, constructed from a hard hat and a long piece of wood and strings. It was one way for him to achieve brief inner peace.

He told me that he disliked being in Greece. He would have preferred Germany or England, because in Greece they treated refugees with callous disregard. Hundreds of Syrian refugees protested in central Syntagma Square in late 2014, demanding permission to leave for other European states. He had been employed as a translator, as he spoke English, Dari, Greek, Farsi, and other languages. His English was excellent because he had worked as a guide to American Christian missionaries who had passed through Greece. He was kind and funny, vehemently opposed to Islam ("My country, Afghanistan, would be much safer if everybody had no religion anymore"). He enjoyed his atheism and feared what would happen when his temporary Greek identity papers expired at the end of 2015. He said he hoped to extend his visa, but it was impossible to know if that would happen. He lived with uncertainty.

Chaman said that attacks on him and his Afghan friends by neo-Nazi Golden Dawn had been worse a few years ago, when the group's leadership was free and its minions roamed beyond political or police persecution. In 2012 countless immigrants were stabbed, beaten up, and killed by far-right hoodlums. Then Golden Dawn candidate Ilias Panagiotaros said: "If Golden Dawn gets into parliament, we will carry out raids on hospitals and kindergartens, and we will throw immigrants and their children out in the streets so Greeks can take their place."

Locals told me that Golden Dawn's power on the streets had reduced, and it less frequently used violence as a weapon. Instead, it had gained political power—perhaps even more dangerous. In the 2015 election, the party reinforced its position as the third-largest in the Greek parliament. It was no longer a minor irritant— a sizable minority of the population responded to the party's fascist agenda.

Human Rights Watch had issued countless reports and statements despairing at the lack of official accountability when racially motivated violence occurred in Greece.[8] The lack of legal or political enforcement of already weak laws left migrants and the vulnerable with no faith that police would pursue attackers. Chaman recounted a story of corrupt and racist police illegally imprisoning him for hours and warning him to stay away from certain Athens suburbs. It was bullying sanctioned by official silence.

Chaman told me of the constant fear that many asylum seekers felt in Greece. As authorities steadily escalated their brutality against them, many lived in a state of limbo and constant stress, unsure when they would be arrested by the police and thrown into a detention center.

The political climate that enabled and demanded brutal action against outsiders was principally the result of a massive debt crisis and elite corruption. Both had built up over decades, with successive conservative governments unwilling to end unofficial oligarchic control of the state. The largest shipping, construction, energy, and football companies paid little tax. The 2008 global financial crisis pushed the nation over the edge. A troika consisting of the International Monetary Fund (IMF), the European Commission, and European Central Bank demanded extreme austerity through massive, unsustainable loans against the Greek population, in a failed attempt to resolve the financial crisis. Mass privatization was pursued, and the economy shrunk by a quarter. Public servants were fired in large numbers. In 2010, the troika falsely predicted that austerity would have little effect on employment and growth. There was an entrenched belief that Greece needed to be punished for excessively high spending.

The results were catastrophic and led to extreme social unrest, poverty, drug use, and prostitution. Popular frustration was taken out on the most marginalized group in society: refugees. It was not only immigrants who experienced the wrath of extreme austerity, but an entire population on whom the failed EU-designed experiment was attempted. Almost every socioeconomic group in Greece suffered—one of the few issues on which the far left and far right agreed. Corporate and privatized solutions became the only medicine that the troika would prescribe, revealing the paucity of vision within the European bureaucracy.

The Greek state found the perfect excuse to appease far-right concerns, and Golden Dawn success, by cracking down on undocumented immigration rather than solving the problem; they simply locked refugees up and hoped that punishment would be an effective deterrent. But, unsurprisingly, considering the grim realities in Syria, Libya, Iraq, Pakistan, and Afghanistan, the flow of migrants continued. In 2015, tens of thousands more migrants in Greece and Italy and thousands died making the deadly journey across the Mediterranean Sea.

But change was in the air. The groundbreaking 2015 electoral victory of the left-wing Syriza party, making Alexis Tsipras prime minister, was a rebuke to years of EU-inspired austerity, while the old parties, Pasok and New Democracy, floundered. On election night, Spain's left-wing Podemos party tweeted: "Greeks finally have a government, not a [German Chancellor Angela] Merkel envoy." It was a remarkable turnaround for a nation whose population had never seriously opted for progressive politics in huge numbers. After decades in which their interests were ignored, Syriza harnessed the disenchantment of young people—whose unemployment rate sat at 60 percent—against corruption and oligarchic tax avoidance. But the party, falling just short of an outright majority, formed a coalition with the right-wing and racist party ANEL (Independent Greeks)—a move criticized by many leftists.

The economics editor of Britain's *Channel 4 News*, Paul Mason, argued after the Syriza win: "What lies beneath the rise of the radical left is the emergence of positive new values—among a layer of young people much wider than Syriza's natural support base. These are the classic values of the networked generation: self-reliance, creativity, the willingness to treat life as a social experiment, a global outlook."[9] Syriza's victory signaled a generational shift away from a politics conducted only by the elites. Its success was also a direct result of the desperation of a people determined to restore dignity to their daily lives.

Syriza was pressured to continue the troika's medicine after the 2015 election.[10] Even after the party's victory, the European Commission urged Greece to pursue further the "reforms"—a euphemism for privatization and cuts to social services—that had been begun by Syriza's predecessors. The ideological gulf between those suffering under austerity and those advocating it had never been deeper.

Tsipras promised to renegotiate the oppressive terms of the troika's conditions, raise wages, create jobs, and restore a feeling of Greek independence among a population who had spent years knowing that their country's destiny was decided in Brussels and

Berlin. But profound questions remained concerning the viability or desirability of supporting a Greek state principally staffed by public servants—a central part of Syriza's vision. During his first policy speech to the parliament in 2015, Tsipras pledged to increase salaries, provide free electricity to those without it, and freeze pension cuts.

Greek finance minister Yanis Varoufakis vowed to destroy the country's oligarchs and their patrons "who viciously suck the energy and the economic power from everybody else." He described the troika's bailout conditions as "fiscal waterboarding."

Many immigrants living a shadow-existence in Greece hoped that Syriza, also known as the Coalition of the Radical Left, would grant them passports, giving them the freedom to live anywhere in the European Union—which, taken as a whole, was now the world's largest economy. Within days of winning office, Syriza granted citizenship to over 100,000 children of migrants born in Greece.

Further changes were promised—though public support for them was not guaranteed. A global study of the International Organization for Migration in 2015 found the Greek people to be the most interested in cutting immigration (followed in Europe by the Maltese, the Spanish, and Italians).

Tragically for the Greek people, according to Reporters Without Borders, the country now also ranked among the worst in terms of press freedom in Europe, having dropped fifty places in the five years before 2014. With growing physical threats against reporters by far-right thugs, including members of Golden Dawn, tabloid hysteria had become the most common method of controlling the public.[11] Every asylum seeker was framed as a threat. In 2013 the Greek government, following pressure from international donors, shut down the nation's public broadcaster in order to reduce the deficit, and only established a new, much weaker state broadcaster after a huge local and international outcry. Syriza announced in 2015 that it would reopen the public Hellenic Broadcasting

Corporation, Tsipras insisting that this would "repair a crime against Greek people and democracy."

Syriza challenged the German-led control of European political and economic policy in support of austerity. During a press conference with his German counterpart, Wolfgang Schäuble, in 2015, Varoufakis made pointed comments about the real-life effects of Berlin's dictates: "No one understands better than the people of [Germany] how a severely depressed economy, combined with a ritual national humiliation and unending hopelessness, can hatch the serpent's egg within its society," he said. "When I return home tonight, I will find a country where the third-largest party is not a neo-Nazi party, but a Nazi party," he said, referencing Golden Dawn. "We need the people of Germany on our side."

The warning was clear: Germany had no right to govern the modern creation of Europe; Greece was its moral and political equal. The ideological and spiritual struggle for the heart of Europe—Germany pushing Greece to insolvency and out of the Eurozone, or accepting a compromise allowing Athens to remain within it—was one of the great questions of the moment.[12]

I was constantly told while in the country that independent journalism was struggling, though social media offered a new way to challenge the dominant narrative. Greek journalist Kostas Vaxevanis lamented that "the only way for the Greek people to know about their own country is through the foreign press"[13]— though even the UK *Guardian* continually called Syriza "radical" in its reporting. Neither public nor private media interests offered much dissent, supporting the close relationship between big business and the state apparatus, and endorsing the authorities' embrace of austerity policies. It was the perfect environment for conspiracy theories, paranoia, race hatred, and reactionary conservatism to thrive. Such an environment made Syriza's victory even more remarkable, convincing a majority of Greeks that there was a viable alternative to living on their knees.

*   *   *

Médecins Sans Frontières (MSF) was one of the few groups that had documented the realities of repressive policies against refugees. Its 2014 report "Invisible Suffering" detailed the lack of state care for asylum seekers and the devastating physical and psychological effects of prolonged incarceration.[14] MSF migrant advisor Ioanna Kotsioni told me in Athens that her organization had started working in Greek detention centers in 2008—the first NGO in the country to do so. "From 2006 and 2007 in Greece," she said, "detention centers started increasing in size." MSF had lobbied the government to improve conditions in detention facilities across the country, and since 2012 the numbers of immigrants being consigned to them—mainly from Syria, Afghanistan, Ethiopia, and Eritrea—had soared.

Here was the problem: there were 4,500 extra beds made available during the economic crisis, but no increase in money or services for refugees in detention. Although MSF had no trouble accessing the facilities, they despaired at the system: more than 7,000 beds were spread across the entire Greek network, as well as thousands more in police stations. Over a thousand unaccompanied minors were scattered across the country, though refugee groups told me that less than 400 beds had been provided for them.

Kotsioni said that the political climate in Greece, and across much of Europe, allowed the state to imprison refugees with little concern about any negative consequences. "Greek opposition to refugees is not just anti-Muslim sentiment," she said, "but also anti-Christian; there's a dislike of brown skin here." The government department in charge of asylum seekers was now called the Ministry of Public Order and Citizen Protection—a name speaking to incarceration and exclusion. Even the Greek ombudsman, after visiting various Greek detention centers in 2013, worried that police were "unable to ensure conditions which respect the fundamental right of detainees, as detention facilities for aliens have turned into sui generis prisons, given the large and escalating number of detainees held for many months."[15]

"I'm often told by asylum seekers: 'We came to Europe for human rights and we're shocked by the conditions here,'" Kotsioni said. You could still buy your way into citizenship—around €200,000 would do it—but this was obviously not an option for anyone other than rich arrivals. "When I first entered detention centers I was shocked," Kotsioni told me. "There's a strange feeling inside. People are put inside and treated like animals, not human beings. The system is indifferent to conditions inside. There are many reasons more asylum seekers don't know the reality in Greece. Many are embarrassed by being detained and can't send money home. They can't provide, and feel rejected by their host country."

Privatization of the detention network was the logical outcome of the nation's political direction when human beings and services could be farmed out to the most attractive bidder. Kotsioni said that another reason for outsourcing was that "too many police are far from home and away from their families, putting pressure on a system to find alternative ways to guard detainees."

During my time in Greece, I spoke to countless Greek journalists who told me that the issue of privatizing the detention system rarely received any attention in the local media. "The state should take responsibility for healthcare and security because the state is locking people up," Kotsioni argued. "Fifteen years ago you would have had news stories welcoming Syrian refugees, but now it's the opposite."

A logic of austerity mandated the demonization of a minority that was unable to fight back. Disaster capitalism completed the job, corrupting both the marginalized and those pursuing their oppression. In Greece many governments had tied themselves so closely to corporations that transparent politics was impossible.

A lack of medical care was ubiquitous, with little public pressure to demand improved access to even the most basic medicines. One day in Perama, a port city in the suburb of Piraeus, near

Athens—privatization plans had been put on hold after the Syriza win—I visited the offices of Médecins de Monde (MdM) to interview doctors who had worked inside the Corinth detention center. It was an overdeveloped area with large boats, shipping containers, and smoke stacks, all styled in a muted beige palette.

The office was in a small street bustling with men, women, and children. Families came to receive medicine because they no longer had insurance, could not afford it, or were unemployed. This was one noticeable effect of the crisis during austerity. Boxes of fruit arrived for children who were not at school and whose parents could not afford to buy healthy food. Because so many Greeks were on the breadline, a "potato movement" sprung up to allow consumers to buy products straight from producers.[16] It was sobering to think that, in 2012, roughly 10 percent of elementary and middle school students faced "food insecurity." In the heart of Europe, malnutrition was rampant among schoolchildren; a cabbage-based diet was now a reality for many middle-class Greeks.[17] Golden Dawn had generated support by providing food to "indigenous" Greeks. Across the nation, its community support had been built through invocations of Greek pride.[18]

Young and old, new mothers with their babies and the decrepit— all waited patiently to speak to a doctor for advice, and hopefully medicine. Doctors told me they usually did not have the required medication, or had just enough for a few days, after which people returned for more but often went home empty-handed. One doctor said that, in some ways, she wished she wasn't giving false hope to people when distributing a few pills or bottles of milk for a baby.

I met three doctors trying to make a difference: Antonios Rompos, sixty-four-year-old neurologist and psychiatrist, who volunteered at MdM, providing for asylum seekers and the poor; Thomas Balkonis, a seventy-year-old dermatologist; and the fifty-year-old Revekka Tzanetea, who worked in internal medicine. They were friendly, greeting me with warm smiles, but furious about what had happened in their country. All of them had started working with MdM in 2013 as volunteer doctors at the Corinth facility because MdM had an agreement with the Greek government. "In my view, it's like prisoners are kept there," said Rompos.

When they had first arrived, they were all shocked by what they saw. There were eighty people in rooms built for thirty, and only ten showers and ten toilets. One bar of soap and shampoo was issued by the government to each detainee every month. In 2013 and 2014 these doctors saw 985 detainees inside Corinth. Their main concern was the rapid spread of tuberculosis and scabies. The authorities demanded that MdM furnish them with the medical records of refugees, though initially the NGO refused. They eventually agreed, even though police and the authorities reading the files mostly did not understand a word, as the records were written in medical jargon.

Most of the men in detention were from Afghanistan and Pakistan, speaking Dari and Farsi, though some were fluent in Arabic. Rompos said they also ran an outpatient clinic providing medication, healthcare, and soap. There were 1,200 people in the camp, and seventy police officers. The authorities were sometimes afraid of refugees, and would racially abuse and brutalize them. "We wondered if some police were Golden Dawn members, because the police there had to choose which refugees deserved to receive medical attention," Rompos said. "Many refugees speak Greek because they've been here for years; there was a political decision to make them 'disappear' into detention." All three doctors despaired at the blatant discrimination that seeped into daily life. "Greek people feel more comfortable for 'cleansing' the area of refugees, and the European Union pays for this activity," Rompos said.

Conditions in detention were brutal. Refugees were handcuffed to the health clinic "for security." The doctors prescribed medicines, but the police would only sometimes supply the drugs to detainees. "Police would accuse us of exaggerating the depression of refugees," Rompos noted. "Medicines are given to police to

administer, handed out sparingly because they're fearful of suicides and self-harm. Refugees were smoking paracetamol to get
high. I gave depression pills, but many refugees said they'd rather
die." The majority of refugees suffered from constipation because
they were given fruit and vegetables only once a month.

The doctors stressed the political game authorities were playing
by locking these people up. "Refugees are released by police in
central Athens, after up to eighteen months inside, and then
sometimes immediately re-arrested for another long period in
detention. Greeks are mostly happy with these policies because
they see fewer refugees on the streets—it's racism. Golden Dawn
support has risen because people are unemployed. Old women
were afraid in some suburbs because they didn't feel safe going
to the shops, and Golden Dawn provided escorts for them. It was
clever PR." Golden Dawn thugs routinely threatened MdM staff
for helping immigrants. The group's secretary responded: "They
will not scare us; medicine does not discriminate."[19]

I asked Tzanetea why Greece had taken such a turn to the right.
"Better education is needed. The youth forget history or don't
know it, and support fascism. People believe Pakistanis are taking
their jobs. I see very few volunteers helping the underprivileged
in our society. Many young doctors at the university I teach in are
sympathetic to refugees but don't want to volunteer because they
fear getting diseases. And this is sixth-year students who should
know better!" MdM no longer worked at Corinth.

Greek citizens knew too well how austerity devastated their
healthcare system. Neoliberal economic policies affected immigrants and the general population equally; disaster capitalism's
massive reductions in public and social services produced few
winners.

The Metropolitan Community Clinic was situated at Helliniko,
on the outskirts of Athens, inside an old US military base. It was
on the last stop on the train line; there was no address, and I had
been given only vague directions. It was relatively quiet inside,

and Christos Sideris, who worked for a shipping company during the day and was the head of communications at the center, showed me around. There were many small offices with medical equipment, a large storeroom filled with thousands of pill bottles and medications, baby food, and refrigerated vaccinations. Volunteer GPs, gynecologists, oncologists, and child, adult, and family psychologists were all provided, though patients had to book in advance. It represented clean, efficient, powerful resistance in the age of austerity.

The idea for the clinic was first hatched in 2011, Sideris told me. During the protests in Athens's Syntagma Square in May, he said, "many of us talked about [starting a clinic], as a form of opposition against economic warfare being waged on us. It was affecting us physically and psychologically." Before the crisis, "public health-care was alright, though not great, and doctors helped patients who needed medication. They broke rules and turned a blind eye."

When hospital services started deteriorating in 2008, the state made a decision that the welfare of its citizens was less important than pleasing international donors. Sideris recalled the horrors: "Citizens without insurance went from hospital to hospital to get medication, and hospitals wouldn't give it to them because they didn't have it. From 2010, we needed to provide alternatives."

The Metropolitan Community Clinic was born. In December 2011 sixty volunteers, starting in the old US army base, used social media to attract interest and volunteers. It was the first community clinic in Athens and the second in Greece. The rent remained free, and the local municipality paid for the electricity and other bills. The task remained daunting, with three million uninsured among a population of eleven million. The clinic had 250 volunteers working every day, and early evenings except Sunday. Between 2011 and 2014, they helped 28,000 patients.

Sideris told me that the clinic had strict rules: "There are no party politics, and we take no money donations. We will receive donations of drugs but won't have Greek politicians with TV crews to look around. The clinic does not advertise who donates drugs—they remain anonymous, and we try not to associate ourselves with the companies, individuals, or NGOs who got us into the financial crisis. We have no leaders; there is a horizontal structure, and an assembly makes decisions on big questions."

The clinic only accepted the poor and unemployed who had no insurance, those on low wages, and the elderly. "We take all ages and sexes," Sideris said, "even former industrialists who have fallen from financial highs. We check people's credentials to make sure they need care, and we have sources in hospitals, government ministries, and local and foreign media to make sure."

It was tough to take this grim reality in a first-world nation. "It's often hard in a European country to see malnourished children," Sideris said. "This fucked up system hasn't even spent a few hours giving citizens their rights as patients, so we provide information to people about what healthcare they can get. We're not trying to substitute for the public health system, and we hope we can close soon, when public hospitals are again well resourced."

Sideris recounted a story that typifies austerity-wracked Greece. In May 2014 a fifty-four-year-old man needed immediate heart surgery, but he was unemployed and uninsured. The hospital initially refused to admit him, fearing it would never be paid, but the man said he would submit the required welfare document when he received it. His doctor convinced the facility that the patient was in need and must be operated on immediately.

The man, whose name had not been released, was lying in the operating theatre waiting to have a pacemaker installed when a person from the hospital's accounting department arrived. Because the patient had not submitted the necessary welfare documents, the accountant forced the doctors to stop the procedure. It was only the next day, after pressure from the Metropolitan clinic, that the man had the life-saving surgery. Instead of acknowledging fault, the Greek Health Ministry blamed the messenger, accusing the clinic of concocting the story. "Patients coming here are often ashamed," Sideris explained, "even scared of giving their stories anonymously to the clinic to publicize the health realities, because they fear retribution from a state that may give them a little money."

After the 2015 Syriza election win, the clinic reminded the world that, "we saw, in our European country in the year 2012, babies that looked like starving children on posters from famine areas. That is when we started to provide baby formula and diapers for infants. We've been doing it ever since. By 2013 we regularly provided for more than 300 babies."

The clinic's founder, Dr. Giorgos Vichas, a suave man with a thick head of brown hair, spoke quietly and with determination about what he saw as his professional and personal obligation: "Cancer patients are often helped by doctors who are breaking the law by giving them medicine [the state doesn't prosecute these doctors]. I never saw tumors this big on people before the crisis, because there isn't enough medicine to treat it now. Studies here have shown that because insulin often isn't available for treatment of diabetes it ends up costing the state more money due to lack of initial care and medicine. This neoliberal ideology is putting money above people's lives."

Vichas had paid a price for his commitment to free healthcare: "My car has been broken into, laptop stolen, papers taken then found, and another time my office was broken into. It's ongoing harassment by thugs. I helped protesters in 2011 in Syntagma Square when they were being attacked by police, and I was hit myself by police." Within days of Syriza's electoral win, the new police minister, Nikos Voutsis—himself a victim of police brutality—removed the steel barriers in Syntagma. "This work gives me strength," Vichas continued, "but I hope this clinic doesn't need to exist in years to come. We have seen too much pain and suffering. The worst thing we can do is get used to this situation." He was damning of his profession, infused with carelessness and selfishness. "The majority of doctors are not interested in community clinics and are critical of our work. I know this attitude among doctors existed before the crisis, so I'm thankful some doctors are helping us."

In such dire circumstances, small blessings were appreciated. In early 2013 the Medical Association of Athens tried to close the clinic down, stating that it did not have the necessary permits. When, in late 2013, narcotics police arrived with a magistrate, she brought a bag of drugs to donate. She could have shut them down.

My time at the clinic was a rare moment during my Greek visit in which I felt hope. It was a sentiment shared by Vichas: "We are romantics at this clinic. We have legality from society, social capital, and we've asked people to help." With little faith in the state or its media—"Goebbels would be proud of the Greek press. We are supposed to be a democracy but we're close to being a financial dictatorship"—he was seeing his idea spreading across an increasingly fragmented Europe. "The first community clinic just opened in Hamburg, Germany—16,000 people uninsured there; so community clinics are growing across the continent."

The decline in government healthcare in free and open democracies provided a warning that extreme financial policies led to social disharmony. Arguably the most serious questions revolved around the role of the euro in Greece's economic crisis. Was it ultimately responsible for the country's decline? Although Syriza pledged to remain in the Eurozone, disaster capitalism became more extreme under its rules. "The euro is simply the deutschmark with little stars on it," investigative journalist Greg Palast wrote after Syriza's 2015 electoral win. Columbia University's Robert Mundell—father both of the euro and of Reagan and Thatcher's deregulation—told Palast that the euro's main goal was to strip parliaments of the ability to control their own fiscal policies. "Without fiscal policy," he explained to Palast, "the only way nations can keep jobs is by the competitive reduction of rules on business."[20]

*   *   *

In Athens, the cover of a major daily newspaper caught my eye. Blazoned across the front page were old color pictures of Golden Dawn leaders performing fascist salutes in front of the Nazi flag and an image of Adolf Hitler. The story, by the country's leading journalist on the movement, Dimitris Psarras, offered undeniable proof that the party's leading figures admired the Nazis, and that this suggestion was not a conspiracy by the "system" intended to smear their reputation, as they routinely claimed.[21]

In recent years the world has been stunned by the rise of Golden Dawn—a brazen neo-Nazi party whose support has grown to make it the third-largest political party in Greece, as was confirmed in the 2015 election. It was impossible to deny that a vocal and sizeable minority of Greek citizens believed that fascism was the best solution for their country. After the May 2012 European elections, which saw the party grow into a force to be reckoned with, only the politically blind denied this reality. In some areas of Athens, among the very poor and very rich, support for the party increased sharply.

Nick Malkoutzis, deputy editor of the Greek daily *Kathimerini English Edition*, commented: "It should come as no surprise that in a country which in the last century has been through two fascist dictatorships, Nazi occupation and collaboration, and a civil war whose wounds never healed properly there should be those who long for authoritarian far-right rule." It had been a "façade" that the nation would inevitably move towards the West and Europe.[22] In June 2014, Malkoutzis lamented "Golden Dawn's version of the Nazi Party's Horst Wessel Song being played outside the Greek Parliament and its supporters wandering through the building's corridors as if it was a Munich beer hall in 1923. How shameful."

I met Dimitris Psarras at his newspaper's offices in central Athens—a second-floor, open-plan space with a few reporters tapping away on their computers. Psarras had a bushy gray beard and an intense stare. During the interview he showed me a 2007

Golden Dawn magazine with an image of Hitler on its cover. The text read: "1945–2007: 62 years since he [Hitler] died."

"Golden Dawn was a marginal group for decades," Psarras told me, "and now there are hundreds of thousands of supporters. It was and is a fanatical Nazi party." The popularity of the party was due to a potent narrative: "Because the government does little against immigrants, Golden Dawn takes action, including pogroms in central Athens. Until September 2013, the Greek state didn't think that they should pursue party leaders, only those carrying out crimes."

In October 2014, with many of the party's leaders in prison for murder, weapons offenses, and countless attacks on migrants, the Greek chief public prosecutor announced that the entire parliamentary party would face criminal trial. I heard many times in Greece that, even if Golden Dawn were disbanded and its hierarchy placed in prison, support for its ideas and policies would not disappear. The poison had already been released, and other groups could deploy it.

The popularity of Golden Dawn had not arisen out of nowhere. Until 2010, the group was akin to a private police force; during demonstrations, its members stood behind official special forces and used knives against protestors and anarchists. The police had a good relationship with them, and many videos showed this intimate dynamic. This was starkly revealed in the 2014 elections, when over 50 percent of police in Athens gave their support to the fascist party, which took 9.4 percent of the national vote.

Psarras started investigating Golden Dawn when it was still a fringe movement. "I began writing about them in the early nineties," he said, "but since the eighties they have had connections to Greece's deep state, such as the church and police. In 2006 the group leader's brother was appointed second in charge of the Greek army. Another brother of the party's leader is a prominent Athens lawyer. Golden Dawn heads are part of the establishment here, not skinheads, and I've known the leadership for decades. Greece never had a de-Nazification process after World War II."

The appeal of Golden Dawn rested on its masterful ability to create a fanciful image of a glorious past being defiled by leftists, gays, Muslims, and immigrants. Although far-right parties had existed and found support in the past, none had surged quite like Golden Dawn. The party's supporters "wanted revenge against the political system," Psarras explained. Its backers were "the most desperate socially, the unemployed, people who don't have an expectation of finding a job, and the party exploits this, saying: We'll kick immigrants out to get you a job." Ironically, in a nation so dominated by disaster capitalism, Golden Dawn offered rhetorical opposition to privatization, but "in reality they're supporting every big capitalist in Greece. In parliament they even voted against a small tax on ship owners"—in 2012 the party sided with the shipping oligarchs on the pretext of encouraging them to hire only local Greeks—"and this is similar to the situation during the Greek dictatorship days, when capitalists were equally supported by the junta." The working class, including unions and political groups, were brutally repressed during that period.

This was all denied by one of the most flamboyant Golden Dawn members I met in Pikermi, nineteen kilometers from central Athens. The seventy-two-year-old Dr. Epaminondas N. Stathis, a losing party candidate in the 2014 European elections (along with many retired Greek generals), lived in an area of rolling hills and few properties, other than large mansions with stunning views. Stathis's house, situated behind a high fence with a G4S tag identifying the private security firm that guarded the place, was expansive. His daughter, a historian in her twenties, welcomed me and took me inside, where he was waiting in the doorway, smiling.

I was shocked by what I saw at the three-story house. The street-level floor had furniture covered by sheets ("We don't use it in summer"), countless paintings on the walls, elaborate rugs on the floor, and eye-level lights and candelabras. As we rode down in a tiny elevator with his fat stomach nearly touching me, we exited into a room that had the curtains drawn. There were a few bare lights shining on countless images of Jesus in a well-appointed library. "I am a Greek Orthodox believer, and I visit church around two times every month," he told me. The Greek Orthodox Church had openly backed Golden Dawn and its fascism.[23] Outside I noticed a large pool and palm trees overlooking the mountains. This was an establishment family, though since Stathis's background was in medicine I wondered how he had earned so much money.

As we began speaking, his daughter brought in a glass of ice water, iced coffee, and ice cream that progressively melted in front of me as the interview progressed. I sensed Stathis wanted to challenge many of the impressions that had circulated locally and globally about Golden Dawn. He said, "You can ask me anything, even something that I may find very offensive." With an intense stare, he repeatedly wiped sweat from his face with a tissue and continuously smoked thin cigarettes. "Property is the expansion of our body—that's my philosophy." He was a retired orthopedic surgeon, in a career that had taken him to London and Ipswich. "I was only involved in science in the UK, and not politics," he said. "I've been fighting for patriotic, nationalist ideas all my life. Greece fought with the UK and Australia against fascism in World War II, and I've always been involved in Greek politics."

It was hard to get a word in, so keen was Stathis to explain his patriotism. He gave an accurate account of the financial mismanagement of his country—"The government has been stealing public money for decades; they're crooks and embezzlers"—but believed that only a strong, hard-right revival would restore Greece's honor. "We are not Nazis or fascists. We are children of the people who fought against Nazism and fascism. My family gave a lot of blood fighting totalitarianism. We are loving and creating humans, and I do not support violence against immigrants."

Stathis was clever, not a simple bigot, and couched his opposition to migrants as nationalism, not racism. His rhetoric resembled what I had heard in the United States, Britain, and Australia from vocal opponents of refugees. "There are 3 million illegal migrants in Greece, and soon we will be strangers in our own country," said Stathis. "Every day more boats come, and Turkey does not take back refugees as they should. Many immigrants are robbing and stealing, with women spreading AIDS and not paying taxes, breaking into houses and killing for a few euros. I've been attacked in my own house, and we are terrified and often not going out at night-time." Stathis said he had no problem with Islam, but feared that the problems in Syria and Afghanistan were being imported into Greece. "We worry about al-Qaeda in Greece, with no checks on who is coming in."

Immigration was a key battleground in Greece, and Golden Dawn had harnessed it with cynical precision. There was truth to the claim that the Greek system failed to adequately provide for the surge in asylum seekers living in the community, and this failure had inevitably led to fear and paranoia. "Political asylum is fine— we should help people from Syria and other places that really need our help; but illegal immigrants must be rejected," Stathis argued. "Illegal invaders must be sent back, and we must sign a new agreement with the EU and Turkey. Areas of Athens are now [violent ghettos] filled with immigrants." He dreamed of the Greek people giving Golden Dawn a majority at a future election. He knew that one of the ways this could happen was through a party program such as talking to employers, encouraging them to fire immigrants and then hire local Greeks at the same rate of pay.

The iconography of Golden Dawn and its adoration of Nazism were key aspects of its identity. I questioned Stathis, who claimed never to have been a member of the party and only a follower, and he denied it all: "The Greek government lies that the Golden Dawn symbol is like a swastika, but it's a Greek symbol." He jumped up and fetched a folded piece of A4 paper, on which one side bore the Nazi swastika and the other the Golden Dawn insignia. "Is this the same?" he bellowed. "Of course not!"

He then disappeared briefly and returned with an iPad, showing me the party's symbol on its website. "You see," he said, "this isn't anything like the swastika." In fact, it was remarkably similar. "We're accused of singing Nazi songs, but they're not— they're patriotic and military songs." He acknowledged that a few members "have made many mistakes over the years, like support- ing Hitler and Nazis." I showed him a Golden Dawn magazine cover from 2007 with a positive image and message about Hitler. "Now we have many intellectuals to help evolve the party." This rhetoric was not helped by countless examples proving it wrong, such as a Golden Dawn MP using a Nazi salute during a party event in Crete in 2014.

Stathis condemned the 2013 murder of Greek rapper and anti- fascist activist Pavlos Fyssas, though he dismissed clear evidence that a Golden Dawn member, Giorgos Roupakias, had been involved. He was in no mood to admit that his party had engaged in countless acts of violence against opponents. Instead, he claimed right-wingers were oppressed. "You must be a leftist to have blood of value in Greece, but the blood of every man in Greece is valu- able." Unsurprisingly, he feared a Syriza-led government.

I challenged him on the party's anti-Semitism and embrace of fascism. He rejected all my allegations, falsely claiming that the local Jewish community had "no issue with Golden Dawn," though overseas Jewish groups did. Unlike some of his colleagues, he did not deny the Holocaust—he was smart enough to know that doing so in front of a Western journalist was not the best move; but "I must not be blamed for what Hitler or Stalin did. I was one of Hitler's victims. Some in Golden Dawn may deny the Holocaust and I engage with them to try and change their minds."

Like many on the right in Europe today, he embraced Israel as being on the frontline of a necessary war against Islamist terror. "I like Israelis, and I don't understand why the Israeli government is against us." He also loved Russian president Vladimir Putin, because "he's a nationalist and loves his country. Europe will be the most powerful continent in the world only when Russia joins the European community." The party's tentacles even extended to Australia, with the occasional fundraising drive; but its support remained weak even though Melbourne contained the largest concentration of Greeks outside Greece.[24]

Stathis was engaging, and clearly determined to try and change my views about Golden Dawn. He offered a well-informed view on the party and its politics. In many ways, as someone who saw himself as an intellectual providing support for the movement, he was more dangerous than a cohort of skinheads. He was the prettier face of the movement, as against the thugs who did the dirty work—though he denied that Golden Dawn did this, insisting that if they did he would condemn it.

With most of the Golden Dawn leadership in prison, I was keen to meet one of the few party parliamentarians living and working on the outside. I interviewed Golden Dawn MP Ilias Panagiotaros in front of the Athens High Court. The morning I arrived, an appeal was being heard related to the party's leadership who remained in prison. There were no flag-waving supporters, but a number of clearly affiliated men came up to Panagiotaros to embrace him and shake his hand. They were large and muscular men with tattoos.

Panagiotaros was a large man with a big stomach, goatee, and bald head. He had his talking points, and he was not afraid to repeat them ad nauseam: "Every Golden Dawn MP believes in country, nation, heritage, pride, and dignity. The cases against our leadership are 100 percent political persecution. At least a dozen Pasok MPs have been found to steal money, and yet nobody says Pasok is a criminal organization. We are Greek nationalists."

A key reason for Syriza's 2015 electoral success was wholesale public rejection of an entire generation of politicians from the old parties. Nationalism had been cynically used and abused both by conservative forces and by Golden Dawn. Panagiotaros was partly correct—countless Greek politicians were on the take and enriching their corporate friends; but his organization was no cleaner.

Golden Dawn also publicly opposed extreme austerity measures, but its plans to resurrect Greece entailed kicking out immigrants, damning Islam, and reverting to an authoritarian past that disenfranchised the masses. This was a message that resonated across Europe, from France to the Netherlands. Economic inequality and racial intolerance threatened the future stability of Europe, and Brussels seemed incapable of responding to the challenge.[25]

A former high-level party candidate giving testimony to the Greek government's magistrate investigating the group explained that Golden Dawn's ultimate aim was a "one-party regime."[26] He claimed that the leadership sanctioned violence against migrants because they would gain electoral "rewards," and that the attacks were "a kind of decoration." Evidence released in 2014 by the Greek public prosecutor showed that countless Golden Dawn members, including some of its MPs, had been involved in violence, arson, blackmail, and murder since at least the 1990s, often with the collusion of the police and the state apparatus.

When challenged on his party's embracing of Hitler, Panagiotaros was dismissive: "So what if our leader was photographed next to a Nazi swastika forty years ago? If you ask every leader in Europe what they were doing forty years ago you may find some interesting stories, too." During my time in Greece barely a day passed without new and recent photographs in the media of Golden Dawn members mimicking Nazi iconography. Panagiotaros wanted the EU to operate "a strict immigration policy," because "illegal immigration is mostly Muslim jihadists who plan to overtake Europe. If Syrians, Libyans, or Iraqis need to go somewhere they should go to the US, the country that caused the wars in their countries. Let the US take these people in."

Panagiotaros claimed to be against rampant privatization, despite the record of his party in parliament backing moves to outsource state services. "Greece has been giving away public assets for years—ports, airports, huge hotels, beaches, islands, roads, bridges. We are against this. We're not against productivity, but

we're 100 percent against giving away free assets. We have trai-
tors in the government here who have done this, sold our assets for
free, and they should face the law and punishment."

The worldview was reminiscent of the twenty-first-century far
right in general: a love for Israel and Putin combined with a hatred
of Muslims, gays, and Western NGOs. Putin's Russia had become
a symbol of admiration for Europe's far right, from France to
Hungary, Greece, and the UK.[27] For some in Europe, looking east,
towards China, Russia, and the Middle East, and rejecting the logic
of Brussels, was an increasingly appealing prospect. Opposing
disaster capitalism had the potential to unite elements of the left
and right, though the latter preferred to demonize and blame
refugees and the marginalized for a country's failings. Even after
Syriza's 2015 election win, leader Alexis Tsipras visited Moscow,
was warmly embraced by the Kremlin, and called for a "reset in
relations" between the EU and Russia.

I was reminded of the words of Greek journalist Dimitris
Psarras, who told me that Jew-hatred had been mainstreamed. A
2014 Anti-Defamation League poll found that Greeks had the most
anti-Semitic attitudes in Europe. It was a cruel twist that groups
that traditionally loathed Jews now embraced Israel as being on
the frontline against Islam. "Anti-Semitism is a big problem in
Greece," Psarras said. "My upcoming book is called *The Bestseller
of Hate: Protocols of the Elders of Zion 1825–2014*. Many mainstream editors and journalists print Protocols-style material here."
Greek Jews mostly welcomed the Syriza win, despite its critical
position on Israel, because they had also suffered from the years
of austerity.[28]

This is why the anti-fascist movement was so important. The
rate of violence and threats against minorities and immigrants was
startling, revealing the complete failure of the state to enforce laws
against oppression. Thanasis Kampagiannis was a lawyer, anti-
fascist activist, leftist, and member of Keerfa, the Movement United
Against Racism and the Fascist Threat: "I've been involved in

some of the most important anti-fascist legal cases against Golden Dawn in recent years, and I came to this work due to my long-standing anti-fascist activism."

Kampagiannis represented the Luqman family, devastated after Golden Dawn thugs murdered their twenty-seven-year-old Pakistani son on his way to work, in January 2013. A Greek couple saw party members just after the attack, and the two men were arrested. Police found Golden Dawn material at their houses. "It was a racist crime," Kampagiannis said. "The men claimed Luqman attacked them, but they had used knives and stabbed him seven times. There was no sign of a fight, the attack took place at 3 a.m., and they were looking for a brown-skinned or foreign person to attack." The public outcry was immediate, with 20,000 people marching through the streets in a protest coordinated by Keerfa. Two years after Luqman's death, in 2015, his father, Khadim Hussein, flew in from Pakistan to commemorate his son's murder alongside hundreds of supporters.

The trial took eight days. "The Luqman trial was important to show that these attacks are racist," Kampagiannis explained. Until 2013, "the police and government gave protection to Golden Dawn." Luqman's killers were found guilty and sentenced to life terms, which in Greece meant sixteen years behind bars.

Kampagiannis had become involved in the trial of Golden Dawn leaders through representing Egyptian fishermen who had been attacked by party members. He was pessimistic about his country's political alliances, explaining that there were clear links between the political elites and Golden Dawn. "There are old ties between the far right and the military, state, and police," he noted. "This goes back to the junta and civil war days. These ties were never broken, and because police still process and manage many refugees, these links are strengthened."

The New Democracy party was rocked in 2014 by a video covertly recorded and released by Golden Dawn that showed then prime minister Antonis Samaras's chief of staff confessing to a

Golden Dawn spokesman that the criminal investigation against the far-right group was solely designed to reduce losses for the ruling party. The chief of staff resigned, claiming unconvincingly that his boss had been ignorant of his dealings.[29]

Unlike many I met on the left, Kampagiannis was only cautiously optimistic about the chances of Syriza being strong enough to tackle Greece's economic woes. "Is Syriza radical enough to deal with Greece's many issues? I worry that they accept the EU framework. Alexis Tsipras thinks you can reform the EU terms on which Greece implements measures against austerity, but Syriza needs to make a decision. The Syriza program, to strengthen wages and collective bargaining, is incompatible with EU demands." It was a view expressed by many who voted for Syriza in 2015—though exiting the euro remained a minority demand. Many in the corporate press expressed concern that a Greek exit from the Eurozone was a possibility.

With popular opposition to the troika never stronger, Kampagiannis wanted his country to consider leaving both the euro and the EU: "The sky won't fall in. The question is who will pay for the transition out of the EU. The danger is that we copy the disaster in Argentina, but I believe we can have a policy where working-class interests are protected, and capital should pay."

Europe's refugee crisis was framed as an emergency requiring regional and global solutions. This was partly true: the war in Syria could not be solved in Athens, but it was also a huge business opportunity. Thousands of poor souls had drowned looking for a better and safer life, as in the tragic boat accident in the Mediterranean in September 2014 that killed around 500, mostly Gazans and Syrians,[30] and Greece was on the frontline. Malta had a policy of mandatory detention, leaving migrants imprisoned sometimes for eighteen months in unsanitary conditions.[31] Frontex Plus was a 2014 idea pushed by the EU to curb the rescuing of migrants at sea in favor of monitoring and controlling

Europe's borders. Dollar signs dazzled the firms that would benefit.[32]

The numbers of people entering Europe were staggering: 15,000 undocumented migrants made the dangerous journey to Greece by sea in 2013, while Italy had to deal with tens of thousands more. The EU's border management agency, Frontex, said that 40,000 asylum seekers arrived in Europe in 2013. This surge fueled resentment, leading to xenophobic campaigns in Greece, such as "Xenios Zeus," designed to round up migrants. Between August 2012 and June 2013, over 120,000 migrants were detained, less than 6 percent of whom lacked legal residency permits. Syriza pledged to abolish the program, shut down detention centers, and establish more open facilities. Serious allegations of abuses against detainees in countless facilities across the country remained unresolved or ignored.[33] The EU was directly responsible for this situation, having provided funds to Greece that it knew were being spent on squalid detention facilities and the repression of migrants. Greece became so dependent on EU handouts that it was forced to do its dirty work.

Research gathered by the Hellenic Foundation for European and Foreign Policy examined the cost of Greece's immigration policy from 2008 to 2013. It estimated that it had cost €16 per day for every detainee—a very low figure compared to equivalent costs in Australian detention centers. With Greece determined to run 10,000 detention centers by the end of 2014, at an annual cost of €57.6 million, the government simply did not have the money to pay for it.[34] Athens repeatedly asked the EU for more funding, for which one of the likely conditions, based on other areas of migrant policy, was privatization of some of the services. Refusing to detain so many people was a policy solution that too rarely entered mainstream debate.

One outcome of this situation was early deterrence. The militarization of the Mediterranean was directly causing the deaths of refugees at sea because Greece and other states were given relative freedom to implement aggressive policies against asylum seekers, with the blessing of Brussels. Martin Lemberg-Pedersen, assistant professor at the Center for Advanced Migration Studies at the University of Copenhagen and an expert on the securitization of European immigration policy, told Inter Press Service that "the Arab Spring brought with it the fall of dictators, who up until that point had been key allies funded by the EU, containing sub-Saharan and Middle Eastern migrants before they could reach European territory." Since then, he said, "it seems that the EU has been looking to establish similar systems of control."[35]

The EU became central in funding, encouraging, and pressuring EU nations to isolate and imprison asylum seekers. In January 2013, Frontex acknowledged that it was working with the world's leading arms and security manufacturers, such as Lockheed Martin and L-3 Communications, to find new ways to repel refugees coming from North Africa and the Middle East. "The European border security policy is going in the wrong direction," German Green MEP Ska Keller told Inter Press Service. "Against a background of pervasive budget cuts and austerity measures, it is unbelievable that the EU is spending millions of euros for 'smart gates,' UAVs [drones] and other surveillance technologies."[36] With little press coverage or other scrutiny, EU member states were being encouraged or forced to buy market-ready equipment from pre-approved firms.

The monitoring and documenting of migrants has generated a large industry. The EU has led the charge in working with corporations that have been very willing to develop and hone methods for repelling the desperate hordes. "Smart Borders" was one tool to identity visa overstayers, which used biometrics and collated a database of personal information. This program was part of EUROSUR, the European External Border Surveillance System, which was designed to build cooperation between Frontex and EU nations. France's Thales and Sagem, leading defense companies, were central to this approach to security and border protection, implemented by a Brussels elite that showed little interest in addressing the root causes of migratory flows.[37] It was much easier to militarize the procedure, boosting a firm's bottom line in the process. Fortress Europe was the result.

In addition, the EU was pushing a burgeoning drone industry to monitor Europe's borders. In 2010, Frontex quietly placed on its website a message asking for expressions of interest in demonstrating "small UAVs (Unmanned Aerial Vehicles) and fixed systems for land border surveillance."[38] The Peace and Security Project, founded by the Institute of Peace Studies, released a report in 2014 that detailed massive Brussels backing "to remove the regulatory and technical barriers that currently limit the flight of drones in civilian airspace." It stated that at least €315 million of EU research funding "has been awarded to drone-based projects, many of which are subsidising Europe's largest defence and security industries and are geared towards the development and enhancement of tools for border surveillance and law enforcement."[39] The Greek government announced in 2014 that it would hire a drone to monitor the Aegean Sea, and remained keen to purchase its own unmanned machines from Israel and other states.

Privatizing security at Greek detention centers was just the first step; British multinational G4S,[40] Mega Sprint Guard, JCB Security, Facility, and Swedish Systems Security all bid when tenders opened in 2014. Although the EU gave nation-states millions of euros annually to assist with processing and taking in asylum seekers, in reality Greece spent the vast majority of its share in 2013 on border security and detention centers. When the European commissioner for home affairs, Cecilia Malmström, visited a Greek detention center in 2013, the Greek press reported it as a signal that Brussels was happy to pay Athens for continuing its harsh policies.[41]

Despite the huge sums of money being discussed, it was unsurprising that Greece topped the Eurozone's poverty rate. The austerity that had been implemented since 2008, including massive reductions in spending on areas such as healthcare and education, had meant that more than a third of citizens were living on less than 60 percent of the 2013 national median income.[42]

Debtocracies, not democracies, were what characterized twenty-first-century Europe. A French committee headed by one of the country's leading economists released a report in 2014 that found 60 percent of French public debt was illegitimate, and that this was partly explained by reductions in the tax burden on the rich over the previous decades.[43] The answer, the authors said, was to acknowledge that much public debt served private interests rather than the common good.

Even the IMF chief economist admitted that his organization's prescription for Greece and other European countries had been a mistake. Olivier Blanchard issued a 2013 paper that acknowledged what went wrong, written in calm and precise language. "Forecasters significantly underestimated the increase in unemployment and the decline in domestic demand associated with fiscal consolidation," it stated.[44] Amazingly, Blanchard wrote that the IMF was largely blind to determining the role of their own economists when implementing its toxic medicine: "The short-term effects of fiscal policy on economic activity are only one of the many factors that need to be considered in determining the appropriate pace of fiscal consolidation for any single country." In other words, there was a human cost to policies drafted in the halls of power. If history was any guide, it was hard to imagine the IMF departing from the neoliberal agenda embedded in its DNA.

The message was clear, if backers of austerity cared to listen: impose brutal policies at your peril. The EU had never been less popular in Greece, or in many other nations across Europe, and the prospect of a united continent far into the future remained less than guaranteed (or even desirable): too many citizens suffered at the hands of Brussels bureaucrats.[45] Dutch-American sociologist Saskia Sassen argued that Greece was undergoing "economic ethnic cleansing"—a tactic that allows the downtrodden to be ignored and shunned in the name of renewed growth.[46]

Opposition to an auction of national assets was strong. Activists and locals challenged the privatization of some of the nation's finest beaches, including on the islands of Elafonisos and Rhodes, in a desperate attempt to raise funds. "We are like a bankrupt housewife forced to sell the silver to save the family," said one eighty-year-old supporter of selling the beaches. "Greece has no choice."[47] This was a view, backing privatization, shared by a minority who understandably craved a better life; but the recent history of outsourcing had been one of dismal failure, and it had not raised the amounts expected. The state had originally aimed to generate €50 billion by 2019, but that figure had been repeatedly revised under previous governments, falling to around €11 billion by 2016.

Insane policies, such as privatizing Greek water utilities, advocated by the Greek government in 2014, were wholly rejected by both the country's highest administrative court and 98 percent of voters in an unofficial referendum on the matter.[48] Interestingly, many Greek courts have opposed the government's attempts to privatize, and slash jobs and salaries, as unconstitutional.[49]

The Canadian mining company Eldorado Gold had wanted to mine in Chalkidiki, in northern Greece, since 2012. Though the rights were sold as a solution to the country's economic woes, locals and environmentalists recognized the destruction the plans would bring. The government pledged at all costs to "protect foreign investment in the country" and yet was happy to receive no mining royalties in the shabby deal (a stance opposed by Syriza).[50] Civil unrest began in 2011 throughout the region and persisted for some time. The state turned on its own people, sending in riot police in 2013 in an unsuccessful attempt to destroy the protest camp. It was another example of ham-fisted policies being made on the fly by a ruling elite who took their instructions from wealthy interests. Syriza moved to block Eldorado's plans when it won government. Convincing the international community that the nation was "open for business"—a mantra heard from Haiti to

Afghanistan—was difficult. This was clear code for deregulation and outsourcing.

The *New York Times* editorialized in 2012 for the Greek people to stop complaining and get privatizing. It was far easier to blame the Greek people and let them suffer than to hold accountable the elites who had caused the crash. "While we sympathize with Greek protests against excessive austerity, we have no patience with politicians [code for Syriza] who continue to drag their feet over pro-growth reforms and privatizations."[51] The paper's tone shifted after the 2015 election, expressing some sympathy with the long-suffering Greek people. It published a travel story on Athens in October 2014 claiming: "the city's self-confidence and creativity are stirring again."[52] The evidence for this was a handful of new cafés and bars.

The biggest fire-sale in the history of state-owned assets started in 2010, when 70,000 lots were up for grabs. Major assets such as the country's third-largest bank, Eurobank, were sold, and the government lost huge amounts of money.[53] From beaches to islands, from vast estates to the government's gambling company, the EU only agreed to release more bailout funds to Greece if it agreed to privatize even more, despite the previous efforts not having brought the benefits that had been promised. From the beginning, the government ignored stark warnings of the risk of rushing to outsource at rock-bottom prices without due diligence, leading to Russian-style oligarchs controlling the batch of assets.[54]

It was hard to disagree with the words of Slovenian philosopher Slavoj Žižek when he explained in 2012 that the Greek people's struggle was central to retaining a decent civilization: "It is one of the main testing grounds for a new socio-economic model of potentially unlimited application: a depoliticised technocracy in which bankers and other experts are allowed to demolish democracy. By saving Greece from its so-called saviours, we also save Europe itself."[55]

Despite the failures, supporters of selling off Greece continued to make themselves heard. The chairman of the Hellenic Republic Asset Development Fund, Stelios Stavridis, told the *Daily Telegraph* that there was no other way to bring Greece back from the brink: "I'm an entrepreneur, not a politician, and I have been screaming my head off that this is all about growth, job creation, wealth creation. I am the anti-bureaucracy man: we need to bring in this money—there is no other way."[56] The manager of a golf course in the village of Afandou on the island of Rhodes, Vassilis Anastasiou, longed for authoritarian rule—a refrain I heard regularly from older Greeks nostalgic for the stability of the past. They made no mention of the accompanying repression, of course. Angry that a clubhouse at the golf course sat unfinished, Anastasiou argued that "at least under the military junta it only took three years to build that site."[57]

But this was wishful thinking. Disaster capitalism in the guise of austerity caused unprecedented social harm. The suicide rate soared; a study from the University of Portsmouth found that 551 men had killed themselves "solely because of fiscal austerity" between 2009 and 2010.[58] These numbers continued to climb in the following years. HIV infection also rose because funding for prevention had decreased. The Labor Institute of the Confederation of Greek Workers found that half of all companies were not paying their staff on time; both public- and private-sector workers suffered.[59] The "cocaine of the poor"—a variety of crystal meth called sisa—ravaged those slipping through the cracks.[60] Police slammed drug addiction by pushing those affected away from the city center. Prostitution was another inevitable byproduct of the crisis. The National Center for Social Research discovered that the number of people selling their bodies had increased by 150 percent between 2011 and 2013.[61] Rates of child abuse were growing. For some, all of this offered a perfect travel opportunity. British-based Political Tours organized a "Greece and the Euro Tour"—a visit to various sites of struggle under austerity.

One day, walking through the middle of Athens, I saw a loud

protest group outside the Greek Ministry of Finance. Hundreds of cleaning women were staging a sit-in to oppose the cutting of their jobs. Riot police had visited the site and made a violent but failed attempt to disperse the group. A G4S truck was parked nearby. Hundreds of protestors converged on the Ministry to offer solidarity with the women. They were determined and passionate as the public face of austerity. Some locals told me that this was the kind of resistance that inspired them. I was handed a flyer about the case: "It is obvious that to the Greek government and the Troika we are just numbers, not human lives." Syriza announced that it would re-hire the cleaners.

A theme running through my time in Athens was the question of identity within Greece and Europe. This was a nation unsure about its place in the modern world, unable or unwilling to relinquish its brutal authoritarian past but led by figures who showed no hesitation in repeating the errors of past decades. Syriza was presented with the opportunity to change this reality. Imagination and bravery were usually in short supply—hardly an exclusively Greek problem. Disaster capitalism was used to impose punitive measures against anyone—immigrants, the working class—who craved a more equal society. Extreme austerity guaranteed a greater urgency in efforts to address the reasons why it was happening.

In Athens, I participated in an event on nationhood organized by a local art collective, the Libby Sacer Foundation, with bestselling Greek-Australian writer Christos Tsiolkas. In the anarchist suburb of Exarheia, in a large room in an upper-floor gallery, a group gathered to hear Christos and I talk about patriotism, asylum seekers, and rights.

I briefly introduced myself as an Australian, German, atheist, anti-Zionist Jew. The Greek-Australian translator for the event, who had lived in Greece since the late 1970s and never returned to Australia, asked me before it started why I was "anti-Semitic," and I had to correct her that I was "anti-Zionist." I explained that

I never really feel part of any community, moving in and out of many, and that I found it hard to feel any sense of pride in Australia because of its consistent breaches of human rights at home and abroad. It was a view shared by many in the room who despaired at the country's rightward turn and Golden Dawn's success. Tsiolkas said that he felt similarly about Australia, arguing that the left routinely failed to speak to the working class in Australia and worldwide.

Much of the discussion for the next two hours consisted of audience members explaining that questions of identity in Europe were necessarily different from those in Australia, being part of a larger debate on European entity, whereas Australia was a continent by itself, though closely integrated with Asia. A number of people asked how we might get past the left's distaste for patriotism, when it was so intimately connected to abuses during peace and wartime.

One of the most striking insights that emerged from the evening was a deep awareness that Greece had a dark, racist past and present. Syriza's rise to power presented a unique chance to unwind decades of entrenched corporate interests, though serious challenges remained—not least that of controlling a police force and military innately disposed to repress the left, while many were sympathetic to Golden Dawn. European power brokers would not release Greece easily from the bonds of financial servitude.

Greece was a traumatized nation—distrustful of all politicians, reeling from years of extreme economic policies and the largest wave of migration since the 1950s. True independence, signifying sovereignty in relation to Brussels, required an accounting for past mistakes, the unraveling of a state apparatus that endorsed and defended bigotry, and the imagining of a nation that would welcome the stranger.

3

Haiti: "If anybody here says they've had help, it's a lie"

The US is doing a lot of good things in Haiti.
Former Haitian prime minister Laurent Lamothe, 2012

I had never seen anything like it. Large parts of the Haitian capital, Port-au-Prince, remained in pieces years after a massive earthquake had ripped through it on January 12, 2010. The sheer devastation made the city look like a war zone, and life at street level was grimmer than I witnessed in Afghanistan, yet here there was no open conflict.

Half-destroyed buildings leaned precariously along the city's roads; the street vendors selling wares in their shadows risked the very real possibility of injury or death. Ivy wrapped itself around cracked concrete, and massive amounts of garbage littered the streets. Water ran everywhere, along with sewage, spilling out of broken pipes that were yet to be repaired. Citizens foraged through the muck for anything useful. Around them roamed bony dogs. The devastating quake had left many roads impassable due to the rubble, while others were accessible but treacherous.

As I walked through the shattered city, I saw Haitians selling whatever they could: mobile phones, schoolbooks, homemade alcohol, belts, vegetables, and fruit. I observed women washing dirty shoes with a hose before dumping them on a pile marked "For sale." I was overwhelmed by the foul smells, but also by the brilliant colors of people's clothing and the structures still standing.

There was a skeleton of a large church that had partially collapsed during the quake and had been sealed with concrete. A few people had made their homes in tents at its perimeter. Men, with their children, begged for money. I was told that people used to shit in the church. When the stench became unbearable, the government locked them all out. Some 80 percent of Haitians were Roman Catholics, but many still practiced vodou, an indigenous faith.

Many other buildings were also still abandoned. A few bank branches had been rebuilt, but there was little evidence of other construction. It all felt decrepit and temporary, but I reminded myself that this was a city where over 700,000 people lived permanently; more people came here daily to buy and sell, to shop and socialize. The situation was grim when I first visited in 2012, and it had changed little on a return trip in 2014.

My white face stood out in Port-au-Prince, as it did elsewhere in Haiti, and many locals eyed me suspiciously as I walked through the destroyed city. I understood that, as a journalist, I was seen as a leech by people in developing countries—we came, we went. But some people approached me, wanting to send a message to anyone who would listen.

A man started screaming at me, then composed himself enough to say that every day his socks and shoes were wet because he could not keep them dry while trying to earn money for his family. He demanded that the government fix the city and make the place livable. He also told me he had little hope this would ever happen.

A woman in her forties wearing a floppy yellow hat and a black top also screamed at me, waving her arms to chase me away. She soon calmed down and explained that she wanted Haitian president Michel Martelly to "do something for me and my two kids, one of whom is crazy." She motioned behind her to where she was forced to earn a living—the squalid, waterlogged space where she tried to sell toys. She lamented that she did not have a house, clearly despairing.

The January 2010 earthquake lasted only thirty-five seconds but wrought incredible destruction. At least three million Haitians were affected—more than a million suddenly became homeless. The exact death toll had never been determined, but the official estimate had gone as high as 316,000. Decades' worth of poorly built infrastructure collapsed, rendering vast swathes of Port-au-Prince uninhabitable. Yet, stunningly, the population rallied together in the Haitian tradition of *youn ede lot*, Haitian Creole for "lending a hand to each other." With little or no government assistance, communities pooled their resources to help save people in the wreckage; keep alive the seriously injured; find food, utensils, and charcoal to burn for warmth; and create sleeping shelters in the streets. Makeshift clinics were established, with shop-owners handing out water, medicines, and other essentials. Young men and women worked to clear the rubble with their bare hands. And although there were some civil disturbances, principally due to frustration over a lack of local and international assistance, the nation did not descend into war.[1]

Haiti had long been portrayed as a country that could not function properly on its own, but the inhabitants' reaction to the earthquake belied this. "The Haitian people put away their economic and political differences and worked together, in dignity and solidarity, to collectively survive," wrote Mark Schuller and Pablo Morales in the introduction to their book *Tectonic Shifts*.[2]

Unfortunately, Haiti, like other poor nations, had long been at risk of exploitation, and the earthquake provided a significant opportunity for this to occur, as was evident from WikiLeaks cables released in 2011. Then US ambassador to Haiti, Kenneth Merten, headlined a February 1, 2010 cable "The Gold Rush Is On." He went on to explain his excitement: "As Haiti digs out from the earthquake, different companies are moving in to sell their concepts, products and services. [Then] President Preval met with Gen Wesley Clark [the former US presidential candidate was working for a Miami-based construction company] and received a sales presentation on a hurricane/earthquake resistant foam core house designed for low income residents." Merten concluded, after seeing countless US firms angling for business, that "each is vying for the ear of the President in a veritable free-for-all."[3]

The gold rush for private enterprise started almost as soon as the earthquake ended, and ultimately meant that only a tiny percentage of USAID's $1.8 billion of funding reached the pockets of ordinary Haitians. At a "Haiti summit" held in a luxury hotel in Miami a mere two months after the quake, private contractors—including the company Triple Canopy, which had taken over the notorious Blackwater's contract in Iraq in 2009—jostled for opportunities.[4]

Lewis Lucke was appointed America's special coordinator for relief and reconstruction in Haiti, and also the head of Washington's earthquake relief effort. He was a veteran of nearly three decades in the US establishment, and a key figure in overseeing billion-dollar contracts for corporations while he was USAID mission director in post-invasion Iraq. Lucke stepped down from his appointments after only three months, but he went on to promote the reconstruction effort during an interview with the *Austin American-Statesman* newspaper, saying: "It became clear to us that if it was handled correctly, the earthquake represented as much an opportunity as it did a calamity ... So much of the china was broken that it gives the chance to put it together in a better and different way."[5]

His motives for quitting became clear two months later, when he inked a $30,000 per month deal with a Florida-based disaster recovery company, AshBritt,[6] and a Haitian firm run by one of the country's wealthiest men, Gilbert Bigio. Lucke promptly secured $20 million in construction contracts and proudly told *Haiti-Liberte* that "just because you're trying to do business doesn't mean you're trying to be rapacious. There's nothing insidious about that ... It wasn't worse than Iraq."[7]

It was just the latest example of canny capitalists sifting through the ashes of a disaster, looking for business opportunities.

"True political freedom is as limited in Haiti as it is anywhere on the planet," wrote Canadian author Peter Hallward in his book *Damming the Flood: Haiti and the Politics of Containment.* "It is limited by the fragility of an economy that remains profoundly vulnerable to international pressure."[8]

The reasons for this fragility were found in the twentieth-century history of the country, when the United States maintained successive brutal dictatorships that benefited local and foreign elites at the expense of the Haitian majority. It was colonialism with the bloodiest of hands. Paramilitary groups were a common phenomenon in Haiti throughout these decades, and they remained a troubling weapon in the current government's armory.[9] Free speech was still far from protected, and journalists faced constant harassment.[10] The reconstitution of the Haitian military in 2014 rang alarm bells for a nation facing no visible external threats and with a history of internal repression against its own citizens.[11]

Haiti was the first slave country in history to overthrow its rulers successfully. February 1794 saw the abolition of French colonial rule, and in 1804 Saint-Domingue became independent Haiti.[12] It was a success constantly mentioned with pride during my visits, a reminder of a period in history when the people stood up and were not answerable to anyone except themselves. It was the kind of sovereignty the country's citizens said they craved again. Unfortunately for Haitians, this period came to an end in 1915, when the United States invaded and occupied the country, paving the way for the installation of the dictator Francois "Papa Doc" Duvalier as president in 1957, and his replacement, upon his death fourteen years later, with his son and fellow dictator,

Jean-Claude "Baby Doc" Duvalier. The CIA had found a willing partner, and Baby Doc was only nineteen years old when he assumed power.

It was a surreal experience driving past the large home of Baby Doc up in the hills overlooking Port-au-Prince, knowing that there was little international pressure to prosecute him for all the brutality and human rights abuses that occurred during his rule from 1971 to 1986. He returned to Haiti in 2011 after years of exile in France and lived in carefree luxury. Duvalier, unlike the many African despots targeted by the Hague, remained a friend of the West and was therefore largely untouchable, though a Haitian court in 2014 pleased survivors of his reign of terror by agreeing a case could proceed to investigate serious allegations of torture and killings. He died in October 2014 having never faced justice. At his funeral, protestors raised signs that read, "You cannot forget what the Duvalier dictatorship did to the country."

In his few media appearances, Duvalier appeared weak but defiant about his legacy. Like all dictators, he claimed he had saved the nation. In 2014, while at the Observatory in Boutilliers, overlooking Port-au-Prince, I fortuitously met Duvalier's lawyer, a large man who was socializing with the Haitian elite. Unsurprisingly, he said Duvalier was innocent of any allegations, though he proudly noted the closeness between two of his clients, Duvalier and President Martelly, a man who had run a popular nightclub for the military and the country's elite during the Duvalier period. Word on the street was that Martelly protected Duvalier because their worlds had been intimately connected for decades.

Documents released by WikiLeaks in 2013 through its Public Library of US Diplomacy revealed that Washington increased sales of deadly weapons to Baby Doc during his rule, weapons that were ultimately used against Haitian civilians.[13] The US embassy's deputy chief of mission in the early 1970s was Thomas J. Corcoran. He wrote in a cable sent from Port-au-Prince on November 23, 1973, that "repression [had] been markedly and genuinely eased" and that there was a "clear desire to do more for the economic development of the country." He argued that the Haitian military, which had been accused of plentiful brutality against their own people, should receive training "which will contribute substantially to advancing a number of our important interests in the region." Decades later, little had changed.

The Duvaliers were devoutly anti-communist during the Cold War, and so Washington lavished them with financial support. Thanks to the financial and military support provided by the superpower, Haiti was ruled with an iron fist—dissent was crushed, the press was muzzled, and many thousands of people were killed. Peter Hallward wrote that in the 1970s, after Baby Doc had taken his lead from his father and declared himself "President for Life," neoliberal policies were ruthlessly implemented, entrenching the state in poverty.

Hallward observed that America's backing deepened

> in exchange for providing the sort of investment climate [Baby Doc's] patrons had come to expect—minimal taxes, a virtual ban on trade unions, the preservation of starvation wages, the removal of any restrictions on the repatriation of profits. In the mid-1980s these measures were supplemented by the beginning of the structural adjustments that would soon reduce Haiti's public sector to a bare-boned shell while stripping its markets of protective tariffs.[14]

The facts of this stark example of American corporate pillaging were startling:

> There were just seven foreign firms in the light assembly sector in 1967; twelve years later there were 51, and by 1986 there were over 300 US corporations working in Haiti. In real terms, average wages fell by around 50 percent between 1980 and 1990, and as import controls were removed, the value of

US agricultural exports to Haiti almost tripled during the last years of the decade.[15]

This was disaster capitalism on a countrywide basis. In the 1980s, however, some organized resistance began to appear: small, local groups—*organisations populaires*—started providing services that the authorities were unwilling or unable to implement. There was also nascent public discussion of how a tiny thugocracy had given both the United States and the International Monetary Fund full access to a population on sustenance employment.

In 1990 the tide turned. A former Catholic priest, Jean-Bertrand Aristide, who pledged to rescue Haiti from decades of misery, was swept into power on a wave of popular support. New schools were built, along with much-needed infrastructure, and higher taxes were imposed on the rich. But Aristide's reforms proved deeply unpopular with elements of the military and the elites who had thrived under the Duvalier dictatorship, and he was overthrown in a coup in 1991. A few years later he became president again, from 1994 to 1996, and again from 2001 to 2004—his last term cut off by a US-led coup.

The French and American governments, which had never been happy about the prospect of a truly independent Haiti, had long been intent on restoring a more compliant leadership in Port-au-Prince, and there was a limit to how much they could take. One of Aristide's greatest mistakes, at least in the eyes of his country's former masters, was to demand of France in 2003 that it pay back the massive amount of money extorted by French gunboats in 1825 for losses of colonial property. Haitian officials estimated that in today's money it was equivalent to $21 billion.[16] Such impudence from a former slave nation was unforgivable.

When he returned to Haiti in 2011 after seven years in exile, Aristide told *Democracy Now!* that the economic disaster of neo-liberalism "didn't destroy the human values of the Haitian people, neither their dreams—not foolish dreams, but dreams of freedom for all, justice for all, food for all, education for all, health for all. Those are like a model, driving the Haitian people, moving forward despite ... political catastrophes."[17]

After the earthquake came the cholera. The first cases appeared in October 2010, and it soon turned into an epidemic. More than 9,000 Haitians subsequently died from the disease, while at least 712,000 had fallen sick. These numbers pointed to the failure of the United Nations and government authorities to solve the problem, and highlighted another aspect of the country's vulnerability to exploitation.

The spread of cholera after the earthquake was expertly detailed by the *New York Times* in March 2012. Journalist Deborah Sontag reported that around 5 percent of the country's population had been affected by the disease. She cited strong evidence that Nepalese troops, who had been brought in to assist the state as part of the UN stabilization force called MINUSTAH, had imported the cholera and contaminated a river next to their base through a faulty sanitation system. Within days, Haitians had begun dying. The UN initially denied the problem. Then, after the organization's secretary-general, Ban Ki-moon, started talking about developing sanitation and water infrastructure, the UN bungled its response and left thousands of Haitians without adequate healthcare.[18] In 2013, the UN remained unwilling to accept culpability, rejecting a legal claim for compensation issued on behalf of the cholera victims, and in 2015 an American judge reaffirmed the UN's impunity.[19] In 2013 the UN was unable even to raise a fourth of the $38 million required to purchase water-purification pills and other hygiene basics.[20] It was a dark stain on the UN's history, despite Ban pledging to raise billions of dollars more during his visit to Haiti in 2014.

Dr. Paul Farmer, co-founder of the NGO Partners in Health, told the *New York Times* that "this unfolded right under the noses of all those NGOs ... Why didn't they throw the kitchen sink at cholera in Haiti?" The answer to this question lay in bureaucratic problems, a lack of proper water-sanitation facilities, inadequate funds for Haitian health workers, and stonewalling by the UN. Basically, too few people were vaccinated and the cholera death toll continued to rise, fueled by other natural disasters.

In 2012, Médecins Sans Frontières (MSF), the world's leading medical humanitarian aid organization, echoed the thinking that Haitian officials did not have the resources to cope with the disease—a fact explained to a large degree by decades of over-reliance on handouts instead of the building up of local facilities. Nonetheless, it demanded a more comprehensive response from the Haitian government, including the provision of clean drinking water and focused care for cholera victims. MSF rightly argued that it was not the organization's purpose "to assume·the respon-sibilities of the Ministry of Health and its international partners in managing the epidemic at a national level,"[21] though they were happy to assist in any way possible. The NGO claimed that, up to that stage, it had treated more than 170,000 cholera victims, roughly 33 percent of the cases across Haiti.[22]

Cholera entered a country with an already poor sanitation system. It was a nation that employed manual laborers called *bayakou* who emptied the filthy cesspools of human waste under Haiti's backyard toilets. Public health was so compromised that there was little government infrastructure to keep food and water away from infected waste (though one of the few Haitian govern-ment departments with a moderately decent record, thanks partly to US aid, was the Health Ministry, especially in the areas of child vaccination and HIV treatment).[23] Around 60 percent of schools lacked toilets. Although a few international organizations, such as the United Nations and the Bill and Melinda Gates Foundation, had argued for privatized projects since the cholera outbreak, there was little evidence of progress.[24] A rare exception was the open-air clinics for cholera patients designed by a firm in Boston, MASS Design Group, and built by Haitians. These facilities aimed to combine clever architecture and health provision to reduce future epidemics.[25]

Put starkly, Haiti was a state that was terminally crooked when other nations were seen as more worthy of donor funding. "Even if the conscience of the world is no longer shocked by Haitian sickness and deaths," the *New York Times* editorialized in April 2014, "the Haitian people still need the world's help."[26] Nonetheless, when Haiti had received lashings of "help," this generosity had done little but enrich foreign companies. To make matters worse, international donors remained unwilling to support a trust fund to allow the Haitian government to eradicate cholera with clean water and sanitation.[27]

The presence of cholera had exacerbated the deep unhappiness that many of Haiti's citizens felt in regard to the presence of UN troops and their mandate to bring safety to the population. UN forces had been accused of countless violations, including the murder of more than thirty Haitians in the Cité Soleil community in 2006 and the alleged rape of a man by Uruguayan troops in 2011. It was therefore unsurprising that a 2012 survey conducted by the University of Haiti found that 70 percent of Haitians wanted foreign armed forces to leave the country within a year.[28]

To many of the nation's inhabitants, the UN troops were just another example of foreign powers imposing their will on Haiti. Canadian academic Justin Podur, in his incisive book *Haiti's New Dictatorship*, viewed this as an indication that Haiti remained a dictatorship and that its people "have no effective say over their economic and political affairs."[29] MINUSTAH, he argued, was an "internationalised military solution offered for what even the UN admitted were problems of poverty and social crime that occur in many places."[30]

A WikiLeaks cable confirmed the real agenda behind the UN force. A 2008 document from the US ambassador to Haiti, Janet A. Sanderson, explained how MINUSTAH was an "indispensable tool in realizing core [US government] policy interests in Haiti."

She argued that one of the main threats that MINUSTAH helped to manage were "resurgent populist and anti-market economy political forces," which could reverse the "gains of the last two years."

Demands for compensation from the UN in connection with the cholera outbreak were growing, along with calls for the international body to develop strategies to protect the population properly, something its troops had so often failed to do. The fact was that although the former US ambassador to the UN, Susan Rice, claimed that UN troops had "helped provide a more secure and stable environment in Haiti, strengthened the country's institutions, protected civilians and safeguarded human rights,"[31] evidence of this was very slim. During my visits to Haiti, I constantly saw armed UN troops standing around in the hot sun, doing little more than sweating as they watched locals lay new asphalt on old roads. For many of the Haitians I spoke to, it felt like another occupation.

In 2014 I witnessed this reality by spending time with armed UN peacekeepers walking through Croix-des-Bouquets on the streets of Port-au-Prince. These men were from El Salvador and Peru, friendly and approachable, though they barely interacted with locals when I saw them, and the amount of time it took to organize the tour proved the degree of sensitivity to any media scrutiny. My questions about cholera, violence, and Haitian attitudes towards the UN were batted away with PR aplomb.

"Haiti is open for business," said President Martelly in late 2011 as he opened a new industrial park at Caracol, in the north of the country, principally supported by Washington to the tune of hundreds of millions of dollars. Standing alongside former US president Bill Clinton, he then praised the huge amount of foreign—mainly US—investment that had entered Haiti since the 2010 quake. The "open for business" slogan was repeated when I interviewed the Haitian minister for commerce and finance, Wilson Laleau, a man who spoke passionately about foreign investment while acknowledging the dangers of not empowering locals.

Ironically, although planning for the industrial park had commenced in 2008, it was not until the earthquake struck two years later that it, and other projects like it, became a reality. The disaster swiftly attracted investment by other countries, in post-earthquake reconstruction or new building projects in which Haitians were barely involved in the decision-making process.

The United States and South Korea, for example, saw opportunities to help their own businesses make a profit by building clothing factories for companies such as Walmart in poor areas of the state. This was all just the latest incarnation of a tired old model that failed to deliver long-lasting benefits to locals, but instead delivered cheap labor to multinationals. This view was reflected in a scathing 2011 report by the media organization Haiti Grassroots Watch, which argued that Haitian workers were earning less than during the time of the Baby Doc dictatorship.[32]

The logic that had been employed was familiar from countries such as Papua New Guinea and Afghanistan. The owner of apparel maker One World, Charles Baker, even admitted to Haiti Grassroots Watch that the salaries he was paying his workers were too low. Baker also said that Washington was happy for foreign firms such as Gap, Levi's, Banana Republic, K-Mart, and Walmart to pay poverty-level wages so that their bottom lines could soar, excusing their actions as a means of assisting Haiti through employment and skill development. After all, Baker claimed, low-level wages and skills were not going to be permanent features of the local economy, but would only be important for the next ten to fifteen years. "It's a step," he said. "We're going up the stairs and it's one of the steps."[33]

The *Economist* was largely positive about the industrial park development, though it cautioned that President Martelly was a "politically inexperienced populist" who needed to change Haiti's image from one of "eternal aid supplicant into one of a hard-working place."[34] The *New York Times* was more circumspect, writing on the third anniversary of the earthquake that the world had failed Haiti and that one industrial park was not a panacea. It highlighted the key problem with the open-for-business mantra: that Haitians felt "like bystanders in their own country."[35]

Bill Clinton, who claimed to have a special connection to Haiti after honeymooning there with his wife Hillary in the 1970s, was appointed by President Barack Obama in 2010, alongside former president George W. Bush, to oversee the earthquake relief effort. But allegations of mismanagement were soon directed at the Clinton Foundation's work in Haiti. The *Nation* discovered in 2011 that makeshift trailers provided by the organization, which were to be used as temporary classrooms and hurricane-proof shelters, had been badly built and contained dangerous levels of formaldehyde. In fact, the company that constructed the trailers, Clayton Homes, was sued by the US government after Hurricane Katrina in New Orleans for providing similarly defective trailers.[36] Corrupt players moved from one situation of exploitation to another—disaster capitalism in motion.

There were exceptions. In 2014 I was taken on a tour of an inner-city Port-au-Prince development along the Champs de Mars by Harry Adam, the government's director of the Unit for Housing and Public Construction at the Prime Minister's Office. Some of the buildings were impressive, and the workers were all locals. Adam explained that they were trying to create a city from the ashes of the earthquake, and to do so sustainably.

Despite all the scandals that had enveloped Bill and Hillary Clinton in Haiti and beyond, they remained darlings of many in the liberal media. When Bill led the Interim Haiti Recovery Commission (IHRC) after the 2010 earthquake, he was answering to his wife in her capacity as US secretary of state. Haitian filmmaker Raoul Peck revealed footage in his 2013 film *Fatal Assistance* of a 2010 meeting when Haitian commissioners confronted Bill and claimed they had been marginalized by Western consultants.

It was just another part of the Clinton gravy-train in Haiti that had started decades earlier, in the 1990s, when friends of the couple bought into Haiti's state-owned telephone network. Clinton "had a particular fondness for places he mucked up as president," former Associated Press journalist Jonathan Katz wrote in his book *The Big Truck That Went By*.

Patrick Elie, a Haitian activist and former secretary of state for public security in the Aristide government, was well aware of the influence of self-interested outsiders in his country. He told *Democracy Now!* a year after the January 2010 earthquake: "Haiti is controlled by a foreign government and foreign interests, the so-called international community."[37]

I interviewed Elie at his home in Peggy Ville, a wealthy part of Port-au-Prince. When I arrived around noon, I found the gray-bearded campaigner drinking Scotch and smoking Marlboro Reds, colloquially known as "cowboy killers." His home was filled with DVDs, books, and photos of his family. A copy of Chris Hedges's book *The Illusion of Empire* testified to Elie's love of history.

"I want to speak for the voiceless of Haiti," said the former chemist who had found his calling in politics. "Since the American occupation of 1915, the US policy towards Haiti has never truly deviated. It has used different tactics—sometimes violence, sometimes more cunning—but it has kept a steady course, which is truly to remove Haiti's independence, its self-determination. It has done so by undermining the Haitian small landowners who are really the anchor of Haitian culture, dignity, and autonomy. I see this project being pursued and accelerated these days. The US saw Haiti from the beginning as a reserve of cheap manpower. In the modern era, the task is how to starve the peasants so they can flock to the cities ... [but] instead of sugarcane plantations, like years ago, there are these factories."

Elie stressed that today's Haitian leaders were little more than representatives of Washington in Port-au-Prince. "It's mostly

America that controls Haiti," he said, although France and Canada were also prominent there. In late 2012, France gave €29 million to Haiti, money slated to implement border security and the rule of law. Canada, meanwhile, has sent more than $1 billion in aid to Haiti since 2006.

Elie also pointed to the new problems that were appearing on the horizon as the country's resources were exposed. There were reportedly billions of dollars' worth of gold, silver, copper, and zinc in Haiti's northern hills. Canadian prime minister Stephen Harper had already encouraged his country's NGOs to partner with mining companies when working in Haiti, in an attempt to pacify local communities about what was to come. Needless to say, according to Elie, the new gold rush, long anticipated by foreign mining companies and the country's elites, would be a disaster. His concerns were eerily reminiscent of what I heard in Papua New Guinea: "It spells serious trouble for this country because the Haitian state is weak and so subservient to the international powers. The companies are greedy. Fertile land is going to be totally destroyed and polluted because they'll be using cyanide and mercury."[38]

"Our subsoil is rich in minerals. Now is the time to dig them up," said then Haitian prime minister Laurent Lamothe in 2012. But the problem was that many of the companies looking to exploit the estimated $20 billion in gold and copper, such as Newmont Mining and Eurasian Minerals, had shoddy records, including Eurasian's compromised copper-mining partnership with Israeli billionaire Dan Gertler in the Democratic Republic of Congo. His company claimed to have found huge deposits of oil there in 2014. Furthermore, the country had signed up to few of the international regulations for extractive industries, the bare minimum required to protect landowners from exploitation. Haiti Grassroots Watch discovered that a former minister of finance was now a consultant for Newmont Mining and had urged a loosening of the already weak mining laws.

Countless licenses had been purchased to explore large swathes of Haiti's north. But, unlike in Bolivia, Peru, or Cuba, where more independent governments placed tighter restrictions on the ability of Western companies to exploit minerals and, in some cases, nationalized their resources, Haiti showed no indication of regulating the behavior of North American mining corporations. If anything, Port-au-Prince seemed happy to follow the West's lead—a common complaint I heard was that white men were turning up in remote areas with a few black Haitians by their side, as if the latter were there purely to support the former's benign plans.[39]

Advocates of a busy resources industry claimed that it was one way for Haiti to reduce its dependence on foreign assistance— the same argument I heard in Papua New Guinea. An alternative view has been articulated by Arnolt Jean, a peasant organizer who worked in an area near the Dominican Republic border. He told Haiti Grassroots Watch in 2012 that "what is underground could make us not poor any more [but] it's the rich who come with their fancy equipment to dig it out. The people who live on top of the ground stay poor, while the rich get even richer."[40] Dozens of Haitian groups agreed in August 2014 to join a movement to oppose open-pit mining in northern Haiti. Collective Against Mining was a local organization that aimed to highlight the fallacy of profitable drilling. Bauxite was exploited in the 1950s and 1960s, but very little of the profits stayed in Haiti. History was often the best guide to the future.

Patrick Elie was passionately opposed to the machinations of disaster capitalism in Haiti, and he spoke frankly. "We are now in a situation where you have a regime that is trying to roll back history," he said, "and go back to an authoritarian period where the people will be kept subdued and business can unfold and make money unchallenged ... When they say Haiti is 'open for business,' they are defining a concept where this country will be run like a [business] enterprise, with the majority of the loot going to the chosen few and their international bosses." A UN envoy to Haiti phrased this a bit differently, saying that the country was "not yet" prepared for foreign investment. Nigel Fisher added: "We can blame external partners for their slowness to pay the promised assistance."[41]

Elie gave me a startling example of the way in which the Haitian government accommodated its overseas business masters, explaining how two mobile-phone companies, Digicel and Voila!, had merged in 2012 and thereby ended up controlling more than 95 percent of their market.[42] "This reminds me," Elie said, "of the Duvalier period, where everything was a monopoly for the friends of the regime. This is being done at the expense of the Haitian people, but also [by] a company in which the state owns 40 percent of the interest." He lamented that, although there had been some vocal resistance to the merger, "a crowd is not a force." Digicel claimed to be giving back to the community, opening a Marriot-run hotel in Port-au-Prince in 2015 and building schools, all plans backed by Bill Clinton.

Elie told me of his admiration for the Castros in Cuba, how they provided free healthcare and education and resisted the United States, offering Haiti an alternative model. He imagined the Haitian peasantry rising up to build a sustainable economy without relying on foreign handouts. This bottom-up strategy, which was anathema to the "solutions" currently imposed by corrupt politicians, was the dream of many Haitians I met. But it did not reflect the status quo enforced by Port-au-Prince and Washington.[43]

A common complaint I heard in Haiti concerned the fact that Washington subsidized its own rice farmers to the tune of billions of dollars, forcing Haitian farmers to sell their produce at a lower price than the imported goods. A more sustainable approach would have been for local rice farmers to expand their production to provide for the whole island, but coherent agricultural policies had not been a priority of the Haitian elites or the international NGO sector[44]—besides which, Washington would not allow it.

As a result, at least 75 percent of the rice consumed in Haiti was imported,[45] which imposed a big financial burden on locals because rice was a key component of the Haitian diet.

Even Bill Clinton recognized the insanity of the policy, blaming his own policies when in office, and calling on Washington to stop subsidizing its rice exports to Haiti. "I have to live every day with the consequences of the lost capacity to produce a rice crop in Haiti to feed those people," he said in 2010, "because of what I did."

Meanwhile, a lack of accountability had developed in the aid industry, especially in relation to USAID. The US government agency pledged $1.8 billion after the 2010 earthquake—the total global amount of support was $13.5 billion, enough to give every Haitian a check for over $1,000; but in reality much of this money ended up in the hands of local and foreign contractors without anything being given in return. USAID's own inspector-general found in 2010 (and again in 2012) that 70 percent of the funds given to the large contractor Chemonics failed to deliver any key goals, and that far fewer Haitians were hired in the process than promised.[46] This was despite Chemonics deliberately lying about its shoddy work in Afghanistan to ensure ongoing contracts. The company was contracted for over $200 million in Haiti.[47] In 2012, *Foreign Policy* discovered that Chemonics, if it were a country, "would have been the third-largest recipient of USAID funding in the world in 2011, behind only Afghanistan and Haiti."[48] Another disappointing case was that of an Inter-American Development Bank–pledged program that was found to have rebuilt earthquake-damaged schools without any seismic protection.[49]

The US government constantly talked about being the world's most generous nation, but its largesse was often intimately tied to military support. Nearly half of the $1 billion in humanitarian aid it provided to Haiti was handled by the Department of Defense. In addition, this money was often directed to contractors that had committed human rights abuses or fraud in Iraq, Afghanistan, and domestically.[50] Although USAID head Rajiv Shah, appointed by Barack Obama, claimed that he was "no longer satisfied with writing big checks to big contractors and calling it development," there was little evidence of change. He left the organization in 2015. Obama signed into law in 2014 the Assessing Progress in Haiti Act, stipulating regular progress reports to Congress, but concrete progress was hard to detect.

One company, Agility Logistics, received more than $16 million in contracts despite being under indictment at the time for overcharging the US army by over $1 billion. Another firm, MWH Americas, which was found to have overcharged the city of New Orleans after it was devastated by Hurricane Katrina, secured a lucrative engineering contract through USAID to investigate the feasibility of port infrastructure in northern Haiti. The US Department of Homeland Security awarded GEO Group a no-bid contract for "guard services" in 2010, despite the company having been found guilty of countless breaches of care in its treatment of prisoners in the United States. The company was one of the biggest campaign contributors in the 2002 and 2004 election cycles, and had given more than $4.5 million to candidates between 1999 and 2014.[51]

The ability of suspect companies to achieve such outcomes was directly related to the huge amount of government lobbying that they performed—for MWH Americas, that meant $1.2 million worth of lobbying in 2010 alone.[52] There was no transparency when it came to such activity. Even US company DynCorp, condemned for its work in Afghanistan and Iraq, was able to secure a $48.6 million contract from the US government in 2013 for providing troops to support the UN Haiti mission.

Another fundamental concern for many Haitians I met was the unwillingness of foreign players to empower local people economically, which would prevent the profits being made from continually flowing out of the country. The US-based Center for Economic and Policy Research (CEPR) found in 2011 that only 0.02 percent of contracts from USAID have gone directly to Haitian companies, while the largest contracts have gone to for-profit development contractors in the form of "high-risk" indefinite quantity contracts. The overwhelming majority of contracts are for companies in the Washington DC area. The percentage that has gone to local firms in Haiti is even lower than USAID's worldwide average, which over the past three years has been 0.63 percent.[53]

Another report released by CEPR, in April 2013, claimed that details of the vast majority of US aid to Haiti were unavailable to the public and resided in a "black box," despite USAID having launched a program called USAID Forward to reform its programs. The report recommended including Haitians in "project design and implementation," increasing contract monitoring, and translating all relevant information into Haitian Creole and distributing it throughout Haiti.[54] Perhaps Haiti should follow the lead of Bolivia, who threw out USAID in May 2013, claiming the organization was conspiring against the country. President Evo Morales said that Washington "still has a mentality of domination, of subjugation."

Hillary Clinton, during her 2009 confirmation hearings for the position of secretary of state, admitted that USAID had "turned into more of a contracting agency than an operational agency with the ability to deliver." It seemed that everyone recognized the problem, but no one seemed willing or able to address the situation. In the meantime, Haiti, whose people craved independence, suffered the burden of innumerable USAID officers whose job it was to manage contractor agreements.[55] Worse still, the companies that had achieved the least continued to win contracts. Somehow, by lobbying the right people in power, they became controversy-proof, immune to the consequences of poor performance.

The only way this situation could improve was if international monies were used to foster local civil institutions and indigenous organizations. If this did not happen, it would be clear that the aid agendas of Washington and its allies were more about enriching donors and friends at home than meeting the needs of developing nations. The simple fact was that too much of the money disbursed to Haiti after the 2010 earthquake to perform essential work had either disappeared or remained unspent, mainly due to corruption and mismanagement.[56] And this went to the heart of the desires of disaster capitalists, whose rhetoric rarely matched reality and whose pledges of financial support were principally about lining the deep pockets of multinationals. Too often, journalists provided media cover for the scam, publishing company press releases as news. Despite decades of American "help," the *Washington Post* editorialized in 2014 that Haiti needed more of it to avoid "predictable calamity."[57] No comment was made on the disastrous outcomes of previous Washington-led interventions.

All of this made Haitians feel invisible. It was a view offered by Yanick Etienne, an organizer with the Haitian group Batay Ouvriye (roughly translated as "workers' fight"), which had been established to protect the locals employed at the country's industrial parks. I interviewed her at her home near the center of Port-au-Prince, where Etienne talked about the curse of foreign aid. She said that tens of billions of dollars had entered Haiti in the last three decades, but estimated that only a few percent had directly assisted residents. She believed that Western private companies and NGOs such as the Clinton Foundation, the UN, and the Haitian government itself had practically colluded to keep the country addicted to privatization and aid. They had done this by continually outsourcing jobs and services to the same inept corporations, and spending too much of their resources on salaries, accommodation, and transport for foreign aid workers. Little time, energy, or money was devoted to developing civil infrastructure and improving the lot of the average Haitian.

"We don't plan here," she said, exasperated. She did not want aid companies to leave tomorrow, but she saw the destructive side of decades of the "same failed policies" being continually implemented. In Haiti, this had resulted in an unofficial unemployment rate of 39 percent, though it was likely far higher. Even where job opportunities had been created, such as in the industrial parks developed outside Port-au-Prince and in the north of the country, poor living conditions—cramped accommodation, a scarcity of fresh water—was the norm.

Etienne was worried that one of the main aims of developments such as the industrial parks was to move people out of overcrowded Port-au-Prince, banishing them to areas with little infrastructure. She also suggested that Washington was keen to point to "progress" in Haiti, after many years of backing dictatorships, and so with the help of multinationals it pushed the Haitian authorities to build showcase factories—using cheap labor, of course.

"We are an occupied nation," Etienne said, referring to the ubiquitous UN, aid organizations, and NGO staff. She was particularly opposed to the presence of UN personnel, whom she collectively deemed a "foreign military force," because they were here, she said, "to make sure the economic and political models are implemented. We receive democracy second-hand. We are not independent [enough] to make decisions. The Haitian government and the International Monetary Fund are complementary, even though they've been implementing these policies for over thirty years without positive [results]. We've still got shantytowns, and poverty is rampant. The so-called investment they're promoting just doesn't work. We need to rally all the forces to oppose this, from the masses of people, and say that another Haiti is possible." Thankfully, after the 2010 earthquake, when the IMF wanted to force new loans on the country, public pressure forced the organization to drop Haiti's existing debt to the group. It was worth $268 million.

Etienne began to talk admiringly of the Arab Spring, of citizens rising up against tyranny. I wondered what she thought about the situation in the Arab world today—engulfed in extremism and authoritarianism, with the notable exception of Tunisia.

I wanted to see the industrial park at Caracol. It was a long journey. I left Port-au-Prince at 6 a.m. with a driver, a man in his thirties who kept a pair of headphones clamped on his ears, and a fixer and translator, Yvon, to help smooth the trip.

It was still dark as we drove through the city. We passed make-shift homes made from mud, sticks, and whatever usable rubbish could be found, desperate constructions that offered little protection against rain, heat, or humidity, let alone another earthquake. This ugly city looked unloved, beaten, and dirty, the air filled with dust. As another day began, shopkeepers—men and women of various ages—sat or stood beside their small wooden stalls. People sold whatever they could, wherever they could. When we stopped at one of the few traffic lights or came to a standstill in the almost constant traffic jam, women appeared with their arms outstretched, offering fruit, vegetables, soft drinks, and little sealed bags of water.

As we reached the outskirts of Port-au-Prince, the sun rose and the landscape changed. The rubbish, filth, and squalor transformed into a vista of lush land and perfectly blue sky. Strikingly green rice fields lay alongside the road. Workers in the distance tended their crops. It was beautiful and calm, but we had little opportunity to enjoy it. The man behind the wheel of our battered old Suzuki four-wheel-drive liked to speed, and he drove erratically. We asked him several times to slow down, but he ignored us, flying over the many speed bumps. Our suspension seemed to be gone, my seatbelt did not work, and the air-conditioning was non-existent. As we approached a market with a bustling crowd, our driver was going too fast to avoid hitting another car. The impact, though minor, was still a shock. As our driver looked back over his shoulder to assess the damage he had caused, he unwittingly steered our vehicle towards another accident. We hit a large bag of charcoal hanging off a truck, sending dozens of pieces in through our windows. Again, the impact was not serious, but it disorientated me—I initially thought we had hit another car, or perhaps a person.

We continued along hot, cracked roads that led over a stunning mountain range filled with rolling hills and coconut palms. We passed many small villages, some with decrepit shacks half-submerged in water. We eventually reached the outskirts of Cap-Haitien, the country's second-largest city, where we saw more shops and dusty tracks. Less than an hour later we reached Caracol. Mountains sat in the distance, and scrub and dirt covered the ground. Signs dotted the roadside displaying images of the shiny new industrial park and praising the facility. We occasionally stopped to ask people for directions to the park, and found that everyone knew exactly where it was. We were told by some of its supporters that it would become one of the country's largest employers.

Ten minutes out from the park, we saw row upon row of houses being built for the facility's workers in various stages of construction. The landscape offered a striking vista, strangely enhanced by the sun shining down on the wooden homes. But while the dwellings probably offered better conditions than many of the workers had experienced before, they were still small, and had little room separating them. A peer review by US architect Greg Higgins found the housing project "extremely dense and monotonous," accusing it of "violating numerous principles inherent to sound urban design"—not least being potentially unsafe during a storm or earthquake. [58] This was hardly a model environment for future prosperity. Critics claimed it would simply be a different kind of slum.

When we started filming the houses, two men sped over and asked what we were doing. We explained we were journalists, which I proved by showing my pass, but they told us we had to leave, that "as journalists you should know that you can't just go anywhere without permission." We asked the men who had been contracted by USAID to oversee the construction whether there was anyone else we could ask about gaining access, but they said it was impossible.

As we left, we passed a housing development that had stalled due to the failure of a Minnesota-based company to produce affordable residences.[59] "Lots of money, few results," commented a local deputy mayor, Pierre Justinvil. "Look, I personally, with my own hands, have just built a whole school for less than the cost of one of those houses, and more quickly. I think we Haitians need to take the wheel."[60] By 2015, Haitians had moved into these properties only to discover they were falling apart. The situation was so grim that the US government was suing the contractor. Even USAID auditors reported in 2014 that the properties "had noticeable problems."[61]

We drove on towards our destination. Suddenly we were on a sealed road, newly laid and smooth—an indication that we were heading in the right direction. We finally reached the entrance to the industrial park, where Haitians were milling around. Nearby were some air-conditioned shipping containers where the facility's executives worked. We met Alix Innocent, a representative of the South Korean company Sae-A, which was running the park.

Innocent was a local man who told us that he would not speak about the politics of the park's construction, only about the efforts being made to address various concerns at the site. "There are social and environmental issues, but we're dealing with this," he told us. "The farmers pushed off their lands are [going to be] paid compensation. I really enjoy working with them, and we aim to replace their livelihood. The Inter-American Development Bank is currently working out a master plan to manage the environmental issues." I asked why this was only happening now, when the site was nearing completion, long after allegations of water pollution and ecosystem damage first arose, but he gave little in the way of a response. Instead, Innocent passed me manila folders full of pamphlets in French explaining the benefits of the park. They included a large map detailing the dozens of factories that would be used by foreign investors such as Gap, Walmart, and Target to produce garments for Western consumers. In 2012, when she visited the site, then US secretary of state Hillary Clinton claimed the project would create 130,000 jobs.

When I visited Haiti in 2014, Caracol's managers, Sonapi, gave me internal documents that outlined the supposed progress of the industrial park, but all they did was confirm the inertia of the project. Sae-A was still the largest employer, with 2,300 workers, and a handful of other corporations were present or considering coming. Around 5,000 workers secured employment. These were paltry numbers, after all the hype.

Ignored within the mountains of self-promotion was the fact that around 300 farmers, who grew produce such as beans, had had their land acquired without consultation. They were simply told to move and were not given any assistance to relocate.[62] Insult was added to injury when the US consulting firm contracted to find a site for the industrial park stated in 2010 that the chosen area had "large stretches of relatively empty land." Even the mayor of Caracol, Landry Colas, was bemused: "I would have chosen another site, given that this one was already occupied by people earning a living. But I'm no expert."[63] One farmer, Jean-Louis Saint Thomas, told the *New York Times* that he had been devastated when the Haitian government started evicting other landowners. "We watched, voiceless. The government paid us to shut us up," he said.[64] Many of the farmers were still waiting for the promised alternative plots of land.

Innocent accompanied us on a tour of the site. We saw massive white warehouses expected to house the thousands of workers. Sae-A claimed that 65,000 people was their goal on the 246-hectare site. Only one of the factories was operating—the rest were still being built; and as we slowly drove past it, we saw large whirring fans on the exterior and hundreds of workers busy inside. We asked to go in, but Innocent said we couldn't without permission from the owner. He took us instead to a nearby, still-empty warehouse, where the only activity was that of trucks rumbling by outside. A guard loitered at the entrance, carrying a shotgun. The empty space inside was surreal because of its size and silence.

We said goodbye to Innocent, but before we left we again tried to get inside the operating factory. Advertising-themed signs decorated the building, such as "Sae-A Loves Kids" and "Sae-A Loves Haiti." It was late afternoon, and hundreds of Haitian workers started to emerge, mostly men in brightly colored clothing. As they streamed towards the park's exit, they checked their mobile phones and talked to each other. We approached the open door, from where the textile machines and their clean surrounds were clearly visible, then walked inside. But a friendly Haitian security guard asked us to leave, saying he would get into trouble if we stayed without permission. It struck me that this nondescript, well-maintained facility would probably not look out of place anywhere in the world, and I wondered if this was the face of the modern sweatshop.[65]

I spoke to some of the female workers as they were leaving. The women, mostly in their twenties and thirties and uniformly thin, earned a paltry $4 per day—$5 was Haiti's official minimum daily wage. Of this money, half went to transport and food, leaving $2 in each worker's pocket. My translator was outraged that his fellow locals were working for such a pittance. He told the women that they should be angry, that they didn't have to work for these low wages. The women just looked at him with a mixture of exhaustion and frustration. Unions were weak in Haiti, and work was desperately needed—a combination that allowed the multinationals to do what they wanted. Workers Rights Consortium released a report in 2013 that found workers at Caracol were being paid 34 percent less than the minimum wage specified by federal law.[66] Although Haiti officially raised its minimum wage to $5.23 per day in 2014, workers at factories producing clothing for Gap and Walmart still found their wages being stolen by unscrupulous employers.

The women piled into a number of tap taps—the small pick-up trucks that served as shared taxis in Haiti. Some travelled to Cap-Haitien, where some housing was provided by Sae-A. Others stayed in makeshift accommodation near the factory. Most had family in areas far away from Caracol and rarely had the chance to visit them.

The industrial park at Caracol was part of an alarming trend in which multinationals targeted cheap labor in countries that had little political will or muscle to protect their workers and regulate development projects. And the trend was growing, thanks to the enthusiasm of businesses like Sae-A. "Investors still do not believe or understand the value and potential of Haiti as we do," said chairman Kim Woong-ki in 2011.[67] Some of the company's executives considered themselves "frontiersmen."[68] Their excitement had been heightened by the fact that, through a public-private partnership, US taxpayers had invested over $100 million in the project. Of course, the backers of the park were not interested in helping poor Haitians get on their feet, although they cited job creation while promoting their company as a good corporate citizen. Rather, their obvious priority was to extract the maximum benefit from the Haiti Economic Lift Program, which allowed textiles to enter the United States tariff-free, as well as the US–Korea Free Trade Agreement.[69]

US scholar Alex Dupuy notes that the Caracol project "has absolutely nothing to do with creating a sustainable growth economy in Haiti," one perhaps based on key farming crops such as coffee, corn, beans, sugar, and rice. "It's about tapping a source of cheap labor. They [corporations] did the same thing in Port-au-Prince, which had people leaving the countryside because of the free trade policies that have devastated the Haitian agriculture sector. So the fear ... that the region will be flooded [by multinationals] is very real."[70]

Economic exploitation had been thrust on Haiti. I obtained

documents from both the World Bank and USAID, published in 2011, detailing "strong investor interest" in the country.[71] One report predicted the creation of 380,000 jobs by 2030, principally through "integrated economic zones," or industrial parks. Two USAID "action memorandums" from April 2011 showed plans to construct a power plant near Caracol in the north of Haiti, to support a US-backed industrial park. In 2014 USAID promoted the success of the plant but conveniently ignored the failure of the park to provide job security or decent wages.

In fact, Washington's role in facilitating Caracol's industrial park was reminiscent of the era of the Duvalier dictatorship, when the US government viewed Haiti as "the Taiwan of the Caribbean." It was a time when massive slums were created to house the workers in Port-au-Prince. History now seemed to be repeating itself. Sae-A had a record of appalling labor practices in Guatemala and Nicaragua, which included crushing unions and threatening employees. But Washington only cared about so-called "progress" in Haiti, whatever the human costs.[72]

These facilities had media backers. The *Wall Street Journal* columnist Mary Anastasia O'Grady, a long-time fan of right-wing South American dictatorships, wrote in 2015 about visiting Caracol. She urged that private companies such as Sae-A be given more latitude to make money in Haiti, with no checks on their labor practices, apparently guaranteeing more jobs for "eager" Haitians.[73]

Powerful Haitians added their support to new developments. I interviewed George Sassine, the founder and manager of the Caracol initiative, who was involved in other projects across the country. Sassine was in his mid-sixties and worked out of a surprisingly dingy, sunlight-starved office in central Port-au-Prince. His desk was buried under piles of manila folders, and next to it was a small table where a PC sat. His assistant hovered around him for the entire interview.

Sassine was a smooth talker. He told me that he and other local businessmen had pushed the idea of Haitian industrial parks and other economic initiatives for years, lobbying various members of the US Congress. In 2006, this resulted in the Hope Act, a set of special trade rules that enabled the tariff-free sale of Haitian textiles in the United States, in exchange for the preferential treatment of American imports. But it was only after the 2010 earthquake that the Obama administration helped him to get the industrial park project off the ground. Naturally, he was quick to seize the business opportunity that the natural disaster presented.

Sassine argued that previous Haitian governments had failed to prepare the country adequately for a sustainable future. He spoke about the restoration of national sovereignty, refuting the suggestion that the United States controlled Haiti and arguing that USAID supported positive programs. As for the Caracol industrial park, Sassine said that there were few environmental issues with it. He also said that Sae-A was vetted and told that it had to abide by certain laws regarding workers' rights and the compensation to be paid to farmers. When I raised the matter of landowners being stripped of their property, he responded loudly with, "Nobody rejected it [the industrial park]!"

"When you have an industrial park, it's like a shopping center," Sassine went on to explain. "You need to have big players. Sae-A is one of the largest garment manufacturers in the world and is vertically integrated, from designing to making their own fabric, so this is the perfect fit for us. I visited South Korea at least eight times over two years. We had a lot of support from the US administration, and if I may drop the name of Ms. [Hillary] Clinton, she convinced former president Bill Clinton, and when he talks people can't say no to him." Both Hillary and Bill, using their long-term connections to Haiti and corporate interests, helped persuade key stakeholders to develop the park.

Sassine predictably argued that less regulation would allow the country to develop. "It means understanding that the investor is a customer," he said, "and the customer is always right ... The foreigner or local is investing and risking his money, and you have to listen to him." True to form, in 2009, when Sassine was the head of an organization of Haitian industrialists, he complained about the Haitian government doubling the minimum wage to $5 per day, claiming it would cost jobs.

Sassine acknowledged that industrial parks were not the only way to get Haiti moving again. He talked about supporting local agricultural projects, adding that the Clinton Foundation regularly backed such ideas. But his main goal, he said, was the mass production of cheap goods for export. Such rhetoric led to his departure from the position in 2013, due to the government being unhappy with his progress and unionists being upset that some of his textile bosses were firing workers for organizing protests.

The theme of unregulated capitalism was repeated at a conference I attended in Port-au-Prince in 2014. "Restore Haiti" was an event mounted by the Christian organization Partners Worldwide, held at one of the city's finest hotels, in the elite suburb of Petionville. It attracted local and foreign business leaders to discuss new opportunities for the economy. Delegates heard how to make money in the Caribbean nation. George Andy Rene, managing director of the government body Investment Facilitation Center, repeated the mantra that had been popular with the government since it had taken office in 2011: "Haiti is open for business." "We need to counter the negative image of Haiti in the global media," he said. Another speaker was delighted to announce that forty more industrial parks were on the cards to "exploit Haitian labor."

However, Texan Christian entrepreneur Fred Eppright, of Bridge Capital, issued a blunt warning: the international image of Haiti remained in desperate need of improvement. By all means support Haiti, he said, but be aware of the risks. He later told me that Haiti needed "saving," and that capitalism was the only way to achieve a brighter future.

*   *   *

The National Palace in the center of Port-au-Prince was a symbol of political freedom to Haitians. Although its latest incarnation was completed by American architects in 1920, during the US occupation of Haiti, it became the place where countless citizens rallied to publicly voice their views. But it collapsed during the 2010 earthquake—video footage of the event showed terrified workers running for their lives as massive pieces of concrete crashed to the ground. Since then, the ruined building had come to represent the lack of sovereignty experienced by many Haitians.

A European filmmaker whom I met in Port-au-Prince, Alice Smeets, told me that an NGO founded by actor Sean Penn, the J/P Haitian Relief Organization, had been charged with demolishing what was left of the palace and removing its rubble. She explained that the fact that Penn's organization was doing the work, rather than a local company, had deeply upset many Haitians. They saw it as yet another sign of loss of control over their own affairs. The federal government, meanwhile, was simply happy to outsource yet another job.

A Haitian friend of Alice's who lived in a poor area of Port-au-Prince wrote to Penn to complain about his organization's involvement in clearing away the palace. Penn responded angrily, writing to tell the man that he did not understand his own country, and that Penn's organization was actually partnering with locals to do important work. This was true, but it did not address the problem of having a foreign company demolish a place about which there was great indigenous sensitivity.

I was in Haiti when the work by Penn's group began. After constantly hassling President Martelly's communications director, Enrique Mari Chaparro, for access to the site, I was allowed in a few hours before flying out of the country. I waited outside the ruins for Chaparro, and he finally appeared, dressed in a suit and tie, his beard carefully manicured. He had worked as a journalist in Spain and France before advising Martelly during the 2010–11 election campaign, and he was now a close aide of the Haitian president.

As workers gathered near some cranes, I noticed Haiti's first lady, Sophia Martelly, standing nearby, and she called Chaparro over for a brief chat. (Later, after looking around the palace, I caught a brief glimpse of the leader himself as he stepped into a dark-windowed SUV, which moved off down the road followed by countless armed men in cars and on motorcycles.)

When I was finally able to ask Chaparro about the palace demolition work, he said, "Sean Penn is an official ambassador to Haiti. He's had experience in clearing rubble and [in] demolitions, so it makes sense." I asked if it mattered that a local group was not involved. "Locals are working on this," he responded, pointing at the site. He was right, but only in the sense that Haitians were doing the hard labor while a number of American and French businessmen ran the show.

The palace was still an imposing building, despite being in a terrible state. Within a few days it was cleared, and the site remained empty until a replacement was eventually built.[74] The structure's famous dome tilted precariously to one side, seemingly about to fall to the ground.

Chaparro said that he was keen to foster international media interest in the country, in that Haiti would be portrayed in a different light. "It's not just disasters and cholera," he told me. "Haiti is now progressing and moving in the right direction. I understand as a journalist that bad stories sell, but there are many good stories here now." I guessed he thought that the demolition of the palace was one such positive story, because it indicated progress and renewal.

But I disagreed. The controversy involving Penn's NGO reflected a deep structural problem in Haiti—something I also saw in Papua New Guinea and Afghanistan. The NGO sector, including the nonprofit groups, often acted as a conduit that ensured business for Western firms. In March 2010, the self-labeled "politically neutral, non-profit" US company CHF International (now called Global Communities) said that "by contributing to Haiti's reconstruction in a lasting, meaningful way, companies will be helping to build a new, more vibrant Caribbean market for their own goods and services." Decoded, this meant assisting US businesses to exploit cheap labor, with US taxpayer dollars supporting the projects. After the 2010 earthquake, CHF ran "cash for work" initiatives that were condemned by human rights groups as being akin to the payment of slave wages.[75] NGOs were not always the benevolent groups we had been led to believe they were.

The NGO-ization of humanitarian relief had been explained as an efficient means of assisting in post-conflict and natural disaster environments. Certainly, smaller organizations could sometimes provide lifesaving aid due to their being nimble and unconstrained by bureaucracy. But the idea that a centralized UN aid service, namely the Office for the Coordination of Humanitarian Affairs, could utilize any number of NGOs to deliver urgently needed help was not borne out by the facts. "In Haiti," wrote the international head of MSF, Unni Karunakara, "the system is legitimising NGOs that claim responsibility for health, sanitation or other areas in a specific zone, but then do not have the capacity or know-how to carry out the necessary work. As a result, people's needs go unmet."[76]

The aid game was often designed to enrich the profiteer. Dr. Paul Farmer, founder of Partners in Health, explained that in Haiti the system was set up to benefit the contractor. "For things to go right, the rules of the road have to be re-written," he said.[77] Farmer's organization founded a well-stocked university hospital in Mirebalais, sixty kilometers from Port-au-Prince, a public facility built by Haitian labor and advised by American volunteers.

In January 2013, a former Associated Press correspondent in Haiti, Jonathan Katz—a rare journalist who realized that his job was holding NGOs to account for their grandiose claims and plans—told *Democracy Now!* that a key problem for the country, and for many other developing nations, was that local institutions were never properly developed, because "donor countries avoid local governments [and] fund through their own agencies, their own NGOs, their own militaries, and that weakens institutions."[78] So when another disaster hit, the state was barely there. Executive secretary of the Platform of Haitian Human Rights Organizations, Antonal Mortime, also condemned the lack of foreign NGO engagement with local partners. "We paid a historical price for being the first black republic in the hemisphere," he told the *Nation*. "I think all these problems are linked to imperialism."[79]

Another negative side-effect of the mass influx of NGOs in Haiti had been the dramatic rise in housing costs across the country, which were affordable for foreigners on high salaries but pushed locals out of the market. This was a common feature of disaster economies, and it was unsustainable because countless individuals and groups only stayed for six, twelve, or eighteen months before moving on to the next global crisis.[80]

In 2014 I visited a new government housing project called Village Lumane Casimir, an experiment in temporary housing for citizens affected by the earthquake. Situated near the massive new post-earthquake shantytown of Canaan on Highway 1, near Port-au-Prince, the colorful though tiny homes represented a small move by the Martelly administration to support struggling families. But residents complained of cracks in the houses. Families were moving in at a painfully slow rate. A planned market and factory had not been delivered. Dominican contractor HADOM Construction had failed to complete even 50 percent of the houses. The public was frustrated, and thousands of protestors vented their frustration with the stalled political process and lack of elections in 2014 (which had been due in 2011) by organizing continual marches through the streets, many of which turned violent. Presidential elections were scheduled for October 2015, with President Martelly constitutionally barred from re-running. His administration was mired in scandal, with many of his closest advisors accused of drug running, kidnapping, and murder.

Talking about assistance was not enough. There was the monstrous example provided by the charity Yele Haiti, founded by the Haitian-born US hip-hop star Wyclef Jean in 2005, but shut down in 2012. The artist wrote in his autobiography in that year that the organization was "Haiti's greatest asset and ally" in helping the country to get back on its feet.[81] The truth, however—uncovered by the *New York Times*—was a litany of corruption and mismanagement, with Haitians missing out on any tangible support after the earthquake.[82] A New York attorney-general's investigation found that millions of dollars in donations had gone to Jean and his friends. A hospitality firm sued the organization in 2013 for $100,000 in unpaid fees. If ever there had been a need for NGOs to be regulated just like banks and mortgage brokers, this was the time.[83]

In the countries I visited for this book, the use of distantly run, globally connected NGOs as a substitute for government planning had eroded the possibility of delivering truly beneficial services and assistance to the people who needed them. By contrast, NGOs that were locally accountable, internationally connected, and financially independent had made a difference and contributed to the greater sovereignty of those nations.[84] A unique model in Haiti was the growth of the renewable and clean energy sector, in which local NGOs partnered with government departments to reduce deforestation.[85]

At least 350,000 Haitians remained in refugee camps more than three years after the 2010 earthquake, though many had been moved elsewhere by 2014. One of the largest camps, which housed around 40,000 people living cheek-by-jowl, was in Port-au-Prince's Parc Jean Marie Vincent, on the site of what was supposed to be a sporting arena. It was called Sou Piste, which means "on the tarmac." I arrived there to see armed UN troops wandering around, though I was later told that their presence rarely kept camp dwellers safe from local gangs and petty criminals. Their mandate—to provide stability—was incredibly vague, and their willingness to help individuals actively appeared to be low.

Entering the camp, I saw a handful of kids in various states of undress running around, tailed by mangy dogs, with bare and dirty feet and soiled faces. For many, their first memories will be of living in a refugee camp in the city of their birth. US and Israeli flags had been painted on a small structure near the entrance, though no one knew why, and a Digicel flag fluttered on a nearby pole. The smell of shit hit me. I walked towards a small amphitheater and found that it was covered in animal and human waste—the refugees came here to relieve themselves. Tents, mostly provided by USAID, dotted the landscape. Many refugees I talked to said this had been the extent of the agency's assistance. "We've never seen anybody from USAID in this camp," one man said. In one area, women stood around holding babies while men sitting at a makeshift table played dominoes. When a game ended, a strange ritual took place whereby the loser took a water bottle filled with small rocks and clipped it to his cheek.

Such was daily life in a Haitian "internally displaced person" camp. This life could quickly change, however, as the risk of forced eviction was ever present. The Haitian government routinely pushed thousands of people out of such camps and onto the streets, with no compensation or assistance.[86] Either way, women faced the possibility of rape, a crime that was endemic inside and outside the camps. There were no accurate figures, but one study performed in 2012 found that 14 percent of Haitian households claimed that at least one female resident had been sexually assaulted since the earthquake, though the actual figure was almost certainly much higher.[87] Officials rarely investigated such crimes, routinely blaming the female victims for what had happened.[88]

The NGO KOFAVIV was a leading female-run organization aiming to tackle sexual assault. The founders, Eramithe and Malya, had lost their homes in the 2010 earthquake and lived for a time in a tent city. They had countless men and women working in the camps to raise awareness of a rape hotline, counseling, and women's empowerment. Tragically, they had been forced to move to the United States due to threats against them. Support from international donors was waning, with many looking for newer disasters to assist. The lack of long-term funding and infrastructure was a constant complaint among a range of local charities and organizations. "The world remembers us only when we are desperate, then moves on," was a refrain I heard a number of times.

Malya told me when I met her in 2014 in Port-au-Prince that there was still a social silence around sexual assault in Haiti, but "the last years have seen authorities, including the police, starting to take the crimes more seriously." One day I walked around the Kid refugee camp in the Christ Roi area of Port-au-Prince with KOFAVIV's Georjhy. Thousands of citizens had been forgotten in this squalid area, where they had remained for more than four years. KOFAVIV's male and female agents walked across the dirty, dusty ground to distribute pamphlets and information to young women, telling them that they had rights, pointing out that they had someone to call if they ran into trouble over sexual violence, promising a sympathetic ear.

Many slums faced similar problems. I spoke to three men at Sou Piste who said they had been at the camp since the earthquake. They were frustrated, saying they had received little support from anyone except the Red Cross, which had recently provided some essentials.[89] As for the Haitian government, despite constantly having made promises to take action soon, it was invisible. The men were understandably opposed to more foreign aid and development money for Haiti because, they said, they never saw it.[90]

One of the men, Wilbert, was thirty-three years old and lived in the camp with his family. His young daughter, dressed in an orange dress and sporting dreadlocks, stood nearby, staring at us. He told me that he was unemployed and had yet to receive anything from his state or president. "Nobody is helping us," he said. "We have heard about organizations helping people, but we've never seen anybody here. Life conditions are very difficult. We're sleeping on the floor. It's a mess. We have to blame the president's office."

Wilbert said that it was not safe to stay in the camp. "The president will not look at me," he added forlornly. "If anybody here says they've had help, it's a lie. We have nothing to do, so we play dominoes all day. You see many kids around you. They are supposed to go to school. We don't have the money to pay for the school fees."

All of the men were opposed to the industrial parks. One said people often had to have sex with a factory boss to secure a job. I also heard that pride stopped many people from taking a job because the wages were so low. This did not strike me as laziness, but rather as people demanding that their government finally take responsibility for them.

Another man invited me into the tent where he lived with his wife and five children. Some members of the family slept in bunk beds while the rest lay down on the rock-and-gravel floor. The man was a stonemason and traveled far every day for work. He was angry. He did not understand why no one had helped move his family to somewhere more secure and permanent. When it rained, everything flooded. He said there was violence over money, food, and other meager resources. I was aware that he was saying what he thought I wanted to hear, but there was no hiding his grim situation.

These camps were a severe indictment of the NGOs and the government in Haiti. Every person I spoke to in Sou Piste seemed politically savvy, yet they did not have any kind words for the UN or other NGOs. Some people said that they wanted the NGOs to leave Haiti because they did not know what they were doing here, apart from awarding contracts to enable various companies to turn a profit.

An aid insider who worked in Haiti but also spoke critically of the aid process was rare, but American anthropologist Timothy

Schwartz was such a man. The intense fifty-year-old loved to talk, which he did profusely during our first meeting, at the busy Muncheez restaurant in the center of Port-au-Prince. Schwartz moved to Haiti in 1994 and divided his time between it, the neighboring Dominican Republic, and the Democratic Republic of Congo. He had written various reports for USAID and had alternately been loved and hated by them. After investigating the death toll from the 2010 earthquake, for example, he claimed it was actually far less than alleged. The official number of dead was estimated at more than 300,000, but he said it was really between 50,000 and 80,000. He contended that the figure had been grossly inflated to gain more international support—a claim that did not go down too well in some circles.

Schwartz explained how the exaggeration of such figures allowed NGOs and corporations to get more funds to solve problems that were not as bad as they claimed. He gave a second example: reports alleging that child slavery was a huge problem in Haiti, which, he said, was "simply untrue … the people doing the reports, claiming 400,000 child slaves in Haiti, know it's untrue." Schwartz said this was done to attract Western donor money, which was then siphoned off to pay for excessive salaries and other perks. This lack of NGO accountability affected every country I had visited during my investigation of disaster capitalism.

I arranged to continue my conversation with Schwartz in his Spanish-style house in Thomassin, an area in the mountains above Port-au-Prince. The drive to his place was along rocky roads with spectacular vistas. It was not hard to see why he stayed here.

After he greeted me, Schwartz picked up where he had left off in the restaurant. "The earthquake was a perfect opportunity for [the Preval government] to do the good things that they [were] talking about, such as decentralization and pump[ing] up peasant agriculture," he told me. "There was no better moment for them to step up and buy all the peasant surplus and bring it into Port-au-Prince, because people needed food. But the international community

flooded the country with food aid, not just for one month but for
the next years. The [UN] World Food Programme rerouted the
food to the maternal child health program.[91] It was a clear flouting
of the Haitian government and what they wanted. It was clear that
Preval wasn't running the country at that stage."

Haiti's sovereignty was again lost on the day the tremors hit, he
told me: "What do you do when you have a country being flooded
with all this goodwill and aid? Stand up and say 'No'? If you do,
you're against the poor, victims, and earthquake survivors. I met
the key World Food Programme senior staff here a year after the
earthquake, and I said that there was no need for all the food.
Everybody simply looked down. I honestly believe that all those
people are sincere. They didn't really understand and they were
getting their information from the press or people on the ground.
One thing that is happening in Haiti is [cries of] 'Give me more,'
from the peasant to the person in the city to the politician to the
NGOs. That's the industry. When it comes to writing the NGO
report, though, everybody does what they have to do—put a
nice spin on it and say it was a success. You can't give a donor's
report and say something was a horrible failure and we wasted this
much money."

I asked Schwartz again about his allegation that the number
of people who were said to have died during the earthquake had
been inflated, which he reconfirmed: "This was just one example
of many of [the] radical inflation[s] of figures in the interests of
more money for the NGOs. They [also] estimated initially there
was ... 10 or 20 million cubic meters of rubble, but the reality was
far lower ... around 3 million cubic meters. But the NGOs kept
on getting the money from donors to clean it up." And, what was
worse, they had been ineffectual in doing so. Vast swathes of Port-
au-Prince were still littered with debris, though less so when I
visited in 2014.

Schwartz said that many USAID people he knew were genuine
in their desire to make a difference here, but that the system was

rigged against them and their plans. Haiti was not an independent country, Schwartz explained, because its policies were decided and dictated by Washington. When asked by academic Justin Podur whether the "aid industry" was doing more harm than good in Haiti, Schwartz had responded that it was, but then said: "We can't cut off the aid because, however we got here, Haiti now depends on it."[92]

In a chapter written by Schwartz in 2013 for a still unfinished book, he wrote that Haiti had a grim history for decades of NGOs invading the country, akin to missionaries. In the 1980s, "NGOs were turned into full-fledged US government, humanitarian aid contractors."[93] Little had improved since.

Indigenous development in Haiti had been largely absent for decades. Attempts were now being made to revive it, but with mixed results.

When I returned to the Sou Piste camp in 2014 I found it completely empty. The masses had been moved by the government to shantytowns in areas near Port-au-Prince, their problems shifted from the center of town to more remote locations. Discarded plastic water bottles and rubbish lay on ground that used to heave with human bodies. The grass struggled to grow in a dust bowl. These citizens were not now living more comfortable lives; they had mostly been transported to slums with little opportunity, farther from the center of Port-au-Prince. One of the prettiest slums from a distance was Jalousie, regularly photographed by visitors due to its multicolored, painted exterior. "Urban botox," wrote journalist Amy Wilentz. In reality, it was a shantytown with few resources.

I visited the main office and factory of the Haitian manufacturer Indepco, situated on Highway 1, on the outskirts of Port-au-Prince. Its head and founder was Hans P. Garoute, an energetic man who had spent his formative years in New York working as a buyer and seller of women's underwear. In 1966, he was caught by the US Coast Guard, along with a number of Cubans, on a boat off the coast of Florida. The group had weapons and was on its way to Haiti to try to overthrow the Papa Doc dictatorship. The result was that Garoute spent twenty years in America on a UN passport that showed he was stateless. He told the story with humor.

Among other things, Indepco organized training for the workers at the Caracol industrial park. One of Garoute's colleagues, Jean Robert Lebrun, who was sitting in on our conversation, told me that he had just returned from Caracol, and that the training of the young men and women there had gone very well. "There are a few women who had never worked before who are now supervisors of over a hundred people. This makes me very happy," he said. He explained that Sae-A had never planned how it would source trained workers, so Indepco stepped in, though only on a three-month contract.

I asked Lebrun and Garoute about workers' rights—in particular, about how a foreign company like Sae-A should treat its employees here. They both agreed that the current conditions were good, and that a unionized workforce should come later, not now. This was expressed in a matter-of-fact way, without enmity. "We had a union leader in this office this morning talking to us about workers' rights," Garoute said proudly, "so don't think it's not a consideration." Neither man seemed worried about the below-minimum-standard pay at Caracol, although Garoute hinted that ideally he wanted workers to receive more money.

Garoute showed me around the Indepco factory, a steaming-hot warehouse with little fresh air blowing through it. Men and women were working on old sewing machines (the brand was "Finger" rather than "Singer") making shirts, dresses, and pants. Some employees were painstakingly stitching colorful heart-shaped vodou patterns. I talked to one young Haitian woman who had grown up in New York and Philadelphia, but whose parents now lived in Haiti, which was why she had returned as well. She wanted to break into the fashion industry and was producing ten different designs for an upcoming fashion show in Jamaica, where she hoped to receive some substantial orders. If she did, Indepco would then help her produce the garments for export. It was one small way in which the company was trying to foster the next generation of productive Haitians.

When I asked about sweatshops in Haiti, Garoute said that the Western idea of worker mistreatment could not be compared with life in his country. He became upset when visiting Westerners complained about such things as a young boy carrying a bucket of water, thinking this was akin to being a slave, when in fact the child was just helping his mother keep the home together.

Garoute was clearly an industrious man and appeared genuinely to care about helping Haiti to become more independent. But he seemed to have one foot in each of two camps: he wanted to encourage much more local production and international investment in the domestic agriculture and textile industries, while simultaneously praising foreign-owned industrial parks for assisting poor Haitians.

In the main office, there was a photo of Garoute meeting George W. Bush and his daughter Jenna here in 2010. He had few kind words for the former US president but was more positive towards the Obama administration. He had no love, however, for USAID. He explained how an Indepco training warehouse at the Sonapi industrial park in Port-au-Prince only operated for two years because USAID provided a manager who did not understand the needs of the project. Nearly $100 million was wasted—no one knew where the money had been spent. Garoute asked why a Haitian person could not have been appointed instead to manage the venture. They would have saved half the money, he claimed, and would have intimately understood the needs of Indepco.

At twilight one day I visited Fort Jacques, which is perched upon a mountain overlooking Port-au-Prince. It was built in 1804, after Haiti had declared its independence from France. The view was hazy but the air clean and unpolluted, unlike in the city center I had left behind. Pop and techno music boomed from some SUVs. Couples snacked and snuggled. A game of soccer began on a rough football field, overseen by an excitable MC whose voice emerged from a makeshift speaker system set up in the stands. It was a beautiful scene of untroubled community life. Seeing it reminded me how easy it was in a country such as Haiti to focus solely on the negatives and not appreciate the daily rhythms of ongoing life. This was not to romanticize poverty, but simply to understand that almost all cultures were connected through music, sport, and family time. I saw this during the hypnotic performance of local band Ram, described as "Vodou rock 'n' roots," playing to a crowd every week at the Gothic-style Oloffson Hotel. The place was infused with the spirit of past guests, like Mick Jagger, and was the inspiration for Graham Greene's classic 1966 book, *The Comedians*.

Another thing I appreciated about Haiti, which all too often was seen as dependent and weak, was its resistance to the economic order. It started with the brilliant graffiti artist Rosembert Moise, who painted across the country. During my 2014 visit, on a bare wall in the expensive suburb of Petionville, I witnessed the artist create a work late one night that depicted a failing economy forcing Haitians to rob each other for opportunities.

Reyneld Sanon was the head of Frakka, a grassroots group that advocated affordable housing. We talked in his office, which was set in a plain house in the suburb of Canape Vert. Sanon was a strong critic of the Martelly government and its pro-business policies, as well as the practices of Washington and USAID. He wanted an emphasis on local producers and farmers, rather than on foreign industries. Opening up Haiti to overseas markets, he said, had only resulted in the country being flooded with imported goods and Haitians being locked out of business opportunities.

Sanon railed against the countless NGOs and UN forces that had been in the country for years yet delivered very little. "The UN soldiers have never done anything to solve the housing issue," he said, "and international NGOs, years after the quake, are still providing weak shelters. It's ridiculous. Some local organizations, with only $11,000, are able to build a good house. In areas near Port-au-Prince, these groups have built over a hundred houses and given the keys to the owners. It shows that there's no will for foreign groups to really help us when they've spent millions of dollars and we don't see anything. The international private sector come here to make money. It's a big business for them."

A rare exception could be the indigenously built computer tablet, Surtab, whose factory I visited in Port-au-Prince to see decently paid workers on a small production line. The founder told me that he hoped to allow young Haitians cheap access to the device, as well as challenging the market dominance of Apple's iPad in America. It was an ambitious target, but I liked his chutzpah.

Haitian economist and activist Camille Chalmers told me that there had been no economic independence in Haiti for the last hundred years. He offered a story about former president Jean-Bertrand Aristide wanting capable Swiss instructors to train the Haitian police, but being told by the Americans that, because of some long-forgotten agreement dating from 1980, Washington had to be asked to approve such a plan. Needless to say, it was rejected.

Chalmers placed Haiti's dilemma in a global context. "We are unable to develop our own models of development and have to get international funding for the neoliberal agenda," he told me. "It's a way to show capitalism that we're willing to work with you, but you're actually destroying our own economy and agriculture."

Chalmers continued: "Haiti is one of the countries they call a 'failed state.' Since 1915, it's been about how Haiti will please the United States, but there are alternatives to industrial parks. If you invest in agriculture and farming, you'll have much better and more sustainable results. There is a finite number of people who can work in industrial parks, but millions of jobs are required. For example, we have over 168 species of mangoes in Haiti, but we don't have the industry that can work on it. That's what the future should be."

Tourism was the latest industry to be sold to Haitians as the answer to the state's poverty, but the early signs were worrying. The small island of Île-à-Vache, off Haiti's south coast, was being promoted, attracting the eye of Madonna and Sean Penn, but massive developers had already claimed huge tracts of public land, depriving thousands of residents of their livelihood. Islanders complained in 2014 that the government had excluded them, and public protests began. Not to worry, said Alex Zozaya, chief executive at Apple Leisure Group, a Caribbean tour operator and hotel investor based in Philadelphia. "Haiti has unbelievable potential," he said. "It's like the Seychelles without the jet lag."[94]

The challenge for Haiti was to reclaim its sovereignty, and it would be a long and painful task. Half of Haiti's 10 million people were under twenty-five, and yet their voices were often ignored in favor of an older elite.

It was hard to disagree with Peter Hallward, who argued that, in places like Haiti, "NGOs provide rich countries [with] a morally respectable way of subcontracting the sovereignty of the nations they exploit."[95] I had seen this NGO-ization of poor nations before, and it was rarely opposed other than by individuals and small groups battling tough odds. The fact that such nations remained economically occupied in some way emphasized how vital was the need for alternatives.

Haiti was an easy target for disaster capitalists, because its inhabitants were caught up in a daily struggle for survival. This was not made any easier by the predatory aid groups, foreign governments, and NGOs that had a one-model-fits-all mindset and refused to assess the effectiveness of their methods. The relationship between USAID and Washington's foreign policy was a case in point—one that prompted understandable skepticism in many Haitians.

When NGOs replaced the apparatus of the state, there inevitably arose the neocolonial mentality permeating far too many Western organizations allegedly working to alleviate suffering. A different model of investment must be possible.

4

Papua New Guinea: "Break our bones, but you can never break our spirit"

We are the "sacrificial lamb" for the few capitalists whose hunger for wealth is quenchless and unceasing … We are not going to sit by and watch capitalists and their Papua New Guinean political allies exploiting us … We have planted the seeds which will germinate soon not only in Bougainville but throughout Papua New Guinea.

Francis Ona, Bougainville resistance leader, 1989

It is like a scene out of *Mad Max*: a post-apocalyptic setting of polluted rivers, corroded equipment, and human scavengers. This was what I saw as I descended in 2012 into the massive old Panguna mine in Bougainville, Papua New Guinea (PNG). One of my companions was a one-time resistance fighter who, along with his fellow combatants, won a brutal battle against one of the world's biggest mining companies, Rio Tinto.

"The Crisis," as locals called it, was a vicious dispute that pitted Rio Tinto and the PNG and Australian governments against aggrieved Bougainvilleans whose lives were being violated by a polluting mine. Tensions had been building between the parties for two decades when, in 1988, negotiations broke down. The Bougainville Revolutionary Army (BRA) was formed, and the

Panguna mine soon closed. The resulting civil war lasted until 1997, devastating the province and bringing both pride and poverty to its inhabitants.

The Asia-Pacific region had never seen anything like it—a fight against a multinational led and won by indigenous people. But another conflict loomed. Moves were afoot to reopen the mine.

To visit what was the center of the conflict, I first traveled via the PNG capital Port Moresby to Arawa, the closest town to the Panguna mine, which was on Bougainville Island. The surrounding Autonomous Region of Bougainville joined with nineteen provinces scattered over various islands and the "mainland" of PNG to form a country with a population of over 7 million people who spoke at least 841 languages.

From the closure of Panguna up until a few years ago, it was nearly impossible for a white man to access the mine pit because of a legacy of mistrust. There was great sensitivity about who I was and why I wanted to visit. But after several days of negotiation with locals in Arawa, I was cleared to proceed. When I returned in 2013 the process was identical, with former fighters still wanting to vet my credentials.

I was picked up early one morning in a jeep driven by a man named John, a former local politician and miner, and Willy, a man in his sixties who was a key figure in the BRA and particularly its militant faction, Mekamui, a still-active defense force that had once fought the PNG army ("Mekamui" means "Sacred Island" and was also the traditional name of the immediate area). Willy was my designated guide for the day. He had a thick gray beard and wore a red cap, a faded purple polo shirt, and gray shorts; a fanny pack was slung across his chest. He was barefoot and had surprisingly white teeth given the widespread tradition of betel-nut chewing in PNG—the fruit of the betel palm was a mild stimulant. Willy died the year after I first visited Bougainville, another of the

older, fighting generation who could no longer impart his wisdom
on the province's future.

I saw abandoned, rusting buildings as we sped along the relatively smooth asphalt towards Morgan Junction; ferns had
wrapped themselves around the old power lines that had been
used when the mine was operational. Waiting for us was a man I
knew as Commander Alex from having scouted the checkpoint the
previous day. He lifted the boom gate to let our car through, and
I went and sat with him in a little booth to discuss the entry fee.
He asked for 300 kina, or about $120 (he had already prepared an
invoice and a receipt), but I said I had been told it would cost only
200 kina. He agreed, but first he wanted to know what I was doing
here, my profession, and how long I would be looking around.
He then proceeded to stamp my documents, took my money, and
smiled. "Welcome," he said. Two years later, in 2013, Alex was
still manning the checkpoint. He remembered me when I arrived,
and his passion for justice had not dimmed. His was the revolutionary spirit in action.

Alex was forty-eight, and it was clear the Crisis was not over for
him. He dreamed of a Bougainville free of mining, and subsisting
on agriculture. He worried that younger people would accept the
reopening of the Panguna mine to exploit its still sizeable reserves
of copper and gold. He said this was a real possibility because many
locals were desperate for economic independence, and mining was
seen as a quick and easy way of achieving it. Alex articulated the
struggle between the PNG government, the mining companies,
and Bougainvilleans over who would benefit from a reopened
Panguna mine. Many locals told me they craved sovereignty, but
how this should be achieved was unclear. Alex's hesitation was
born of experience, reflecting a cynicism towards past and present
corporate promises and distrust of the local government.

Alex was shy, but his attitude reflected that of a committed activist. He claimed he had to continue to man the community-run
checkpoint around the clock, living in makeshift conditions, until

compensation was fully paid to all those who deserved it. "The checkpoint was a symbol of what happened in Bougainville, the revolution," he said. "It's to let the world know that the cost of the revolution is about mining and independence."

Driving towards the mine, we soon saw the large buildings that had been used to process copper in the 1970s and 1980s. A massive swimming pool was without water and overflowing with ferns. Lush greenery surrounded the sealed road, but I knew that vast tracts of this land were blighted after Rio Tinto had dumped huge quantities of the dredged waste called spoil. If left untreated, spoil sat in the ground for thousands of years. The company had never cleaned it up.

In 2013 I still saw the results of this pollution, with locals calling for assistance. The United Nations Environment Programme announced that it would help clean up the asbestos, mine tailings, acid-rain damage, and heavy metals. The estimated cost was in the billions of dollars. No date had been set for the work.

Willy had mixed feelings about the prospect of the mine reopening. Like Alex, his ideal was that agriculture would sustain PNG. But he was also a realist. "People are being educated, and they need employment to sustain their living," Willy said. He also told me that Bougainville was experiencing a massive baby boom, and that this population explosion required urgent action. It was obvious where he thought the money would come from. "They say there's still a lot of gold here that could last for forty years of mining," he told me.

Willy hoped that whoever ran the mine would clean up the environmental damage it had caused, such as the pollution in the soil and rivers, and ensure that the mistakes of the past did not happen again. He was skeptical that this would occur, however, citing mines in other PNG provinces and internationally where ecological destruction had taken place. Willy made particular mention of the gold- and copper-producing Ok Tedi mine in PNG's Western Province, which since the 1980s had caused enormous environmental destruction and social upheaval affecting tens of thousands of nearby residents. Even PNG's attorney-general had admitted that the mines in his country had been allowed to use unsafe methods of waste disposal that had been banned in many other countries.[1]

Willy and other Bougainvilleans could not escape the paradox. They were desperate to establish an independent nation and knew that four decades of copper and gold profits could help fund the new state. But the clash between the desired independence, economic freedom, sustainability, and raised living standards, and a lack of PNG and foreign support, meant that the matter was not a simple one for locals.

The average age of Papua New Guineans was twenty-one, and 30 percent of the population was under thirty, making education and employment significant issues in the country. Regarding the former, adjusted for inflation, the current funding for every PNG student was one-fourteenth of the level in the late 1970s.[2] These issues were arguably especially important in Bougainville, whose so-called "lost generation," the young people whose parents had died during the Crisis, urgently needed rehabilitation, tuition, and jobs.

In March 2012, a protest march took place in the streets of Arawa, with the participants demanding that the Autonomous Bougainville Government build schools and universities so that local students would not have to leave the region to get educated. The march came on the heels of a three-day government conference in 2011, supported by Australian government aid (AusAID) and the New Zealand Aid Programme, that began developing a land policy for Bougainville. A key point was that, in a region that had lost years of potential development during a civil war, "there has been little adaptation of customary ways with modern processes, which has contributed significantly to the level of confusion."[3]

AusAID then funded a reconciliation meeting in February 2013 that discussed, among other things, the reopening of Panguna.

The return to operation of the mine, which was still controlled by Bougainville Copper Limited (BCL), whose largest shareholder was Rio Tinto and whose second-biggest investor was the PNG government, was favored by the country's political establishment as one of the fastest ways of generating employment (though PNG prime minister Peter O'Neill reportedly threatened in 2014 to expropriate and nationalize Rio's controlling share). So it was no surprise that the media narrative that emerged from this meeting cited local positivity about the mine. But a PNG blogger who visited Arawa after the conference challenged this. He claimed that most people he spoke to would prefer agriculture to thrive.[4] In 2014, an increasing number of community forums were organized by the Bougainville government, all designed to convince former fighters and average citizens that the mine should reopen. They were not persuading many people.

When I was back around the mine in 2013, I heard mostly negative sentiments about the pit. Without serious consultation or compensation, locals wanted alternatives. An articulate young local woman, Theonila Roka, told me as the sun set on the polluted Kavarong river that mining simply was not necessary to bring Bougainville independence. "In many ways we're already independent," she said. "Most people are self-sufficient, growing their own food on their land."

A report by Australian NGO Jubilee in 2014 detailed the myriad of voices in Bougainville, largely ignored by the media and local government, who opposed the mine. Dozens of villagers were surveyed, and there was "near universal" opposition to its reopening. The results were so damaging to Rio Tinto's cause that Bougainville president John Momis himself, in long letters secretly written by Australian government advisor Tony Regan, disparaged its findings.[5]

One reason for local hesitation was that people remembered the violence that resource exploitation often brought. A lecturer in criminology at the University of Ulster, Kristian Lasslett, produced

evidence that BCL had placed intense pressure on the PNG government to send police squads to Bougainville in 1988 to quell
unrest, despite their shocking human rights record. According
to the minutes of a meeting held on June 8, 1989, the company
was told by PNG's minister of state that "brutal firepower" was
to be used against the resistance movement. BCL welcomed this,
hopeful that it could continue its mining work as soon as possible.[6]

In his 2014 book, *State Crime on the Margins of Empire*, Lasslett
expanded his research and revealed even more damning evidence
of official Australian complicity with BCL and its desire to crush
any resistance. "Australia wanted to demonstrate to its allies, particularly the US, that it could underwrite stability in the South
Pacific region and ward off trouble on its patch," Lasslett argued.[7]

The mistrust directed at BCL in Bougainville did not stop when
the fighting ended, and for good reason. In 2011, the company
appointed to its board Sir Rabbie Namaliu, PNG's prime minister from 1988 to 1992, and the man who had directed his security
forces to terrorize the population of Bougainville by torturing and
killing its citizens, as well as imposing a blockade on the province.[8]

The BCL chairman told the Australian parliament in 1999, in
comments tinged with patronizing colonialism, that his company
had a "non-interventionist position during the conflict." It was
a lie. Besides, "Bougainville probably has two generations to go
before it gets over this, assuming it starts now."[9] He hoped for a
pliant younger citizenry.

A current senior BCL manager, who was present in Bougainville
before the Crisis erupted, told an Australian NGO in 2013 that he
had never understood why the locals revolted. Requesting anonymity, "John" said that when the conflict erupted in 1989, "we
were astonished. Things were so good there. Relations between
the company and the people were always harmonious and coop-
erative." John denied any BCL complicity in violence against local
people, highlighted the "positive health and education benefits
experienced by Bougainvillians," and pledged to close the mine

properly because "our legacy is important." I met no one in the province who believed this promise.

The stance of the president of the Autonomous Bougainville Government, John Momis, had added to the uncertainty. When he was serving as a minister in the PNG government during the Crisis, Momis had argued: "It is important to understand the significance of holding Rio Tinto responsible for its actions"—indeed, Kristian Lasslett interviewed eight managers who had worked for BCL between 1987 and 1992, and they all openly admitted that the company had provided whatever weapons and logistics the PNG military had requested.[10] Momis went further: "PNG took its direction from BCL's management."[11] Momis wrote a letter in 2001, composed for a US-based legal action against Rio Tinto, that detailed the deep complicity between Rio Tinto, BCL, and the PNG government at the height of the brutality against the people of Bougainville. "I was aware of one meeting," he said, "where BCL management instructed PNG to 'starve the bastards out.'"

However, by 2013 Momis was advocating the reopening of the mine. Recent legislation he had proposed, drafted thanks to a large AusAID grant to an Australian academic, Tony Regan, who denied the complicity of BCL in the Crisis, argued that some landowners had the right to veto mining projects, but permitted the institution of large-scale mining nonetheless.[12] Regan was involved in drafting mining legislation for Bougainville in 2013 (and again in 2014, opposed by virtually every civil society group), but the secrecy caused key stakeholders to revolt publicly, accusing AusAID and the local government of collusion in pushing through a failed law and ushering BCL back in. Landowners were not given full rights over their lands. Former resistance leader Sam Kauona said it was drafted by "rich, white lawyers." Regan did not help matters by telling Radio New Zealand in 2014 that Panguna was the best option for the province, and he dismissed agriculture as an alternative. The Bougainville government finally pushed through its mining legislation in 2015.

One of Regan's colleagues, Griffith University's Professor Ciaran O'Faircheallaigh, had direct links with Rio Tinto—receiving unspecified amounts of financial support from the company —while he had also been contracted by Coffey International, another corporation close to Rio Tinto.[13] Between 2010 and 2014, Regan was paid $968,120 as a "legal advisor," according to official documents. This was significantly higher than any Australian government assistance towards agriculture. Canberra met so frequently with Rio Tinto, the Bougainville government, and BCL representatives that officials claimed that "to collate such a list and provide the level of detail requested [on the number of meetings between the parties] would entail a significant investment of resources." In 2014 and 2015 alone, the amount of Australian aid money given to legal and mine advisors spoke volumes about Australia's priorities.[14]

Attempting to absolve the earlier PNG administration of any responsibility, Momis told Australian ABC Radio's *PM* in March 2013 that Rio Tinto and the Australian government were to blame for the original crisis. He said that in "their zeal to generate revenue, [they] completely ignored the people's way of doing things."[15]

In theory, the people of Bougainville would choose whether or not the Panguna mine would reopen once their independence had been achieved. But it was not a choice centered on sustainability and economic empowerment, but rather a toxic dilemma between further environmental devastation or poverty. These alternatives stemmed from a war that followed intensive mineral exploitation, all of which had deeply disrupted the well-being of the current generation of Papua New Guineans, not to mention the prospective welfare of future generations. This was the legacy of predatory capitalism. Environmental vandalism should not be the price tag for "progress." Bougainvilleans were savvy enough to realize that they were carrying a weak hand into negotiations with the mining companies and the governments that supported them.

The anger towards the Panguna mine had been there since its birth in the late 1960s, partly because Australian companies had been exploiting PNG's minerals for decades before this. By 1975, when PNG gained independence from Australia, the fully functional operation was the biggest non-aid earner in the country. The new state lived and breathed through Panguna—at its most productive, the mine contributed 20 percent of PNG's national budget—even though the mine was simultaneously destroying any chance of resource sustainability. But the citizens of Bougainville, despite suffering ecological devastation, had received less than 2 percent of the profits to assist their own communities.

In addition, PNG workers did not enjoy equal employment opportunities in the mine—a common situation in other mines across the country. A type of workplace apartheid was established by BCL, with much better facilities and pay offered to white workers than to locals. The Australian administration of the late 1960s also excluded landowners from the bargaining table, dealing only with the Australian government and Rio Tinto. In 1969 an article in *Canberra Times* explained how the Australian government, then in control of PNG, "could not allow a handful of people to block the Bougainville copper project on which the future of more than two million people depends."[16] Decades later, the rhetoric remained exactly the same.

In the late 1980s, the quiet fury boiled over. The BRA demanded independence from PNG, an end to the environmental damage caused by the mine, and compensation for being excluded from the initial negotiations. The mine was shut down in 1989 after continued sabotage by the BRA, but the bitter conflict continued for another eight years, by which time between 15,000 and 20,000 locals (about a tenth of the population) had died, principally from a PNG-imposed blockade and fighting. Many families were still searching for their loved ones' remains. Bougainville was economically ruined. This was the price of the BRA's decisive blow against multinational colonization—a rare example of a mining company being forced to accept defeat despite receiving support from two national governments.

We arrived at the Jaba River, close to the center of the mine site, a waterway that was filled with glowing blue copper tailings—the end result of many years of BCL dumping chemicals and heavy metals in the area. We watched as dozens of men, women, and children panned the river for gold in a desperate attempt to earn a living. It was their only form of income—one gram of gold could earn around $30—but this primitive form of resource extraction was taking place in Panguna's toxic waste. The villagers knew the health risks, but they had no other options, although even this would be denied them if the mine reopened. They had set up very basic temporary shelters on the banks of the river to house themselves for short periods while they were panning, before they headed back to their villages. During my 2013 visit I saw locals, including children, still washing in the polluted water, condemned to a fate of sickness and irritated skin.

We drove a short distance across rocky, uneven gravel to the main part of the tailings. No vegetation grew there. It was desert-like, with sand as far as the eye could see—an abandoned wasteland. All that was visible were small mountains of dirt around which polluted water ran, and old batteries and tires with weeds growing through them, as well as a crane that had fallen on its side. It was a depressing sight.

Willy said that he had no idea how the area could be properly rehabilitated. He told me of the times he had hunted animals there in the 1960s, when it was a lush forest with a healthy river running through it. Now he could only look around in disbelief.

Another short drive took us to the mine pit. It was massive, seven kilometers across at its widest part, and layered like an inverted wedding cake, with trees and bush slowly taking over its upper levels. At the edge of the pit were two large processing centers, both overgrown with plants. John, who worked in one of the centers in the 1980s, remarked that the buildings were slowly disappearing as scrap-metal seekers worked their way through them.

At Panguna's inception, it was one of the world's biggest working open-cut mines. Now, abandoned earthmovers and cranes lay rusting across the vast expanse (by 2013 Chinese scavengers had removed most of this equipment to be shipped and sold as scrap metal overseas). In the middle of the pit was a patch of bright blue water that almost glowed on the overcast day, while green slime covered the surrounding rocks. Amazingly, there, too, people had built makeshift huts and were panning for gold. They lived and worked in the shadow of a deserted mine, eking out an existence that bordered on the inhumane.

The heart of the mine emitted a deafening, machine-like sound. It came from a large, rusty column that was busily sucking air into a pipe that transported water outside the mine. For twenty-four hours a day, every day for the past quarter-century, this had ensured the mine did not fill up with water, particularly when it poured during the rainy season.

Willy looked shocked by what he saw. He said he had never been to the center of the pit before. Both he and John naively wondered whether, should BCL have no interest in reopening the mine, the company might help to fill in the hole to allow locals to grow crops there. As we walked back to our jeep, John picked a purple flower. He said he wanted to prettify his home with a reminder of our day together. He laughed when he told me this, but I think he was serious.

Willy was hungry, so we drove to Panguna town, which before the war had sustained 3,500 people and included supermarkets, cinemas, banks, and schools. Now it had little more than a bare-bones general store. Inside the dim wooden room, American hard-rock music played from a stereo, and a young girl sold children's clothes and fizzy drinks. I paid $12 for Chinese biscuits, soft drinks, and tinned pork for my traveling companions. Nearby was the closest port to Arawa, once a busy hub of export but now a decrepit place infused with abandonment. I saw the derelict hulks of three power plants, while fuel tanks leaked oil close to the sea. Pieces of metal were strewn over ground that had accumulated nothing in the last twenty-five years but moss and weeds.

The final place the men wanted to show me was the Arawa runway, which, currently disused, had recently been flattened and cleaned up. No one seemed to know who was going to use it, but the consensus was that it would be politicians, miners, or scrap-metal workers. Willy told me that local landowners had disputed the use of the ground and were fighting for the right to grow cocoa there.

Sitting and standing on the runway, our group talked about the future of PNG. Prime Minister Peter O'Neill's government had announced that all education in the country, from the earliest years until Year 10, would either be free or subsidized. (He claimed in April 2014 that his "fee free policy" had brought 85 percent of children into school.) Willy said the money for this would be sourced from mining and the country's biggest energy project: a 407-kilometer, $19 billion ExxonMobil LNG pipeline, which opened in 2014 and funneled gas to buyers in China, Taiwan, Japan, and beyond. This was part of what was being called a resource boom in PNG. Port Moresby recently welcomed an ANZ Bank–commissioned report that found the country had the potential to export resources to the tune of $38 billion a year until 2030. Prime Minister O'Neill said the challenge was to develop such assets responsibly.[17] By late 2014, however, reality hit, with global oil and gas prices diving and the government's revenue reduced.

"I don't care where it comes from, as long as my people are educated," Willy said. I challenged this position, asking if it mattered whether these resource-exploitation projects were affecting the environment and local communities, as happened in Bougainville, and if so, whether they should be opposed. But Willy and John maintained the pragmatic line I had heard earlier. In particular, although they cared about other provinces and communities, both argued strongly that Bougainville, after decades of providing massive wealth to PNG, now deserved payback in the form of financial compensation and free education for its children.

Willy then warned that Australia should play its cards right and not just think of its resource companies. He said that Canberra had already supported the wrong side too many times in the past. It was nothing like a threat—more a faint hope that Australia would start thinking beyond money and mining.

When I first visited Bougainville in 2012, I expected a desolate and isolated province. That is what I mostly found, along with anger that the world, and the key instigators of the conflict such as Rio Tinto and Australia, had ignored their responsibilities to clean up the place.

When I returned in 2013 the situation had barely improved. I saw a few more examples of foreign aid, roads and basic hospitals; but unemployment, social inertia, and political incompetence remained dominant features. Arawa town was still eerily quiet, with poor residents working, talking, and drinking in the shadow of burned-out buildings. There was now a modern bank with an ATM machine near the center of town. The Autonomous Bougainville Government was ramping up its public rhetoric in an attempt to sway a skeptical public that the Panguna mine was the only viable way to achieve independence from 2015 when a referendum could be held to decide on the future.

I left in 2012 with little hope for a peaceful future, but in 2013 I was partly swayed by my time with a remarkable twenty-four-year-old local woman, Theonila, and her now husband, Nathan. Her father was murdered during the Crisis, in 1993, and she lived with her mother and sisters in refugee housing. Violence was all around them. Today her family lived near the mine, in Makosi in Panguna District, having witnessed the brutal fighting and deprivation during the worst years of the conflict, and she and Nathan had started a school teaching basic reading and writing to children who were yet to enter formal schooling. Education was the best form of modern resistance and inoculation against governments aiming to convince locals that large-scale mining was the best way to bring liberation.

In the shadow of Panguna, I met Theonila's siblings, mother, and the rest of her family for a homemade meal as the rain hit the huts under which we sat and talked. They all rejected any consideration of the mine reopening. They were still waiting for compensation, an apology, and justice for the myriad of crimes committed by Rio Tinto's allies. This was still the dominant view across the province. Every day, they saw history's shadow before them. Near their home, a sign reading "Pit Drainage Tunnel July 1985" sat above a rusting passage, running straight from the center of the mine.

The mine itself looked barer, with fewer old, rusting trucks still in the pit, though nearby I saw massive old vehicles being consumed by large spiderwebs and ferns. I witnessed the sun set behind the tailings, and was almost seduced by the beauty as the light faded on the horizon. But I stopped myself, remembering that this was the sight of environmental destruction, pollution, and destitution. There was no allure here. A limping young boy played near me, fascinated by my presence and my white skin. Theonila said he was probably disabled due to the mine's pollution still leaking into the water and land.

There was no romanticizing the pit or its dirty legacy. With frequent talk of reopening the mine now a constant source of discussion and frustration—communication on Bougainville remained sketchy, though smartphones, in even the remotest areas, were allowing connected locals to be informed far faster and more reliably than the pro-mining mainstream media—the lack of consultation between the key stakeholders was an even stronger sentiment in 2013.

I visited the remote village of Guava, often enveloped in clouds and rain, above the mine, to find a community implacably opposed to large-scale mining. This was where the Bougainville resistance was born and where the leader Francis Ona lived. The spirit of quiet defiance had not dimmed. Bougainville president John Momis made a visit to the village in 2014 in a futile attempt to reconcile with locals and gain their support for the return of Rio Tinto.

What haunted me was whether people like Theonila were strong enough to withstand the powerful political forces supporting the mine reopening. These voices of opposition inspired me—the descendants of revolutionaries who refused to bend to the will of foreign corporate interests and their local proxies. But were they organized enough to forge an independent path in a damaged province?

PNG had long been aware of the dangers of an overreliance on the mining industry. In 1975, the year in which PNG gained its independence from Australia, a constitutional planning committee reported:

> We believe that since we are a rural people, our strength should be essentially in the land and the use of our innate artistic talents. We caution that large-scale industries should be pursued only after very careful and thorough consideration of the likely consequences upon the social and spiritual fabric of our people. The basic concept in our society with regard to the use of natural resources is that one generation holds and uses resources in the capacity of trustee for future generations. We, the generation of today, cannot squander our country's resources. We would clearly be failing in our responsibility if we sold our resources to foreigners for our own short term benefit, without regard to the needs of generations after us.[18]

It might have been written today.

Unfortunately, from its first day of independence, the fledgling PNG state had little bargaining power in its dealings with the foreign mining and timber groups that were keen to exploit the nation's abundant natural resources.[19] It could be argued that PNG was ill-prepared for its break from Australia, in that the transition resulted in lenient laws that gave foreign corporations undue influence over a largely unregulated state.

During World War II, PNG was a major battleground on which over 215,000 men—Japanese, American, and Australian—were slaughtered. The assistance that New Guineans gave the Western forces created an enduring relationship, at least in the Australian consciousness. However, since its independence, there had been little development of an understanding of PNG, which was mostly characterized as a poor nation teetering on the edge of collapse despite its abundance of natural resources—a state reliant on outside help and plagued by institutional corruption. Australia's dumping of asylum seekers on PNG's poor Manus Island, with justified local anger, strengthened the foreign narrative of a failed state.

The new nation's first prime minister, Michael Somare, was fondly remembered by some young locals as the man who commenced negotiations with Australian prime minister Gough Whitlam in the early 1970s to begin the decolonization process. But he was mostly seen as having delivered few long-lasting projects that had assisted all inhabitants of PNG. He was certainly unpopular in Bougainville, viewed as having contributed to many alleged corrupt, business-as-usual practices that now blighted the state. Somare's "look north" policy (towards China) had been particularly prominent. Critics accused successive PNG governments of giving companies that had close ties to Beijing preferential access to resource projects. In fact, the country had become a battleground for a proxy war over access in the Pacific, as Washington became increasingly engaged in the region.

Neither the United States nor Australia were pleased that

another power was trying to gain influence over what each saw as its own turf—PNG's wealth was apparently not to be shared further afield. In statements she made to the US congressional Foreign Relations Committee, former US secretary of state Hillary Clinton was direct. "Let's put aside the moral, humanitarian, do-good side of what we believe in and let's just talk straight, real politics," she said. "We are in a competition with China. Take Papua New Guinea—huge energy find." Clinton then accused Beijing of attempting to "come in under us" and stated that it would be a "mistaken notion" to think that America would retreat from "the maintenance of our leadership in a world where we are competing with China." Perhaps this was why Prime Minister Peter O'Neill announced increased military ties with Washington in 2014, as a way to keep the United States and China in competition for his affection.

Australia had been giving aid to PNG since 1975—$461 million in the 2014–15 period alone—but very little of that money had been seen by the local people. Rather, many corrupt PNG officials enjoyed the largesse of the Australian taxpayer because of this aid, and countless billions found their way into the pockets of Australian corporations—as so-called "boomerang aid." Michael Somare claimed in 2010 that 60 percent of Australian aid ended up back in the coffers of Australian companies—firms such as Coffey International, SMEC International, GHD, JTA International, and Cardno ACIL. The money had also disappeared further afield. In 2013, PNG's forestry minister complained about how Canberra had hired a US-based environmental group, the Nature Conservancy, to spend $6 million on a sustainable forestry project without consulting Port Moresby.[20]

Some of this aid went towards assisting school enrollments, training midwives, and providing anti-HIV drugs, police training, scholarships for students, disability programs, and other forms of essential care. But I regularly heard that corruption ate up far too much of the money and that, as a result, locals who had spent decades watching Australian firms exploit the nation's resources had become extremely cynical and angry. This had led to calls for Australia's aid to be far better managed, reduced, or even canceled. An attempt was made to address this issue through performance-based aid programs, which were worth tens of millions of dollars annually, but these were often public relations exercises designed merely to give the impression that Canberra was concerned about stolen funds.

The truth was that Canberra had been content to pay hefty fees to white Australians working in PNG while offering far less to local workers. In 2010, a review found that half of Australia's aid budget to PNG was being spent on consultants who were routinely receiving six-figure salaries, though this figure had dropped to around 20 percent by 2012. It was very similar to the situations in Haiti and Afghanistan.

A 2012 study by Sydney's *Daily Telegraph* newspaper also found that seven companies had earned over $1 billion in Australian taxpayer–funded contracts in recent years.[21] These so-called "private sector corporations" were the beneficiaries of an aid industry that had been the subject of little political oversight or media scrutiny, and one through which a handful of multinationals raked in vast sums of money. This arrangement was encouraging foreign firms to establish Australian arms in order to win lucrative contracts; one example was the US-based company URS, which won a $110 million contract to deliver services in education, health, and gender training in PNG.

It seemed that the Australian government had never lost sight of its main goal in PNG, which was to ensure that Australian corporations had a ready market in which to turn a profit. Needless to say, the financial and political assistance given to foreign mining companies to operate in PNG had ultimately done nothing to alleviate the many problems that existed in a resource-rich but infrastructure-poor nation.

BHP Billiton, for example, was one of the world's largest

mining companies and had worked in PNG for decades. In 1995, the corporation—known as the "Big Australian," due to its former status as a domestic steel producer—helped draft a bill in the PNG parliament that invalidated the right of PNG citizens who were negatively affected by the polluting Ok Tedi mine in PNG's Western Province to seek legal redress in court. *Multinational Monitor* magazine—a nonprofit publication founded by US political activist Ralph Nader in 1980 to document the global economy—highlighted what was going on:

> In August 1995, BHP drafted legislation for the PNG Parliament that subjected anyone who sued BHP to fines of up to $75,000. Even more remarkably, the bill also applied the same fines to anyone who attempted to challenge the constitutional validity of the proposed law in PNG courts. The bill made it an offence to commence compensation proceedings against BHP, to assist a person to do so or to give evidence at compensation proceedings.
>
> In an attempt to seduce the landowners, BHP offered to establish an $82 million fund to pay out compensation and benefits to plaintiffs over the life of the mine. This package would provide $180 per landowner per year over the mine's remaining 15-year life.[22]

Copper mining used a procedure involving cyanide and was virtually guaranteed to bring ecological destruction. So BHP had good reason to anticipate that locals would eventually try to seek legal recompense for the fallout from its mining activity at Ok Tedi, a campaign that continued. Bizarrely, despite the well-documented environmental destruction that BHP had caused, the PNG government gave the company a good corporate citizenship award in 2011—though, by 2013, Port Moresby's relationship with the Ok Tedi mine was more fraught.[23]

Canberra had always been keen to assist Australian companies to expand their activities overseas. It was worth remembering that the foreign affairs division of the Australian government was intimately involved in trade, which is why one of its departments was called the Department of Foreign Affairs and Trade. This would explain why assorted environmental groups had little success when calling on the federal government to impose tighter restrictions on potentially destructive operations undertaken by Australian companies overseas and to force those corporations to abide by local environmental laws.

The Australian Greens, for instance, unsuccessfully argued in 2011 for legislation to prevent Australian mining companies working overseas from behaving in ways that would be illegal at home. The then Greens' leader Bob Brown had just visited the highly polluting Chinese- and Australian-controlled Ramu nickel mine in PNG's Madang Province, which he said was "an appalling indictment of modern technology being brought to Papua New Guinea without the safeguard that you would get in the home countries against this sort of destruction of marine eco-systems."[24] I saw evidence of this pollution during a trip to lush Madang in 2012. Increasing attacks by locals against Ramu as well as the Porgera mine in the PNG Highlands, owned by the Canadian company Barrick Gold, signaled growing public resistance to exploitative industries. Barrick Gold agreed to pay eleven PNG women compensation in 2015 after security guards and police at its Porgera mining site raped them in 2010.

There was also ongoing tension over the billions of dollars of Australian aid delivered to PNG that had been spent on supporting the mining and petroleum industries at the perceived expense of agriculture, which had the potential to benefit many more people. According to a paper released by the Australian National University in 2009, "over 75 percent of PNG people rely on agricultural exports for their livelihood." Furthermore, the paper stated:

As the PNG government and Australian corporations [and government] pursue profits from the operation of PNG mines and petroleum stations, they have largely ignored the environmental impact that the mines have had on the PNG people ... The development of the resource sector has benefited Australian corporations and PNG officials at the expense of the PNG people, who suffer the financial, social and ecological effects of their activities.[25]

Recognition of the role that PNG officials had played was important. After 1975, Papua New Guineans were rarely asked what they wanted. Policies were imposed by a corrupt Port Moresby elite, Australian bureaucrats, and parochial media. Civil disturbances over low pay and poor working conditions, as well as a lack of employment, were common, but there was little improvement in the standard of living of the majority. Forty years after its independence, PNG's vital statistics remained some of the poorest in the Asia-Pacific region. The World Bank estimated that close to 40 percent of the population was below the poverty line, the average life expectancy was barely sixty years, and only 33 percent of rural citizens had access to an adequate water source.

Nearly everyone I discussed these figures with in PNG wondered why conditions for most of the country's citizens remained so inadequate, considering the international support that had been given to the nation in the last four decades. This support was tailored to those with vested interests, and PNG's political elite were content to leave the country on an aid drip-feed, increasingly dependent on outside forces.

It was another form of disaster capitalism: predatory corporations—supported by foreign-aid payments and tax concessions, and insulated from media scrutiny or political criticism—acted solely to benefit international shareholders and prevented a nation from truly exercising its independence. I saw similarly dysfunctional relationships in Haiti and Afghanistan, where great influence was wielded by the multinationals at work in those countries. PNG would never enjoy real sovereignty unless the ties that bound it to corporations and foreign aid were severed, or at least changed, and the capacity to create self-sufficient businesses was allowed to flourish.

A January 2013 story in Rupert Murdoch's *Australian* newspaper perfectly illustrated this problem. The article spoke about Canberra and Port Moresby becoming increasingly close, but the Papua New Guineans themselves were completely ignored in the article. All that mattered, it seemed, was ensuring that the resource pipeline remained open.[26] The article's author, Rowan Callick, was a guest of Australian bank ANZ in PNG in 2013, and again rehashed the tired talking points of foreign businesses exploiting the nation's resources. Once again, the locals were invisible.[27]

Bougainville had been a model for resistance to this ugly reality, an island province that foreign interests had expected to bow down and simply accept having its resource wealth exploited, only to face irrepressible opposition. But that was not all that set it apart.

The 1970s saw the emergence of a Bougainville secessionist movement that opposed the province being part of an independent PNG, claiming it had far more in common with its near neighbor, the Solomon Islands. During my visit, I was repeatedly told of the area's deep racial, spiritual, and cultural connections with the Solomons.[28] The BRA then reignited the independence movement in the late 1980s, and it still burned. The Bougainville Peace Agreement, signed in Arawa in 2001 by Port Moresby and Bougainville's leaders, dictated that a free vote on independence must be held between 2015 and 2020. The PNG elites largely opposed any move towards independence, and Canberra was equally nervous, using friendly reporters to issue warnings of chaos if Bougainville dared go its own way.[29] Australian foreign minister Julie Bishop instructed Bougainville in late 2014 that the province was not ready. She added that Australia, New Zealand,

and other countries "who are responsible, if you like, for this part of the world" had concerns about independence. Colonial lecturing remained alive and well in the twenty-first century.

A fundamental concern of those who embraced the sovereignty cause had been PNG's adoption of the Australian state-ownership approach to resources, instead of the more culturally appropriate Melanesian system of landowner rights. The latter involved fair negotiations with the relevant landowners, whereas under the state-ownership model, landowners' wishes were ignored and community-based protection of the land was often sidelined. A 2014 report published in the *Proceedings of the National Academy of Sciences* in the United States found that this was a common problem across the world, with mining and hydrocarbon companies routinely failing to discuss the effects of their work with local communities.[30]

Debate about the desire for independence always occurred within the context of a sustainable economic base, which explained the heated discussions about the potential reopening of the Panguna mine. History cast a long shadow over these arguments. The Panguna Landowners' Association supported mining by local landowners who could then choose to work with foreign companies if they wished. In keeping with this ideology, in March 2012 the PLA released a statement that challenged the PNG Chamber of Mines and Petroleum over its support for state ownership of the country's resources. Association secretary Lawrence Daveona outlined a number of reasons why it was impossible to trust the promises made by Rio Tinto, or any other multinational. "No adequate controls had been in place," he said, "to insure that royalties, taxes, environmental law compliance, and human rights" were upheld, and that foreign investors in PNG paid their dues.[31]

And yet times changed. When I met Daveona in Arawa in 2013, he told me that he supported the reopening of the Panguna mine on strict conditions and said it was the only viable way for Bougainville to achieve independence. Serious allegations of corruption surrounded Daveona,[32] and his seemingly newfound desire to work with Rio Tinto could be connected to the company's financial largesse. He was just one more key stakeholder that the mining company had worked assiduously to buy off in its campaign to operate again. For this treachery, Daveona said he now had to travel with bodyguards. By 2015, the PLA faced growing public opposition to mining, further isolating it from the people.

Samuel Kauona was one of the leaders of the BRA in the late 1980s, alongside the now deceased Francis Ona, a man who had led his people against BCL. He was smeared as a terrorist and obstructionist by the Australian media, but in a 1989 letter he correctly explained that the PNG government was "not for our peoples which would secure their freedom of their rights. It is in fact a government for the economy of PNG and Australia."

These sentiments still burned into Kauona. I met him in Arawa's District 17, whose name had been carried over from the mining era. The soft-spoken Kauona was in his late forties and highly articulate. He told me about his twin visions for the island: independence and sustainable mining. For him, keeping the region's enormous mineral wealth in local hands was essential. "This is why we fought the war," he said. It is also why, in 2012, he presented the Autonomous Bougainville Government with a mining exploration application. He wanted to examine land that he believed contained gold and silver.[33]

Kauona, who played an integral part in the peace process that ended the war in the late 1990s, believed that the citizens of Bougainville had to reclaim what was rightfully theirs. When new resources were found, he said, Bougainvilleans should receive appropriate compensation for collaborating with outsiders. He argued that the power dynamic this time must clearly lie with the locals. In 1994, with the civil war still raging, Kauona wrote: "Papua New Guinea and international interests came and took our land without asking, destroyed it and tore it apart, poisoned our streams and made our people sick ... You can break our bones, but you can never break our spirit. The land of Bougainville is ours. We will not give up this land."[34]

This determination, he explained to me, was instrumental in Bougainvilleans' war victory against seemingly overwhelming odds. I asked him whether he saw any similarity between his war and those fought by the United States in Afghanistan and Iraq. He did, saying it proved that local knowledge was a powerful weapon when fighting a better-armed adversary.

Kauona resented the fact that Australia supported his opponents, namely the PNG government and its army, during the Crisis through annual aid payments.[35] "I would stop all the aid tomorrow," he told me. "It's not making people self-sufficient." He also had little time for the older men who dominated both the Port Moresby and Bougainville parliaments. "We need young people to lead," he said.

Kauona's desire to make sure mineral development benefited locals first was shared by other influential Bougainvilleans, including ex-militant and Mekamui spokesman Philip Takaung. On hearing that a number of landowner groups in Bougainville had begun inviting exploration companies onto their lands, he said that environmental management had to be the priority. "We mustn't let money lure us into disaster, and damage our natural habitat by destroying the eco-system [so that] we will be evacuated somewhere [else] to live." Takaung had a different message for former BRA fighters:

Don't be fooled by money, and remember what we all fought for, because when a lot of people see money, they become greedy and forget about the others. A lot of us, especially us the ex-combatants, I can admit right now that we are very greedy. We have lost our soul and vision of what we fought for.[36]

I asked Kauona about leading the revolution. He said that no one expected it to last so long or to inflict the damage it had—particularly the loss of so many lives. He said he spent most of those years constantly on the move, rarely staying in the same spot for any period of time. His wife had given birth to two girls during the Crisis, and they now had two grandchildren.

He laughed when I mentioned the Sandline controversy. When the PNG government requested military support from Australia and New Zealand, both countries refused, so Port Moresby started negotiating with a London-based mercenary company called Sandline. Run by a former British army officer, Tim Spicer—who headed the mercenary company Aegis and secured hundreds of millions of dollars in contracts in the "war on terror" after 9/11—Sandline was hired to crush the BRA by force. But the plan became public, and the members of the private army, who were mostly hired through a South African group called Executive Outcomes, were disarmed and arrested in PNG before they could cause any damage. "We would have beaten them in two weeks if they had come," Kauona said proudly. Remnants of Executive Outcomes continued to thrive in the twenty-first century, with former members hired by the Nigerian government in 2015 to fight Boko Haram militants.

When I saw Kauona again in 2013, he remained as defiant as ever against the prospect of Rio Tinto reappearing in the province. I sensed that he saw himself as a potential future leader of an independent Bougainville, and his pedigree made him a possible candidate (he ran for president in the 2015 elections). Kauona's demand had not changed since our last meeting—namely, compensation from Rio Tinto and accountable legislation that allowed mining, but only on a scale that gave ultimate power to the landowners. He was optimistic that he would achieve his goals.

It was a Sunday morning, and rain was falling as I wandered the muddy streets of Arawa in the stifling humidity. The town's roads were potholed. Old Mobil and Shell service stations lay in ruins, covered in graffiti. Grime smeared the façades of apartment blocks originally intended for police but that now sheltered locals. Few of the town's 25,000 inhabitants were out and about. Sunday was when the predominantly churchgoing public attended prayer services. Arawa had been established by Australians as the main service hub for the Panguna mine. But when the Bougainville civil war broke out and the mine was closed, the place was neglected. Now, decades later, it looked and felt like a ghost town. I wondered why the countless millions of dollars of Australian aid had not made any difference here. When I returned in 2013, Arawa still looked forlorn, untouched by development for decades.

I encountered Leonard, a teacher in his fifties. He had betel nut–stained teeth and a sizeable gut. I asked him for his thoughts on the reopening of the Panguna mine and Bougainville's potential independence. "More than 50 percent of young people here are illiterate and don't really understand what's going on," he said. "I worry that they would be voting for something and not get why. Our people need to understand ourselves better before we do that."

I asked Leonard why almost everyone talked about a "crisis" rather than a "war" or "conflict" when discussing the brutal fighting that had taken place here in the 1990s. He just said: "We all call it that. Because of this crisis, so many children weren't educated. We have so much to still do before we can move on."

One of the as-yet-unresolved issues that came to mind was the dangerous legacy of the large number of wartime weapons still circulating in the community. I learned about this from the head of the Autonomous Bougainville Government's Veteran Affairs and Weapons Disposal division, Aaron Pita, whom I had visited in Bougainville's comparatively functional capital, Buka, a four-hour drive from Arawa on a rough road. Pita spoke fluent English, having studied in the United States in the early 1980s. He told me that his job was to find and decommission the countless weapons used during the war and to document on a computer database the names and details of all former combatants, of whom he guessed there might be between 3,000 and 5,000.

The Australian foreign minister Julie Bishop wrote without irony in June 2014 that Canberra was trying to stamp out the spread of illegal weapons by mentioning how "destabilizing" they had been in Bougainville in 1980s.[37] She knew that Australia had been a key player in the militarization and arming of that conflict.

During Bishop's visit to the province in late 2014, she pledged $57 million in aid because "Australia comes as your friend. I'm so impressed by the commitment and energy shown by the people of Bougainville to peace building. The government of Australia will always be a partner and will support everything that is done for the good of Bougainville and its people." She conveniently omitted mention of the mine. Australia announced in 2015 the expansion of its diplomatic mission in Buka, a clear attempt to deepen its influence over the island's resources. PNG responded with anger, imposing a travel ban on Australians wanting to visit the province.

Skepticism was rampant on the ground. Pita was ambivalent about the reopening of the mine, fearful, like Leonard, that the issues that had created the backlash against it in the first place had not been resolved. Compensation from Rio Tinto was essential, he said, as was the consent of the landowners of the area and the people of the island. It would be a long process, he told me. He did not seem convinced that mining was the solution to Bougainville's problems. He said that people who were his age—he was fifty-seven—remembered how badly things had gone the last time around. "Nobody wants to return to that," he said.

As I wandered around Arawa, women were visible on the streets, and I was able to speak to them in markets, shops, and hotels to get their views. Generally, though, women struggled to be heard here. Politically, PNG was a man's country—only three of the 109 members of the PNG parliament were female at the time of writing. This reflected a trend throughout the Pacific, which was the region with the lowest level of female political participation in the world. It had been stated that women comprised only 4 percent of politicians in the sixteen-country Pacific Island Forum; this compared with 18 percent across Asia, and nearly 15 percent in the Arab world.[38]

PNG's decidedly patriarchal society was also reflected in the fact that sexual assaults and domestic violence against women were common. Médecins Sans Frontières estimated in 2012 that 70 percent of PNG women would be either raped or sexually assaulted at least once in their lifetime.[39] Equally disturbing was PNG's maternal mortality rate, which, according to the United Nations, was one of the highest in the world, at 733 deaths per 100,000 births.

I stayed at the Arawa Women's Training Center, a basic tourist and worker accommodation unit that also assisted local women to learn domestic skills. It was run by Josephine, a woman in her fifties. She explained that the center had been formed in the wake of the Crisis by a group of women from various political factions. They were united by the desire to help the women who had suffered during the war to gain essential "home management skills," such as basic accounting, cooking, and sewing.

"Women were the bread-and-butter earners in the family" during the Crisis, Josephine told me. "The women suffered more than men … because they were the backbone of the family and often the opportunity for women to look after their families wasn't there. There was a blockade with few medical facilities, and basic items like soap, salt, and household needs weren't around."

Josephine opposed any return to mining on the island, preferring the development of adventure tourism such as hiking and diving. She believed that tourism combined with agriculture, such as cocoa and copra production and traditional gardening, could fulfill the nation's economic needs. The ecological record of the Panguna mine was so bad, she explained, that it was almost unimaginable that it could reopen.

This last concern was echoed in 2011 by Patricia Tapakau, president of Panguna Women in Mining, a group representing women in thirteen mining-affected areas. Tapakau told Inter Press Service that her members were nervous about the future. "What sort of mining and with what process will [Panguna] reopen?" she asked. "We need to know, because we don't want any more destruction. We have had enough of that."[40]

Bougainville Women in Mining, a female advocacy group of six mining lease areas, submitted a report in 2014 that demanded its voice be heard before any serious discussions were entered into over a reopened mine. "Bougainville is a matrilineal society," they concluded, after condemning male authority at all levels.

It was clear that reopening the Panguna mine was one of the most contentious and emotive issues in Bougainville. There was no consensus on the island about how to move forward. One former Mekamui commander, Moses Pipiro, summed up the disagreement when he said in 2012 that the redevelopment of the mine site was inappropriate until the people of Bougainville were educated about what options were available to them.[41] These obviously included forgetting about the mine and focusing on agriculture. After all, people had noticed that the fertility of the soil in certain areas around the mine had improved in the last two-and-a-half decades, and that coconuts had reappeared in many villages. Also, BCL had yet to explain how it would remove the huge amount of toxic waste still polluting much of the site.

Still, a new beginning for Panguna was firmly on the agenda at an initial meeting between the Autonomous Bougainville Government, BCL, and landowners in July 2012. Soon afterwards, the interim chairman of the Panguna Landowners Association, Chris Damana, told *Radio Australia* that all stakeholders wanted Rio Tinto to return. "BCL will … reopen the mine but needs to tidy up a lot of things before they come," he said. "We all agree that BCL will come back because they have learned their mistake

... and maybe we can start on a new slate."[42] He added that, for the mine to reopen, it was vital that a reconciliation ceremony be held and "belcol money" (compensation) be paid to those who had suffered in the region. All interested parties apparently expressed satisfaction with the discussion.

Bernadine Kirra, the chairwoman of the lower-tailings land-owners, the 3,000-strong group that had suffered the most while the mine was open, also told Radio Australia in July 2012 that it was vital that Panguna again operated, so that BCL could "build maybe some schools for a better standard [of education] and maybe better hospitals for Bougainville."[43]

These were all understandable desires on the part of Bougain-villeans. The question was whether or not the mining companies could be trusted to fulfill them. Unsurprisingly, the chairman of BCL, Peter Taylor, was enthusiastic about his company's prospects, telling a shareholders' meeting in Port Moresby in May 2012: "There is widespread agreement today that Bougainville's economic future needs mining if it is able to fund services for the people from its own resources."[44] However, he made no mention of the environmental destruction that occurred the last time the mine was running, nor of how this would be addressed, despite claiming it would cost around $3 billion to reopen the site. He was still sticking to the commercial positives in April 2013, when he said that the mine would employ around 2,500 workers and yield its valuable minerals for roughly twenty-four years; according to Taylor, it would take six years to ready the mine for production. One mining expert, Gavin Mudd, told Radio Australia that it would cost at least $1 billion to clean up the environment in Bougainville.[45] Although it was not guaranteed that BCL would ever return to Panguna, Taylor said in 2014 that he knew his company was the "preferred devil" of the Bougainville authorities.[46]

Market doubts concerning BCL, in particular about the negotiations to resume mining activity on Bougainville, led to the company recording a financial loss in 2011. "Uncertainty is poison," said

European Shareholders of Bougainville Copper president Axel
Sturm in March 2012, before demanding that the PNG government invest heavily in Panguna to get it moving again.[47] The
resources at stake were likely to continue to win over investors—
BCL announced in 2013 that Panguna contained up to 5 million
tons of copper and 19 million ounces of gold, worth $41 billion
and $32 billion respectively. Sturm, photographed with BCL head
Peter Taylor in Singapore in 2013, claimed without evidence that
"the majority of Bougainvilleans are aware that their personal
future depends on the reopening of the Panguna mine by a trustful
organization like Bougainville Copper Limited."[48]

The PNG government welcomed the renewed interest shown in
PNG by Rio Tinto and other resource giants such as Shell, mostly
because Port Moresby was desperate for foreign investment. The
minister for petroleum and energy, William Duma, said that this
was "a demonstration of the trust and confidence multinationals
around the globe have for PNG ... We as a country stand to gain
more and we can't go wrong."[49] Prime Minister Peter O'Neill,
officiating at the opening of a Shell office in the capital in February
2012, reassured foreign investors that "despite the perception of
political instability, unlike many other countries of the world,
PNG has been able to maintain the confidence of the business
community."[50]

But the governor of PNG's Gulf Province, Havila Kavo, voiced
his concerns, asking why Shell was being welcomed back to the
nation after the company had described PNG as a "failed state" a
decade earlier. "They [Shell] ripped off the country and left," he
said. "What infrastructure have they left and what positive development have they left before departing? Such companies have no
confidence in the country."[51] It seemed that Shell had decided to
retract its previously held views in order to participate in PNG's
developing gas industry.[52]

It was rare that a poor country could resist the charms of a multinational offering substantial investment within its borders. This

was an option open only to strong economies and institutions. The Norwegian government, for example, divested from Rio Tinto in 2008 to the tune of $1 billion, for its "grossly unethical conduct" at its mine at Grasberg in West Papua, which involved "severe environmental damage."[53] In September 2012, the New Zealand Superannuation Fund also pulled its investment from the Grasberg mine, in which Rio Tinto holds a 40 percent stake, explaining that its key reason for doing so was the human rights abuses committed by Indonesian forces against locals.[54] In 2015, the global union IndustriALL, representing 50 million workers globally, launched a campaign to highlight Rio Tinto's awful record on the environment and employee rights. The Australian Tax Office investigated Rio Tinto and BHP Billiton in 2015 for allegedly avoiding tax due to some of their operations being based in Singapore.

Sometimes, though, the legacies of the past were challenged. A US lawsuit filed in 2002 against Rio Tinto by landowners in Bougainville, who claimed that the company had been involved in the commission of war crimes and genocide during the Crisis, was dismissed in 2013. An attorney for the landowners, Steve Berman, told Radio Australia in November 2011 that Rio Tinto had "financed the helicopters and troop carriers and communications devices, and the means that the [PNG] government used to try and suppress the uprising."[55] The class action represented up to 14,000 Bougainvilleans, and Freedom of Information requests revealed that the Australian, British, and US governments had lobbied for its failure. Australia wrote to the US State Department in 2001 that the case "would be an unsettling and destabilizing event in circumstances where the need for stability and certainty on the island is paramount."[56] It is unsurprising that Rio Tinto, a multinational with 66,000 staff, would be so keen to quash legal action, as it is a corporation constantly pursuing its mining agenda against local communities around the world, from Madagascar to Indonesia, Mongolia, and the United States.[57]

Documents uncovered by the London-based Corporate

Responsibility Coalition in 2014 revealed that the British government had consistently "supported [Rio Tinto] in ducking out of
scrutiny in the US courts."[58] Business lobbying trumped human
rights every time.

There were additional concerns in PNG today about a "mobocracy." That was the word used by Sam Koim, the chairman
of PNG's Task Force Sweep, which was set up in 2011 to look
into government corruption. "A mob is beginning to dominate
the resources at the expense of the majority," he said. Koim has
accused Prime Minister Peter O'Neill of corruption.[59] Documents
released by WikiLeaks confirmed the belief that the PNG political establishment was a "totally dysfunctional blob" and that
the country was trapped in "Ponzi politics." Such honest statements ran counter to the usual comments by Australian officials,
who spoke of "institution building."[60] The problem extended to
Australia, where money laundering by PNG politicians and other
officials to the tune of tens of millions of dollars was common.[61]

One good piece of news in 2012 was the announcement of a
sovereign fund that would save some of the huge wealth created
through oil, gas, and mineral exploitation in PNG. But, again,
critics worried that a corrupt government was ill-equipped to
manage it, and at the time of writing the idea remained unfulfilled.
"The real challenge is keeping sticky fingers out of the revenues
pot," wrote former PNG prime minister Mekere Morauta.[62] The
2013 announcement by the PNG government to consolidate
state-owned companies and the country's oil and mining assets,
including Bougainville Copper and Ok Tedi, into a new corporate
structure was heralded as a better way of maximizing the benefits
to the people, although without proper oversight the mistakes of
the past were destined to be repeated.[63]

The worrying backdrop to all of these factors was Australia
itself, which appeared to be thwarting the autonomy of its northern neighbor in order to protect its significant vested interests.
This sentiment was articulated by then Australian foreign minister

Bob Carr in March 2012, when he warned PNG against postponing upcoming elections, as that would "place Australia in a position where we'd have no alternative but to organize the world to condemn and isolate Papua New Guinea." Carr subsequently backed down in the face of PNG anger—by late 2012, he was claiming that PNG could be a regional leader[64]—but the outburst was instructive of the mentality that resided in the Australian political elite.

Australia paid lip service to the idea that PNG was an independent nation, but its actions over the last few decades—not least making a poor nation dependent on its largesse in the form of aid—had made sovereignty close to impossible. "PNG has a way of holding itself together but we do have to be watchful," the Australian high commissioner to Port Moresby, Ian Kemish, said patronizingly before the country's 2012 election. A few years earlier, PNG's high commissioner to Australia, Charles Lepani, had critically reviewed Australia's John Howard government as "proselytising the values of Western society without attempting to understand the values of Pacific islands culture."[65]

Successive Australian governments had seen PNG as a problem that could be managed through aid agreements, which were currently worth more than $500 million annually. Canberra even appeared willing to tolerate the loss of funds to PNG corruption, despite spending more than $160 million on Australian advisers in the first decade of the twenty-first century to "strengthen governance."[66]

In 2011, AusAID introduced a "Mining for Development" initiative, which claimed to "provide countries with the expertise they need to build a sustainable mining sector, making better use of revenues, improving socially and environmentally sustainable development, and growing the economy." All fine words, except that in PNG they were completely contradicted by the facts on the ground.[67] Canberra had even brought out politicians and bureaucrats from across the world, mainly Africa, on "study tours" to see how apparently model corporations such as BHP Billiton and Rio Tinto conducted their business. In November 2012, ten women from five African countries toured Queensland and Western Australian mines and their communities. Sylvie Gilbert, a provincial director of Madagascar's interregional department of mines, told the ABC: "One of the things I am hoping to learn from this study trip is better governance principles as well as a better income stream for the country."[68]

A PNG blogger, Martyn Namorong, called this idea "neo-colonization" and asked what kinds of positive development PNG locals had seen in the areas where mining was occurring. He wrote that the Australian government, through AusAID, had been pursuing a clear agenda for years: "to act in Australian mining company interests as they did in Bougainville." He also damned the PNG "elite," who were trained in Australia and "run the country" only with regard for the interests of outside forces and themselves.[69] Resistance to this agenda was growing both internally and outside PNG. One important development was the Australasian Centre for Corporate Responsibility moving resolutions at the 2014 BCL Annual General Meeting demanding an independent review of the role and responsibility of the company in Bougainville.

Privatized aid was too often sold as the answer. The think-tank Australian Strategic Policy Institute released a report in 2013 that called for greater Australian aid for Bougainville, claiming civil unrest would occur without it, completely ignoring the complicity of Canberra in the province's troubles during the Crisis. Sending more AusAID money would not make locals forget who backed the polluting mine in the first place. Even stranger was that AusAID released a 2008 report that recommended against reopening the mine—"the mine community's attitude to profit-seeking foreigners is dour"—and advocated agriculture. This message had been ignored because of the closeness between Canberra and Rio Tinto.

Australia's adoption in 2011 of the global Extractive Industries Transparency Initiative (EITI), welcomed by the NGO Jubilee

Australia, was viewed suspiciously by critics in PNG. There was a lack of solid evidence that the plan, which aimed to provide transparency concerning company revenues in countries where extractive industries were important, had helped the nations that had signed up, which included Liberia, Niger, and Mongolia. In fact, the *Financial Times* reported in 2013 that countries in Africa that were involved in EITI, such as Mozambique, continued to struggle with endemic corruption.[70] The United States announced in 2014 that it would begin reporting under the scheme.

But there were some in PNG who wanted even more Australian involvement in the country. I spent some time in Port Moresby with an employee of Oxfam who told me he wished that Australia would again take control of PNG. He said the nation's independence in 1975, pushed by Michael Somare, had come too early, and that not enough local people were equipped to manage the new country. This had led, in his view, to the current malaise whereby corrupt politicians were wasting PNG's vast natural wealth. He said his father still spoke longingly about the pre-1975 days, when Australia supposedly treated PNG in a respectful way.

This man claimed that his view was widely shared across PNG, though I had only come across a handful of other supporters. I had never before heard of a formerly colonized people wanting to be once again controlled by their former colonizers, but it was not hard to see the logic. How else to repair a troubled state with poor public services and wasted or stolen resources when there was little faith that locals could solve the myriad of problems? Though whether an army of well-meaning Australian aid workers on high salaries would do any better was clearly arguable.

PNG needed a new model of investment—one that did not treat the country's natural wealth as jewels to be admired and then taken. If this was not forthcoming, the horrors of Bougainville might be repeated. When I walked around the old, decaying mine in Panguna, I imagined the rusted trucks being replaced with new models and the whole cycle of exploitation beginning again, the resource curse striking anew. Riches were there for the taking, and there was currently little incentive for Western corporations to behave any differently unless a public campaign of naming and shaming took place.

A truly sovereign Papua New Guinea—sovereign not simply in name but in reality—was not created in 1975. Disaster capitalism was ingrained in the new regime from the very beginning, something for which Australia bears a deep responsibility. Today, there is an obligation to assist Port Moresby to break free of the aid trap and develop far more sustainable practices—most obviously, agricultural ones. The people and tools are already there. All that is now needed is investment in infrastructure, training, and education—and a change in mindset.

PNG should not be condemned to remain a land that offers little to locals and much to Western shareholders. Twenty-first-century independence is surely possible.

Part II

5

The United States: "The land of the free has become a country of prisons"

Follow the money. Never mind what privatization does or doesn't do to state budgets; think instead of what it does for both the campaign coffers and the personal finances of politicians and their friends. As more and more government functions get privatized, states become pay-to-play paradises, in which both political contributions and contracts for friends and relatives become a quid pro quo for getting government business. Are the corporations capturing the politicians, or the politicians capturing the corporations? Does it matter?

Paul Krugman, *New York Times*, 2012

America incarcerates a higher proportion of its population than any other country in the world. It operates a system that demonizes and stigmatizes African-Americans and immigrants on an unprecedented scale, resembling a social experiment in population control. In her book *The New Jim Crow: Mass Incarceration in the Age of Colorblindness*, US writer Michelle Alexander explained that the "war on drugs" had crippled entire communities. In thirty years, the prison population had soared from 300,000 to more than two million. Meanwhile, the globally expansionist and violent "war on terror" that followed 9/11 brought greater division and repression at home.

The Obama administration made a small though welcome change in 2014 to allow around 50,000 nonviolent federal drug offenders to seek lower sentences; at the same time, however, a battle against immigrants surged—a battle that had forced millions of refugees to pass through detention facilities since the 1980s. In December 2014 President Obama issued an executive order that might save 5 million immigrants from being deported.

"No other country in the world imprisons so many of its racial or ethnic minorities," Alexander wrote. "The United States imprisons a larger percentage of its black population than South Africa did at the height of apartheid. In Washington DC, our nation's capitol [sic], it is estimated that three out of four young black men (and nearly all those in the poorest neighborhoods) can expect to serve time in prison."[1] These facts are mirrored across the country. The Vera Institute of Justice released a study in late 2014 that found mass incarceration to be "one of the major public health challenges facing the United States," due to millions of people suffering acute physical and mental problems both in prison and once they were free.

"The land of the free has become a country of prisons," Human Rights Watch noted in 2014, issuing a report that outlined the absurd number of Americans facing jail time for minor and non-violent crimes.[2] The *New Yorker* writer Adam Gopnik assessed that there were "more black men in the grip of the criminal justice system—in prison, on probation or on parole—than were in slavery [in 1850]. Overall there are now more people under 'correctional supervision' in America—more than six million—than were in the Gulag Archipelago under Stalin at its height."[3]

Private prison corporations saw a unique opportunity to make a financial killing from the explosion in numbers of men and women behind bars. A bipartisan belief that incarceration might solve America's social problems has been an abject failure—but don't tell this to the firms turning a profit. California, for example, dealt with its overcrowded prisons and lax medical care for inmates by opening more centers run by the Geo Group, one of the country's biggest contractors. The revolving door between such firms and the federal government was highlighted in 2014, when the company appointed Julie Myers Wood to its board. From 2006 to 2008, she was the Department of Homeland Security assistant secretary running ICE (US Immigration and Customs Enforcement).

Rather than examining the reasons so many people end up behind bars, in 2014 California made the decision to allow Geo to open a women's center in Bakersfield. It was estimated that this new center would increase company profits over a four-year period from $38 million to $66 million.[4] Geo had a history of allowing sexual abuse and poor medical care at its facilities. The long list of failings included serious allegations of sexual assault on the part of Central American women at a Geo-run center near San Antonio.[5] Thankfully, California voters saw sense in the 2014 mid-term elections and supported Proposition 47, which reclassified nonviolent crimes as misdemeanors. As a result, tens of thousands of people would either be freed or not convicted in the first place.

The number of private prisons across the nation has increased by a factor of twenty since the 1990s, and the inmate population stands at thirty-one times what it was then. Corrections Corporation of America (CCA) was established in 1983 and ran its first prison in Texas in that year. Between 1999 and 2010, there was an 80 percent surge in private facilities, including a 784 percent increase in federally administered prisons and a 40 percent increase at the state level.[6] The prison industry was not only building cells and managing the facilities, but also producing equipment, paints, body armor, military helmets, and ammunition.

A number of states, including Ohio, have ended their relationship with private prison operators. They have realized that the risks and costs of outsourcing far outweighed any initial benefits. The ACLU reported in 2011 that Ohio's private prisons offered few rehabilitation courses, resulting in higher rates of recidivism.[7] However, in a rare piece of good news, the Federal Bureau of Prisons announced in 2015 that it would not be renewing its contract with CCA for the Northeast Ohio Corrections Center in Youngstown. Poor conditions at the facility, riots, unsanitary food, and lax security were all good reasons cited for closing the center down.

The reasons for the US obsession with imprisonment are not very mysterious. Politicians have feared being seen as "soft on crime"—a fear driven by a tabloid press that celebrated harsh sentencing. Attacks on the poor and underprivileged neatly dovetailed with the popularity of lengthy mandatory minimum sentences and the "three-strike" laws that put people behind bars for life for stealing a chocolate bar. Enormous numbers of people were jailed without any chance of parole. The National Research Council released a 464-page report in 2014 detailing why these policies had been enacted: "Deeply held racial fears, anxieties and animosities likely explain the resonance of coded racial appeals concerning crime-related issues."[8]

The possibility of serious sentencing reform has remained distant, because prison contractors lobby legislators for tougher judgments, improving their revenue. According to the former director of the Oklahoma Department of Corrections, Justin Jones, "The bottom line is that private prisons' current business plans simply cannot coexist with meaningful evidence-based sentencing reform. If we want a fair and smart system, we have to cut these dangerous pushers [contractors] out of the deal entirely."[9] Without meaningful sentencing reform and removal of the commercial imperative, the United States will be left with around 160,000 people serving life sentences, some of whom are innocent and don't deserve to never again see freedom.[10]

Immigrants have faced similar problems. The 9/11 attacks heightened anxieties that an unknown threat must be contained. Steve Logan, CEO of Cornell Companies, an immigration detention business, told a Wall Street analyst in 2001 that these new circumstances were "positive for our business. The federal business is the best business for us. It's the most consistent business for us and the events of September 11 are increasing that level of business."[11]

Little has changed since, except that more people are in detention. Prisons for criminals and facilities for immigrants were separate, and yet the business logic behind them was the same. Ironically, despite the rhetoric of privatization advocates praising the wonders of the market, firms like CCA and Geo Group are leeching off government contracts.[12] In 2014, CCA was caught falsifying staff hours to boost its profits in Idaho. The company escaped with a minor fine.[13] It remains the country's largest private prison contractor.

The situation was so out of control that it constituted a national crisis. It is why the *New York Times* editorialized in 2014 that "the American experiment in mass incarceration has been a moral, legal, social, and economic disaster. It cannot end soon enough."[14] The paper urged states to find alternatives to prison, improve rehabilitation, and reduce sentences. Notably, there was no mention of the companies encouraging the maintenance, or even growth, of the prison population. CCA sent letters to forty-eight states in 2012 offering to buy their prisons—on the condition that the states guaranteed 90 percent occupancy and a twenty-year management contract.[15] Some states did deals with the Geo Group to ensure contractually that 100 percent of prison beds would be filled every night.

Some states, such as Georgia, even outsourced the killing of prisoners. After the execution of black man Troy Davis in 2011, the Southern Center for Human Rights filed a complaint against a company called CorrectHealth for the underhanded means it had used to obtain the drug used to kill him.[16]

Racism was central to an understanding of why Georgia was the state with the highest proportion of adults under correctional control in the nation. A 2014 report by the ACLU and other civil society groups proved that ICE had increased its arrest rate of immigrants between 2007 and 2013 by 953 percent. People of color were disproportionately targeted: in 2013, 96.4 percent of all detainees had a "dark or medium complexion."[17]

Profit-seeking companies were benefiting from this reality. Sadly, the problem went well beyond incarceration. For-profit corporations found a new way to make money in Georgia and beyond, privatizing misdemeanor probation—allowing a company representative to supervise people who were unable to pay minor fines. Jail was used as a threat to make vulnerable citizens pay up. Contractors stood accused of abusing their role by linking a probation officer's earnings to the collection of payments from those on her or his caseload.[18]

Human Rights Watch published a major report into this scam in 2014, showing that probationers were forced to pay companies for "supervision" services while their debts were settled.[19] It was a burgeoning industry that included private halfway-houses, pension funds, electronic tagging, and prohibitively expensive phone cards for detainees. Geo Group ran a range of such "community re-entry services."[20]

The outcome of these failed policies was clear. Louisiana had been the world's prison capital since 2012, with a higher incarceration rate than Iran or China (though by 2015 the number had slightly fallen due to sentencing reforms and a re-entry program for inmates). This was due to a rigged legal system in which sheriffs, judges, prosecutors, and politicians benefited, politically or financially, from close ties to private prison outfits. Facilities avoided having empty beds because sheriffs ran the entire enterprise for profit, then diverted the money to their law-enforcement section. Despite such high levels of imprisonment, or maybe because of it, the state was still one of the poorest in the nation.[21]

A landmark 2011 study by the Arizona Department of Corrections found little evidence that privatized prisons saved the state any money. In fact, statistics showed that private facilities appeared less expensive because they only housed the relatively healthy. "It's cherry-picking," said Arizona's state Democrat representative, Chad Campbell. "They leave the most expensive prisoners with taxpayers and take the easy prisoners."[22] This left an army of mentally ill inmates rotting away in state-run prisons that were often in worse shape than when they had arrived, according to a 2014 report by the Treatment Advocacy Center.[23] According to a 2012 study by the same organization, 356,000 mentally disturbed people were held in prisons nationwide, while only 35,000 were housed in psychiatric facilities.[24]

This is how it worked. The American Legislative Exchange Council (ALEC) was a body that brought together conservative legislators and the private sector to draft market-friendly policies around the country. In Arizona, ALEC routinely indulged politicians making decisions about immigration policy with parties and exclusive access to sports events—and yet the politicians only needed to disclose that they had attended an ALEC conference. Lobbying greased the wheels of a faltering democracy, handsomely filling re-election coffers.[25]

In recent years, Arizona's approach to immigrants has been one of the most repressive. In 2010, a law allowing police to stop and imprison people who could not show evidence they had entered the country legally was drafted by the private prison industry. CCA was involved, and its lobbyists donated funds to local politicians who co-sponsored the bill.[26] A 2011 report by the Justice Policy Institute (JPI) found concrete examples of CCA, Geo Group, and others directly financing politicians. CCA donated $1.9 million in political contributions between 2003 and 2012, according to the National Institute of Money in State Politics.[27] Paul Ashton, co-author of *Gaming the System*,[28] said that the JPI report showed that "private prison companies' interests lie in promoting their business through maintaining political relationships rather than saving taxpayer dollars and effectively ensuring public safety."[29] In 2013 CAA's revenue reached nearly $1.7 billion, with a profit of $300 million. All of this money had come from government contracts; it was a nice form of subsidized socialism, if you could get it.

It was not as if the companies hid their agenda. In 2010, CCA's annual report boldly stated that a "relaxation of enforcement efforts" would reduce "demand for our facilities and services." Geo Group's annual report in the same year expressed concern at the growing movement towards "decriminalization of drugs and controlled substances" and how it might "potentially reduce demand for correctional facilities."[30]

But making money from prisons remained an appealing option for venture capitalists. The Geo Group received millions of dollars from the Gates Foundation, founded by Bill and Melinda Gates, despite pressure from activists for them to withdraw their money because of company abuses. The foundation defended its actions. In 2014 its media spokesperson said: "We understand the passion of people standing up for injustice. That is what motivates us all at the foundation every day," going on to explain that the foundation was contributing billions of dollars to good causes around the world.[31]

A more humane system for prisoners and immigrants is bad for the bottom line and would be fought bitterly all the way. But this reflects an ideological position: an insistence on placing a price-tag on every aspect of life. The United States has exported this philosophy to the world with remarkable success. Failures at home—glaringly obvious if examined—are routinely ignored in the rush for "efficiency" and "cost-cutting." The harm caused to human lives is collateral damage.

The conference hall was huge and the atmosphere buzzing. Heavily made-up women and men in badly fitting suits stood around soliciting interest from the thousands of delegates. Hundreds of companies were exhibiting their products in Salt Lake City at the American Correctional Association (ACA) conference in 2014. With money to make, and wardens and sheriffs arriving from across America and internationally to source new products to deck out their public and private facilities, business was booming. The ACA was the world's largest and "oldest association developed specifically for practitioners in the correctional profession." The terror threat was hyped daily in the media, so a massive market existed to keep a sense of insecurity permanently afloat across the country.

Wandering around the exhibition hall, I saw a Homeland Security Evidence Collection Kit for $1,000, which included a range of objects, including tweezers, a tape measure, and a urine specimen jar—apparently the perfect accessory for police authorities in the post-9/11 environment.

While I was in Salt Lake City there were riots in Ferguson, Missouri, over the police killing of a young black man, Michael Brown. Television images showed a militarized police force looking as if they were equipped to face insurgents in Iraq. A Department of Defense program allowed the transfer of excess military equipment to local police forces. With massive budget hikes, local law enforcement increasingly claimed that it needed to prepare for war and terrorism. The streets of Missouri increasingly mirrored the war zones of Baghdad.

Avon Protection produced "respiratory protection system technology specializing primarily in military and law enforcement." It was exactly the kind of equipment worn by police in Ferguson. I asked its rep if such outfits were increasingly popular with law enforcement, and he said that they were, because the threat level had risen on the streets and in prisons.

This was why the annual Urban Shield conference, held across the country, was the country's biggest first-responder event, at which police forces purchased billions of dollars' worth of SWAT gear. At the 2014 event in Oakland, California, the Department of Homeland Security, together with corporations such as Verizon, Motorola, and Uber, participated enthusiastically in an industry that was experiencing phenomenal growth, assisted by the decades-long "war on drugs." Items on sale included advanced drones and a device designed by Shield Defence Systems that temporarily blinded a suspect, facilitating their apprehension. When *Mother Jones* reporter Shane Bauer asked an Urban Shield representative if the United States was becoming a police state, he replied: "I think there is some validity to that."[32]

There was a great deal of money to be made at the Salt Lake City event. With many prisons still being built in the country, "green technology" was used to reduce correctional costs—a mixed blessing. It was a positive step that sustainability was now a consideration in such facilities, but it could also be viewed as greenwashing. For example, the founder of Green Prison, George H. Berghorn, was friendly—"I'm politically slightly right of center, but not Tea Party crazy"—and committed to building new, sustainable prisons. I asked him whether he should consider constructing fewer prisons, rather than striving to make them more "green." He declined to engage in a political discussion.

Despite the number of companies turning a profit from the prison industry, the number of adults in some form of correctional arrangement has continued to fall marginally. Though it is not the impression you would get from the tabloid media, crime and incarceration rates have continued to decline. In 2013 the federal prison population fell by 4,800 inmates. Perhaps this was why prison contractors such as CCA and GEO Group were the only companies at the event unwilling to share much information with journalists—they were cautious about saying anything that might jeopardize their lucrative trade.

I saw products that remained unavailable anywhere else. Crossbar produced a plastic e-cigarette designed exclusively for prisoners. Executive Vice President Greg Crockett told me that neither he nor the product's inventor were smokers, but that in the eighteen months since its launch, interest in the product had been massive both domestically and globally—1 million units had been sold. Released inmates had asked to buy the product but had been told it was unavailable for retail. Tobacco possession was illegal in detention facilities, so Crossbar had designed a system that allowed prisoners to get their hit while enriching wardens with a legal kickback. One jail administrator in Kentucky said it had provided his prison with more than $7,000 in additional revenue every month.

Droneshield manufactured a device advertised to protect prisons from drones smuggling in contraband. Users received alerts by email or text message at a cost of $1,000 per service. An employee said that the company had also received interest from farmers, including in Australia, who wanted to protect themselves from animal rights activists using unmanned aerial vehicles to monitor cattle.

Avera eCare was a model providing prisons with tools to administer medical care to inmates, though the company's representative said that prisoners could still be taken to the hospital if necessary. The company's brochure stated: "The cost of an inmate transfer plus average emergency room charges can exceed $4,000." There were many similar companies at the conference claiming to assist prisons in providing healthcare, though it was hard not to conclude that they were motivated less by the priority of helping detainees than by saving funds for the state-run or private penal institution. Many firms offered services for prisons to treat sex offenders. These were expensive programs that would once have been provided by the state or not at all.

One of the effects of disaster capitalism is the reduction of even marginal state oversight, allowing officials to outsource services that were once under their control. I saw smartphone apps designed to give drug tests to "clients" on probation. The spokesperson from Eramnow said it was almost impossible for a participant to fake clear eyes—the technology assessed the redness of eyes to detect drug use—unless "you take eyedrops before looking at the camera." Not so foolproof, after all.

Washington State Correctional Industries used inmate labor to make clothes and furniture, and the "Programming Security

Chair" allowed prisoners to be chained to a seat. Its PR casually noted: "The offender is able to sit and work easily under full restraint." The company told me that a number of inmates could be in the seats, in a classroom setting or in solitary, completely incapacitated, "under full restraint." The man was proud of his company's work, though he acknowledged that the inmates received a pitifully small wage for their work. "It's all about the experience that they can then take with them when they're back in the outside world," he explained.

Grainger is one of the world's biggest providers of equipment for firemen, the military, and police forces. Its large catalog featured items ranging from spit masks to tactical vests. Josh Schofield, the company's government program manager in public safety, told me that the use of this equipment had massively increased in recent years, with SWAT teams becoming the normal tool for addressing many community policing issues that years ago had been managed in a less confrontational way. This cultural shift had provided a business opportunity.

Tex-Net used netting around a prison perimeter to prevent contraband entering the facility. Its rep, Annette Scarperia, said she was confident that it was nearly impossible for anyone to breach her firm's product, though she admitted that the use of drones complicated matters; another company would have to tackle that problem, she explained.

PPSS build the "world's toughest cell extraction vest." The vest was worn by a stout English employee who had previously worked in the British army and in a prison in the north of England that had been closed down. Hammers and nails lay nearby to test the strength of the vest. "Nothing gets through it," he proudly declared, "including needles." I picked up a nail and tried to pierce the vest, without success. According to the PR, the vest was designed to protect officers from some of the "most hostile, brutal, vicious, and irrational human beings on the planet."

The event was held in a large conference center on a humid

August day in the heart of Salt Lake City—the capital of
Mormonism, surrounded by mountains. Many of the participants
were overweight, though it was not clear whether this was a function of the national trend or of the industry they were in. Smiling
and friendly, they all appeared to enjoy their jobs and were proud
to share their ideas about the corrections business.

They were predominantly male and included whites, Hispanics,
and African-Americans. These were the wardens, prison contractors, sheriffs' department employees, spin-doctors, and armies
of consultants and auditors from prisons in the US and around
the world. Many expressed a desire to improve conditions for
detainees, and it would obviously have been glib to imagine that
the thousands of participants were all sadists; but there was little
serious questioning of the harsh, punitive ideology underpinning
US "justice."

In session after session, speakers outlined their vision for dealing
with potential suicides, bad media coverage, and healthcare. My
journalist colleague Shane Bauer—we saw no other media in
attendance—had visited the preceding conference, held in a different city. After I left, he was thrown out by the ACA in Salt Lake
City for allegedly failing to disclose that he was a reporter, though
I had never seen him conceal the fact. Bizarrely, a photograph of
Bauer appeared in the next edition of the ACA magazine, as a participant. He said he had met a number of people in the industry
who professed a desire to liberalize the ways in which individuals
were incarcerated, and that some had succeeded in making minor
changes. But the dominant imperative remained punishment for
profit. I heard a lot of hardline Republican-type talk in Salt Lake
City, voices critical of minorities, with little sympathy expressed
for inmates.

Bauer knew all about the emotional turmoil of being behind
bars, having been imprisoned for twenty-six months in Iran after
he, his wife, and a friend had accidently hiked into Iranian territory from Iraq, in 2009. On his return home, he investigated

solitary confinement in US prisons and found that conditions there were more isolating and brutal than what he had experienced in Tehran's Evin prison. When Washington last released data on prisoners held in solitary confinement, in 2005, the figure stood at 80,000. Many had been isolated, with little prospect of release, for crimes such as reading left-wing books and black literature.[33] California officials had cited the possession of such material as evidence of gang affiliation and thus determined that solitary confinement was appropriate. In South Carolina, prison officials send inmates caught using Facebook to isolation for years.

Children under eighteen continue to be subjected to solitary confinement in many US states. Figures for 2011 released by the Department of Justice revealed that, of the 61,423 minors in youth detention, one in five were in isolation—while 95,000 more juveniles were held in adult prisons. Studies have demonstrated the profound mental and physical torture of this experience—inflicted in both public and private institutions.[34]

The ACA did not speak of such things, preferring to present itself as an enlightened, reforming organization. During a meeting of the ACA Committee on International Corrections, they expressed pride at having established a scholarship program for poor people in developing nations who wanted to attend the next ACA conference in California—one way, perhaps, to soften the image of the prison business in the eyes of the general public.

I attended one session on the lessons that could be drawn from the experience of Scandinavian prisons. Jim Conway, a retired superintendent from the infamous Attica Correctional Facility in New York—where at least forty-three people died during an uprising in 1971—had toured the region's jails, none of which were privatized. He was amazed at the conditions for prisoners, the number of guards employed, the well-appointed kitchens, and the use of solar energy.

But Conway was not sold. Nordic nations had a "focus on inmate privacy. In the US the right to privacy was gone. Society is supposed to be normal, not prison. Privacy is a right you gave up when you came in. They put people in solitary for no longer than one week to ten days. In the US we don't think twice about putting someone away for one year." A male member of the audience shared Conway's skepticism. "It's a different culture over there," he said. "It's an open-border system, so anybody who arrives gets benefits and assistance."

Another session featured two doctors employed by the private operator Corizon, which turned a profit from inmate health-care. They both argued that their company was doing a "great job" reducing the rate of suicide inside jails, though it remained stubbornly high—one of the leading causes of inmate deaths, responsible for more fatalities than drugs, alcohol, or homicide. A man named Frank Smart died in a jail in Pennsylvania in 2015, and his mother accused Corizon healthcare staff inside the facility of not giving her son his required medication. Smart suffered from seizures and had not yet been found guilty of any crime. Corizon obtained the contract at the Allegheny County Jail after promising to cut healthcare costs for $1 million.

One of the final events was an insightful guide to media man-agement. Karla West, director of communications at Davidson County's sheriff's office in Nashville, Tennessee, was a bubbly presenter. She urged wardens and sheriffs to be honest and not to duck journalists' questions. "When we contract out prisons to CCA, it's important that we as a sheriff's department have the same talking points as the private contractor," she explained. "Sometimes a media story appears that shows we haven't coor-dinated our message." West suggested prison contractors use "PR words to soften meaning of actions." I had observed this trend in the immigration debates in Britain and Australia. For example, "restricted housing" means solitary confinement. The term "Shu," popularized on the TV show *Orange Is the New Black*, stands for "Security Housing Unit"—in other words, complete isolation.

In the evening, I attended a party with Shane Bauer organized by GTL, a provider of communication and technology to prisons. At a venue called the Green Pig Pub, near the center of town, we congregated on a rooftop bar overlooking the mountains as the sun was setting. Filled with mostly white men with substantial bellies, the bar offered free tacos and alcohol to lubricate the conversation—courtesy of GTL.

Those in attendance were friendly, and many of those in company uniforms were keen to chat and relax. Greg worked for GTL and had been in the communication business for prisons for eighteen years. He loved his job, as he was keen on technology and reveled in the chance to promote it. "This industry hasn't changed for over 100 years," he told me; it was run "by men who didn't see any need to do so. But new technology is forcing these shifts, and my generation is at the forefront of it."

Scott worked for the British company Call Sense. With only seven staff in America, it was a small operation with good growth prospects. It sold a metal detector that was highly sought after in prisons for finding mobile phones, knives, and guns. Scott told me that he had previously worked in stem-cell research but was attracted to a business that allowed him to travel. He loves "the corrections business because it was friendly and helped people."

It was a revealing evening, where individuals in profitable businesses socialized and talked shop. Everyone I spoke to said that they attended every ACA conference, always twice a year in two different cities, to share ideas and meet colleagues with whom they sometimes competed in the market. These men (and some women) had jobs, and they did not question the ethics of the business model under which they operated. This did not make them immoral, just happy to work in an industry that had not existed a few decades before but now operated seamlessly with the cooperation of countless sheriff's departments across the country. The self-perpetuating business model—with increased political lobbying leading to growing demand—ignored the wider social cost of warehousing millions of Americans.

On the last day of the conference, I took an ACA-organized tour of Utah's oldest prison, the Wasatch County Jail. It housed murderers, rapists, and fraudsters. The setting of the center was spectacular, with soaring mountains on the horizon, though the facility's buildings were mostly old and forbidding.

Wasatch was a public prison but was nevertheless governed by the profit motive. Utah Correctional Industries (UCI) was based here—a business employing prisoners at low wages to produce furniture, printing services, and license plates for the people of Utah. Its stated aim was to teach prisoners the vital skills they would need upon release, but the labor overseen in the prison had more to do with profit than rehabilitation. I asked whether labor costs had to be so low but was told that detainees were pleased to be kept busy.

I was shown the various UCI workshops, which included sophisticated printing presses and facilities producing large and small furniture. The factories were large warehouses that had a peaceful atmosphere. I saw no guards around the prisoners, though a number followed our visiting group. I was told that only well-behaved inmates were allowed to work and train with UCI. The men were paid a pittance—from forty-five cents an hour to a few dollars, but mostly under $1. This was akin to slave labor.

The Stewart immigration detention center was situated on the outskirts of Lumpkin, Georgia—a ghost town every day of the week. Visitors and detainees arriving at the nearly 2,000-bed center were greeted by a huge painted sign on an outside water tank: "CCA: America's Leader in Partnership Corrections." It was one of the largest privatized immigration facilities in the country.

My tour of the center took in everything except the isolation ward. I was allowed to take my camera, a notepad, and a pen, but no mobile phone. My possessions were X-rayed by the

African-American female staff, and my sunglasses and phone placed in a locker. Five men followed me everywhere: one from CCA, the center operator, and the rest from ICE. This entourage looked and felt like overkill. They were jumpy the entire time, worried about my questions, concerned something unexpected might happen, and nervous that I might see something that could embarrass them. Down a long hallway, lit brightly with neon lights and smelling of paint and detergent, lines of inmates walked past me—some smiling, some waving, and some looking forlorn.

Barack Obama has been dubbed the "Deporter in Chief" for the record number of detainees his administration has forcibly removed from the country. The Migration Policy Institute (MPI) issued a 2014 report noting that, in his first five years in power, Obama deported over 1.9 million people—nearly as many as the Bush administration had deported in its two terms in office (2 million). Although Obama introduced important prosecutorial discretion to manage the enforcement program, and 2014 saw a slight drop in deportations, MPI argued that "more humane enforcement is fundamentally in tension with stricter immigration control," and that "a more robust enforcement system inevitably inflicts damage on established families and communities."[35]

The *New York Times* found that two-thirds of Obama's deportees had committed minor infractions, such as traffic violations, or no crime at all.[36] Those suffering the most from expulsion were Guatemalans, Hondurans, and Salvadorans who were in the US unlawfully; these three countries comprised roughly 29 percent of ICE federal removals. In 2014 alone, around 90,000 children arrived at the US border fleeing poverty and the US-fueled drug war in Central America. The southern border had thus become a militarized space, where corporations, including arms manufacturers Raytheon, Lockheed Martin, and Boeing, as well as the leading Israeli arms company Elbit Systems, earned billions of dollars trying to keep immigrants out.[37]

The average inmate stay at Stewart was thirty-eight days—far less than most prison sentences—so it was virtually impossible for detainees to establish any sense of routine. While it was positive that long-term detention was largely avoided (unlike for asylum seekers in Britain, Greece, and Australia), inmates were often moved from one facility to another, while others were deported back to their country of origin in a process that lacked transparency; they were just numbers to be processed, bodies to be moved elsewhere.

On the day I visited Stewart, 1,766 detainees were behind bars—the vast majority from El Salvador, Honduras, Mexico, and Guatemala, though sixty other countries were represented, including Bangladesh, China, Nicaragua, Peru, and Somalia. Many inmates lived in large, barred pods, with a maximum occupancy of sixty-two. Others stayed in smaller rooms, or in the segregation unit. I spotted a few female CCA staff inside the pods with male inmates. A sign next to one of the rooms read: "Upon Entering Detainee Pod All CCA Female Staff Will Announce Female in POD."

Another pod had its lights dimmed because the inmates had started working in the kitchen at 5 a.m. and were now resting. CCA paid $4 per day for inmates to perform kitchen duties, and less for other jobs (barbers receive $2, for example). ICE proudly told me that the law only mandated that the state pay $1 per day, so CCA was doing a fine job. These were slave wages, justified simply because inmates had so little political power to demand more. Meanwhile, prison corporations advertised inmate labor, sold at knock-down rates to Fortune 500 companies such as IBM and Bank of America.[38]

Men in a different, brightly lit pod were lying on their bunk beds under blankets and sheets. A microwave, cable TV, sink, Playstation, and Wii were inside. One man was wearing headphones to listen to the TV in front of him. Basins and toilets were behind a curtain. Metal tables and seats were fixed to the floor.

"I'm not saying it's like the Hilton here," an ICE manager told me—though he explained he was proud of what his center offered. Signs in English and Spanish read: "Keep Detention Safe: ICE has zero tolerance for sexual abuse and assault."

A notice listed a phone number for inmates to call if they needed assistance, but activists claimed this was little more than window-dressing in a system that aimed to penalize immigrants. Telephones were available for inmates to call lawyers, embassies, and friends, though the cost was exorbitant because of price-gouging by companies selling phone cards to detainees. It was a massively profitable business—just one of many markets to be exploited within America's incarceration system. It was common for local sheriff's departments to make money from these costly phone calls, a commission that cost inmates dearly. It cost roughly $15 for prisoners to buy less than thirteen minutes of talk time.

During the tour, ICE or CCA employees—I couldn't tell which—suddenly appeared, said a few words about the center, then disappeared. I asked one how inmates received a free haircut, and he said that he gave priority to detainees who were keen to clean up before a court appearance. There were no hair or beard restrictions, and an ICE manager said that some Jamaican men had long dreadlocks, and that was just fine.

The library was stocked with countless Bibles and romance novels. Detainees played soccer and basketball, both inside and outside, under the bright blue sky. They had two hours each day to enjoy the outdoors. "We try to keep them busy," one ICE manager told me, "because we know if they're not doing anything there will be trouble." Men sat around in their variously colored clothes: blue meant no security risk, while orange signified slightly higher risk; red uniforms were not in view, as they were worn in a different section.

In the medical center, I saw an inmate in an orange jumpsuit and orange Crocs hooked up to a drip. The medical officer refused to tell me about his condition. I wondered if it was sickness, or suicide risk. As soon as I saw him, we were moved on.

Stewart was waiting for a full-time physician. Two full-time dentists and sixty-two medical staff were employed. The medic said it was hard to recruit staff because the center was so remote. Antidepressants were sometimes prescribed to detainees, because people coming from prisons into immigration detention suffered increased mental health issues. The state deliberately placed these facilities in remote areas where poor health and conditions were inevitable. In one of the hallways hung a picture of a man ascending an icy mountain, with the message: "You can't finish what you don't start." Whether this Oprah-esque messaging was designed for the inmates or guards was unclear.

I was told that the food hall, or "chow line," provided three meals a day, planned by a dietitian. I saw hundreds of men lining up in a queue to be served. Men sat at tables with trays in front of them; I observed some men praying before eating. On the tray were brown bread, macaroni and cheese, carrots, celery, salad, and a small sweet cake. Everyone received the same meal, except if they wanted a special or religious meal, and ICE managers said that Muslim, Jewish, and Buddhist inmates were catered for on request.

In June 2014 many inmates participated in a protest about the food, including a hunger strike, complaining that it contained maggots. ICE told me that this was false, and that in fact what had been thought to be maggots were a type of bean sprout that looked remarkably like maggots. It was impossible to determine the accuracy of the ICE allegations, but I heard similar criticisms from immigration activists in Georgia. A handful of major corporations, including Aramark, produces and sells food to prisons and detention centers across the country. There were constant reports from detainees of sickness and hunger.[39]

A daily medical examination included checks for tuberculosis, and ICE said that heart and eye conditions were regularly improved in detention, as many detainees had not seen a doctor for a long time, if ever. "Great medical care here," the ICE manager said proudly. "We're fixing them when they came in broke." But this was a highly contested view. The reality of privatized detention is one of services cut to the bone, offering the barest minimum of care. Detention Watch Network issued a report in 2013 that examined 250 facilities across the country, many of which were run for profit, and found that none of them could guarantee basic medical care or appropriate protection against sexual and physical abuse. A lack of official oversight exacerbated the problem, along with the 1996 Illegal Immigration Reform and Immigrant Responsibility Act, which allowed inmates to be punished for minor crimes as if they were serious felonies.[40] Punishment, not rehabilitation, remained the corporate and governmental focus, as it was more profitable. CCA refused a simple proposal in 2015 from former prisoner and associate director of the Human Rights Defense Center, Alex Friedmann, for the company to commit an additional 5 percent of its net income to reducing recidivism.[41] Public opposition to these companies was growing; the Interfaith Prison Coalition launched a campaign in 2015 to boycott and divest from firms that made profit from prison labor and charged exorbitant prices for prisoner phone calls.

The system was rigged to benefit companies like CCA. There are more examples than can be cited here to demonstrate the company's unwillingness to enforce the barest standard of care, while the falsification of records was not uncommon.[42] ICE and the Department of Homeland Security regularly refused to investigate persistent breaches, so cases went unpunished involving female prisoners giving birth prematurely because CCA guards had ignored their cries for help, and incorrect medication being given to inmates, causing sickness and death. In one instance in a long list of abuses, forty-five-year-old Pamela Weatherby died in 2010 from diabetes-related complications because CCA staff at the Dawson state jail in Texas had given her cheap insulin instead of her prescribed medication. Her family sued CCA for neglect. Understaffing, combined with poor training, had been the cause of such tragedies, which had too rarely prevented firms like CCA from getting more work.

The reality of privatized detention revealed itself in the smallest of details. CCA used to provide tennis shoes for inmates at Stewart, but they now bought them Crocs instead, because this saved money. CCA explained that it was easier to just hose down the Crocs when they were dirty. Water for showers was sometimes rationed to save money, and I heard allegations that water had been switched off at Stewart, though this was denied by ICE and CCA. CCA did not allow visitors to touch detainees in a meeting room at Stewart, because guards would need to be trained in managing these personal interactions. More training meant increased costs for CCA. In some other CCA facilities direct contact occurred. In some, the glass window in the visiting room was removed. Activists continually pushed for the rules to be loosened.

At Stewart, I passed a guard staring into a darkened cell. He looked through a small window at a seated inmate who was focused straight ahead, with his eyes wide open. He was not handcuffed but sat perfectly still in a flame-retardant suicide smock, resembling a straitjacket. It was not clear what he might have used to set himself alight when locked in a cell on his own, with a guard watching him like a hawk. The medical officer said that suicide watch was not always necessary, but that, with the high rate of removals from Stewart, a detainee's state of mind was often fragile.

Another door led to the center's own court, where claims by immigrants wishing to remain in the country were assessed. The courts were under the executive, not the judicial, branch of government, and serious questions existed over its lack of transparency for lawyers, activists, and detainees. Many decisions were not even written down, hearings were secretive, and access to lawyers was sporadic. Almost every immigrant brought before the court was issued with a deportation order. Competent legal representation was rare, and many immigrants appeared before the court without any knowledge of their legal rights. The local town of Lumpkin boasted only one lawyer. Eighteen out of fifty-eight immigration courts in the US were housed within immigration detention centers. The public, it seemed, was barely interested—let alone involved—in proceedings.[43]

Unlike the US prison population, among whom drug and alcohol abuse were common, ICE told me that these problems did not exist at Stewart. Throughout the visit I never witnessed any abuse, violence, or racism. My hosts were friendly and attentive, and dismissed inmates' numerous claims of assault and degradation. Solitary confinement was still used against many immigrants, and at least two people had died while housed in Stewart, including Roberto Martinez Medina, in 2009, from over a treatable heart condition.

Solitary confinement was rampant. Across the country, there were thirteen Criminal Alien Requirement (CAR) prisons, run for profit, that housed around 25,000 inmates without legal documentation to be in the United States. The conditions were often appalling—prisoners lived in cramped and putrid conditions, and there was even an "isolation cell" quota, according to which facility managers were incentivized to send inmates to solitary confinement for complaining about poor food or medical care.[44] Following an investigation that lasted several years, the ACLU discovered that immigrants in these for-profit centers suffered from overcrowding as well as poor access to education and rehabilitation. One facility in Willacy County, Texas, consisted of tents in the searing heat, which suffered from insect infestation. The contract to run it was awarded in 2006 to a Utah-based company, Management and Training Corp, in a no-bid contract for $65 million. Suspicions of corruption among county officials hung over the process that had delivered the contract.[45] One of the terms of the deal guaranteed a minimum payment of $45 million based on a 90 percent capacity rate—even if the prison stood empty. In 2015, inmates protested poor conditions and set fire to the facility, destroying much of it. It was shut down and prisoners were transferred elsewhere. Willacy County, despite being promised riches from the contractor for the center, faced financial uncertainty.

Gaining access to Stewart was a curious process. Like most detention centers in the world, it was closed to the public except for brief detainee visits. With a private company running the facility and the government reluctant to allow journalists inside, accountability was low. I contacted ICE months before arriving to assess the viability of obtaining entry. For a freelance journalist this was an almost impossible task, so I used my status as a *Guardian* columnist to begin the process. Both CCA and ICE claimed that the facility was not run like a private prison, but in reality it operated like one.

On the day of my Stewart visit I met the ICE representative, Vinnie, at Peachtree City, one hour from Atlanta. It was a city with armies of golf carts, which minors were allowed to drive around town. Vinnie was my host for the day, and he drove us in his SUV for two hours to Lumpkin. He had worked in PR for all of his professional life, from the US military in Kuwait to the US National Park Service. He was skeptical of foreign military interventions, was a supporter of journalist Glenn Greenwald and former NSA whistle-blower Edward Snowden, and said that the immigration system needed urgent reform. He was not the typical representative of a hardline government department known for brutally expelling immigrants.

Vinnie said that the Stewart center had provided essential economic opportunities in Lumpkin, an undeveloped town. The detention center parking lot was filled with vehicles when we arrived. Vinnie parked in the section designated for ICE staff, and nearby was a padlocked enclosure where visiting law-enforcement officers left their weapons upon entry.

During my tour I was unable to speak to any detainees, who looked at me with confusion, humor, and blank stares. A local group assisting immigrants, El Refugio, gave me the name and number of an inmate willing to see me, so at the end of the visit I was taken into a small visiting room with white walls. A glass window divided the space.

A man in an orange jumpsuit appeared, displaying a slight smile. His name was Linden Headley, a fifty-two-year-old black man with a gray beard and dreadlocked hair. Born in Georgetown, Guyana, he had been in the United States since 1975 and spoke with an American accent. He told me that he was happy to share his details and that I could publish anything I wanted. There was a small black block at the bottom of the window between us that could be removed to exchange documents. This was the room where lawyers consulted with their clients, and during our meeting Headley passed me a number of files, which I photographed.

Headley had been charged with a number of drug offenses and told me that he feared deportation back to Guyana, which he had not seen in decades. After serving with the US military in Lebanon and Japan in the 1980s, he had worked in various jobs, despite having PTSD. He had many children with different women. Although he was a lawful permanent resident, ICE claimed he had repeatedly violated the terms of his residency and should be deported because he had never become a full US citizen.

"I've been inside Stewart for three months," he told me. "Life is miserable. I'm a vegan, and every meal every day is beans, rice, and starch. ICE is trying to get me deported to Georgetown, where I haven't been for four decades. My pro-bono lawyer, recommended by a fellow inmate, keeps telling me that I'll be deported because most people here are."

Headley said that if he was released, he would work as a carpenter or construction worker, marry his girlfriend, and move on peacefully with his life. ICE gave me information that claimed Headley was a danger to society, including countless claims of drug possession and dealing. He claimed he had only been caught up with marijuana.

"I'm scared of returning to Guyana because of violence there," he said. The large file he had brought to show me included the 2013 State Department Human Rights Report and CIA World Factbook on Guyana, and they both listed abuses, police brutality, and corruption.

It was impossible to assess the validity of Headley's story. He spoke calmly about his situation and clearly wanted to convey his desperate situation. Insisting that I talk to him through glass seemed unnecessarily draconian, as he was not a convicted killer, or even dangerous. Remarkably, after his ICE hearing in September 2014, Headley was released into the community, his arguments having been accepted. It was a rare case of leniency by a system that aimed to deport individuals at a steadily increasing rate. The Stewart court had a 96 percent rate of deportation.

Nonetheless, Stewart would be trumped by the nation's largest immigration facility, run by CCA, opening in 2015 in a small town in Dilley, Texas, and set to house 2,400 women and children. Inmates imprisoned there faced at least a twelve-month wait for their asylum hearings. The vast majority would not have legal representation, though evidence proved that finding a lawyer would hugely increase the chances of refugees receiving asylum. *Democracy Now!* visited the family detention center in Dilley and found town residents were being sold on economic security and jobs, while imprisoned detainees told of being separated from their children in prison-like conditions.

For Dilley, CCA advertised a range of amenities, such as spacious classrooms, play areas, and lounges. But the management contract for Dilley was problematic, with Obama officials rushing to seal the deal and establishing the facility under conditions set for a CCA prison in Eloy, one thousand miles from Dilley. Eloy officials stated that they had no intention of visiting or monitoring Dilley.[46]

During Obama's two terms in office, his administration continued to outsource more facilities to CCA and other corporations that ignored federal laws and abused human rights. Alex Friedmann, an activist investor and former prisoner who held CCA shares, told CNN: "Investors see this as an opportunity [the government imprisoning migrants]. This is a potentially untapped market that will have strong demand."[47] Disaster capitalism was the winner. Silky Shah, co-director of the Detention Watch Network, slammed the Obama administration's decision to expand privatized facilities, arguing that "family detention is an abusive and inhumane practice that erodes family bonds and undermines children's wellbeing."[48]

Out in Lumpkin, the roads were empty. The shops on Main Street were mostly empty, paint peeling on their window-panes. A taxidermy outlet was one of the few open businesses. The town, in one of the country's poorest counties, was all but unknown to most Americans. Its population barely broke 1,000. A barbecue was being dismantled near the police station. A large African-American woman told me that it was never busy in Lumpkin, and she liked it that way.

I met a man in his twenties, either high or drunk, who was hanging out at a petrol station with his friends. He had a tattoo on his bare chest: "Me Against The World." He told me he had been visiting Miami. "It's so much better there," he said. He had only been there for a short visit.

The town's dwindling youth population was leaving for greener pastures in bigger cities nearby. CCA started building Stewart in 2004 and sold the idea to ICE and the local community years later as both an economic benefit for local residents and a deterrent in a state traditionally hostile to immigrants. As a result, CCA's share price had soared for years. Although the company's financial results were strong, the benefits never arrived in Lumpkin. Many staff members did not live in the town but commuted from other cities. Lumpkin reminded me of crumbling towns next to other detention facilities I had seen in Australia, Britain, and Greece.

The same failed promises from the same companies and state authorities had been made in those nations, too. The economic promise of a local detention center usually turned out to be a lie.

Even in the detention center itself, CCA's own employees struggled financially to make ends meet. I met one guard who was selling potato chips, bottled water, and chocolates to raise money from staff to support struggling CCA employees around the country. Although it was admirable that people wanted to help, it was revealing that the company, rather than raising wages, facilitated the sale of junk food to help poor staff. In tough circumstances this kind of charity was all that people had. In Lumpkin, a small, Christian-run volunteer group, El Refugio, supported the visitors and families of detainees coming to town. Open since 2010, it operated a basic weatherboard house over the weekends very close to Stewart, providing free meals, accommodation, and donated clothes and shoes. This kind of humanity was sorely missing from much of the immigration debate in the United States, which was generally defined by toxic rhetoric from Republicans and timidity from Democrats.

I visited El Refugio and talked to the volunteers who donated their time. Founder Katie Beno Valencia told me that almost all of the participants were church-goers. Maggie, a large and friendly woman who lived near Atlanta, said she was outraged at not being allowed to touch detainees physically: "It shouldn't be like this in America. These people should have more freedom."

Resistance to Stewart was growing. On November 22, 2014, the largest-ever protest occurred outside its entrance. Nearly a thousand activists converged in Lumpkin and marched to the facility. Five activists were arrested and charged for nonviolent civil disobedience. At the event, Georgia Detention Watch coalition founder Anton Flores declared: "the depth of a loving society is going to be marked by how quickly we can close these facilities down."

*   *   *

"It's a racist mindset, like white supremacy." In Georgia, Adelina Nicholls, executive director of Georgia Latino Alliance for Human Rights (GLAHR), had a low opinion of the mentality within the immigration detention industry. GLAHR was one of the leading immigrant activist groups in the state. "It's more profitable to behave this way when immigrants are treated like second-class citizens. Criminals have more rights. Migrants have no access to lawyers, and if they do they're often acting like mass-produced tortillas," barely caring about their clients.

The group's office was in an industrial park on the outskirts of Atlanta and was filled with Spanish newspapers and signs declaring: "Not One More! Stop Deportations!" On the wall and floor was artwork used at public actions and protests. "We now have only one generation of Latinos here—it's a new community," Nicholls said. "There are now around 1 million Latinos in Georgia." Nicholls spoke with passion and energy, and justifiable anger—especially with President Obama, despite having voted for him twice. She had been in America since 1996, when she married a resident. She explained how GLAHR had started in 1999, doing outreach work in Georgia. It launched a campaign for Latino workers because 90 percent of them arrived undocumented.

"Many live in the shadows due to the fear of being caught," she said. "Many are processed for deportation, and it's a three- to four-day process when people are put in detention. We put pressure on the police to not hold people for more than forty-eight hours. We have a campaign, the 'Georgia Not One More' coalition, aimed to educate 150 county sheriffs and change their policies."

Nicholls painted a grim picture of institutional racism against the Latino community. "Our community is afraid to confront police because officials blame-shift. We receive 600 calls a month on our hotline, and it's Latinos asking for help because it's hard getting effective pro-bono lawyers." Nicholls offered a convincing narrative around America's predicament and the poor who suffered under Washington's dictates: "US immigration is based on supply and demand. Drugs and crimes are destroying the Latino countries. [The North American Free Trade Agreement] has devastated local communities and the Mexican corn industry. The US doesn't care about bad trade deals for Latino farmers."

A key source of immigrants was Honduras—a country that suffered a US-supported coup in 2009 and now held the dubious status of being one of the murder capitals of the world. Tens of thousands of unaccompanied children were surging across the US border to escape a Washington-backed dictatorship.[49]

Nicholls continued: "We need to go to the root of the problem. The US doesn't want to resolve immigration because here people often care more about hunger in Ethiopia than poor Guatemalans in the US. If you cross our US border they will care, but Americans believe they can take our oil, gas, resources, food, and people. The perception in the US of immigrants depends if you arrive by plane or cross a border by foot. It's about class."

The Stewart detention center was a major point of contention. Nicholls told me: "It hurts us deeply. Many detainees inside have been in the US for years, and they ask, Why are gringos doing this to us? We're treated unfairly. These workers have been here for years in farms and restaurants. Anger is growing, along with desperation. We are trying to mobilize resistance and civil disobedience."

It was the lack of transparency inside privatized detention facilities that grated the most: "As [it is] run by CCA, the state, and ICE, it's hard to know in Stewart how to get answers. It's like a game, and we regularly see breaches of the Fourth Amendment of the Constitution [the prohibition of illegal searches and seizures]. Many sheriffs haven't even reviewed ICE rules." The number of detentions was soaring, with bail often set at $20,000. "This is an insult to the immigrant community at large. There's too much bureaucracy to get inside Stewart. With around 1,800 detainees and only six booths for visiting people, many inside have never been in jail and are there for minor traffic violations. The ICE office has super, God-like powers."

Nicholls explained that the demonization of the Latino minority was one of the reasons why so many Americans supported locking them away in privatized prisons and detention centers. It was a case in which racial bigotry aligned neatly with the profit imperative.

There was surely no better example of this omnipotence than a little-known 2007 Congress-approved law compelling 34,000 immigrants to be imprisoned by ICE every night across America while the government resolved their status. It was designed to send a strongly deterrent signal, but resulted in many innocent people being rounded up and placed in beds at an annual cost of $2.8 billion. The process was so corrupt that ICE lawyers were complicit: higher levels of government funding depended on hitting a target. Private detention operators made serious money from this arrangement. The *New York Times* slammed the quota in 2014: at a time when millions of Americans "can't find work and have lost their unemployment benefits ... there is no shortage of money when it comes to hunting down unauthorized immigrants."[50]

The reality of the "bed mandate" was a boon for disaster capitalism. Lobbying by for-profit companies ensured that the country's privately run facilities were filled with foreign-born, legal US residents convicted of mostly minor crimes who could be deported at any time. This dragnet did nothing to ensure public safety, but instead satisfied a Republican House that embraced punishment as a response to tepid immigration reform.

Azadeh Shahshahani, ACLU Georgia's former national security and immigrants' rights project director and president of the National Lawyers' Guild, was one of many calling loudly for this inhumane and arbitrary law to be axed. She told me at her Atlanta office: "The bed quota is tied to corporate profit to ensure 34,000 immigrants are in beds every night. There's no law enforcement evidence it does any help." Shahshahani was a tireless campaigner for immigrant rights and opposed privatized provision. Born in Iran, she arrived in the United States in 1994 and said she could relate to the immigrant experience more easily because of her background.

It was this spirit that infused a 2012 ACLU Georgia report on "Prisoners of Profit," which showed how ICE officials and immigration judges routinely forced detainees to sign removal orders that they did not understand.[51] The ideology behind outsourced incarceration was Shahshahani's target, and she was proud that CCA disliked the ACLU for its tireless work. Changing the minds of Georgia's politicians, "keen to be effective in their anti-immigrant rhetoric and laws when the state has tried virtually all anti-immigrant legislation," represented a significant challenge. "CCA says it brings economic development to towns, but these are myths," Shahshahani said. "In Stewart and Irwin County [the location of another detention center in Georgia], the contractor tries to convince the local community of the benefits of a detention center, that they'll bring jobs, but it's a con and the community discovers when it's too late. CCA is exploiting the insecurities of poor communities. Stewart and Irwin should be closed down. The privatizing trend can be reversed if we stop incentivizing imprisonment."

Silky Shah, co-director of Detention Watch Network (DWN), a nationwide coalition dedicated to humanizing the immigration system, explained to me in New York that the business of mass incarceration was not the only challenge: "Ankle monitoring is now big. [One company providing it], Behavioral International, [has been] bought by Geo Group. The fear is that reduced detention will lead to greater surveillance of immigrants via monitoring."

DWN started in 1996, when mandatory detention was expanded radically in relation to misdemeanors. Deportations accelerated, in response to which DWN campaigned to eliminate the 34,000-bed quota and all detention facilities. "The companies build facilities on spec, like Stewart," Shah told me. "They lobby Congress. The

US environment is so skewed post 9/11 and since Barack Obama's election as the first black president there's been a space opened up for the right wing to exploit fears."

Shah's principled position reminded me of refugee activists in Britain and Australia who never accepted a partial solution: "I do not believe people should be deported. Deportation causes trauma. At the moment the burden is on the detainee to prove why they should stay, but the burden should be on the government to justify expulsion. They should assess if the immigrant has community support."

Private prison and immigration contractors play a major role in maintaining the culture of mass incarceration in the United States. People of color are disproportionately represented in facilities across the country. CCA and Geo Group have spent decades successfully lobbying states to guarantee "occupancy quotas" and contracts whereby taxpayers are penalized when not enough beds are filled. The human rights conditions entail the gratuitous infliction of suffering on millions of men and women.

But times are slowly changing. Federal prison populations are slowly shrinking. Kentucky took a major step in 2014 by not renewing a contract with CCA for its facility in Marion County, saving money and sending prisoners to state-run centers after changes in policy reduced jail time for nonviolent drug offenses. There is now serious talk of public campaigns to divest from private prison firms such as CCA and Geo, and pressure is being placed on politicians like Democrat Chuck Schumer and Republican Marco Rubio to stop receiving electoral funding and investment from these and similar firms.

What I saw in America offered a small window onto a problem too vast to imagine. Many of the worst facilities never admit journalists or members of the public. They are hidden, operating in big cities and small towns without scrutiny, yet they comfortably align with Washington's self-image as protector of the world's weak and dispossessed. In reality, only a select few are welcome. The lobby-ists who sustain the Fear Inc. industry know that without strong government support, their business model would collapse. This is capitalism underwritten by socialist principles.

The business imperative of contractually guaranteeing a fixed number of beds in a prison or detention center has created a permanent, invisible, and tightly controlled underclass. African-Americans, Latinos, foreigners, immigrants, and "terrorists" challenge America's conception of itself as a global superpower that welcomes the stranger. Millions of men, women, and children become like processed meat in a grinder. Short of systemic cultural and political change, Fortress America is set to expand.

6

The United Kingdom: "It's the outsourcing of violence"

I am very passionate about our values and building this company not to make a profit. If profit is an immediate byproduct, then that's wonderful. If you can make it have an impact on society, people's lives and make it fun, crumbs, then we don't have to worry about making this profit or that. It happens naturally.
Former Serco chief executive Christopher Hyman, 2006

I was driven to a poor suburb to the north of Sheffield, in South Yorkshire. Children and parents played in the street. The houses looked shabby, some painted various shades of red, with boarded-up windows. I arrived with local activists at a nondescript property. Michael, who was from Cameroon, opened the door and welcomed us warmly in fluent English.

The house was managed by British multinational G4S. It was a damp-smelling, three-story building with steep stairs. Though the tenants received little money from the state and were not legally allowed to work, they had to buy cleaning products and other essentials for themselves. Clearly, this was not a priority. In the kitchen I saw the effect of leaking water, grimy around the sink. A mop stood in the corner, though I was told the floor remained stained even after washing.

The back garden was overgrown, with rubbish in the tall grass, and old cushions, a washing machine, and boxes were piled up in a small shed. The shower was covered with mold—there was usually hot water, but there had been a period in the winter when it ran cold for three months.

In the living room, a form bearing a G4S logo noted the times when a G4S Housing Officer had visited, together with the list of asylum-seeker tenants, who had originated from many nations. The Housing Officers visited once a month, and although Michael said they were often friendly, they rarely took action to remedy the property's many problems.

Since he had been in the place for nine months, I asked Michael why he had not cleaned it up. He would have to buy gloves to do it, he said—another expense—and it was easier to ignore it. The carpet on the stairs was peeling, posing a danger to residents and visitors.

Most bedrooms were occupied by two people, each with a single bed. Every room had a lock on the door. Michael said he got along with his housemates—a small mercy in the cramped space available—and he was lucky to have the attic on his own, which afforded a view over the drab city. The room contained a Bible, a laptop—though no chair—coins, shoes, suitcases, soap, and shampoo. Water had leaked from the ceiling for months, and G4S had not fixed it. It was cold and depressing, though I was visiting in July, at the height of summer.

Michael was on a cocktail of drugs for anxiety and depression, awaiting a decision on his asylum claim after a re-application. He said he could not return to Cameroon as a result of political repression against his family. He did not want to speak on the record, and I understood why: he felt vulnerable. Nonetheless, Michael was articulate, bright, and despairing. The state of his housing and the limbo in which his asylum claim languished made him deeply unhappy—though he was one of the lucky ones, receiving state-provided weekly counseling. Many others were left to fend for themselves, often ending up on the streets.

A cool breeze ran through the property. The heaters worked in the winter, but with leaking water, living with other migrants in a similar state of inertia and with no paid work, the situation was guaranteed to generate fluctuating moods—which was surely the point. Michael sometimes volunteered with a local NGO to talk to schoolchildren about asylum seekers, in order to occupy his mind.

This G4S house was a disgrace, but it was nothing out of the ordinary. Little money or care had been expended on it, or many others like it, because that would require funds whose use would damage the bottom line of a company whose sole aim was profit. A 2013 Home Office committee, convened to investigate why G4S and Serco had not fulfilled their contract to provide decent housing, while allowing subcontractors to bully tenants, heard from James Thorburn, Serco's managing director of home affairs, who explained: "We care for a lot of vulnerable people and we run two immigration centers, so we understand the immigration market."

Thorburn gave an almost identical statement in late 2014, when Serco won another contract to continue running the Yarl's Wood detention center. Although the 2013 Home Office committee had elicited admissions from officials that it was not sensible to grant housing contracts to organizations with no experience running them, the contracts had already been signed, and G4S had no fear of losing them. As elsewhere, unaccountability functioned as a core value of disaster capitalism.

We later drove a short distance to another G4S property. It was a three-story building with nine tenants, in better condition and tidier than the first. An Iranian man, Bozorg, said his housemate had cleaned the place for Ramadan. There was a G4S sign in the entrance hall that read: "This house has now been professionally cleaned: Please keep it clean and tidy at all times." The G4S "House Rules" read like a prison manual for good behavior. The company barely provided anything of use, and Bozorg said that nothing had been done about an infestation of mice. He had clashed with an African housemate, and did not feel secure. The back garden was overgrown and dirty, and G4S had not sent anybody to clear it up.

Bozorg had been in Britain for six years, and had not seen his wife and two children during that time. He broke down when recounting a conversation with his wife in which she had told him that his sons, twelve and eight, had been teased at school in Iran because he was in Britain and not around to support them. "What can I do?" he begged, seeking answers from me that I was unable to provide. I turned away, embarrassed. He was on heavy medication to manage the depression and anxiety. Because of a bad back, he was unable to sleep on a bed, so he lay on a mattress on the floor.

A local NGO requested that Bozorg be moved to another G4S property, because his physical condition meant that he could not climb the stairs in the middle of the night to relieve himself. He showed me the plastic bottle into which he urinated. He showered every three days, when he found the strength to pull himself up the stairs.

He had been waiting for years for a final resolution of his asylum claim, but his previous solicitor had not represented him properly. Bozorg was now filing a complaint against him. It was common for lawyers, paid badly by the state, simply to give up on cases, leaving their clients without representation. Successive governments have progressively cut legal aid, leaving thousands of asylum seekers with no real chance of success. The system is guaranteed to leave asylum seekers in limbo, while enriching the countless corporations that leech off it.

Bozorg was keen to tell me his story. He was a Christian and this caused him political problems in Iran. There was no way to verify his story or that of Michael before him. Robert, the local campaigner, knew both men and said it was likely that they would eventually both be granted asylum, though it might take some years. But there was no excuse to house people indefinitely in inadequate accommodation while they awaited resolution of their cases.

This property was in far better shape than the one I had visited earlier; but with nine people living in a relatively small place, only two working burners on the stove, and not enough refrigerator space for everyone's food, Bozorg was desperate to move.

Asylum Help was a service that advertised itself as helping refugees to understand the asylum process. I saw an A4 sheet of paper advertising it in the hallway. Anyone who called the number was put on hold for at least thirty minutes, and the services then offered were barely satisfactory. This situation was repeated across the country, with few of the asylum seekers having a chance to be heard. The media was largely uninterested, and the Home Office and charity bureaucracy resented having to talk to journalists and migrants at all. Activists and immigrants all told me that the system was close to useless.

This reality of privatized housing for refugees was linked to the country's housing crisis, both for asylum seekers and for the general population, but not for the reasons its defenders claimed. It had not brought greater freedom in the market; it had simply allowed profiteers to thrive, because the mantra of "self-reliance" for the poor—another term for hanging the underclass out to dry —had become official government policy. A select few companies —G4S, Taylor Wimpey, Barratt Homes, Persimmon, Bellway, Redrow, Bovis, Crest Nicholson—had captured the market.

Housing demand in Britain had soared, but the number of properties being built remained stagnant. British journalist James Meek argued that former British prime minister Margaret Thatcher and her successors had "done all they can to sell off the nation's bricks and mortar ... only to be forced to rent it back, at inflated prices, from the people they sold it to."[1] Asylum seekers were just the latest group to pay the price for this cultural shift towards slumification for the masses.

John Grayson was a friendly and passionate sixty-nine-year-old activist. Over the years he had worked in adult education, as an independent researcher, teaching and researching on housing and social movements, and as a solidarity campaigner. He was now a member of Symaag, the South Yorkshire Migration Asylum Action Group. "Councils used to provide housing through public funds," he told me. "Then this all went through privatization by Labour and the Tories, and Labour often pushed for more privatization of asylum-seeker services. Now private contractors do the dirty work for the state, but it's the outsourcing of violence. The state should have a monopoly on these tasks."

The rot deepened from 2012 onwards. Britain started privatizing asylum housing, the Home Office giving most of the contracts to G4S and Serco. There was a plan to "nationalize providers," and the country was divided into separate territories for the purpose—and Yorkshire was allocated to G4S. Asylum housing was only for those waiting for an outcome of their asylum claim, but many others were homeless. Grayson recalled a 2012 public meeting about the proposed plan at which a Zimbabwean man said: "I don't want a prison guard as my landlord. I've seen G4S in South Africa."

The G4S-run Angel Lodge in Wakefield, West Yorkshire, situated in the grounds of Wakefield prison, was dirty because the company would not pay for better services. The rooms were home to rats and cockroaches. Pregnant women were placed in poor housing with steep stairs. Food poisoning was common. Some private contractors did not pay council fees, and tenants quickly discovered that heating and electricity had been disconnected.

The British press rarely reported these conditions, instead highlighting the "four-star" treatment given to migrants. The *Daily Mail* claimed in May 2014 that asylum seekers were being treated by G4S to luxury accommodation because the Angel Lodge "specialist hostel" was full.[2] In truth, Angel Lodge was a grim facility that generated constant complaints from its residents.

* * *

In 2000 British journalist George Monbiot published *Captive State: The Corporate Takeover of Britain*—a book that proved eerily prescient, both documenting and predicting the drift towards privatization that would characterize the direction of the country's public services, by bipartisan agreement. At the 1999 Labour Party Conference, with Prime Minister Tony Blair at the helm, delegates had to walk past sixty-two corporate stalls. Lord Whitty, a minister at the Department of the Environment, told the BBC that exhibitors were not buying access to ministers. "You buy access to the whole party," he said. "I think he was trying to reassure us," Monbiot noted.[3] In 2012, Monbiot argued that there was little room in the public sphere to challenge mindless outsourcing. "So effectively have governments, the media and advertisers associated consumption with prosperity and happiness that to say these things is to expose yourself to opprobrium and ridicule."[4]

It had been a coup d'état, Monbiot rightly argued—and often a botched one. When the British government sold off the Royal Mail, in 2013, the National Audit Office later found that it had cost taxpayers £750 million in a single day, because the government had vastly undervalued the company.[5] Millions more could have been secured, but business secretary Vince Cable did not lose his job over the fiasco. Instead, he established a review into how governments sell off public assets, as a way to distract critics of his mismanagement. The report found that the Tories should have received a further £180 million from the sale. Absurdly, the leader of the UK Independence Party (UKIP), Nigel Farage, said that having Cable in government was like a "Marxist in charge of the business department."

The business press featured approving quotes on the privatization, however, instructing critics that they should be patient. The *City AM* newspaper—"business with personality"—told its readers: "It should ... be remembered that the aim of the Royal Mail sale was not to raise revenue for the government, but to move a service from the state sector to the private sector where it could become a flourishing business."[6] By 2015, Royal Mail's prospects for delivering a decent business for all of Britain were in doubt, with Scottish citizens in particular experiencing unreliable service.

Advocates of privatization made wildly inaccurate claims about its benefits. Scottish historian Niall Ferguson—an enthusiastic supporter of rehabilitating the supposed benefits of US and British colonialism—articulated the thoughts of the privatizing mind. "The mystery is why freedom-loving Americans are so averse to privatization," he lamented, "a policy that has been a huge success nearly everywhere it's been tried."[7] This was the mainstream consensus, echoed by many in the media and major political parties—that privatization was essential to continued growth.[8] But Ferguson was fundamentally wrong. He cited Britain, from Margaret Thatcher's period of office onwards, as an ideal model, conveniently ignoring the fact that the wage gap between the highest and lowest earners in the UK had widened in the preceding quarter-century,[9] and that the number of working people living in poverty had never been higher.[10] By 2014, it was calculated that the number of British households falling below minimum living conditions had doubled in the preceding thirty years, despite the UK economy having doubled in size. Poverty and deprivation were soaring.[11]

Britain had perfected so-called shadow personnel, orchestrated by job agencies pushing for contract and cheap labor. Millions of workers toiled for minimal pay, in poor conditions and without job security, in factories and retail outlets across the country. This was a "workforce that is breeding unpeople by the hundreds of thousands," wrote *Guardian* journalist Aditya Chakrabortty.[12]

It was vital for citizens to understand why this had happened, though many experienced it directly every day. This is not to idealize the public sector, which could also be wracked by inefficiency, corruption, and abuse. The state increasingly used surveillance against its own citizens (with the help of corporations), refused to be transparent in its dealings with business, launched unprovoked wars over resources, and blithely funded militarized police forces. This was not the only alternative, and it was arguable that the supposed Western democratic ideal represented in Britain, the United States, Australia, and Europe was not democratic at all, disenfranchising millions by limiting economic options and debate. Noam Chomsky has rightly argued that "the United States has essentially a one-party system and the ruling party is the business party."[13]

This was a view shared by clear majorities across the Western world. According to 2013 poll by YouGov-Cambridge, Britons, Americans, French, and Germans all believed that their economic situation was declining and felt pessimistic about the future. Respondents were questioned as to whether they were "basically confident that our children's generation will end up enjoying a better standard of living than our generation, just as our generation has mostly been better off than our parents." Only a tiny minority in all countries answered in the affirmative.[14]

One of the key arguments used by Thatcher and her supporters since the 1970s, along with US president Ronald Reagan from the 1980s, to justify placing public assets in private hands was the alleged excessive power of the trade unions and meddling bureaucrats—and it was true that some unions ferociously protected their turf. The point was made that Britain was not fulfilling its potential because leftists hated the idea of private enterprise. The changes resulted in hundreds of thousands of workers being sacked in the name of "efficiency." Millions of Britons then bought shares in the corporations that became an integral part of the British state.

But the results were disappointing even in the terms pushed by advocates of privatization, leading to greater inequality and poverty. Thatcher herself wrote that "privatisation was one of the central means of reversing the corrosive and corrupting effects of socialism ... the state's power is reduced and the power of the people enhanced ... privatisation is at the centre of any programme of reclaiming territory for freedom."[15] In reality, Britain never became a country filled with eager shareholders, as only a minority were able to consider acquiring a share portfolio.

Thatcher naively, or maliciously, argued that privatization was a panacea for a broken society and that managers would become beacons of virtue. The catastrophic failures of the global business class during the 2008 financial crisis demonstrated the danger represented by faceless executives running the world. The new regime, in Britain and other Western nations, was one in which users had no choice but to pay for essential services, from airports to water, through tolls and added fees. It was a case of democratic totalitarianism.

In his book *Private Island*, James Meek wrote that the myths surrounding privatization continued to dominate public debate despite the lack of evidence to support its supposed successes. Disaster capitalism had its own armies of defenders who were undeterred by failure—though, in their way of thinking, making large sums of money at the expense of job security represent a dazzling success. As Meek argued, "Privatisation failed to demonstrate the case made by the privatizers that private companies are always more competent than state-owned ones—that private bosses, chasing the carrot of bonuses and dodging the stick of bankruptcy, will always do better than their state-employed counterparts," while politicians "struggled to separate their ambitions for Britain from their own ambitions and their families' ascent into the six-figure-income class."[16]

Extraordinary salaries for the elites in Britain illustrated the failure, though a 2015 report by a Belgian business school showed that German executives were for the first time getting paid better than their British counterparts because there was "more scrutiny on pay in the UK from institutional investors." In both countries, executive salaries for bosses in the FTSE 100 and top German firms had climbed to well over £3 million, and it was encouraging that some pushback was being exerted against rising corporate pay.[17]

The list of outsourced work was staggering both within Britain's borders and among British companies contracted around the world. G4S is a behemoth, operating in 125 countries with over 657,000 employees, whose work has included guarding prisoners in Israeli-run prisons in Palestine. In 2014 the company predicted huge growth in the Middle East, especially in Egypt and the Gulf states. In Britain alone, G4S controlled countless police tasks from 2012 onwards, in a partially privatized system whereby police officers continued to make arrests, but G4S staff processed suspects in their own "custody suites."[18]

In 2014, G4S won a $118 million contract to deliver "base operating services" at the US military base at Guantánamo Bay, in Cuba.[19] G4S ran countless private prisons across Britain, despite being routinely fined for failing to meet its agreed targets. Occasionally, mainstream politicians criticized Serco, G4S, and other providers, but they did little to enforce greater accountability.[20]

Founded in 1929, Serco has been ubiquitous in British life, running ferries, London's Docklands Light Railway, the National Physical Laboratory, prisons, defense contracts, education authorities, waste management, and a host of other operations. It has over 100,000 employees globally and controls prisons in Australia, New Zealand, and Germany. It operated with a $1.25 billion contract from the Obama administration to implement Obamacare, despite a Serco whistle-blower having alleged that its staff had "hardly any work to do" during a botched program.

Both Serco and G4S were complicit in overcharging by tens of millions of pounds for the electronic tagging of prisoners—some of whom were found to have been dead at the time—from the 2000s onwards. The Serious Fraud Office was tasked in 2013 with investigating, and in late 2014 Serco was forced to reimburse the Ministry of Justice to the tune of £68.5 million.

The government's solution to this fraud was not to address the reasons that privateers had been able to deceive them—loosely written contracts and little appetite for enforcement—but to hand over the contract to a Serco and G4S rival, Capita. This corporation, formed in 1994 with 64,000 staff, has become the largest beneficiary of outsourcing in Britain. By 2015, it ran all Cabinet Office civil-service training, as well as contracting with the Criminals Record Bureau to manage and maintain criminal records, plus many others.[21] A "clean skin," relatively speaking, Capita operated without the recent controversies surrounding Serco and G4S, and it appealed to governments craving commercial secrecy for services traditionally run by the state.

The Home Office dispensed with the services of the UK Border Agency in 2013 for failing to manage properly a huge backlog of asylum cases. It then appointed Capita, with a £40 million contract. The company bungled its delivery, sending hundreds of text messages to individuals who were in the country legally, reading: "Message from the UK Border Agency: You are required to leave the UK as you no longer have the right to remain." Others who had chosen to leave Britain were sent messages by Capita wishing them a "pleasant journey."[22]

This callousness was highlighted again during a 2015 inquiry that showed Tascor's medical staff, operated by Capita, ignoring health warnings about a Pakistani man, Tahir Mehmood, before he died at Manchester airport in 2013. Corporate delays and incompetence caused Mehmood's death, because contracted employees did not see information about his ongoing chest pains.

Never miss a good opportunity to make money from disaster—this was the unofficial mantra of Capita boss Paul Pindar, when he told the Public Accounts Committee in 2013 that the reason army recruitment was down was the "disadvantage that we actually have no wars on."[23] These words were spoken before the battle against Islamic State militants had commenced. Capita was given the Ministry of Defence contract to manage advertising, marketing, and the processing of application forms for the army. Pindar's brutally honest admission—that war was good for business—was refreshing. The fact that all of the conflicts Britain had engaged in since 9/11—including Iraq, Afghanistan, and Libya—had been catastrophic failures was not mentioned as a factor in Pindar's skewed reasoning. There was good reason for many citizens to be wary of further foreign engagement.

Another major contractor is Mitie, a company that in 2014 quietly became Britain's largest provider of immigration detention centers. It is a FTSE 250 contractor with over 54,000 staff. It works for Eurostar and Heathrow Airport, provides cleaners for government departments, and manages data centers and security guards for Marks & Spencer and the British Museum. Founded in the 1970s, Mitie has grown to become a company worth billions of pounds. It hosted an annual Mitie's Got Talent competition to identify its most talented staff. (G4S had a theme song—as awful as you might expect.)[24] This was a corporation that wanted to display a human face while it benefited financially during an economic downturn. "It is a tough time to be in business, but outsourcing has always been positive during recession," CEO Ruby McGregor-Smith told *Management Today*.

Cutting corners was an inevitable practice within these massive organizations. Ronald van Steden of Vrije University Amsterdam, an advisor to the Dutch government, told the *Financial Times* that companies like G4S "follow a salami technique: slicing off a small part of public services to see how far they can go."[25] The British group Social Enterprise, which assists businesses with a social conscience, released a report in 2012 entitled *The Shadow State*. It found that the explosion in privatization, the biggest wave since the 1980s, meant that "government policy can be undermined or become irrelevant when commissioners have little choice over whom they can purchase services from."[26] The problem was exacerbated when neither governments nor corporations could be trusted to manage public services responsibly without thinking about profit.

Mass privatization and job losses were leading to generations of youth disappearing through the cracks of reduced opportunity. A

2014 Oxfam report revealed that Britain's five richest families controlled more wealth than the poorest 20 percent of the population. Another Oxfam study found that eighty-five global billionaires had resources equaling those of half of the planet's population—3.5 billion people.[27] In 2015, Oxfam warned that the world's top 1 percent would own more in 2016 than the other 99 percent. *New York Times* economics columnist Paul Krugman sagely argued that Britain's austerity push "isn't really about debt and deficits at all; it's about using deficit panic as an excuse to dismantle social programs."[28] This was the definition of disaster capitalism.

The New Economics Foundation found in 2013 that Britain had recently seen the biggest drop in living standards since the Victorian era, most severely affecting public sector workers and women.[29] The bald facts of this austerity craze were enough to indicate that something was horribly wrong with modern politics. British prime minister David Cameron felt the need, in 2013, after years of austerity and falling living standards, to teach schoolchildren about the glories of capitalism—which seemed like a defensive impulse. It was vital, he said, to celebrate a culture "that values that typically British, entrepreneurial, buccaneering spirit."[30]

Multinational corporations spent the twentieth century gradually reducing their obligations in the various jurisdictions in which they operated. When national and international laws became obsolete or could be circumvented, the relationship between the company, the state, and the public changed irrevocably. This occurred because of ideological lobbying, and accompanying political and media pressure.

Britain's immigration policy had played a key role in generating profits for privateers. Britain had had an Immigration Act since 1971 that allowed the incarceration of asylum seekers in detention facilities or jails, and by the 1990s there was public pressure to manage the growing number of arriving migrants more stringently. The Murdoch press and *Daily Mail* convinced many citizens that a nation with a harmonious past was being swamped with criminals. Activists argued that it was wholly inappropriate for individuals fleeing repression to be held in prison-like conditions; punishment as a deterrent had been the default setting for years, and yet it had not stemmed the flow of people. Refugees continued to arrive because the global crises that were the cause of the influx persisted.

In October 2014, the House of Commons Public Accounts Committee detailed the 11,000 asylum seekers waiting in Britain for at least seven years to hear if they would be allowed to stay; the further 29,000 migrants still awaiting official assessment of their applications; and the 50,000 immigrants who had had their claims rejected, then disappeared.[31]

The mad rush to privatize seemingly everything had few limits in the minds of its advocates. Since 2000, there had been lucrative investments in residential homes for the needy and mentally disturbed. Utilities were routinely outsourced, and prices increased. "Welfare to Work" contractors were lining their pockets, with little evidence of success. Despite public opposition, there were growing moves to privatize public libraries, schools, child protection services, and forests. University courses, the fight against climate change, and foreign aid were all endeavors that were routinely framed as having to serve commercial interests, rather than the common good.

Prime Minister David Cameron has outsourced hundreds of medical services during his time in power, including non-emergency ambulance services and community care.[32] Robots were increasingly replacing nursing staff—a development welcomed by companies looking to cut costs. Reductions in government funding for public hospitals led to the chief executive of the NHS Confederation, Rob Webster, warning in 2014 that the NHS would have to start charging patients £75 per night for a bed—an unthinkable measure in a supposedly public system.[33] In 2015, Britain's only privately run NHS hospital, Hinchingbrooke, dropped its contractor, Circle Holdings. This was unsurprising, because a 2014 report found that there had been little oversight of the facility, as well as "poor hygiene levels." and major problems in the emergency department.[34] Taxpayers were forced to shell out for yet another tendering process.

The prioritization of market competition over quality healthcare had become the default setting of forces pushing for the privatization of the NHS itself, against the strong opposition of medical experts and the public.[35] Even the US defense company Lockheed Martin was keen to bid on a £1 billion GP support service contract.[36]

According to journalist John Pilger, what the country had witnessed was "the replacement of democracy by a business plan for every human activity, every dream, every decency, every hope, every child born."[37]

"I love, live and breathe outsourcing," Ruby McGregor-Smith told *Management Today* in July 2014.[38] McGregor-Smith, Mitie's CEO, is an Indian-born former accountant, who previously worked for Serco. The publication wrote that her industry was a "low-profile, low-glamour business that doesn't attract big, flamboyant egos. Some might call it dull ... Outsourcing is the child of recession."

I met Britain's first Asian CEO for a rare interview at the Mitie office in central London. In a boardroom overlooking the Thames, McGregor-Smith was friendly and approachable, keen to show the organization in a positive light. "Our passion is service," she told me. "Increasingly, as we do more public sector work, our client base becomes the general public—38 percent of our work is now public sector." Her annual salary and company shares amount to millions of pounds.[39]

When, in 2013, she became the chair of the Public Service Strategy Board—a body of private company heads tasked with "rethinking how public services can operate more effectively and efficiently," she said in the press release: "We demonstrate the positive impact that the private sector can make in transforming services and generating value for taxpayers through greater competition." In other words, the institution offered political cover to justify and defend the acceleration of outsourcing.

Despite this, McGregor-Smith expressed surprise that there should be a demand for total transparency in the privatization process, and that complaints were made about the board's opaque dealings. "The fact that the public believe that we are the extension of government and should be answerable to them directly has not been something that has ever really been raised or discussed as an issue." It was revealing that there was so little consideration of the end-users of services other than as "clients."

Mitie's focus was primarily inside Britain, with a handful of interests overseas. McGregor-Smith was enthusiastic about her company's ability to run detention centers, although she insisted: "We are more risk-averse than some of the other contractors. Personally, as an outsourcer, I do not believe everything should be outsourced unless I think it's for the right reasons. In the case [of] detention centers, it's who can best run them with the skills and experience, and I think the private sector brings a lot to the way you can support the individuals inside those environments. If you see our work at Campsfield [a detention facility near Oxford], from the art rooms we build to the football pitches, we're trying to keep the individuals while [they are] there in a secure and safe environment. It's important that it's not a prison environment, and it's a difficult thing to do. We will not be perfect."

Since Mitie assumed control of Campsfield in 2011, the center has experienced a fire, a suicide, and three mass hunger strikes. Corporate Watch discovered that the key figures running the facility were veteran detention managers who had previously worked for Geo Group and other providers.[40] Mitie had just rebranded the old, discredited face of detention outsourcing with a new, brighter face in an attempt to convince the public that something had changed in immigration detention.

Mitie offered to arrange for me to receive a guided tour of its Campsfield detention facility, in order to bypass the bureaucratic obstacles to my entry. The company told me that the Home Office had to approve the visit—a revealing insight into who really controlled these privatized facilities. However, the night before I was to go, a PR official contacted me to say that the Home Office press department had suddenly decided to block my trip, nervous about journalistic scrutiny. No further explanation was given. I spoke to Mitie the following day, and they sounded frustrated and apologetic. "The Home Office talks about wanting to be more open and transparent," the Mitie PA told me; but the reality, she acknowledged, was the exact opposite. "We'll be chasing this with the Home Office because we don't want this to happen again," she said. She realized the impression this experience had left me with: one of immigration bureaucrats striving to hide their handiwork from public view.

McGregor-Smith told me about a man who always came to the Mitie annual general meeting and expressed concern about conditions at Campsfield. "I said to him, Come and see it and tell us how to make it better. If you want to offer a philosophy that says the detention center shouldn't exist I can't answer that for you, because that is not my decision. He came to my AGM for three years, and by year three he said, 'I'm still not with it that they should be open, but if they're open I'm happy you run it and nobody else.'" She was pleased to tell me this story, hoping it would convince me that her facility was the best in the industry. "My personal view [about detention] is more as a mother rather than as a business. If the private sector can add innovation then it should do it, but anything that puts me at loggerheads with the public will make them wonder why it's being outsourced. Whole tranches of the NHS should never be outsourced. I personally see doctors and nurses being state-run."

There was a fire at the Campsfield center in 2013, and serious charges were leveled against Mitie that it had not appropriately protected staff and detainees. It was a charge vehemently denied by McGregor-Smith, though she acknowledged the absence of a sprinkler system—a key failing in the privatized facility. "We weren't asked to put a sprinkler system in," she countered. "We took the center over, and there wasn't one there. If I take over a center which is owned by the Home Office and it doesn't have a sprinkler system, and I'm not asked to put one in, that's their call. A Home Office assessment then changed their mind [a sprinkler has now been installed]. It is not for me to say that's right or wrong—it's their call. My opinion would be that facilities should be as safe as they can be. Did anybody predict that one individual's actions would cause what happened?"

I asked McGregor-Smith whether Serco and G4S, and their constant presence in the media for breaching human rights, were tainting other contractors by association. "Controversies over these firms have made us all realize that you're only as good as the weakest part of your organization," she said. "Many talk of the opportunities it can create. I sit there and think that's really interesting, but only if you're capable of delivering. There is a perception, and I don't know if it's right or wrong, that G4S and Serco have gotten too big, or they're doing too much."

The secrecy of the system, and the difficulty for the public and media of scrutinizing how public funds were being spent, were becoming an increasing concern. Mitie's profits decreased in 2014 after losses in some of its construction contracts, but the business press reported the difficulties as little more than a blip in what would become a rosy future. "When there are problems, we expect they'll be managed in private, not public," said McGregor-Smith. "We don't expect it to be all public-domain information. The only thing we've learned from the G4S and Serco controversies is that maybe we do need to open up and talk to more journalists, and get to be known more about the kind of companies we run."

I questioned McGregor-Smith about the commercial-in-confidence clauses in contracts—an arrangement whereby contractors and governments keep the details of their agreement private and inaccessible to the public, which suits both the government and the contractor. "Most of our contracts preclude us from talking to anybody," she admitted, "but we're currently discussing whether we should be more open, because otherwise we become a ridiculous area of interest when there isn't any interest really; we're just a bunch of people delivering services. You attract the wrong kind of media if you don't explain what you're doing."

With all the controversy around privatized immigration detention and the abuses associated with it, McGregor-Smith assured me: "We have adopted a gentler approach to detention; some have questioned why we've done that. We would say, they could be our kids." She wanted Mitie to be a transparent organization, unlike G4S and Serco, and believed freedom-of-information legislation should be reformed to encompass private companies' records. She condemned the "prison culture" of major contractors and said that the facilities she ran were not jails, but detention centers. In Mitie's 2014 annual report, McGregor-Smith proudly explained how the "landmark [immigration] contract" to run Colnbrook and Harmondsworth detention centers "would release significant savings for the taxpayer." There was no mention in the £180 million, eight-year contract of providing decent care for detainees.

Injecting more accountability into the system was the stated goal of Julian Huppert, Liberal Democrat MP for Cambridge, whom I met at his parliamentary office (he was defeated at the 2015 general election along with countless other Liberal Democrat MPs). After his election in 2010, he was leading a campaign to release children from detention. "Under the previous governments, literally thousands of children were detained for the purposes of immigration for months on end," Huppert said. "These were not people who had committed a crime. We have ended routine detention of children." This was true, though some children were still incarcerated around the country. He argued that ongoing scandals at Yarl's Wood, the Serco-run detention center in Bedfordshire, had "contributed to raising the issue of children in detention up the agenda."

Huppert despaired that mainstream British political and media culture celebrated punishment as a legitimate form of deterrence: "There is a view that says if we don't detain children then people are more likely to come to this country illegally. There's no real evidence that refugees check out the refugee benefits [of all possible countries in great detail] before making a rational decision where to go to. Some want to make it a hostile area for asylum seekers [to deter them], and saying you might lock up their children is a hostile way of treating people. I don't want this to be a country where we deal with our immigration policies by being actively unpleasant to people."

It was an indictment of democratic societies that there was energetic debate over whether refugees should be isolated, locked up indefinitely in poor conditions, or, conversely treated with respect. Huppert praised a facility called Cedars, run by Britain's largest children's charity, Barnardo's, near Gatwick Airport. It was opened in 2011 in response to concerns over abuses at Yarl's Wood. Cedars provides short-term accommodation for families about to be deported. "It is not run to be a cheap way of managing people," he said. "This is for people where there has been an effort to get them to go voluntarily. That has failed. Cedars is a very high-quality space."

But a 2014 Barnardo's report found that children were often separated from their parents in the facility, and that police in protective armor were routinely arresting and escorting traumatized families to the center.[41] The Chief Inspector of Prisons released a report into this center in 2012 uncovering a litany of problems—from self-harm, lack of legal representation, child distress, and the excessive use of force.[42]

But Huppert was unbowed: "A colleague said that we shouldn't encourage the right-wing press to look at [Cedars], because they'll complain how nice it is and how we're spending too much money looking after these people. Barnardo's come to this with an angle of child protection. Several of the detained women at the center who were spoken to during an inspection said to me it was very helpful to have a place to get used to the fact that they were leaving the UK."

Huppert's vision for asylum policy was moderate, and he eschewed the racism so common in today's debate: "We have to have immigration controls—we can't have an open-borders system. I find the concept of open borders intellectually interesting, but you can't combine that with a welfare state and free healthcare. You can't do both."

I asked him about the private sector running refugee facilities, and he argued that his focus was reducing the number of refugees behind bars, rather than obsessing over who managed them: "One of the reasons you get the private sector in is because they at least say they can run it for less money. But a better way to see it is to have less people in there. At the moment we have the situation where people are locked up in detention for months and years. And some of these people will then be released into this country. So we will have spent tens of thousands of pounds in some cases detaining people who will actually then be allowed to be here. The Liberal Democrats' policy is about reducing immigration detention rather than focusing on privatized facilities."

A culture of demonizing refugees remained rampant in Britain, and Huppert believed that Labour, the Conservatives, and UKIP were competing to outdo each other in finding new ways to isolate and punish those seeking asylum. "We're even seeing xenophobia against Caucasians, which is relatively new here," he lamented. "I think privatized immigration detention should be open to appropriate freedom of information. If they're running a good service they would benefit by being able to demonstrate that." Despite my constant prompting, Huppert remained hesitant about seriously criticizing any of the companies making money from detention.

The Liberal Democrats tried to show vehement opposition to the growing trend of disaster capitalism—in 2014, the party pledged to protect Britain's forests from privatization; but their rhetoric did not match the reality. A dossier was leaked in 2014 that showed one in five Tories and Liberal Democrat politicians had received donations from individuals pushing for NHS privatization.

In sharing power with David Cameron since 2010, the Liberal Democrats were either powerless or complicit in the ongoing sell-off of public assets. In the most dramatic change in outsourcing ever to affect the criminal justice system, 2014 saw companies Sodexo and Interserve sign contracts worth £450 million to run 70 percent of the probation service. (Serco and G4S withdrew their bids after the emergence of their involvement in overcharging the government for electronic tags.) Freedom of information laws were bypassed by the secretive contracts, and the wife of the chief inspector of probation, Janine McDowell, was promoted in November 2014 to run Sodexo. Conflicts of interests abounded, and in 2015 the chief inspector of probation, Paul McDowell, resigned.

On a gray and rainy summer day I caught a train to Bedford, one hour from London, to visit Yarl's Wood detention center. The notoriety of this center—colored by years of reports of sexual abuse of detainees by guards, deaths in custody, self-harm, and Serco mismanagement—was well known, and yet it remained open. The UN special rapporteur on violence against women, Rashida Manjoo, was denied access to Yarl's Wood in 2014 on instructions, she said, emanating from the highest levels of the Home Office. In 2014 Serco was awarded another eight-year contract to manage the facility.

Yarl's Wood is located in an industrial park around twenty minutes from Bedford. Alongside factories and the Bedford Pet Cremations, the detention center is a nondescript set of buildings with Serco signs at the entrance telling visitors that the company "brings service to life." A brochure in the foyer helpfully informed visitors about biometrics, and why they use them to document everyone entering the facility. Blank complaint forms sat nearby.

A number of lawyers and visitors were milling around outside, some smoking, others talking on their mobile phones. I entered, registered my fingerprints and photo with a Serco employee, and told him the name of the couple I was there to see. This center, unlike many others in the UK, allowed men and women to live together. I progressed to another section, pressed my fingers on the print scanner and was body searched and patted down after being told that I could not take anything into the visiting area. Security guards radioed to get permission to open one door or unlock another. The frustration and fatigue of the guards was exactly the same when I had visited detainees in the Mitie-run facilities at Colnbrook and Harmondsworth, near Hearthrow Airport. *Channel 4 News* aired secretly recorded footage in 2015 that revealed Mitie was locking detainees in their cells for longer periods every day under a so-called efficiency measure.

The visiting center was much like any other around the world: a children's area with toys; a small room where detainees had to see people behind a glass window; many low tables and chairs for visitors. A Sinhalese couple arrived, Thehan and Sathi (not their real names), and approached me, smiling. We sat down and talked for an hour about their situation. Sathi spoke quite fluent English, though her husband was less confident. She was seven-and-a-half months pregnant, and was crying and obviously distraught. She explained how they had arrived in the UK four-and-a-half years previously, after paying an agent in Sri Lanka to escape to somewhere, anywhere, away from a regime that they said made it impossible for them to stay. She had studied to be an accountant, working as a teacher in Sri Lanka, and they found a way to survive by renting a room in an apartment with an Indian couple who had a small child.

When they had formally applied for asylum, they were both arrested and brought to Yarl's Wood. They looked shell-shocked at the way in which this had happened. They had a Sri Lankan lawyer, but it was unclear how effective he would be in getting them out. According to Home Office policy, pregnant women should not be in immigration detention beyond the twenty-fourth week of pregnancy, and yet Sathi was twenty-nine weeks pregnant, for which no explanation or justification had been offered. She had suffered two miscarriages in the past and was scared that the same thing might happen again.

The environment inside this privatized detention center was making her sick and mentally unstable. She said she had considered committing suicide. She had recently thought she had a blood clot, but doctors were unable to clarify where it was. While she recounted these stories, tears ran down her cheeks and she shook. The cruelty and futility of the process was startling. There was no reason to keep them both here other than for punishment or as a supposed deterrent—but they both insisted that they could not return to Sri Lanka.

Sathi said she that had often received decent medical care from the hospital. Sometimes the Serco staff believed her when she explained that she needed to visit a hospital, and at other times they did not. If she was away at the hospital during meal times, she would miss food and be hungry, even though she hated what they would often serve—chips, chicken, vegetables, and fruit. Sathi's treatment was not unusual. A pregnant South African woman at Yarl's Wood in 2010 had been refused a scan for four days and had to apply to the High Court to pressure authorities to grant one. Even then, officials initially refused to comply with the court order.[43] Pregnant women imprisoned at Yarl's Wood continue to suffer both neonatal and mental complications. *Channel 4 News* smuggled cameras into the facility in 2015 and found a callous disregard by guards towards these vulnerable prisoners.

In the visiting room one couple was kissing, and families that had been separated were briefly reunited. Colorful murals with Disney characters were painted on the outside walls, but Yarl's Wood was run like a high-security prison—soulless, tough, unfriendly, and cut off from the rest of society. A former mental-health nurse told the BBC in 2014 that the facility was unsafe for women. Many women had died under suspicious circumstances on the site. "The system wasn't driven for mental health," mental health nurse Noel Finn said. "It was more driven about, 'Are they fit to fly, physically?'"[44] Allegations of sexual assault by guards were commonplace.[45] Imprisoned women were paid fifty pence an hour to carry out menial tasks.

It was not lost on detainees that they were unable to work legally in the community while Serco was happy to accept their labor inside the center.[46] Corporate Watch used the Freedom of Information Act to demonstrate that Mitie, Geo Group, Serco, and G4S paid hundreds of detainees little more than £1 an hour for cooking, cleaning, and other jobs within detention centers across Britain.[47] The problem was wider than just in immigration. Corporate Watch revealed in 2015 that a Mitie-owned company, MiHomecare, one of Britain's largest contractors for the elderly, was paying workers less than the minimum wage.

It was the personal stories that left the deepest impression on me. I expressed sympathy with the couple's plight, asked questions, and said that surely they would soon be released. What they would then do remained unclear. A privatized system that offered no indication of when court hearings would be held served to prolong the mental anguish, which was even worse when a woman was pregnant. Happily, the couple was released the day after our visit, to an undisclosed location.

Many activists campaigned tirelessly for the closure of Yarl's Wood. Emma Mlotshwa, in her late forties, ran the NGO Medical Justice and lived in Bedford in a large house where many asylum seekers recently out of detention rented rooms. It was a huge property—one room had African artifacts, and there was a large mural in the living room on the theme of freedom and justice.

Mlotshwa's anger at the immigration system had begun when she witnessed her town transformed. "I saw Yarl's Wood being built. The plans for the center made me outraged," she told me.

"I felt a comparison with World War II camps and a need to do something. This was in 2000, so I educated myself and visited other anti-detention groups. I was still working as an electronics seller. Initially we called our group 'Campaign to Stop Arbitrary Detention at Yarl's Wood.'" Yarl's Wood opened in 2001, and already there was a riot and a fire in 2002. The police and Group 4, the company then running the center that eventually became G4S (it was contracted to Serco from 2007 onwards), fared badly in the trial relating to the fire. "I had naively expected that Yarl's Wood would be closed due to public awareness," Mlotshwa said. "I used my house in Bedford as a place for then relatively easily released detainees." It was a time when immigrants were not locked up for such long periods of time.

Anger burned within her, and Medical Justice was launched in 2008. At that stage, no independent doctors were going into detention centers, and the new group had to negotiate with the Home Office for access. The group's 2014 annual report detailed 448 detainees being assisted with "serious medical issues." The organization's doctors "helped a hunger-striker who the Home Office had the power to detain until 'death is unavoidable.'" Mlotshwa explained that it was important to have independent doctors in detention centers, because countless asylum seekers were lost inside a privatized system that skimped on even minimal medical checks. Victims of torture told her that they were being traumatized all over again in detention, and that their mental health issues were ignored. A 2013 report showed a severe shortage of immigration detention staff who were able to diagnose mental illness.[48] Detainees with serious illnesses, such as those needing HIV treatment, were either ignored or given irregular help. A 2011 Medical Justice report found that detaining HIV refugees "puts them at a high level of risk that is so severe that they should never be detained."[49] "These are all reasons why detention is worsening the personal situation of those inside, especially the old, severely disabled, pregnant women, and the sick," Mlotshwa told me.

A 2013 report revealed that the Home Office did not know how many pregnant women were in detention, and evidence indicated that Yarl's Wood's Serco staff routinely refused to treat these women with appropriate sensitivity. Medical Justice demanded that the Home Office no longer detain pregnant women at all.[50] Another report, in 2012, had demanded that asylum seekers who had been tortured should not be placed in privatized immigration detention. Rule 35, formulated in 2001, was designed to avoid this possibility, but it was ignored.[51]

Medical Justice fought against a system that gave refugee care a low priority. I heard stories of detainees being taken to the hospital in handcuffs. In 2014, G4S was forced to compensate a seventy-nine-year-old disabled former serviceman they had handcuffed during a fourteen-day hospital stay in Liverpool.[52] The British government did not treat people humanely, Mlotshwa said, "with guards often in the room alongside the asylum seeker and doctor, removing confidentiality. After years of demonizing refugees, private staff in hospitals, on planes, and at airports suspend caring and turn a blind eye to abuse."

Since becoming a full-time immigration activist, Mlotshwa had witnessed a range of problems with outsourced work: "The lowest price wins the contract, which leads to cutting corners, less care, and lower-paid and -qualified staff." A key problem with this kind of disaster capitalism, reminiscent of similar cases in Australia and the United States, was the "deliberate aim to fudge responsibility between Serco and the Home Office. With mostly male guards looking over [guarding] women at Yarl's Wood, Serco often tries to stop us visiting, saying detainees can't be found or we have the wrong paperwork." Mlotshwa said that the male staff often tried to intimidate women inside and outside the facility. Medical Justice knew of a "shit-sheet" kept by Serco on its visiting medical practitioners, making it difficult for them sometimes to get access.

I asked Mlotshwa about the political culture that allowed refugees to disappear into an unaccountable bureaucratic maze, becoming invisible. "The Home Office are not very helpful. They see us as a hassle and are not interested in real dialogue. Their staff aren't reading judgments when a judge finds a detainee is being treated in a cruel and degrading way and should be released or moved. The British political mood has demonized migrants so effectively. The Home Secretary has given the green light to damn immigrants, giving permission from the high elites to the lowly thugs who work for Serco and G4S."

The system was gamed by G4S, which routinely poached former civil servants who subsequently moved back into government, in a revolving-door system that incentivized all involved to protect it from scrutiny.[53] A 2010 British government–released Advisory Committee of Business Appointments noted that several former ambassadors, a Ministry of Defense chief of staff, and the general manager of the National Offender Management Service had all moved seamlessly to G4S management after leaving government employment. The cronyism was entrenched.

Jimmy Mubenga was an Angolan man killed by G4S on a British Airways flight in 2010 as he was being deported from Britain. Three G4S guards were charged with manslaughter and acquitted, despite evidence emerging at their 2014 trial that they had forcibly held Mubenga down while he screamed: "I can't breathe." G4S whistle-blowers told a Home Office committee after Mubenga's death that the company routinely hired individuals who were not trained appropriately, or who showed insensitivity towards vulnerable detainees. The potentially lethal technique used to restrain Mubenga had been flagged as dangerous, but this had been ignored by management.[54] Other deportees also complained of rough handling by G4S employees, including a Zimbabwean man who alleged that he had been punched and kicked while handcuffed and wearing leg locks.[55]

The Mubenga case was a perfect example of corporate unaccountability. At the end of the 2014 trial, Mubenga's widow,

Adrienne Makenda Kambana, pledged to pressure the Home Office "to make sure there is an independent monitor on each deportation so they can observe what is going on. I can't stand by and watch this happen to another family. I have to do that for Jimmy." After four years of investigations and public shaming of G4S, Amnesty International commented that it was still impossible to "know which of these [dangerous restraint techniques] are still being used today or if the UK government has actually delivered on its promise to introduce new and safer methods and training. Once again a migrant has lost their life in detention, and once again no one will ultimately be held to account."[56]

At the heart of this tragedy was the role of G4S and its hiring practices. Although, at the 2014 trial, text messages from the guards had inexplicably been deemed not to have "any real relevance"—as was the testimony of a whistle-blower who told an earlier inquiry that a form of banned restraint known as "carpet karaoke" was used to forcibly restrain Mubenga and push his head down—two of the three defendants had sent dozens of messages that displayed hatred towards Muslims, Asians, and Africans. One of the guards, Stuart Tribelnig, 39, had written: "Fuck off and go home you free-loading, benefit grabbing, kid producing, violent, non-English speaking cock suckers and take those hairy faced, sandal wearing, bomb making, goat fucking, smelly rag head bastards with you."

With so many cases of G4S having hired racist employees, and report after report having found that the company had employed a disproportionate number of staff who displayed a callous disregard for people of color, it was reasonable to ask why the firm was not charged with corporate manslaughter when a person died in its care.[57]

Racism had become endemic within an economic system that produced dehumanization while suppressing transparency and neglecting proper training. An anonymous account of a Serco guard working at the remote Curtin detention center, in Western

Australia, explained: "If you start off a bit of a cunt when you arrive, you're a major cunt by the time you leave." As for the G4S guards hired to transport Mubenga, poorly vetted and intolerant, an aggressive attitude and a contempt for non-whites was often a prerequisite. Although guards dealt every day with the most vulnerable members of the community, they were, the Australian guard said, there because they "need[ed] a job that will last a few months, pay well, employ immediately, and requires no expertise."[58]

Mubenga's coroner, Karon Monaghan QC, understood what outsourcing meant in reality. In a far more humane assessment of the case in 2013, which forced a criminal trial after the initial inaction of the Crown Prosecution Service, Monaghan wrote, after reading the racist texts, that "the potential impact on detainees of a racist culture is that detainees and deportees are not 'personalized.'" The sheer scale of the problem, exacerbated by years of state inaction, was revealed in a 2015 Institute of Race Relations report, *Dying for Justice*, identifying Mubenga as one of over 500 minority individuals who had died after an interaction with the police, prison, or immigration services, or one of their privatized proxies, since 1991.[59]

G4S lost the contract to deport foreign nationals after the Mubenga debacle, but in 2011 the government awarded the work to another contractor, Reliance, which had an equally disturbing past. After many G4S staff had been hired under European employment regulations, countless incidents emerged of guards allegedly assaulting detainees.[60]

There had been warnings for years. Medical Justice released a scathing 2008 report into the "outsourced abuse" of countless men and women who had been denied medication, beaten, punched, and subjected to racist abuse by contracted guards.[61] Since 2001, roughly 800 flights had been used to deport around 30,000 people from Britain, often back to repressive states. Stories of detainees being abused and assaulted by private security guards on the flights were infamous.[62] As far back as 2008, Britain's former chief inspector of prisons, Lord David Ramsbotham, had issued a report finding the government responsible for the abuse of hundreds of asylum seekers at the hands of thuggish private security officials.[63]

G4S excelled at securing contracts in a range of diverse fields, increasing revenue and reducing financial troubles in another part of the business if one contract, such as deportation, was lost. For example, it ran a Welfare to Work program on behalf of the Department for Work and Pensions. On its website it claimed to represent "a unique opportunity to transform lives and communities across the UK; an opportunity not only to support people into secure and lasting employment, but to make enormous inroads into eradicating child poverty and kick-starting social mobility." That was the spin, but the reality had more to do with punishment and coercion. The Conservative government established this G4S plan to assist the long-term unemployed, but activists in Sheffield explained to me how it had exacerbated poverty and disillusionment. Numbers of food banks and welfare recipients were soaring.

The *Guardian* investigated the G4S-run program in 2012 and discovered that countless contractors and subcontractors had run the initiative with little transparency. Unemployed and vulnerable people were pushed to accept unpaid work and told that paid work might be provided in the future. G4S earned more money if it found jobs lasting two years or more. The newspaper saw only a few secure jobs in Hull and noted that it was "hard not to keep wondering how assistance with CVs and motivational pep talks, however heartfelt, can overcome the stark local unemployment statistics."[64] Imagining private-sector jobs that did not exist, at a time when both public and private industries were struggling, was a tactic that had clear benefits for the G4S PR department.

Brutally but accurately, Conservative employment secretary Chris Grayling explained: "What we have tried to do [with the Welfare to Work program] is create a situation where our interests and the interests of providers are really aligned. They can make shedloads of money by doing the things we would absolutely love them to do."[65] It would be hard to find a more a succinct definition of disaster capitalism.

In Sheffield, where the G4S program was deeply entrenched, activist John Grayson said that the corporation had "synergy" with the government agenda. "Will the state run job centers in years to come, or will G4S run all aspects of welfare?" he asked. The militarization of society, achieved through the seamless transfer of influence and power from the public to the private sector, had not achieved any of its stated goals, other than its primary aim of enriching friendly companies at the expense of the general population.

In 2015, even the body representing the companies making money from the Welfare to Work program, including G4S, Ingeus, and Serco, reported that the "sanction first, investigate later" policy against social security recipients had failed. It left people impoverished, did nothing to help them get jobs, and thus kept them on benefits longer.[66] Such problems were the reason why opposition grew. A coalition of local activists petitioned Sheffield Council in July 2014 to sever all ties with G4S because of its "gross human rights abuses." The group City of Sanctuary operates across Britain to assist asylum seekers and educate the public about their plight. Grayson submitted a scathing report to the Home Affairs Committee inquiry into asylum in 2013 that documented "the appalling neglect of vulnerable asylum seeker tenants through unsuitable allocations and degrading treatment by G4S/subcontractor housing workers."[67]

A female asylum seeker with newborn twins in West Yorkshire was threatened by G4S for daring to complain about living in squalid conditions. A pregnant migrant was evicted on the day she was to be induced and left with no transport to the hospital. Countless female immigrants reported sexual, racial, and privacy breaches by G4S staff. These are just a small list of abuses suffered by asylum seekers across Britain in a system that demonizes the vulnerable.

In the heart of London, near London Bridge station, was the nondescript Becket House immigration enforcement reporting center. Vans with the words "Immigration Enforcement" on both sides sat outside. This was where immigrants were forced to sign in weekly to make sure they had not disappeared. More ominously, the vans visited workplaces daily around the city, grabbing suspected undocumented immigrants and bringing them to this center for processing, before sending them on to privatized immigration detention facilities around the country. Becket House was for short-term detention, and the building had countless cameras filming passers-by.

Corporate Watch's Phil Miller said that people regularly protested outside the building. Prime Minister David Cameron was being advised by the Australian polling firm Crosby Textor, famed for inflaming racial tensions in the pursuit of political power, and the Conservatives had become far more brazen in their efforts to crack down on immigrants. Having "Immigration Enforcement" vans driving around London was one Crosby Textor idea to signal a tough line against perceived dangers to public security. The Home Office dispatching of "Go Home" immigration trucks was another. The vehicles carried large posters with a message and phone number, alongside an image of a set of handcuffs: "In the UK illegally? Go Home or Face Arrest." The Home Office reported that its staff subsequently responded to countless bogus calls.

These actions were one of the Conservative Party's responses to being spooked by the sudden rise of UKIP that had resulted from burgeoning anti-immigrant sentiment. They were also guaranteed to enrich numerous corporations that were only too keen to profit from the ever-growing number of outsourced services. A key principle of disaster capitalism was keeping the public in a state of perpetual fear and insecurity, and then claiming to know how to soothe society's anxious mind.

Nick Hardwick, Britain's chief inspector of prisons, might privately agree. Occupying the post between 2010 and 2015, he was a cautious and friendly man. When I met him, I sensed that he did not want to speak too critically of government policy, as he knew the acceptable boundaries of debate that his position allowed. Hardwick's job was to report on conditions in prisons, immigration detention centers, and police custody. His role was independent of government, and he stressed: "What I report on is the outcome for prisoners and not the management of the prison. I'm not really interested in how these places are run."

I asked Hardwick about his assessment of the differences between public and private facilities. "The question of where prisoners or detainees are treated better, in public or private facilities, is the wrong question," he said. "From my inspection findings, you can't find any difference between the public and private sector. The critical difference is that on the whole a new prison, public or private sector, will have difficulties for some years after it's set up. So a newly established private prison will initially perform worse, but after time they'll likely become better than something running in an old, crumbling Victorian ruin."

Hardwick was unafraid to question the moral underpinnings of outsourcing punishment: "One of the best prisons now is the Parc Prison in Wales, run by G4S. It's a phenomenally well-run facility with a stable management team. But that doesn't answer whether it's an ethnical decision to privatize the system. A small private sector can innovate, more so than the public sector. But it should be an exception rather than the rule [to privatize prisons]." The dangers of profiteering were starkly highlighted in a late 2014 report by Hardwick that had found that five Serco-run prisons were likely still to be illegally monitoring inmates' phonecalls with their MPs.

Hardwick opposed the government-imposed austerity that had

led to cost-cutting and human-rights abuses. In October 2014, he noted that a rising prison population, combined with budget cuts, had resulted in soaring numbers of prison deaths—the highest in thirty years—and levels of violence. "At its worst, overcrowding means two prisoners sharing a six-foot-by-ten-foot cell designed for one, with bunks along one wall, a table and chair for one, some shelves, a small TV, an unscreened toilet at the foot of the bunks, poor ventilation, and a sheet as a makeshift curtain. A few prisoners might spend twenty-three hours a day in such a cell."[68]

Running an Inspectorate that would arrive unannounced at various centers around the country, Hardwick had seen an improvement in the behavior of Serco, G4S, and other contractors in recent years. "What causes peoples' despair in immigration removal centers, the bulk of them, why they are such unhappy and sad places, is because of people's distress in how their immigration case is being handled. It's not generally about the center itself. This is not just down to Serco—that's an easy cop-out. You have to confront the hard questions about your detention policy."

Hardwick told me that he had not found rampant abuses at Yarl's Wood, despite having read countless media reports suggesting otherwise. However, "if you place a woman who's had some trauma and abuse in the past in that position where the power imbalance between the woman and the detention officers is so extreme, where you place them in an establishment which is behind closed walls and where the women may have difficulty raising concerns about their status due to language difficulties, you're placing them in an incredibly vulnerable situation. We are not careful enough, and we don't take seriously enough how we put and keep women in a situation that is inherently dangerous and risky."

His ideal vision for detention, if it happened at all, was to reduce physical tension for refugees. "The first principle is that people are not there because they've committed an offence, therefore every prison-like aspect needs to be individually justified. It should be as un-prison-like as possible. It's about the design, what uniforms people wear, access to the internet, can you move around the place freely. One of the great surprises of this job is seeing how many people are locked up without ever going before a court. A lot of these people are locked up essentially on the say-so of a relatively junior civil servant as an administrative convenience. There needs to be a much higher level of oversight of the decision to detain and the need for continuing detention."

Hardwick was critical of many facilities but believed he had identified two centers that should be copied by others: "In Scotland there's a place called Dungavel, run by Geo Group. They're a big local player that attracts good local talent. It's a long way away from the bureaucracy, and it runs in a very civilized and humane way. It's very cheerful compared to other places, and people get really good-quality advice about their immigration cases. It's about reassurance and treating people in a dignified way. Because of that you don't get the tensions. You could have more places run like that."

He was also supportive of Cedars, the family detention facility run by Barnardo's, though I told him I had received reports of ongoing abuses. "If you talk to families there—we do when we inspect—they say that if we're going to be removed forcibly, this kind of breathing space for a couple of days is important for us. They run it in a very child-centered way. Levels of individual care are very good. It's still a difficult time for people, so there's high levels of self-harm, but there's a focus on care. I don't think you should detain more children, but I think the principles that are applied at Cedars, for the vulnerable, you could apply to other settings as a whole."

I found myself questioning Hardwick's judgment, however, when he released a positive assessment of the Mitie-run center at Campsfield in 2015, despite finding a litany of faults there: a child had been locked up for sixty-two days "by mistake"; overcrowding was rampant; kitchen hygiene was criticized; torture victims were detained despite Home Office rules forbidding it; and legal services for detainees were inadequate. The Practice, the medical company contracted to provide healthcare, was found to have cut corners and to operate with insufficient staffing.[69]

Despite all of these problems, Hardwick's report praised the facility: "Overall, this was a very positive inspection. Staff and managers at Campsfield House should be congratulated in dealing professionally and sensitively with detainees who were going through what, for many, was a difficult and unhappy time."

Disaster capitalism is thriving in Britain because the forces opposing it are so weak. While the privatization boom continues apace at home, London is exporting the ideology behind it, providing more than £600 million—packaged as development aid—to help local companies such as Unilever and Monsanto to take over vast tracts of land in Africa. Small farmers, women, and agriculture-reliant communities are exploited in the name of helping Africa. In the guise of development, Britain is recolonizing the continent all over again—this time with friendlier rhetoric and fewer guns.[70]

This exploitation will inevitably increase inequality, as even the OECD seems to agree. In a 2014 report, the Paris think-tank argued that wealthy nations must accept that capitalism's glory days were over, and that poor countries would discover this reality by 2060. This was because discrimination would surge globally, with climate change starting to have profound effects on agricultural sustainability. The OECD's proposed solution consisted of the kind of thinking that increased the abuses reported in this chapter: privatization and further austerity. "The ultimate lesson from the report is that, sooner or later, an alternative programme to 'more of the same' will emerge," wrote Britain's *Channel 4 News* economics editor Paul Mason. "Because populations armed with smartphones, and an increased sense of their human rights, will not accept a future of high inequality and low growth."[71]

There is some reason to be hopeful. After a public campaign in 2014 by writer and comedian Russell Brand to highlight plans by

US asset management firm Westbrook Partners to evict dozens of families from the New Era housing estate in London, the company shelved its proposal and sold its stake to an affordable housing organization. It was a small but significant win, undeniably strengthened by the profile of Brand, and a rare example of disaster capitalism being challenged and beaten back. With this success, Brand wrote that he had "inadvertently wandered into the heart of a truly accessible and exciting movement to oppose pointless government and tyrannical big business ... I was compelled to stay ... [b]y something I didn't even know I was grieving; the loss of community, our connection to each other."[72]

Such successes are why public resistance is essential to ensure a British future not designed by corporate bosses and their political friends. Humanity must not be outsourced to the highest bidder.

7

Australia: "If you have a pulse, you have a job at Serco"

We have here an environment that is inherently toxic. It has characteristics which over time reliably cause harm to people's mental health.

Dr. Peter Young, former Australian head
psychiatrist for detained asylum seekers

It was a strange feeling to leave the Australian mainland by plane without needing a passport or visa and land on an Australian-run island three-and-a-half hours later.

There was a diverse range of people who boarded the plane in Perth, Western Australia, for Christmas Island: Pacific Islanders, burly white men, Asian Muslims, and hijab-wearing women. I saw two Serco staff sitting next to a refugee with a bushy goatee—a man likely from Iran or Iraq. He was reading a *Where's Wally?* book and wore a T-shirt with "No Prisoners" written on the back. We made eye contact; I smiled, and he returned the courtesy.

The expensive flight was a beautiful trip over blue sea with occasional atolls ringed by perfectly white sand. Flying across the Indian Ocean, I half expected to see an asylum-seeker boat on its way to Christmas Island being intercepted by the Australian Navy. My first glimpse of the island was of steep hills and a striking coastline. Its small airport turned out to be little more than a large room—a shop that sold duty-free alcohol and cigarettes. This isolated island was where Australia warehoused asylum seekers under the profitable gaze of the British multinational Serco.

The humidity was high as I left the tiny terminal; outside, a sign welcoming me to the island stood alongside a tall pole flying an Australian flag. At the desk of a rental-car company, a young Chinese-Australian man gave me a photocopy of a hand-drawn map of the island and said, "You can't get lost here, mate. It's basically just one big circle."

The drive from the airport into Flying Fish Cove, the island's main town, revealed luscious greenery and washed-out 1960s-style low-level apartment blocks with clothes strung across their windows and doors. Near the water there was a mosque with a small minaret and more grubby apartment buildings, tightly packed together; rust infested the structures. An Australian Navy ship was docked at the waterfront, and its officers dived into the glistening water from the short pier. A sign on the pier read: "Warning: This Is A Customs Controlled Area. Persons Must Not Enter Without Appropriate Identification."

Arriving on Christmas Island felt like stepping into a time warp, as there were no noticeably contemporary buildings. The place looked tired and unloved, and its remoteness reminded me of other detention centers in Australia, Britain, and America. It was no accident that these were the locations governments had chosen to house asylum seekers—out of sight and out of mind.

I checked into a hotel overlooking the ocean, less than fifty meters from the site of the tragic accident that occurred on December 10, 2010, when an asylum-seeker boat struck the coast in bad weather and forty-eight people died. Residents could only stand by helplessly and watch as refugees perished in the rough waters below. Another tragic accident occurred offshore in March 2013, with at least two asylum seekers dying when their boat capsized. This made the national news for a few days, then disappeared. Public sympathy extended only as long as the media cycle.

There were approximately 1,500 permanent residents on the island and about 600 Serco and Australian Department of Immigration and Border Protection (DIBP) staff, who came and went (it was called the Department of Immigration and Citizenship—DIAC—until 2013). One of the latter's facilities, the "Construction Camp," sat opposite the sports center where the workers who built the first Christmas Island detention facility lived. At the time of writing, all refugee families—around 100 men, women, and children—had been removed, though when I visited there were around 200 people, also families, despite a surge in capacity allowing up to 300, in very basic accommodation such as dongas (temporary dwellings) and rusty shipping containers. Single men were placed in the much larger detention center, which was a short drive from town. The site was eerily quiet, though I could hear a few voices in the distance. There was low-level security, and the green shrubbery behind the prefabricated structures was the only sign of color in the area.

Getting access to these facilities was a tortuous process, and Serco and DIBP staff deliberately gave me the runaround. I arrived on Christmas Island after being told on the Australian mainland that I would not be allowed to meet any detainees, despite knowing asylum seekers had requested to see me. Independent oversight, by journalists or the public, was seen as a threat to a secretive system.

Despite the transformation of Christmas Island from mining outpost to detention facility, there remained a unique multicultural mix on the island. One evening I attended a Buddhist ceremony— an event held annually—at a hilltop temple near the detention center. Flags were fluttering in the wind, and stretching to the horizon was a gorgeous view of the sparkling Indian Ocean. The sun set with a brilliant red flourish. There was mainly a Chinese-Malay crowd in attendance; it was this community that raised the funds each year to bring two shamans over from Malaysia for the occasion. But there were also representatives of the island's other ethnic communities, as well as some Serco staff.

The temple was packed with Buddhists, many of whom were taking photographs of one shaman in a red smock rocking back and forth in a trance. He wrote prayers on small pieces of paper while keeping his eyes closed. Many candles were burning, and incense wafted through the air. A local man drummed hypnotically throughout the afternoon and evening. Outside the temple, a banquet that had been prepared for the ceremony's 100 participants was on a long trestle table—noodles, rice, chicken and other meats, huge quantities of everything. We all lined up and helped ourselves.

The final part of the ceremony saw one of the shamans leading a procession across a small bridge that had been constructed in front of the temple. People paid money to hold incense sticks, and then removed their shoes to receive a blessing.

I talked to Simon, a tall, lanky British man who taught young children in detention. He had arrived with high hopes of being able to change the system from within, and he said the children had undoubtedly benefited from the regular classes. But he also thought that uncertainty over the length and outcome of detention had an adverse impact on their mental health. Simon said that Serco staff were friendly enough to him, then shared a revealing anecdote. His school had put together an induction manual and given it to Serco to examine. The company's response was that some of its officials were unable to complete the task because they could not read or write. Education options for island children had been limited, the Catholic Education Office of Western Australia establishing a school for asylum seekers only.

Also at the ceremony was Harry, an Australian who has been on Christmas Island for nearly two decades and rarely returned to the mainland; there had been a gap of eighteen years between his last two visits. He told me that he opposed the detention center because of the environmental degradation caused by the amount of resources, such as water and timber, required to run the place. He was against having a privatized "prison" on the island and thought refugees should be put in community-based detention. "Politicians and the media whip up a fear of asylum seekers, but only a few thousand are coming over a year," he lamented. "Are we saying as a nation that we can't handle this small number?"

The following day I met Gordon Thomson, formerly a Christmas Island councilor and now general secretary of the Union of Christmas Island Workers (UCIW). He was in his mid-fifties, with a cheeky grin and crazy white hair. He had been on the island for more than fifteen years, outstaying his wife and daughter, who had left years before. Gordon loved the place. He had always opposed the detention center and told me that it divided the island's residents into two groups: the few who were benefiting, and the many who were not. He was having a row with Serco over improving the conditions for detention-center workers. He said they were a stingy bunch of managers.

Gordon drove me across the island. As we motored along the main shopping strip, where Christmas Island's sole post office and bank were located, he explained the mix of Malay, Chinese, Thai, and Anglo people who lived here. Roughly 60 percent of the population was Chinese, 20 percent Malay, and the rest mainly Caucasian. Buddhism was the predominant religion. Before the reopening of the detention center in 2008, the island received around 2,000 tourists annually. But in the years since that number had declined to around 1,500.

The annual migration of the red crab was taking place, and as we headed out of town we saw countless crabs, large and small, scurrying across the road. It could be so dangerous for drivers that Parks Australia closed some roads at different times of the year. Most locals respected such directives, but a common complaint I heard during my visit was that Serco's fly-in, fly-out (FIFO) officials often ignored them and ended up killing many crabs, fueling resentment towards the multinational.[1]

Gordon took me to a lookout point. It was a stunning view. There were beautiful booby birds and mountains and ocean all around me. Some 63 percent of Christmas Island was designated as national park. Another 14 percent was under a phosphate mining lease—an industry established in the 1890s. During my visit, mine workers were on strike over pay demands, causing tension in the community due to about 180 men not earning a wage. The miners were refusing to accept poor salaries at a time when two liters of milk cost $19.50, and while on-site DIBP officials each received an allowance of around $30,000 per year to cover such expenses.[2] From the lookout, I saw signs of mining damage across Christmas Island's pristine environment—large areas of excavated land and massive mounds of dirt.

Gordon next took me down a road framed by lush forest to show me the detention center, which was situated at North West Point, around seventeen kilometers from Flying Fish Cove. He pulled over to show me a winding path that led to a hilltop spot with a clear view of the detention center; with help from Phosphate Resources, DIBP had tried to block the entrance to the path with large piles of gravel. From beside the road, we glimpsed the center, which had a clinical look to it. Large satellite dishes dotted the grounds, and there were many signs reading "No Unauthorised People Past This Point."

A few days later, I skirted the gravel mounds and hiked for fifteen minutes to the viewpoint. I was rewarded with a striking vision of the entire detention center as it glistened in the late afternoon sun. Situated near the ocean, it was accessible by one entry road. I saw a few people moving around inside the center. Its massive size surprised me. At its peak, the place had housed over 3,000 detainees, though at the time of writing it had between 100 and 200, as many had been transferred to the Australian mainland, with an uncertain future.

The voices of Christmas Island residents were rarely recorded because so few reporters make the journey out there, but my trip gave me the opportunity. When I attended a UCIW executive meeting, chaired by Gordon Thomson, I asked the attendees about their attitudes towards the detention center and Serco. There were twelve people in the fluorescent-lit room—eleven Asian men and one Indian woman.

Christmas Island shopkeepers were happy with the detention center, as food prices kept going up. Demand sometimes outstripped supply, but the FIFO workers had a lot of disposable income, so the shop owners could inflate prices accordingly. Everyone was also pleased that the new Serco roster had its employees staying for six- to twelve-month blocks on the island. "Short-term Serco staff have no sense of belonging on the island," one man said.

The people at the meeting were mostly sympathetic to refugees. Their anger was directed more at the distant bureaucrats who were putting undue pressure on their island. They wanted more houses built for locals, for instance. They were also upset about the millions of dollars spent on the inquiry into the boat disaster in December 2010—money they believed would have been better spent on infrastructure. A young man told me that "when detention centers are built in remote areas, locals usually suffer, and hire cars, hotels, and better food are only easily obtained by fly-in, fly-out staff. The facility has killed off other industries for the island, like tourism, and Christmas Island's image globally is of a prison."[3]

Australia's modern asylum-seeker network had a sordid history. Its status as a colonial nation that committed genocide against its Aboriginal people partly explains the fears of non-British outsiders. In August 2001, the *Tampa*, a Norwegian ship carrying 438 people, predominantly Hazara Afghans who had been rescued from a troubled fishing vessel in international waters, was refused entry into Australian waters by the military, and was eventually steered to the Pacific island of Nauru. This prompted the conservative John Howard government, in the days before the 9/11

attacks, to announce its Pacific Solution, whereby it would establish detention facilities on Christmas Island, Nauru, and Papua
New Guinea's Manus Island—offshore locations that would house
refugees well away from the Australian mainland and the prying
eyes of the public and media. A temporary detention facility was
established on Christmas Island in late 2001 in an attempt to send
the message that asylum seekers arriving on the Australian mainland would be processed offshore, not near population centers,
and made to suffer long periods behind bars.[4]

This regime endured from 2001 to 2007. A new Labor government, initially stating that it would humanize and soften the system
by closing offshore centers, reopened the Christmas Island facility
in late 2008, and the whole Pacific Solution began again in 2012.
The plan, which received bipartisan support in the Australian
parliament, involved excluding countless islands from Australia's
migration zone, and using the Australian Navy to stop refugee-
carrying boats. Asylum seekers were removed and processed in
other countries, often waiting for years in poor conditions for
their refugee status to be determined. In May 2013, the federal
parliament legislated to remove the Australian mainland from its
migration zone—meaning that all asylum seekers arriving on the
mainland could be sent to offshore facilities in Nauru or Papua
New Guinea. Both nations accepted facilities on their territories
because Australia used the oldest form of persuasion in the book:
heaps of money. In 2014, Cambodia, one of the poorest and most
corrupt nations in Asia, was also bribed to take some refugees that
Australia did not want.

Offshoring was an ingenious innovation that heralded an
ominous development in mutated economics. It meant one less
level of accountability to cooperate with regional partners known
for graft and brutality. Papua New Guinea and Cambodia could
not provide for their own citizens and refugees, let alone manage
people Australia rejected. Sovereignty was skewed. When questioned about the problems inside the camps on Nauru and Manus

Island, Australia falsely claimed that it was not their problem and suggested asking the officials of these "sovereign" states. Australia pulled the strings, multinationals made the money, and former colonial outposts were left with the problems (though they were handsomely rewarded for the imposition).

This did not bother Canberra. The opposite was true because, by restricting media access to the contested sites, both the government and privateers were able to work mostly without interruption. The system even inspired others. The United Nations announced in 2014 that it was considering establishing holding camps in Egypt, Libya, and Sudan to manage the huge influx of refugees into Europe. It was entirely unworkable, but it proved that Australia's ruthless efficiency had friends in the most unusual places. The European Union in 2015, facing a huge increase in unwanted migrants, announced a military-style solution to the crisis, mirroring Australian policies.

Throughout this entire process in Australia, over two decades the amount of money being made by contractors soared. These were the perfect conditions for disaster capitalism to thrive. International companies such as Serco and G4S—multinationals with virtually no accountability in the Australian parliament—sold their competence to successive Australian governments, despite routinely failing to care for their staff or asylum seekers. Serco and G4S executives rarely appeared in the press or before government committees. While they lobbied behind the scenes for more work, they played no direct role in local Australian politics. This was typical of globalized corporate culture. Ultimate responsibility for breaches or abuses lay thousands of kilometers away in Britain—an arrangement that suited both the firms and the government.

It was a time of brutal politics and inhumane policies that were condemned by the United Nations and every reputable human rights group in the world. This period never ended. The UN Human Rights Council Commissioner, Jordanian prince Zeid

Ra'ad Al-Hussein, slammed Australia in September 2014 for a "chain of human rights violations" and "arbitrary detention and possible torture following return to home countries."

But the Pacific solution was not unpopular with the Australian public. After 9/11, boat arrivals were constantly framed as potential terrorists who needed to be treated with suspicion. Australians still nurtured this prejudice, milked by many commentators and politicians. A poll in early 2014 found that many Australians wanted harsher treatment against boat arrivals, because they did not believe the new arrivals were genuine refugees.[5] In reality, the vast majority of asylum seekers arriving in Australia were found by immigration officials to be deserving of legal protection. In the 1970s there was anxiety about Vietnamese and Lebanese refugees fleeing war and persecution. In the twenty-first century it was Muslims and Tamil "terrorists" allegedly importing sharia law, division, and violence. G4S and Serco did not care about this race-baiting, though many of their staff racially abused people in their care. In many ways, privatization had no moral code, apart from making money; and if contracts were available, then the large companies felt obliged to bid for them.

Central to Australian immigration policy had been its association with the corporations that carried it out. Both major political parties, Labor and Liberal, supported outsourced detention centers, though the Labor party, nominally more progressive on some social issues, had occasionally expressed discomfort with it. It had been in effect, along with mandatory detention of refugees, since the 1990s. (Figures released in 2014 found that refugees were being kept in detention for an average of nine months—far longer than international standards allowed.)[6]

The Christmas Island detention center began to take shape when the Howard government's minister for territories, Wilson Tuckey, arrived on the island in March 2002, and delivered the following news: "You're going to get a new detention center and I'm not here to argue." Regular environmental assessments were waived to get the project moving as fast as possible. In 2014 locals still complained about not being consulted about anything, including services and the hospital. "Sometimes we feel as though we are the forgotten island," says Linda Cash, Christmas Island Tourism Association's marketing manager.[7] Christmas Island and the Cocos Islands were essentially colonies controlled by Australia. In the 1990s a casino brought riches to Christmas Island, but closed due to the Asian financial crisis. Some locals wanted it reopened. Boat arrivals had made at least ten people millionaires on Christmas Island—savvy beneficiaries of the detention business.[8]

Building commenced in 2006, and the facility was initiated with roughly 800 beds at a cost of $400 million. But the cost increased, and private contractors still had not completed all the work when John Howard was voted out of office in 2007. The center finally opened in 2008 under Labor's watch. The government awarded Serco a contract in 2009 to manage all of Australia's detention centers, for $370 million over five years. The boats started surging soon afterwards. DIBP heralded the company's "strong alignment with the department's values and the government's directions in detention." Serco maintained the contract in 2014, despite years of mismanagement. It was worth around $1 billion over five years—a huge increase, due to the far greater numbers of people the company had to manage.

The conservative Tony Abbott government, elected in 2013, pledged to "stop the boats," and at the time of writing it had mostly succeeded, though at a high human cost.[9] Operation Sovereign Borders was the Orwellian-named government program designed to implement the policy. Then immigration minister Scott Morrison, a practicing Christian, was given unprecedented powers to push asylum-seeker boats back into the sea, to block them from making refugee claims on dubious "character" grounds or in the name of "national interest," with no oversight over the government's decision-making process, and to deport people to nations with horrendous human rights records. His decisions were beyond review.[10] He played God, and apparently enjoyed doing so. Afghans and Tamils, sent back to Afghanistan and Sri Lanka, were beaten and tortured, and sometimes simply disappeared. Morrison continued the Guantánamo Bay–style indefinite detention of dozens of asylum seekers, some of whom had been incarcerated for more than five years. None were allowed to know the reasons that ASIO, Australia's intelligence service, was keeping them in detention.

Secrecy was central, with little information publicly released. When asylum seekers made the treacherous boat journey from Indonesia to Australia, Australian customs vessels apprehended unspecified numbers of them. Some were transferred to small orange lifeboats to be sent back to Indonesia in a "turnback" maneuver. They were cramped, and refugees alleged rough handling by Australian naval officers. Others were held below deck on customs vessels for long periods of time without seeing sunlight. Public outcry in Australia was muted. Outrage against the corporations working with the government to implement these policies was minimal. Their corporate names were only occasionally referenced in media reports, and that was the way they liked it—remaining almost invisible to the public, yet being integral to the government's plans.

Australia exported a privatized culture to overseas detention centers. Serco had managed some facilities on the Cocos Islands, and G4S was initially given the contract to manage the site on Manus Island. Nauruans had been paid $4 per hour by the contractor Transfield Services to work at the center there—ten times less than the hourly rate received by Australian citizens employed in the same facility.[11] Australian contractors had been enjoying Canberra's decision to build permanent structures on Nauru to the tune of more than $70 million,[12] though a visit by a journalist from Rupert Murdoch's *Australian* newspaper in 2013 found very basic conditions. Serious allegations of sexual abuse, as well as threats of rape by guards at the center, continued to surface, and in September

2014 detainees' self-harm soared. Female asylum seekers claimed they had to expose their bodies if they wanted to shower for longer than two minutes.[13] This story caused no national scandal, and simply disappeared. A government-appointed review released in 2015 heard allegations from detainees on Nauru that private security staff had sexually exploited them, along with evidence showing the sexualization of children in the cramped, dirty conditions. Save the Children aid workers, present on Nauru, claimed the Abbott government knew about the sexual assault of detainees since 2014 but ignored them.

In 2004 I interviewed a Kuwait-born Palestinian, Aladdin Sisalem, when he was the sole detainee on Manus Island. He was clearly mentally traumatized by the experience. After Manus had been reopened, he condemned it as an island of lawlessness. "When you are there, you are worth nothing," he said. "You are not protected by law."[14]

The presence of asylum seekers had also brought irreversible changes to Manus Island itself. There was no local consultation. "We heard about it on the radio," said political leader Nahau Rooney.[15] When detainees protested their long-term detention and poor conditions on Manus in January 2015, after leaked official figures for 2014 found refugees being placed in medical isolation at a rate of nearly one a day, Australian Immigration Minister Peter Dutton thanked local authorities and Transfield for removing the "threat" of legitimate protest. No further mention was made of the company's role, and journalists were still refused access to the site. The only images the media showed was footage shot surreptitiously by asylum seekers, revealing men who had sewn their lips together and passed out from being on hunger strike. Transfield made more money the longer the refugees remained behind bars. The company imposed a draconian policy on its staff working on Nauru and Manus Island, telling them they could be sacked depending on who followed them on social media or for being part of a group or party opposed to Australia's refugee policies.[16]

Detention was costly for taxpayers. The figures contained in a DIBP brief for the federal government in 2010 revealed that offshore processing at Christmas Island was five times more expensive than holding refugees on the Australian mainland. The $471 million earmarked for this task included $109 million for "service delivery" and $358 million for "administration." The brief showed that the government had arrived at these numbers by assuming that boat arrivals would slow down in the years after 2011.

The opposite occurred, however. Sixty-nine boats came in 2011, and at least 205 boats arrived in 2012, compared with 134 in 2010. By the end of 2012, the number of asylum seekers who had arrived in Australia by boat since Labor assumed office in 2007 was over 13,000—just shy of the number who had arrived during the entire twelve years of the Howard government. In May 2011, the Labor government publicly acknowledged that its previous costings were less than was needed, and that about $1 billion would need to be allocated in the mid-year budget.[17]

Of course, this money was "found" without additional public scrutiny. It seemed that no amount was too much for the Australian government to pay to process asylum seekers as far away from the mainland as possible. Australian journalist David Marr pithily wrote that undisguised racism lurked behind this willingness: "The budget for reassuring Australians is bottomless."[18]

Australasian Correctional Management (ACM), owned by the US prison company Wackenhut, which previously managed at least six detention centers in Australia, revealed in 2000 that its annual turnover was $100 million, with an after-tax profit of $7.5 million.[19] In 2010, Serco's revenue was $369 million, and its after-tax profit was $40.5 million. The following year, this jumped to $756 million in revenue and a $59 million profit.[20] In 2013 Serco's revenue rose to $1.25 billion, and yet its 2013 financial statement showed a relatively stagnant profit. Results were murky, because G4S and Serco did not abide by Australian accounting rules. By 2014, Serco's global position was faltering, its share price having crashed by a third. Happily, though, the firm's Australian detention contract partially insulated them from disaster.

G4S was rolling in it, charging $74,792 per detainee per year on Manus Island. It was cheaper to place an asylum seeker in a room in the Sheraton hotel in Sydney than for one night on Manus under G4S control.[21] Australian construction firm Decmil increased its contract to expand the Manus facility in 2014 from $137 million to $253 million.[22] A source contracted to Decmil told me in 2015 that the company had bid to replace Transfield and Wilson Security on Manus Island and Nauru and wanted to apply a different, less aggressive approach. "We do not see the task as security, we see it as welfare and care," my source said.

The scale of the growth of the private detention center industry had been massive. Countless companies and individuals were reaping the rewards, including charter airlines, a pub on Cocos Island providing temporary accommodation for asylum seekers, and construction firms. "Stopping the boats" had the potential to affect the bottom line negatively. Since 2003, four companies—G4S, Serco, Transfield, and Toll Holdings—had been given more than $5.6 billion in detention work.[23] Overall, since 2007, contractors, including the Salvation Army and Canstruct, had won up to $10 billion in detention-related jobs.[24]

Transfield scored the massive $1.2 billion contract to run Nauru and Manus Island in 2014, after G4S had badly botched the work and was rightly blamed for a riot in February 2014 that led to the murder of Iranian refugee Reza Berati.[25] No senior G4S staff were charged for the crime. Serious allegations of rape, abuse, and violence were commonplace at the center, one Australian officer labeling the facility a "horrendous chicken pen."[26] Guards locked asylum seekers in solitary confinement for days on end, without communication.[27]

"There was nothing like a crisis to stimulate a bit of change," said former G4S head Nick Buckles in 2010. By "change," he meant the privatization of services under the guise of efficiency and cost savings for the government. Buckles told an analysts'

meeting in March 2011 that losing a contract here or there was not
such a big deal, because there were "a lot of outsourcing opportunities and not many competitors."[28] It was an unhealthy power
balance. Richard Harding, who was Western Australia's chief
prison inspector for a decade, told the *New York Times* what was
at the heart of the problem: "These global companies [like Serco]
are more powerful than the governments they're dealing with."[29]

The mystique of these companies was enhanced by the almost
complete absence of media appearances by their spokespeople,
although they seemed unwilling to admit this. In a rare 2011 interview, then chief executive of Serco Asia-Pacific, David Campbell,
remarked: "To be described as a secretive organization, I was
completely gobsmacked." He also told *Perth Now* that he was personally pained by the death of any asylum seekers, but they did
"everything in our power to look after these people." Referring to
a recent Tamil death in detention, he asked, "Is it in our power for
no one ever to pass away under those circumstances? Actually, no.
It's not in our power, we're not God."[30]

Yet secrecy was the hallmark of the system. In 2011 I co-wrote
a story that leaked for the first time the 2009 contract between
DIBP and Serco. Unauthorized media access to detention centers
was shown to be a "critical" event, given the same status as a
hostage situation, bomb threat, or death, while detainees' clinical
depression and voluntary starvation of under twenty-four hours'
duration were "minor" situations.[31] Keeping tabs on the media was
a high priority.[32]

Matthew J. Gibney, a political scientist at Oxford University,
argued that the explosion of outsourced incarceration since the
1990s was politically driven: "When something goes wrong—a
death, an escape—the government can blame it on a kind of market
failure instead of an accountability failure."[33]

It could be that the outsourcing of prisons and detention centers
in Australia had also been influenced by its relationship with the
United States. In 1988, a successful meeting took place between

various Australian government officials and the leading US private prison company CCA. "The decision to go private was not precipitated by problems such as overcrowding, litigation, or lack of public funds," wrote Australian professor Eileen Baldry, but the "client state nature of Australia's relationship with the US," which encouraged firms to seek contracts in Australia.[34]

It was another hot and humid day on Christmas Island, and I still hadn't gained access to the detention facility. But I was about to talk to some of the detainees.

A few days earlier I had met Joan Kelleher, a sister who worked with the Christian aid organization Australian Mercy, and a resident of the island since March 2010. She was also a daily visitor to the refugees in detention. Sister Joan was a true humanitarian. She opposed mandatory detention and took asylum seekers with fragile mental states on brief excursions, for activities such as cooking and swimming. She told me that she oscillated between despair and inspiration, but unfortunately felt more of the former. Then she recalled a Tamil man who had been inside the detention center for twenty-six months—he had been granted refugee status but was waiting to receive security clearance. "I'm inspired by those who survive what this system throws at them," she said. "And those who stay strong."

Sister Joan then told me that she would be taking four Afghan Hazara refugees to the beach for a barbecue in a few days' time and suggested I come along. I arrived to find the sister and the quartet of men wading barefoot in shallow water—one man dipped his entire body underwater, fully clothed. It was a beautiful day, and the color of the water alternated between green and blue. There were a few fishermen and some boats on the horizon, but little else. The men were aged in their thirties and forties, all married with children, their families still in Afghanistan and Pakistan. They had all been rejected for refugee status twice by DIBP and remained in limbo in Australia, claiming they would be injured or killed if they were sent home (bombings and attacks in 2013 and 2014 targeted the Hazara people in Quetta, Pakistan, where all the men had family). They appeared pleased to see me—a new person to talk with. Despite the grave threats to the Hazaras, Australia started sending refugees back to Afghanistan in 2014, some of whom were tortured by the Taliban on their return.[35] Australian prime minister Tony Abbott said in 2015 that Iran should take back its citizens who failed to gain asylum in Australia, despite the grave risks faced by returnees.

The men collected rocks of different colors to send to their children. One man, Abdul, could not speak English, and he told me that he had been in detention for twenty-two months, in Darwin on the north coast of Australia and on Christmas Island. He took six different antidepressants daily. His left eye was bloodshot, and he showed me injuries on his body that he claimed had been inflicted by the Taliban. He smiled as we talked but said he was sad because of uncertainty about what would happen to him, and that he had never been given any definite information on his case— including a timeline of when it would be resolved—from either DIBP or Serco.

I talked to all the men, but with varying degrees of success because of language difficulties. They said they wanted to be allowed to live in community detention—a policy implemented by the Labor government in 2012 and deepened by the Abbott regime in 2014, permitting asylum seekers to live freely but in limbo under a "temporary protection visa" that expired after three years. It offered little security. Babies born in Australia were classified as "unauthorized maritime arrivals" and could not live in Australia, but were settled offshore. This system was better than being in a high-security prison, but it still left refugees in an emotional abyss. The men talked about the difficult existence of a detainee—the monotony of daily life, the lack of excursions or visitors, the humid weather. They told me that the boredom caused trauma. This was borne out by the facts: self-harm and attempted self-immolation had soared among asylum seekers in detention in 2013 and 2014, as shown in figures released in 2015.[36]

Refugee desperation was financially exploited at every level of the journey, from people smugglers taking refugees' life-savings to corrupt officials needing to be bribed along the route. I knew many asylum seekers who recounted awful stories of harrowing boat journeys from Indonesia to Australia. People often drowned all around them. Arriving by boat in Australia did not end the nightmare, because new multinational actors entered the picture to atomize and privatize their lives. Everything and everyone had a monetary value. Spending months and years in a remote location, managed every day by a careless or racist guard employed by a private company, compounded the feeling of hopelessness. Tamils, Pakistanis, Afghans, and Iraqis, among others, moved from an authoritarian hell to a bureaucratic maze, in a nation they had wrongly assumed was fair and democratic.

I was walking back to my hotel when something out at sea attracted my attention, and I stopped at the exact spot from which Christmas Island's residents watched helplessly in December 2010 as refugees drowned in heavy seas. I could see a clearly over-crowded boat on the horizon, and it was heading towards shore. Two large Australian ships and a few smaller vessels shadowed the boat. A few people gathered, to film and photograph the boat. Those around me, a mix of tourists and locals, were largely unsympathetic towards the incoming refugees. One said, "I bet they'll find wads of cash in their pockets." Two older couples said they were sick of so many boats arriving in Australia.

This had been a regular occurrence on the island until 2013, when boats largely stopped arriving, but it was the first time I had seen it. It was difficult not to feel sympathy for people who had sailed across dangerous waters to reach somewhere safe.

I went down to the jetty, where several dozen DIBP, Serco, police, and customs officials, as well as interpreters and ambu-lance staff, awaited the arrival of the refugees. A number of island residents and tourists were there too, mostly middle-aged or older. The ones I talked to all expressed opposition to refugees. They were "illegals" who might come and "take over," like "what's happening in parts of Europe." One person said, "They should be pushed back to Indonesia, where they will be safe. Why are they coming to Australia? What if terrorists are on the boats? We have poverty here and people living in bad conditions on Christmas Island, but they come and are treated better than Australians." I mentioned Serco and asked whether anyone cared that a private company was making money from greater numbers of refugee arrivals. One older man said he felt uncomfortable about it; a tourist was unaware of the fact.

The refugee boat stopped around 200 meters from the shore, and a speedboat raced out to meet it. After a short while, around fourteen refugees wearing life jackets were brought to the jetty, then more were brought ashore. I saw a woman in a wheelchair (I was later informed she was pregnant), an exceptionally tall man, a young girl, a woman wearing a hijab, and a teenage boy—all Middle Eastern in appearance. They were frisked and their bags collected.

There was something moving about this piece of theatre. I did not know the refugees or their stories, but after hearing little but demonization of them for years, the first contact between asylum seekers and the government struck me as a deeply human exchange. Sadly, the refugees were about to be politicized, privatized, and silenced by bureaucracy.

The process on the jetty looked orderly, and the various officials treated the asylum seekers with respect. I heard one woman near me say, "See how they always come with men and boys first, and then bring their families later?" As I walked back to my car, I started talking to a local Chinese man who was watching the proceedings. "They people, all bad Muslims," he told me. I asked him how he knew they were Muslims. "I've heard they are, and they're not like the others."

Arriving back at my hotel, I saw an Australian ship alongside the refugee boat. The latter was to be set on fire and destroyed. I had been told the oil from such fires often floated to shore, damaging the coastline.

A businessman explained the economic logic of Serco managing Australia's detention network. He had been employed by DIBP in 2006 to find a new contractor to run the system. This task continued until after the 2007 election of Labor prime minister Kevin Rudd, despite his party being officially opposed to privatized detention. My source, Clive (not his real name), who requested anonymity,[37] was a supporter of Serco—after all, he had been involved in the company's successful tender. But he attributed this partly to DIBP being "filled with incompetence and no accountability." His search started with 400 firms who could possibly run the system, but it soon came down to a choice between Serco and Global Solutions Limited (GSL); no other corporations could handle the scope of the work.

DIBP believed that privatizing detention centers was one solution to the refugee issue—a way of processing asylum seekers away from the public gaze that also pleased politicians looking to isolate new arrivals. But it knew that GSL—which was bought by G4S in 2008—had a troubled record in dealing with asylum seekers. In 2006, the Howard government announced that it would not extend the GSL contract beyond 2007. It argued that the system needed to be retendered principally because countless reports had found that health and psychological services had been botched by the private firm.

The list of problems was long, both with the bungling immigration department and GSL. Two egregious cases caused huge controversy. Cornelia Rau had been unlawfully placed in detention in 2004 and 2005, while Vivian Alvarez Solon had been unlawfully deported to the Philippines in 2001, and officials had covered up the fact. In 2005 GSL was fined $500,000 for transporting five people in a van for hours without food, water, or toilet breaks. An auditor general's 2005 report condemned the minimal health services provided in detention.[38] The government capitulated to public pressure and dumped GSL, but left office in 2007 still committed to outsourcing. It was a PR exercise—keeping the same economic order while changing the public face of the service provider.

Serco was always going to be near the top of the pile, due to its extensive work with asylum seekers in Britain. But Clive said it won so easily simply because G4S had been a "disastrous contractor" for six years during the Howard and Rudd administrations. He also said that DIBP "knew it but kept on outsourcing more jobs to them." This was the rewarding of failure because the alternatives, such as investing in publicly run services, were politically unpalatable.

Labor, when in opposition, had pledged to put the country's detention centers back into public hands if it won office; this had been part of the party's electoral platform during the 2007 election. But it reneged on this promise in 2009, when Prime Minister Kevin Rudd awarded a massive $370 million contract to Serco to run all seven detention centers in Australia. There were then only a few hundred refugees in detention. In 2015 the company ran many facilities across Australia (though other companies also managed aspects of incarceration).

Clive described to me how he had once met then Serco chief executive Christopher Hyman when he visited Australia. Hyman was "treated like royalty," and he "made it clear that profit was king."

Welcome to the world of cash for care.

Clive believed that Serco "should run all levels of immigration detention because they're more efficient than the department." He thought that private companies like Serco were keen to maintain their contracts with the government, and so were more responsive to demands for change if problems arose. He also said that privatization brought more transparency, "as does Serco," but added that the company was "wary of speaking out about problems due to possible government fines." This, he argued, guaranteed cover-ups, something I heard about during my visits to Curtin detention center in remote Western Australia and Christmas Island.

Nonetheless, Clive believed that Serco was doing "a terrific job under very difficult circumstances." He chastised me for suggesting that Serco staff often mistreated refugees in their care and that remote centers ensured abuses because of the lack of necessary resources. "You seem to ignore the fact that decisions regarding where people in detention go [are] entirely the government's," he said. "A feature in the contract, which is very tightly controlled and was drawn up by the government, is the gag on public comment by Serco." This cute comment ignored the fact that both parties in the agreement benefited from this silence.

Clive said that "no other organization, be it public or private, is better placed nor more capable of providing these services. That Serco continues in good faith to provide services, under extremely difficult circumstances that have been forced upon it by the government, speaks volumes for the organization's integrity and commitment. Yes, they are making money on this service delivery, but the last time I checked they competed in an open market economy for the contract through a process designed by the Commonwealth, won it on merit, and are having to comply with some of the most onerous abatement regimes in place anywhere in the world. I know this because, as you know, I ran the early part of the tendering process and designed the service penalties regime."

Clive argued that Serco should be held accountable for any breaches, including the alleged abuse of detainees and the treatment of vulnerable asylum seekers as if they were being warehoused in a high-security prison. But he blamed the government for mismanaging the large influx of asylum seekers that had put undue pressure on Serco. The company, he said, "would never back out of its contract because it would affect its global reputation."

Clive concluded with an insight gained from countless

conversations with DIBP: "The department would not, under any circumstances, want a return to delivery by public servants." Government officials believed that Serco, with all its faults, was far preferable to an underfunded public service that would have to be more responsive to daily challenges, mainly because a private operator was a convenient scapegoat for systemic failures.

Another high-level source, who still worked for Serco, opened up to me in 2014 about his experiences in Australia, when he helped secure the 2009 immigration detention deal with Canberra. David (not his real name), who also requested anonymity because of the nature of his insights, said that his company's vision was to transform the facilities into "administrative detention and not treat people like criminals in a prison." But then, he told me, "the numbers of boats shot up, and basically we spent a year fire-fighting, trying to cope with the high numbers and the new [immigration detention centers], which were opened with very little notice. Frankly, both Serco and DIBP were overwhelmed, and, much to my personal disappointment, we were unable to implement fully the changes I wanted. I think Serco had some fault here. We should have said no to more, as we couldn't operate them satisfactorily to our vision. However, as you can imagine, in a commercial company it is difficult to turn down work."

I asked David about his "vision" for the immigration centers. "More recreation and activities," he said, "less institutionalized buildings, more internal freedom of movement, and recruitment and training of staff with a social-care ethos rather than just security guards." None of these benefits ever materialized in Australian facilities.

In 2013 a Serco source leaked a cache of internal documents to me that detailed massive price-gouging of the federal government by the multinational, extreme rates of self-harm among detained refugees across the country, the non-reporting of mistakes to avoid government abatements, and a work culture designed to ignore the rights of asylum seekers in order to maximize profit.

My contact, Sean (not his real name), who asked for anonymity due to the sensitivity of his revelations, had worked within senior Serco management in Canberra for a number of years. He told me that, when Serco had won the detention center contract in 2009, it was a relatively well-managed arrangement with the Immigration Department. The situation was "positive-values driven," and public servants mostly seemed keen to assist asylum seekers and visa overstayers.

The policy of the Labor government at the time was that as few individuals as possible would spend significant time in detention. But the relationship between Serco and DIBP quickly deteriorated when the number of refugee boats began surging in 2010. Sean recalled being given only two days' notice to open a new center— the company received the order on a Friday and was expected to prepare an existing but as-yet-unused facility by Sunday. The work was completed, for a hefty fee. Sean also revealed that Serco was given less than three months' notice by Canberra that the Curtin detention center was to be reopened—a facility in the middle of a desert. He said that such short-term planning had become commonplace because successive federal immigration ministers were petrified of making decisions due to "complex politics around the issue ... [They] didn't want to announce new centers until the last minute." The result was policy made on the run, and refugees' living conditions were not a major factor in the government's considerations.

Serco was occasionally asked by the federal government if it could manage the increasing number of detainees in its system. It always said yes, Sean told me, "because we're in the human warehousing business." (When he had complained about the ways in which asylum seekers were being treated, senior management had informed him that he was not "taking a corporate enough view.") A senior official in the Department of the Prime Minister and Cabinet told Sean that the government regretted giving Serco a monopoly in the detention-center business, but that once more boats started arriving, Canberra decided it had no choice but to rely on Serco to manage the huge influx of people, despite the fact that the existing system had been designed for far fewer individuals.

The most serious charge Sean leveled against Serco was that the company was "playing the system" and "making a killing." He explained that the firm "won't spend money on anything that they're not being paid for, such as assessing the relationship between the company and clients. There's little to no oversight of this aspect. Serco has no desire to do so."

Serco gamed the system so well that it was able to exploit the federal government's mismanagement of immigration detention while providing the bare minimum of trained staff to manage asylum seekers. An internal Serco document revealed that, across the country, in every center, the rise in revenue was not met with an increase in hiring. Staff numbers remained relatively constant in 2011—less than the bare minimum required for decent care, Sean argued—despite boat arrivals increasing to over 4,500 people in the same year.

Sean confirmed what I have reported elsewhere in this book—that Serco training was minimal, and cultural training within the detention centers was "almost non-existent." Racism among junior staff was common. He recalled an incident in 2010 in which a number of refugees staged a protest on the roof of Sydney's Villawood Immigration Detention Centre. Serco had no negotiation experts on staff and no idea how to respond, so the situation escalated. To address this deficiency, the company brought in hostage negotiators from the UK to train local staff for all of one month. Another incident in 2012 saw Villawood staff using axes to try to get refugees down from the roof, but in the process they allowed the asylum seekers to get hold of objects that could be turned into weapons.

Years of damning human rights reports had done little to humanize the system. It was revealed in 2014 that hundreds of refugees were being placed in solitary confinement at Villawood by staff without appropriate qualifications. Some were being kept isolated for months on end.[39] The standard of care inside detention was so poor that a call was made by doctors in 2014 to boycott working inside the facilities.[40] The private company running all healthcare facilities in detention, International Health and Medical Services (IHMS), had made billions of dollars from offering substandard care. In an unprecedented move, the former chief psychiatrist for the company, Dr. Peter Young, spoke out in 2014 to condemn detention conditions as "inherently toxic." He accused the process inside the facility of being akin to "torture" and said that "strong coercive pressure" had been applied to asylum seekers to abandon plans to settle in Australia. "Suffering is the way that's achieved."[41]

IHMS was dogged by scandal. A radiologist wanted in America on child sex charges was hired by the company to work on Christmas Island. Another doctor, an anesthetist, was hired despite having engaged in medical misconduct in Britain.[42] Despite these breaches, officials pressured IHMS to be less sympathetic to detainees and comply with "government requirements"—principally, reduced standards of care.[43]

The mental health of detainees was another hugely significant problem. A DIBP document, in a section titled "Self-Harm Risk Assessment Interview," provided only the most basic of instructions to staff, such as to ask how detainees were feeling. Sean said his company's staff were mostly untrained and ill-prepared to manage such tasks. "If you have a pulse, you have a job at Serco," he said.

Accurate figures on self-harm were rarely officially released to the public, but I obtained detailed Serco information about incidents that occurred between 2009 and early 2012. Although it was impossible to be sure that the figures were completely accurate, as a staff member had to note down an incident for it to be recorded, the numbers were shocking. From January 2011 to January 2012, when the number of people in detention fluctuated between 3,994 and 6,520, there were 2,974 "network incidents," including what Serco called "actual," "attempted," or "threatened" events. According to the documents I saw, the vast majority of these incidents were only threatened. Little had changed by 2014, when rates of self-harm and violence soared on remote Manus Island. Many asylum seekers had sought financial compensation for mental and physical trauma after being dumped in these remote centers. Neither the government nor the private contractor were keen to take responsibility—a classic example of unaccountable outsourcing.[44]

Of course, it was not just refugees who suffered under this arrangement. The nature of Serco's subcontractors' work at Villawood Centre, in suburban Sydney, was highlighted when I was contacted by a number of guards employed by MSS Security in early 2011. I had written some articles about asylum seekers, without considering the pain and suffering of the staff working in extremely stressful situations among traumatized detainees. The guards' stories were illuminating. I was moved by what I was told, despite the toxic language often used to describe refugees; racism was not unusual. These men and women had been thrown into a volatile detention center with only the barest minimum of training—a constant complaint was that no cultural training had been undertaken, which resulted in greater anger felt towards asylum seekers. The staff felt abandoned and believed the asylum seekers were being treated better than them. Guards on remote Christmas Island had suffered especially, one trying to take her own life, and others showing a high statistical risk of self-harm.[45]

John (not his real name) was a fifty-three-year-old former Scientologist who had worked for MSS Security for nearly fifteen years. He spoke in a soft drawl and seemed desperate to share his experiences with me—experiences that were later corroborated by other MSS guards. He revealed a litany of Serco failures during his time at Villawood, including inadequacies that persisted after Wilson Security acquired the contract for the center in 2011. (Wilson also won the contract to manage security for the Australian detention facility on Nauru, where evidence emerged in 2013 that several asylum seekers had attempted to hang themselves.[46] The company was also caught up in unrest on Manus Island in 2015 and stood accused of assaulting protesting detainees.)

John said that his first job had been to monitor the outside fence. He alleged that Serco routinely saved money by not carrying out a proper assessment of the facility, which meant that people had escaped. John told me, "I had said there should be a risk analysis of the place, but nobody wanted to do so because you need to spend this much more to adhere to safety regulations." John reported errors that had been committed by Serco, but each time the blame was shifted to MSS: "Whenever there was a bungle on their part, they blamed us." He claimed that, during a protest at Villawood, "Serco didn't respond for five hours, by which time eleven [detainees] had got onto the roof. Serco just didn't want to confront the situation, therefore there was inaction for so long."

Working conditions at Villawood were grim. There was plenty of evidence of asbestos at the site, and Liberal and Labor governments, ACM, Serco, and MSS had all pledged to clean it up. But John said he was disturbed at constantly seeing signs that read: "Danger: Asbestos." In 2002, Villawood was declared safe from asbestos; but in 2006 the toxic substance was rediscovered, only for the site soon to be declared safe again. "Why were there still signs telling us about asbestos if there's no danger?" John asked. I asked DIBP about these serious allegations, and they claimed that "extensive monitoring over a number of years has consistently found contaminants are well below the accepted levels for asbestos."

The MSS guard's attitude towards asylum seekers was negative. "I don't know any refugees complaining about the conditions at Villawood," he told me. "Many in maximum security aren't refugees—they're visa overstayers. Some come back to detention because they can't afford life on the outside. Inside, they get three meals and free internet access." In his opinion, the Australian Army should have managed detainees, because companies like Serco "baulk at a problem and remain eternally paranoid about losing the contract with the government, hence always blaming MSS." He said this resulted in an aggressive culture, in which "MSS managers are paranoid" and "don't really protest."

John was appalled, for instance, when an MSS colleague was sacked at the end of a forty-degree day for complaining about the heat and for not working to his full capacity. "He had been in that heat for four hours," he said. "I've been calling for more breaks in summer, because we can't get out of the sun at all. It's often twelve hours in the open with no shade. People looked sunburnt when coming off a shift. WorkCover [an Australia government system designed to protect workers' health and safety] has said it's a disgrace, but nobody is doing anything about it." John concluded: "One day I was keeling over from the heat, and my supervisor said, 'Where's your tie?'"

Other MSS guards contacted me after John told them I would guarantee their anonymity—they feared retribution from their employer if they spoke out publicly. Sharon (not her real name) said that she resented all the benefits given to asylum seekers at Villawood: "They get free English classes, computer classes, hairstylist, dental, glasses, mental health, doctors, and hospitalization or operations as soon as required. Clients have internet access with no one looking at what is being accessed." Sharon repeated a key complaint I had heard from other MSS workers: "Serco staff treat clients more as a buddy than inmates or detainees. Because of our legal system, it takes a long time to verify truth or lies ... so if the clients do not like you they will make it very hard for you to work there. Clients have more rights, and they know their rights and play them to a T."

After I had interviewed a number of MSS employees, I again approached DIBP and also Serco to get some answers. MSS failed to respond to multiple requests for comment. But once more I encountered the inadequate assumption of responsibility within a privatized system. A DIBP spokesman refused to email any responses and would only say over the phone: "Serco remain responsible for the subcontracted staff as they are for their own employees. It is a commercial decision for Serco on whether to engage a subcontractor to take up certain security tasks."

Serco spokeswoman Emma Needham emailed me what was clearly a pro forma response: "We have a zero-harm policy in place to ensure every employee returns to their home unharmed. If there was evidence of a subcontractor failing to meet these required standards, they risk penalties or termination." She did not answer my questions about the company's responsibility towards MSS and its employees.

I had been hassling DIBP's regional manager on Christmas Island, Scott Matheson, and he finally granted me access to the detention center on my last day on the island. But he told me that only one of the detainees I had listed on my application form, Hayatullah Mozafari, would see me. "You can't bring a video camera, camera, or mobile phone, and because you're a journalist not even a pen or paper," Matheson added. At the time of writing, the Abbott government had officially allowed no journalists inside the Christmas Island facility since 2013.

As I pulled up in the detention center parking lot early in the morning, all that was visible was a large satellite dish next to the main reception, high fences in front of compounds reminiscent of a prison, and a collection of automated lockers in which Serco staff and visitors could stow their belongings. Two bulky MSS Security staff worked the reception desk, and I showed them my photo ID. There were Serco brochures "welcoming" visitors to the center. I signed in and went through an automated revolving door to find Matheson waiting for me. "I wanted to make sure you got in alright," he said. He talked to me about recent boat arrivals and how the Australian Navy always gave asylum seekers proper life jackets when they were escorted to the island. I sensed Matheson was giving me special treatment, wanting to show me that the system could be friendly and approachable.

We walked down a path lined with fences and were met by Sally, a senior DIBP case manager who supervised the twenty assessors on Christmas Island. She was normally based in the country's capital, Canberra, but regularly did stints in detention centers such as those at Sydney's Villawood, Melbourne's Maribyrnong, the remote Curtin in Western Australia—where I had seen 1,000 male refugees living in the middle of the Katherine desert on an old army base run by Serco—and Christmas Island. She had arrived on the island just after the March 2011 riots, when detainees had protested their incarceration. Sally and I walked through high-security doors and into an area where the "clients" had meetings with caseworkers and refugee assessors. The meeting room was clinically clean and furnished only with a single table and a few chairs. We sat down to talk.

Sally was doing the best she could in tough circumstances. She said she understood why people traveled to Australia by boat. She seemed to care about refugees and spoke at length about trying to process people quickly. She said things had greatly improved since the Howard years, that there was "better care and less punishment." I asked about Serco, and she was full of praise for the company, saying they were "essential partners" because "the public service simply aren't capable of handling security, intel gathering, and other services." She said Serco staff were well trained and much better than those of previous contractors G4S and ACM. Sally argued that DIBP had the power to sack any Serco staff who were not behaving properly, such as when they treated refugees with disrespect. "This happens very rarely," she told me.[47]

Sally said that most people who passed through the system were genuine refugees, and that processing times were getting shorter. I asked her how she could argue this when asylum seekers sometimes languished for two years behind bars. She remained adamant but conceded, "I wish it was faster, but the system simply can't handle all the people here." I asked if the arrival of more boats would strain the system even more. "Yes," she said, "but we're trying to keep less than 1,000 people here on Christmas Island." She stated that the current number of asylum seekers was manageable and allowed refugees to be given more personal treatment; she worried about what would happen if they had to reinstitute the use of tents to manage an excess number of arrivals.[48] Sally also claimed that DIBP and Serco offered refugees activities such as English classes, internet access, trips out of the center, and tailoring classes—though Sister Joan disputed that the authorities did much of this. In reality, there were endless negotiations in order to allow asylum seekers irregular visits to the public swimming pool, and the local cricket club had banned them in 2010.

I asked Sally if she supported the privatization of the detention system, and she replied that although "it isn't perfect, contractors have to control certain aspects the government simply cannot." Cannot or will not, I wondered. The idea of Canberra hiring and training more detention center staff was fanciful. Rather, it seemed there would be an ever-increasing reliance on Serco. Sally gave me the impression that DIBP and Serco were trying to address the negative public image of the system. She agreed with me, for instance, that when the media reported the arrival of a boat, it simply fueled a paranoia about, and hatred of, refugees in the wider community. "The media should be profiling the people in here," she said, "and they'll see that most of them are fleeing from persecution and coming [here] for a reason." I presumed she knew how difficult her superiors made this process for the media.

Sally asked if I wanted to see Hayatullah in the meeting room or in the center's courtyard. When I suggested the courtyard, in the hope of chatting with other detainees, she remembered that Thursday was "visa day," and that the space would be crowded with people wanting to come and talk with me. She also said that the man I was visiting "won't be getting a visa today, so it wouldn't really be fair for him to see the others celebrating."

Hayatullah, a Hazara man, finally arrived. He was one of the men I had seen on the beach with Sister Joan. He looked forlorn and barely made eye contact with me. I was told he was on anti-depressants and had trouble getting out of bed—this even happened when he knew he had a visitor. Hayatullah's teeth were crooked and yellowed from smoking, and he had a small hunch, which caused him to lean forward and look down when talking.

Through a translator, Hayatullah told me he had been in detention for twenty-two months and still had no idea when his situation would change; he was awaiting a court date for a judicial review. I asked if he would consider returning to Afghanistan, or perhaps going to Pakistan, but he said there was nothing for him there. He recounted flatly that his fifteen-year-old son had recently been killed in Pakistan.

Hayatullah gave short answers, and I could tell his despair was sensed by the translator, though he did thank me for visiting: "It gives me some comfort." I asked if the Hazara community in Australia had reached out in any way, but he said no one had made contact. He had become friends with other detainees on Christmas Island but told me: "Ultimately everybody was out for themselves and desperate to get refugee status."

It was a difficult conversation. I tried to show empathy for his situation—I did not know his exact story or its validity, but I could see he was in a bad way. At one point, he said, "It won't matter if I get out if I've gone crazy in here. It will make no difference on the outside." Here was a man who had lost hope, and privatized detention had been a key factor in that process. He briefly smiled when I got up to leave, and I said I hoped to see him soon on the outside.[49] He now lives in Darwin, in Australia's Northern Territory.

Hayatullah had left Pakistan because of communal violence and a lack of opportunities. He believed that Australia would offer a refuge, with peace and jobs. His new home was not officially at war, but it had declared its opposition to any and all boat people (those many asylum seekers arriving by plane were conveniently ignored in the toxic debate). Income inequalities in Pakistan were endemic, with a tiny elite owning vast swathes of the country. This was a global problem, though the degree of disparity differed from country to country. Thousands of asylum seekers formed an underclass in Australia—the exact number was unknown, but it was in the tens of thousands—due to a lack of opportunities and housing, poor public funding, and isolation. It was not exactly the environment men such as Hayatullah would have imagined.

Sally walked with me to a fortified gate that led to an oval mostly comprising brown dirt. She said that it was greener when the rain was more frequent, after the height of summer had passed. The detainees played cricket and soccer later in the day, when it was cooler, but at 10:30 a.m. it was quiet. A refugee in a purple shirt sat silently beyond the gate, just watching. Serco and DIBP staff greeted each other as they passed near us.

Around the oval, Sally explained, were various compounds painted in different colors, the "most secure" painted yellow or white. She said that if the men behaved in the white compound, they were gradually moved to less secure areas. She suddenly looked at me and said, unprompted, that the detention center looked like a "maximum security prison, and it is." She went on: "If it was built more recently it would be different, softer, less like a jail."

I said to Sally that DIBP and Serco had done themselves no favors by not being more transparent about their activities. "We've been burnt too many times" by the media, she responded, mentioning a recent *60 Minutes* TV story that featured aerial shots of the center obtained by a remote-controlled helicopter and the testimony of disgruntled former staff, their voices muffled. It aggravated everyone and distorted the reality of the Christmas Island detention center, she claimed. It was hard to have any sympathy, because DIBP and Serco had colluded to keep personal and moving stories from the public, citing the privacy concerns of refugees (something I also heard in the United States and Britain). It was revealed in 2015 that the Abbott government had reported journalists who critically investigated the situation of asylum seekers to the Australian Federal Police, aiming to uncover their sources—in particular, whistle-blowers.[50]

Australia is a first-world nation and should not have been blind to the reality of the current detention center system. There was no evidence that privatization had improved transparency or saved money.[51] A study in Canada found that refugees living in the community cost the government around C$10 to C$12 per day; the cost of keeping an individual in privatized detention in Australia was at least $179 per day.[52] The Community Assistance Program in Australia, which assisted vulnerable asylum seekers, cost around $38 per day; an equivalent program in mandatory detention cost $125.[53] Imprisoning refugees behind bars had nothing to do with saving money and everything to do with keeping the problem hidden from the eyes and minds of urban Australians. Responsibility was kept at arm's length to allow plausible deniability for governments, officials, and corporations. The result was the punishment of asylum seekers by governments that believed their electorates wanted them to be tough on boat arrivals. Sadly, with such widespread misinformation about the background and plight of asylum seekers, there was some truth to this assumption.

Resistance did emerge, however. In 2014, artists exhibiting in Sydney's Biennale, Australia's largest outdoor event, protested financial sponsorship by Transfield—a key contractor within the government's detention policy. The initial response by the media, government, and many arts administrators was anger that allegedly ungrateful artists had dared raise ethical concerns in a political climate where arts funding was limited.[54] But the campaign worked—the Biennale partially cut ties with Transfield, and the public had the chance to see a healthy debate over the role of companies trying to deflect scrutiny from its ugly but profitable work as "good corporate citizens." It was one of the more successful attempts at challenging public inertia over the policy of privatizing the asylum system.

It was a real challenge for the media and politicians to investigate and monitor any corporation looking to turn a profit from managing vulnerable asylum seekers—a challenge that neither group had risen to. Serco, Transfield, and the federal government worked together with virtual impunity, and there were few consequences attached to their shared unaccountability. The idea of placing detention facilities in public hands was rarely raised in public debate, though the federal Green party advocated it.

After two decades of successive Australian administrations wanting the perceived problem of refugees to be managed away by private companies, it was time the country established a more open system that put the care of asylum seekers above profit.

Conclusion

Breaking the Spell

Somewhere along the way, capitalism reduced the idea of justice to mean just "human rights," and the idea of dreaming of equality became blasphemous. We are not fighting to tinker with reforming a system that needs to be replaced.

Arundhati Roy, 2014

The History Channel described its reality-TV show *Bamazon* as "eight out-of-work Alabama construction workers locked in the fight of their lives, risking everything they've got on a long-shot chance to find gold in the Amazon jungle." Set in Guyana in South America, the program featured "aggressive jaguars, venomous snakes, malarial mosquitoes, and countless miles of impenetrable mud." One of the main characters, Tim Evans, explained how he and his US colleagues came to the Amazon every mining season to "take the gold."

This was depoliticized entertainment that mainstreamed disaster capitalism for the sake of sensationalism and the ratings it would bring. All that mattered was the excitement of the chase, the broadcasting of a carnival of grime and grit to an audience who would learn nothing about why resource hunting could be so destructive. The History Channel, wrote environmental academics Nathan K.

Lujan, Devin D. Bloom, and L. Cynthia Watson, "exploits habitats as a backdrop for glorified plunder."[1]

Missing from the program was any mention of the human rights abuses committed by mining corporations against indigenous communities and the damage done to delicate ecosystems by the excessive pillaging of resources such as gold.[2]

TV cameras were not there to record this exploitation in the depths of Papua New Guinea, Afghanistan, Pakistan, or Haiti, or inside detention centers and prisons in Greece, the United States, Australia, and Britain. The predatory behavior of multinational executives, government officials, and complicit NGO staffers is the defining feature of what I record in this book: profit at any cost. The methods vary from country to country, but the strategy is the same: exaggerate a threat, man-made or natural, and let loose unaccountable private-sector contractors to exploit it.

If there is economic uncertainty, let foreign companies mine any available resource, and then sit back and watch as most of the money leaves the country. Make sure that wars, including those started for tenuous reasons, last as long as possible to ensure ongoing work for mercenaries, guards, and intelligence officials. Industries such as mining, construction, and security feed off each other. It is a global gravy train—when one country is sucked dry, it moves off to the next lucrative destination.

During a visit to Greece in 2013 to investigate the reality of extreme austerity and those workers resisting it, Canadian writer Naomi Klein issued a stark warning: "We really are in a midst of what I've come to think of as a final colonial pillage for the hardest to reach natural resources in some of the most beautiful protected parts of the world using some of the most dangerous and damaging extractive practices."[3]

Nothing remains untouched. "The privatisation of everything," writes Arundhai Roy, "has also meant the NGO-isation of everything." She rightly celebrates the "remarkable, radical work" undertaken by many NGOs, as I show in this book, but questions "the corporation and foundation-endowed NGOs [as] global finance's way of buying into resistance movements, literally like shareholders buy shares in companies, then try to control them from within."[4] The commodification of human rights, at a time when market forces are putting a monetary value on everything, requires us to be highly skeptical of agendas pushed by think-tanks, NGOs, and civil libertarians. Many do fine work, but many others advocate for the maintenance of American empire at the expense of the developing world. That we do not see or hear these groups daily does not mean we are doing no harm.

In light of the declining abilities and constricting self-interest of the Western corporate press, it is up to the individual—the citizen blogger and the Twitter and Facebook user—to document the effects of disaster capitalism, to provide what is missing from the mainstream media: a view from the ground.[5] The challenge could not be greater; of the 175 largest economic entities in the world in 2011, including nations, 111 were multinational corporations.[6]

A Haitian villager now has the ability to connect quickly electronically with an activist in Sydney and inform her of a chemical spill at a mine. An Afghan blogger can describe to a worldwide audience the corruption of a government official. Awareness does not necessarily bring change, but it is the first, vital step in doing so. What we do with this information, living in nations with power, is our choice.

Reversing the trend of exploitative capitalism also means offering an alternative to its apparently seductive charms.[7] This is an urgent challenge, I realize, when witnessing the ideology at work in places like Haiti, where industrial parks are promoted as the ultimate opportunity. The answer is not more outsourcing of services or privatization of resources. Listening to locals and empowering them is a better option. This means challenging the orthodox view that the West has all the answers.

There were countless times during my travels when I felt helpless, overwhelmed by the stories recounted to me. I often questioned the usefulness of journalism itself, keenly aware of the limitations of the medium to bring significant changes where they were needed. In particular, I was struck by how often people felt like slaves to an economic system over which they had no control. Financial consultant Satyajit Das writes that "the rule of extreme money is that everybody borrows, everybody saves, everybody is supposed to get wealthier. But only skilled insiders get richer, running and rigging the game."[8]

This book uncovers these covert players, exposes their tactics, recognizes the financial, social, and political groups that have created this mess, and makes the case for change. But bringing this change requires first an acknowledgement of what we are fighting, and who we are. In his book *The Divide: American Injustice in the Age of the Wealth Gap*, *Rolling Stone* journalist Matt Taibbi argues that the problem begins at home: "We [Americans] have a profound hatred of the weak and poor, and a corresponding groveling terror before the rich and powerful, and we're building a bureaucracy to match those feelings."[9] In copious detail, Taibbi shows how key instigators of the 2008 financial crisis have not just been spared jail time but have benefited and been protected, while untold millions of needy men and women are crunched through an unforgiving legal system. With a few exceptions, such as the Occupy movement, there has been no public protest movement to demand prosecutions for Wall Street fraud.

Taibbi goes to the heart of an economic, social, and legal system that underpins the abuses documented here and explains why they are allowed to happen. "We're creating a dystopia," he explains, "where the mania of the state isn't secrecy or censorship but unfairness. Obsessed with success and wealth and despising failure and poverty, our society is systematically dividing the population into winners and losers, using institutions like courts to speed the process."[10] It is this carelessness and cruelty, amplified through the corporate media, that allows companies in the United States and globally to behave badly against the poor. Will we act to make them accountable? After all, many UK local councils are now wholly privatized, operated by companies with no knowledge about the regional area.[11] It is a cold process that has unfolded without public consent.

The challenges remain profound. While former British prime minister Margaret Thatcher, a key architect of today's neoliberal destruction of the public sector, died in April 2013, mass privatization, market fundamentalism, and support for dictatorships friendly to the West, which were championed by her and like-minded capitalists, continue to thrive. Both main parties in British politics still subscribe to private contracting as a responsible way to manage the state. But opinion polling consistently shows that the British public much prefer services run by the public sector. The challenge is transforming that attitude into action.

Noam Chomsky, in a 2011 follow-up to his classic 1967 essay on the "responsibility of intellectuals," explains what role we should take when fighting established power, and that we face the choice of either embracing or challenging it. "If we are serious about justice," he writes, "we will focus our efforts where we share responsibility for what is being done."[12]

It is essential that greater transparency is demanded from those institutions that create or perpetuate crises. This includes the organizations that run prisons for asylum seekers and those that undermine the autonomy and livelihoods of local peoples in pursuit of the resource dollar. It also includes those that sell questionable intelligence to US forces in the "war on terror." They mask their greed with claims of helping the United States win its battle against terrorism, when it is obvious that patriotism and global stability are not behind their actions.

Resistance to predatory capitalism is occurring all over the world, enacted by affected communities in Haiti and Papua New Guinea, refugee activists in Australia, NGOs in Afghanistan, and the Syriza victory in Greece. There is increasing opposition to the fact that the West has become little more than a heavily fortified gated community, exploiting resources and people in its pursuit of increased profits and a self-serving notion of peace. A vision is evolving of how the world can be ordered differently, with true democracy thriving from the ground up. The ambition of developing collective solutions, with public and private interests reducing inequality, poverty, and disease, is not a Communist throwback to the twentieth century, but the prerequisite for a realistic and necessary future.

There are countless examples. Consider Hamburg, Germany's second-largest city, voting in a 2013 referendum to take back control over the heating, electricity, and gas networks sold to private operators decades before. Municipalities in France and areas in Africa and Asia have ended the failed experiment in outsourced water.[13] This was achieved by grassroots organizing, using evidence showing that cost savings and environmental sustainability would be better served by managed state ownership.

Let us never forget the humanity of the people and communities craving a more equitable world. It is too easy to erase personalities and talk instead only about dollars. I like the thinking of US writer Rebecca Solnit, who writes in her book *A Paradise Built in Hell* that the challenge for modern societies is to view humans as more than just consumers. She explains how disasters, while horrific, can bring communities together in ways that show the best of us all. "You can read recent history as a history of privatization," she writes,

> not just of the economy but also of society, as marketing and media shove imagination more and more towards private life and private satisfaction, as citizens are redefined as consumers, as public participation falters and with it any sense of collective or individual political power ... Economic privatization is impossible without the privatization of desire and imagination that tells us we are not each other's keeper.[14]

What I witnessed while researching this book was people strug-gling against overwhelming odds—the invisible, the unpeople, the undesired, the expendable, the broke, and the poor. Their battle is our battle, because it is our choice to hold our own companies and governments to account for making money from cruelty and exploitation. Disaster capitalism is the ideology of our age because we have allowed it to be. We can change it. A more equal economic system and truly representative democracy must be our goal.

Now is the time.

Acknowledgements

This book has taken me to places that fundamentally challenged my belief in journalism and what I've been doing professionally for over a decade, questioning the impact of reporting on issues where power is so unbalanced. And yet bearing witness is something I take seriously; raising public awareness is a noble duty.

There was no other response to visiting devastated nations such as Afghanistan, Haiti, and Papua New Guinea than listening, learning and striving to find the best way to convey the horrors and the grim humor that accompanies the telling of them. It was difficult witnessing how Western states such as Australia, America, Britain, and Greece punish the most vulnerable in their privatized detention centers and prisons. But in the end I believed such reporting was an important contribution to revealing the ways in which our world is being sold to the highest bidder without public consent.

This book is the result of five years of work and has been made possible by the countless people across the globe who've wanted their voices heard. It has been a collaborative process and I could not have done it without the dedication, passion, and bravery of the journalists, activists, writers, and citizens who graciously gave me time, information, and support. Thank you. There are some people whose identities I must not reveal, to protect their safety (I have used pseudonyms when referring to these people in the text), but I acknowledge them here, too.

Investigative journalism is a painstaking endeavor for all involved, though it too often sees the writer taking all the glory. The following people around the world provided invaluable guidance, links, friendship, support, research, and information: Yasmine Ahmed, Maryam Alavi, Anthony Arnove, James Arvanitakis, Conor Ashleigh, Spencer Austad, Zubair Babakarkhail, Wendy Bacon, Rosanna Barbero, Heather Barr, Shane Bauer, Kaye Bernard, Yaara Bou Melhem, Reuben Brand, Neesha Bremner, Alice Brennan, Adam Brereton, Linda Briskman, Alison Broinowski, Simon Butler, Matthew Carney, Chaman, Thom Cookes, Marni Cordell, Amy Corderoy, Pamela Curr, Sharon De Silva, Peta Doherty, Helen Durham, Paul Dwyer, Katherine Fallah, Paul Farrell, Neil Fergus, Clinton Fernandes, Caroline Fleay, Luke Fletcher, Elena Fon, Benjamin Gilmour, Anand Gopal, John Grayson, Nicky Hager, Rebecca Harrigan, Ansel Herz, Matthew Hoh, Emily Howie, Liz Humphrys, Julian Huppert, Michael Grewcock, Kim Ives, Mark Jeanes, Thanasis Kampagiannis, Jeremy Kelly, Matt Kennard, Glen Klatovsky, Ioanna Kotsioni, Melissa Lahoud, Barry Lalley, Oliver Laughland, Kristian Lasslett, Rebecca Lichtenfeld, Julie Macken, Narelle Mantle, Amelia Marshall, Victoria Martin-Iverson, Nathan Matbob, Brit Mehta, Jay Mehta, Phil Miller, Emma Mlotshwa, Anastasia Moumtzaki, Paul McGeough, Sally McMillan, Omar Musa, Martyn Namorong, Thor Neureiter, Adelina Nicholls, Rachel Nicolson, Lizzie O'Shea, Mike Otterman, Selena Papps, Andre Paultre, Colin Penter, Tom Peter, Vinnie Picard, Dimitris Psarras, Maria Psara, Mustafa Qadri, Justin Randle, Jessica Reed, Warren Reed, Lee Rhiannon, Jen Robinson, Theonila Roka, Juan Carlos Riaz, Ian Rintoul, Clare Sambrook, Elina Sarantou, Susanne Schmeidl, Sterling Seagrove, Silky Shah, Azadeh Shahshahani, Bozorgmehr Sharafedin, Nick Shimmin, Tim Shorrock, Christos Sideris, Charandev Singh, Mikey Slezak, Peter Slezak, Jack Smit, Jorge Sotirios, Jeff Sparrow, Andrew

Sully, Jessica Sumaryo, Helga Svendsen, Gordon Thomson, Tad Tietze, Inga Ting, Brian Toohey, Daniel Trilling, Christos Tsiolkas, Eugenia Tzirtzilaki, Damian Mac Con Uladh, Katie Beno Valencia, Corinne Vernizeau, Kath Viner, Emily Wilson and Yugan.

Leo Hollis at Verso has warmly welcomed me into the Verso family. A publisher unafraid to piss off the powerful, it's a natural fit. Thanks also to Mark Martin, copy editor Charles Peyton, and the whole Verso team.

Thanks to my agents Benython Oldfield and Sharon Galant from Zeitgeist Media Group for believing in my work and understanding the importance of this material gaining a global audience.

My former agent, Mary Cunnane, was instrumental in formulating some of the ideas in this book.

Thanks to my Australian publisher, Melbourne University Press, for continuing to back my vision. Louise Adler, Elisa Berg, Sally Heath, Paul Smitz, and Penelope White have all contributed hugely to the vision in your hands.

I continue to be inspired by a range of journalists and groups whose work informs my own: Julian Assange and WikiLeaks, Pratap Chatterjee, Glenn Greenwald, Amy Goodman, the late and great Michael Hastings, Naomi Klein, Dahr Jamail, Chelsea Manning, George Monbiot, Greg Palast, John Pilger, Jeremy Scahill, Edward Snowden, and Matt Taibbi.

Alison Martin is a truly unique woman who constantly challenges, provokes, and loves me. Her intelligence, insights, and warmth run through this book. Our life journey together is one of the best damn things to ever happen to me. Thank you, my love.

My parents Violet and Jeffrey give me endless support, backing, and love. Our small family means we're closer than many others and it's something I cherish deeply. They are the best parents in the world.

This book aims, in the words of the campaigning British website Media Lens, "to correct the distorted vision of the corporate media." My hope is that it generates a global debate, challenging the silencing of the majority by the media, business, and political elite that claims to represent them.

Resistance is never futile.

Bibliography

Assange, Julian, *When Google Met Wikileaks*, OR Books, New York, 2014.

Benns, Matthew, *Dirty Money: The True Cost of Australia's Mineral Boom*, Random House, Sydney, 2011.

Briskman, Linda, Susie Latham, and Chris Goddard, *Human Rights Overboard: Seeking Asylum in Australia*, Scribe, Melbourne, 2008.

Chandrasekaran, Rajiv, *Imperial Life in the Emerald City: Inside Baghdad's Green Zone*, Bloomsbury, London, 2007.

—. *Little America: the War within the War for Afghanistan*, Bloomsbury, London, 2012.

Chang, Ha-Joon, *23 Things They Don't Tell You about Capitalism*, Allen Lane, London, 2010.

Chatterjee, Pratap, *Halliburton's Army*, Nation Books, New York, 2009.

—. *Iraq Inc.: A Profitable Occupation*, Seven Stories Press, New York, 2004.

Cleary, Paul, *Mine-Field: The Dark Side of Australia's Resource Boom*, Black Inc., Melbourne, 2012.

—. *Too Much Luck: The Mining Boom and Australia's Future*, Black Inc., Melbourne, 2011.

Coll, Steve, *Private Empire: ExxonMobil and American Power*, Penguin, New York, 2012.

Cromwell, David, *Private Planet: Corporate Plunder and the Fight Back*, Jon Carpenter Publishing, Oxfordshire, 2001.

Das, Satyajit, *Extreme Money: The Masters of the Universe and the Cult of Risk*, Portfolio, Melbourne, 2011.

Dwyer, Paul, *The Bougainville Photoplay Project*, Currency Press, Sydney, 2010.

Elliot, Jason, *An Unexpected Light: Travels in Afghanistan*, Picador, London, 1999.

Funk, McKenzie, *Windfall: The Booming Business of Global Warming*, Penguin, New York, 2014.

Gopal, Anand, *No Good Men Among the Living*, Metropolitan Books, New York, 2014.

Grewcock, Michael, *Border Crimes: Australia's War on Illicit Migrants*, The Institute of Criminology Series 29, Sydney, 2009.

Hager, Nicky, *Other People's Wars: New Zealand in Afghanistan, Iraq and the War on Terror*, Craig Potten Publishing, Nelson, 2011.

Hallward, Peter, *Damning the Flood: Haiti and the Politics of Containment*, Verso, London, 2010.

Hatherley, Owen, *A Guide to New Ruins of Great Britain*, Verso, London, 2010.

Hastings, Michael, *The Operators: The Wild and Terrifying Inside Story of America's War in Afghanistan*, Blue Rider Press, New York, 2012.

Hughes, Solomon, *War on Terror Inc.*, Verso, London, 2007.

James, C. L. R., *The Black Jacobins*, Vintage, New York, 1989.

Katz, Jonathan M., *The Big Truck that Went By: How the World Came to Save Haiti and Left behind Disaster*, Palgrave Macmillan, New York, 2013.

Klein, Naomi, *The Shock Doctrine: The Rise of Disaster Capitalism*, Penguin, London, 2007.

—. *This Changes Everything: Capitalism vs. the Climate*, Allen Lane, 2014.

Laslett, Kristian, *State Crime On the Margins of Empire: Rio Tinto, the War on Bougainville and Resistance to Mining*, Pluto Press, London, 2014.

Mason, Paul, *Why It's Kicking Off Everywhere: The New Global Revolutions*, Verso, London, 2012.

Monbiot, George, *Captive State: The Corporate Takeover of Britain*, Pan Books, London, 2000.

Palast, Greg, *Vultures' Picnic: A Tale of Oil, High Finance and Investigative Reporting*, Constable, London, 2011.

Parenti, Christian, *Tropic of Chaos: Climate Change and the New Geography of Violence*, Nation Books, New York, 2011.

Podur, Justin, *Haiti's New Dictatorship*, Pluto Press, 2012.

Rosen, Nir, *Aftermath: Following the Bloodshed of America's Wars in the Muslim World*, Nation Books, New York, 2010.

Roy, Arundhati, *Capitalism: A Ghost Story*, Haymarket Books, 2014.

Scahill, Jeremy, *Blackwater: The Rise of the World's Most Powerful Mercenary Army*, Serpent's Tail, London, 2008.

—. *Dirty Wars: The World Is a Battleground*, Nation Books, New York, 2013.

Schuller, Mark and Morales, Pablo (eds.), *Tectonic Shifts: Haiti Since the Earthquake*, Kumarian Press, Sterling, VA, 2012.

Shorrock, Tim, *Spies for Hire: The Secret World of Intelligence Outsourcing*, Simon and Schuster, New York, 2008.

Schwartz, Timothy T., *Travesty in Haiti*, BookSurge Publishing, Charleston, SC, 2010.

Singer, P. W., *Corporate Warriors: The Rise of the Privatized Militarised Industry*, Cornell University Press, New York, 2008.

—. *Wired for War: The Robotics Revolution and Conflict in the 21st Century*, Penguin, New York, 2009.

Solnit, Rebecca, *A Paradise Built in Hell: The Extraordinary Communities that Arise in Disaster*, Penguin, 2010.

——. *Men Explain Things to Me*, Haymarket Books, 2014.

Sprague, Jeb, *Paramiltarism and the Assault on Democracy in Haiti*, Monthly Review Press, New York, 2012.

Taibbi, Matt, *The Divide: American Injustice in the Age of the Wealth Gap*, Scribe, 2014.

——. *Griftopia: Bubble Machines, Vampire Squids and the Long Con that Is Breaking America*, Scribe, Melbourne, 2010.

Trilling, Daniel, *Bloody Nasty People: The Rise of Britain's Far Right*, Verso, 2013.

Walker, Frank, *The Tiger Man of Vietnam*, Hachette Australia, Sydney, 2009.

Notes

Introduction

1 Jo Confino, "It Is Profitable to Let the World Go to Hell," *Guardian*, January 20, 2015.

2 Peter Coy, "The Richest Rich Are in a Class of Their Own," *Business Week*, April 3, 2014.

3 Ned Resnikoff, "Food Pantries Stretched to Breaking Point by Food Stamp Cuts," *Al Jazeera America*, November 24, 2014.

4 David Leonhardt and Kevin Quealy, "The American Middle Class Is No Longer the World's Richest," *New York Times*, April 22, 2014.

5 Matt Taibbi, "Bank of America: Too Crooked to Fail," *Rolling Stone*, March 14, 2012.

6 Matt Taibbi, "Bank of America Is a 'Raging Hurricane of Theft and Fraud,'" Occupy Wall Street day of action, February 29, 2012.

7 Justin Wolfers, "All You Need to Know About Income Inequality, in One Comparison," *New York Times*, March 13, 2015

8 David Halperin, "The Perfect Lobby: How One Industry Captured Washington DC," *Nation*, April 3, 2014.

9 Cecilia Olivet and Pia Eberhardt, *Profiting from Crisis: How Corporations and Lawyers Are Scavenging Profits from Europe's Crisis Countries* (Amsterdam Transnational Institute/Corporate Europe Observatory, March 2014).

10 Aditya Chakrabortty, "New Era Estate Scandal: Families at the Mercy of International Speculators," *Guardian*, November 20, 2014.

11 James V. Grimaldi and Robert O'Harrow, Jr., "In Egypt, Corruption Cases Had an American Root," *Washington Post*, October 20, 2011.

12 Jennifer Schuessler, "In History Departments, It's Up with Capitalism," *New York Times*, April 6, 2013.

13 Andrew Hussey, "Occupy Was Right: Capitalism Has Failed the World," *Observer*, April 13, 2014.

14 Gillian Tett, "Anxiety in the Age of Inequality," *Foreign Policy*, November/ December 2014.

15 Naomi Klein, *The Shock Doctrine: The Rise of Disaster Capitalism* (London: Penguin, 2007), pp. 3–21.

16 A poll conducted by Essential Research in 2012 found that a majority of Australians believed that the economic "reforms" introduced by successive governments had "[most] benefited" corporations; only 5 percent thought that "ordinary Australians benefited." Essential Research, *Economic Reforms*, June 4, 2012.

17 Naomi Klein, "Super Storm Sandy—A People's Shock?" *Nation*, November 5, 2012.

18 Andrew Martin, "Hurricane Sandy and the Disaster-Preparedness Economy," *New York Times*, November 10, 2012. "Disaster economics," writes a *New Yorker* columnist, "should ensure that the state prepares for disasters before they happen, rather than just dealing with them after they have hit." James Surowiecki, "Disaster Economics," *New Yorker*, December 3, 2012.

19 Mariah Blake, "How Hillary Clinton's State Department Sold Fracking to the World," *Guardian*, September 11, 2014.

20 Naomi Klein, "Climate Change Is the Fight of Our Lives—Yet We Can Hardly Bear to Look at It," *Guardian*, April 23, 2014.

21 Bill McKibben, "Global Warming's Terrifying New Math," *Rolling Stone*, August 2, 2012.

22 George Monbiot, "Forbidden Planet," *Guardian*, December 3, 2012.

23 McKenzie Funk, *Windfall: The Booming Business of Global Warming* (London: Penguin, 2014), p. 10.

24 James Risen, "The Post-9/11 Homeland Security Industrial Complex Profiteers and Endless War," *Truthout*, November 16, 2014, at truth-out.org.

25 Rick Wallace, "Ex-Ambassador Frustrated by Post-Tsunami Silence," *Australian*, March 10–11, 2012.

26 Klein, *Shock Doctrine*, pp. 391–4.

27 Mark Anderson, "Aid to Africa: Donations from West Mask '60bn looting' of Continent," *Guardian*, July 15, 2014.

28 Felicity Lawrence, "Alarm as Corporate Giants Target Developing Countries," *Guardian*, November 23, 2011.

29 Hannah Beech and Oyu Tolgoi, "Hesitant Steppes," *Time*, August 20, 2012.

30 Thanassis Cambanis, "Could Aid to Syrians be Prolonging the War?" *Boston Globe*, June 1, 2014.

31 In 2010, the *Washington Post* reported that an estimated 854,000 people held Top Secret security clearances. Dana Priest and William M. Arkin, "Top Secret America," *Washington Post*, July 19, 2010.

32 Jeremy Scahill, "Former CIA Spy on How US Intelligence Became Big Business," *Nation*, July 7, 2010.

33 Pratap Chatterjee, "Iraq War Logs: Military Privatisation Run Amok," *Guardian*, October 23, 2010. In 2010, I uncovered evidence that Australian special forces, along with the forces of other countries, were undertaking covert actions, possibly assassinations or kidnappings across the Muslim world, without accountability. A training center in Paris, Alliance Base, was established in the wake of 9/11 to coordinate these missions. Antony Loewenstein, "Elite Oz Soldiers in Covert Operations for Top Secret Alliance Base," *Crikey*, November 22, 2010, at crikey.com.au; Brian Toohey, "Troops' Secret Role in Iraq," *Australian Financial Review*, August 28, 2004.

34 "Jeremy Scahill Testifies before Congress on America's Secret Wars," *Nation*, December 9, 2010; Tim Shorrock, "America's New Mercenaries," *Daily Beast*, December 15, 2010, at thedailybeast.com.

35 Jane Mayer, "The CIA's Travel Agent," *New Yorker*, October 30, 2006.

36 Rupert Neate, "Lloyds Own Stake in US Firm Accused of CIA Torture Flights," *Guardian*, May 6, 2012; Ian Cobain and Ben Quinn, "How US Firms Profited from Torture Flights," *Guardian*, August 31, 2011.

37 Jo Adetunji, "British Firms Urged to 'Pack Suitcases' in Rush for Libya Business," *Guardian*, October 21, 2011.

38 Kim-Jenna Jurriaans, "UN Increasingly Reliant on Private Security Contractors," *IPS*, July 12, 2012, at ipsnews.net.

39 Tim Shorrock, "The Afghanistan War Is Still Raging—But This Time It's Being Waged by Contractors," *Nation*, February 4, 2015.

40 Eli Lake, "Contractors Ready to Cash In on ISIS War," *Daily Beast*, September 13, 2014, at thedailybeast.com.

41 Dan Lamothe, "Let Contractors Fight the Islamic State, Blackwater Founder Erik Prince Says," *Washington Post*, October 9, 2014. In 2014, after a long legal battle, four former Blackwater employees were found

guilty of murder, manslaughter, and firearms charges after the killing of fourteen Iraqis and the wounding of seventeen others in Baghdad's Nisour Square, in 2007. It was a rare case of delayed justice.

1 Pakistan and Afghanistan

1 Paul McLeary, "New Day for Private Security in Afghanistan," *Defence News*, October 9, 2014.

2 A leading Western human rights advocate in Kabul tells me it is absurd that the US is "doing development through private companies … People who have often never left America, coming to Afghanistan and telling them how to run their justice system while working for private foreign contractors."

3 The reality could be different, however. The European Union announced in 2012 that it would spend up to €50 million on private security in Afghanistan until 2016. Andrew Rettman, "EU to Spend €50 Million on Private Security in Afghanistan," EUobserver.com, May 11, 2012. The transition to Afghan security forces after 2014 has made many foreign NGOs nervous about security, though most say they will stay in the country, albeit with a reduced presence. Matthew Rosenberg and Graham Bowley, "Security Fears Lead Groups to Rethink Work in Afghanistan," *New York Times*, March 10, 2012.

4 Lynne O'Donnell, "What's to Become of Afghanistan's Mines?" *Foreign Policy*, April 2, 2014.

5 Most Australian journalists who visit Afghanistan are embedded with Australian forces, and the coverage they offer is severely limited. The practice guarantees little more than "boys' own adventure" stories—tales of men fighting the Taliban with little context. "Embedding in Afghanistan," ABC TV's *Media Watch*, October 5, 2009; "Media access and Afghanistan," ABC TV's *Media Watch*, April 19, 2010.

6 Solomon Hughes, *War on Terror, Inc.: Corporate Profiteering from the Politics of Fear* (London: Verso, 2007), pp. 115–16.

7 Kim Baker and Stephen J. Hedges, "US Paid for Media Firm Afghans Didn't Want," *Chicago Tribune*, December 13, 2005.

8 Diana Farsetta, "The War on Terror Meets the War on Drugs," PR Watch, May 11, 2006, at prwatch.org.

9 Influence in Washington, DC, is what explains the ability of some failure-prone Beltway consultancies to continue winning government contracts.

10 The Associated Press revealed in 2012 that the US military was not reporting all Afghan attacks against American soldiers, and was therefore denying the extent of the hatred of the occupying forces. Robert Burns, "US Not Reporting All Afghan Attacks," Associated Press, April 30, 2012.

11 The Special Inspector General for Afghanistan Reconstruction continues to issue damning reports. In July 2014 facilities built by the US Army Corps of Engineers for the Afghan army, worth $1.57 billion, were found to be defective. A 2013 report made the startling suggestion that "US anti-corruption activities in Afghanistan are not guided by a comprehensive US strategy." This was twelve years after the American invasion.

12 Jacob Siegel, "The Real Winner of the Afghan War Is This Shady Military Contractor," *Daily Beast*, April 24, 2014, at thedailybeast.com.

13 Laura A. Dickenson, *Outsourcing War and Peace* (New Haven, CT: Yale University Press, 2011), pp. 137–43.

14 Charles Glass, "The Warrior Class," *Harper's*, April 2012.

15 Ibid. A DynCorp employee in Afghanistan sent the following missive about his company's work in 2011: David Isenberg, "A DynCorp Contractor in Afghanistan," May 11, 2011, at mssparky.com.

16 Pratap Chatterjee, *Halliburton's Army* (New York: Nation Books, 2009), p. x.

17 Ibid., p. 73.

18 US Department of Defense statement, November 8, 2012.

19 Walter Pincus, "Profiting in Afghanistan," *Washington Post*, February 23, 2012. An examination of the US Department of Defense website, where details of awarded contracts are listed, reveals the huge amounts of money offered to companies to undertake work in Afghanistan and beyond. Meanwhile, a former employee of Mission Essential Personnel claimed in 2010 that more than a quarter of the translators working with US soldiers in Afghanistan had failed basic language tests but were sent into the field regardless. Matthew Mosk, Brian Ross, and Joseph Rhee, "Whistleblower Claims Many US Interpreters Can't Speak Afghan Language," ABC News, September 8, 2010.

20 Scott Higham, Jessica Schulberg, and Steven Rich, "Doing Well by Doing Good: The High Price of Working in War Zones," *Washington Post*, May 5, 2014.

21 Sarah Stillman, "The Invisible Army," *New Yorker*, June 6, 2011.

22 Sam Black and Anjali Kamat, "After 12 Years of War, Labor Abuses

Rampant on US Bases in Afghanistan," Al Jazeera America, March 7, 2014.

23 Chatterjee, *Halliburton's Army*, p. xii.

24 Tabassum Zakaria, Susan Cornwell, and Hadeel Al Shalchi, "For Benghazi Diplomatic Security, US Relied on Small British Firm," Reuters, October 17, 2012.

25 Tim Shorrock, "Exclusive: New Document Details America's War Machine—and Secret Mass of Contractors in Afghanistan," *Salon*, May 28, 2014, at salon.com.

26 Declan Walsh, "Made Rich by US Presence, Many in Kandahar Now Face an Uncertain Future," *New York Times*, December 9, 2014.

27 In the ten months between June 2009 and April 2010, 260 PMCs employed by the Defense Department were killed in Afghanistan, while 324 US troops died. Justin Elliot, "Hundreds of Afghanistan Contractor Deaths Go Unreported," *Salon*, July 15, 2010, at salon.com.

28 "Warlord, Inc.," US House of Representatives report, June 2010. Countless other reports reached the same conclusion. For example, in August 2011 the US military awarded more than $1 billion in new contracts for military transport after previously employed firms were accused of funding militants. Karen DeYoung, "US Military Awards Contracts in Afghanistan to Get Money Away from Insurgents," *Washington Post*, August 16, 2011. Another report, also released in 2011, found that "US taxpayer money has been indirectly funneled to the Taliban under a $2.16 billion transportation contract that the United States has funded, in part to promote Afghan businesses." Karen DeYoung, "US Trucking Funds Reach Taliban, Military-Led Investigation Concludes," *Washington Post*, July 25, 2011. Dion Nissenbaum, "Roads to Nowhere: Program to Win Over Afghans Fails," *Wall Street Journal*, February 10, 2012.

29 Aram Roston, "How the US funds the Taliban," *Nation*, November, 11 2009.

30 Rod Nordland, "Top Afghans Tied to 90s Carnage, Researchers Say," *New York Times*, July 22, 2012. Countless US-backed warlords have terrible human rights records, but none of this bothers Western forces in the battle against militants who oppose the occupation. Commander Azizullah and Abdul Raziq are just two Afghan warlords who, despite being accused of murder, extortion, and drug smuggling, have received millions of dollars in US support. Julius Cavendish, "Afghanistan's Dirty War: Why the Most Feared Man in Berman District Is a US Ally," *Time*, October 4, 2011. Matthieu Aikins, "Our Man in Kandahar," *Atlantic*,

November 2011. Heela Achakzai, a senator from Oruzgan province, told me that the warlord Matiullah Khan controls all PMCs in his area, and that the Australian troops stationed there are "fine with it." The *New York Times* investigated Matiullah Khan in 2010 and found evidence he had backed insurgents and ran an unaccountable PMC. Dexter Filkins, "With US Aid, Warlord Builds an Afghan Empire," *New York Times*, June 5, 2010.

31 P. W. Singer, *Corporate Warriors* (Ithaca, NY: Cornell University Press, 2008), p. 50.

32 Ibid., pp. 231–2.

33 Ibid., p. 232.

34 Ibid., p. 238.

35 John Reed, "The Contract Airlines that Quietly Move US Troops and Spies Around the World," *Foreign Policy*, May 2, 2013.

36 Ibid., p. 234.

37 "US Wasting Billions While Tripling No-Bid Contracts after Decade of War in Iraq, Afghanistan," *Democracy Now!*, September 2, 2011, at democracynow.org.

38 Barack Obama speech on procurement, March 4, 2009, at whitehouse.gov.

39 *Democracy Now!*, "US Wasting Billions."

40 Edward Wong, "Exploring a New Role: Peacemaker in Afghanistan," *New York Times*, January 14, 2015.

41 "US Army Investigated Soldiers over Suspected Drug Use in Afghanistan, Data Show," Associated Press, April 21, 2012.

42 "UNODC Reports Major, and Growing, Drug Abuse in Afghanistan," press release, June 21, 2010. There were plans to move addicts to a facility at Camp Phoenix, the site of one of the biggest US bases in Afghanistan.

43 Tahir Qadiry, "Afghanistan, the Drug Addiction Capital," BBC News, April 10, 2013.

44 Alissa J. Rubin and Matthew Rosenberg, "US Efforts Fail to Curtail Trade in Afghan Opium," *New York Times*, May 26, 2012.

45 Matthieu Aikins, "Afghanistan: The Making of a Narco State," *Rolling Stone*, December 4, 2014.

46 The role of USAID in Afghanistan remains largely unreported, but its failures are clear. David Rohde writes in the *Atlantic* about the confused efforts in Helmand Province to get two large dams operational with the assistance of private security companies and contractors with little cultural or political understanding. David Rohde, "Visit Afghanistan's 'Little America,' and See the Folly of For-Profit War," *Atlantic*,

June 2012. McClatchy Newspapers have done some of the best reporting of how US-backed contractors have been responsible for shoddily built offices, power plants, and police stations while overcharging for the work. Marisa Taylor and Dion Nissenbaum, "US Keeps Funneling Money to Troubled Afghan Projects," McClatchy, July 12, 2011; Dion Nissenbaum, Warren P. Strobel, Marisa Taylor, and Jonathan S. Landay, "Flawed Projects Prove Costly for Afghanistan, US," McClatchy, July 12, 2011; both at mcclatchydc.com. Perhaps one of the most shocking cases involved revelations that a US-run hospital in Kabul had "Auschwitz-like" conditions, and senior US officials had tried to cover it up. "Congressional Probe Reveals Cover-Up of 'Auschwitz-Like' Conditions at US-Funded Afghan Hospital," *Democracy Now!*, August 1, 2012, at democracynow. org.

47 Matthieu Aikins, "Last Tango in Kabul," *Rolling Stone*, August 28, 2014.

48 A typical US media response to alleged corruption in Afghanistan is to blame the Afghans for failing to carry out foolproof US plans. Matthew Rosenberg and Graham Bowley, "Intractable Afghan Graft Hampering US Strategy," *New York Times*, March 7, 2012. A contradiction at the heart of Barack Obama's Afghan policy was highlighted when the *New York Times* discovered that one of President Hamid Karzai's aides had been accused of serious corruption while being on the CIA payroll. Dexter Filkins and Mark Mazzetti, "Key Karzai Aide in Corruption Inquiry Is Linked to CIA," *New York Times*, August 25, 2010. A 2014 Amnesty International report detailed countless examples of US forces in Afghanistan torturing detainees, covering up crimes, murdering civilians, and refusing to investigate any of it properly. It was a damning report that received relatively little international media coverage. A 2014 investigation by journalist Matthieu Aikins found US-backed militias complicit in murder, rape, and various other abuses. Militia commanders told Aikins that, despite the various allegations, the US continued to provide arms and salaries. Matthieu Aikins, "A US-Backed Militia Runs Amok in Afghanistan," Al Jazeera America, July 23, 2014.

49 Some American and Australian special forces will remain in Afghanistan after 2014 to work with the CIA to target "militants," but the status and legality of this work remains unclear. Brendan Nicholson, "A Tentative Transition," *Australian*, May 15, 2012.

50 The Afghanistan Analysts Network released a report in October 2011 that questioned the validity of the ISAF night raids (which applied a so-called "kill or capture" strategy) by showing how NATO's claims of

having killed militant leaders were often exaggerated—the definition of the word "leader" "was so broad as to be meaningless." Julian Borger, "Nato Success Against Taliban in Afghanistan 'May Be Exaggerated,'" *Guardian*, October 13, 2011. The Western counterinsurgency tactics in Afghanistan are reminiscent of the Vietnam War's Phoenix Program, which led to the torture and murder of countless Vietnamese in the name of fighting communism. Jeff Sparrow, "Australia's Vietnam-Style Killing Program," *New Matilda*, May 12, 2009, at newmatilda.com. I have had email communication with former Australian lieutenant-colonel Barry Petersen, who worked with the CIA in Vietnam to train locals as guerrillas against the Viet Minh. What he explained to me in detail sounds remarkably similar to what the West is doing in Afghanistan: arming and training insurgents to beat the Taliban, and failing.

51 Alissa J. Rubin, "Retiring Envoy to Afghanistan Exhorts US to Heed Its Past," *New York Times*, July 28, 2012.

52 David Bosco, "The War over US War Crimes in Afghanistan Is Heating Up," *Foreign Policy*, December 3, 2014.

53 Graham Bowley, "Fears of the Future Haunt a Budding Generation of Afghan Strivers," *New York Times*, February 11, 2013.

54 Felisa "Farzana" Dyrud and Davood Moradian, "Trust Fall," *Foreign Policy*, October 2, 2012.

55 Matthew Rosenberg, "Karzai's Office Gets Bags Full of CIA Cash," *New York Times*, April 28, 2013.

56 Matthew Rosenberg, "US Suddenly Goes Quiet on Effort to Bolster Afghan Forces," *New York Times*, January 29, 2015.

57 Wardak province remains a contested area, where the Taliban's influence endures. The relationship between US forces and Afghan troops there is bitter, with almost no trust between the two sides. Alissa J. Rubin, "Reporting a Fearful Rift Between Afghans and Americans," *New York Times* blog, October 24, 2012.

58 A 2010 US congressional report found that the Watan Group had bribed Afghan officials to secure a vital NATO supply route in southern Afghanistan and had also paid the Taliban not to attack the highway. "US Blacklists Afghan Security Firm Tied to Karzai," Associated Press, December 9, 2010. The Watan Group hired high-profile lawyers to smooth its relations with the US government. A 2013 report in the *New York Times* documented yet another Afghan company with ties to the Taliban still receiving US contracts. The company, Zurmat Group, undertook work on a US-controlled facility while being found to have passed bomb-making

equipment to insurgents. Matthew Rosenberg, "Afghan Companies with Insurgent Ties Still Receive US Contracts," *New York Times*, November 12, 2013.

59   Zubair tells me that a great Western media myth is that the Taliban forced women to wear the burqa during their rule. He acknowledges that the Taliban encouraged women to do so but says it is a tradition here that stretches back many years. "Some girls [wore] one because their mothers did, and others didn't because it wasn't something that existed in their families," he says. However, my fixer's claim flies in the face of plentiful evidence that the Taliban did not tolerate exceptions to the burqa.

60   "Afghanistan: US Should Articulate Women's Rights Strategy," Human Rights Watch, October 19, 2012.

61   Afghanistan's defense minister claimed in 2011 that it would cost $5 billion a year to support the country's army and police—more than three times Kabul's domestic revenue the previous year. World Bank figures estimate that 97 percent of Afghanistan's $15.7 billion GDP comes from foreign sources.

62   The Afghan ambassador to Australia told the ABC in 2011 that his country had no choice but to exploit its mineral wealth, and that it wanted to approach Australian firms such as BHP and Rio Tinto to invest. Stan Correy, "Afghanistan Wants Help to Kick-Start Mining Boom," ABC's *Background Briefing*, December 19, 2011.

63   "Afghanistan's Mineral Deposits," *Money Morning*, June 15, 2012.

64   Maria Abi-Habib, "Iranians Build Up Afghan Clout," *Wall Street Journal*, October 25, 2012.

65   "Afghanistan Aid Boost Welcome, Checks Needed on Support for Mining Industry," Greens Senator Lee Rhiannon, press release, July 9, 2012. It is hard to have any faith that Kabul's current crop of politicians will deal fairly when it comes to the country's mineral wealth. In October 2012, Minister of Mines Wahidullah Shahrani announced that 200 mining contracts would be made public, which was a first. The minister was praised by the United States for the action but condemned by political rivals at home. Graham Bowley and Matthew Rosenberg, "Mining Contract Details Disclosed in Afghanistan," *New York Times*, October 15, 2012.

66   Many companies claim to conduct surveys of the Afghan population and then sell this information to Western forces. One example is Glevum Associates, which was hired by the US military to help it better understand the local population. But there is no evidence that the company, which had no previous experience in Afghanistan, ever provided any

useful information. April Joyner, "How I Opened an Office in a War Zone," *Inc. Magazine*, September 7, 2011, at inc.com.

67 Countless ISAF reports for the Human Terrain System found that locals felt foreign troops showed no cultural sensitivity towards them and that the bombing of villages inflamed anti-government sentiment. Spending millions of dollars on this program seems bizarre when serious research is not needed to know how Afghans will feel when attacked by outsiders.

68 This story was first broken by Jeremy Kelly in London's *Times*, but he gave few details of the privatized intelligence. Jeremy Kelly, "Afghan Spy Network Tells NATO Bitter Home Truths," *Times*, March 24, 2012.

69 A WikiLeaks-released document explained the existence of Task Force 373, a US-run assassination squad in Afghanistan that had a hit list with over 2,000 names on it. Many civilians are believed to have been victims of these secret missions. Pratap Chatterjee, "Manhunters, Inc.," Tom-Dispatch.com, August 19, 2010, at tomdispatch.com. The CIA also hired Blackwater in Afghanistan to run an assassination unit, starting in 2008. Conor Friedersdorf, "The Terrifying Background of the Man who Ran a CIA Assassination Unit," *Atlantic*, July 18, 2012.

70 "Obama's Lists: A Dubious List of Targeted Killings in Afghanistan," *Der Spiegel*, December 28, 2014.

71 Mujib Mashal, *Bloomberg Business*, December 18, 2014.

72 S. M. Hall, "US Trojan Horse," *Nation*, March 28, 2012.

73 Ewen MacAskill and Declan Walsh, "US Gives Fresh Details of CIA Agent who Killed Two Men in Pakistan Shootout," *Guardian*, February 21, 2011. Evidence emerged in late 2012 that indicated the CIA and Inter-Services Intelligence had struck a deal in 2011 allowing the swift passage of Raymond Davis to the United States in exchange for the United States dropping investigations into former director-generals of the intelligence agency, who were allegedly complicit in the 2008 Mumbai terror attacks. Amir Mir, "The Inside Story of the CIA-ISI Immunity Deal," *The News*, December 21, 2012, at thenews.com.pk.

74 Salman Siddiqui, "Private Security Companies Operate Under 'Law of the Jungle,'" *Express Tribune*, March 25, 2012.

75 Ikram Sehgal, "Private Security Business," *The News*, March 8, 2012, at thenews.com.pk.

76 Karin Brulliard, "Khyber Club's Bartender Had Front-Row Seat to History in Pakistan," *Washington Post*, February 7, 2012.

77 Many USAID contracts in Afghanistan are undertaken with the assistance of private for-profit companies. The situation is similar regarding

Australian aid, the effectiveness of which was seriously questioned when the Australian Defence Force admitted in 2012 that it had spent more than A\$255 million to deliver only A\$27 million in aid. Brendan Nicholson, "\$27m Aid to Kabul Delivers \$255m Bill," *Australian*, October 9, 2012. In 2010, Australia announced it had awarded a \$20 million contract to Hart Security to guard diplomats in Kabul—double the cost paid to the previous provider, Control Risks Group. Dylan Welch, "Australian Troops Ruled Out of Guarding Embassy Staff in Kabul," *Sydney Morning Herald*, December 6, 2010. Mark Graham, "USAID in Afghanistan," *CounterPunch*, December 5, 2012. I gave testimony to an Australian Senate committee on the future of aid to Afghanistan in December 2012. Antony Loewenstein, "My Evidence at the Senate Committee on Australia's Overseas Development Programs in Afghanistan," at antonyloewenstein.com.

78 Jeremy Scahill, "The Secret US War in Pakistan," *Nation*, November 23, 2009.

79 Contractors are often forced to take more risks than soldiers, such as when transporting goods or people, and some pay the ultimate price for it. The commercial imperative often trumps security.

80 In 2006, *The Age* estimated that between 200 and 300 Australians were working as contractors in Iraq. Nick McKenzie, "Armed and Ready: Private Soldiers in Iraq," *The Age*, July 1, 2006.

81 A former director of BLP International, a private training company registered in the UAE, told ABC Radio in 2007 that the PMC industry was filled with "cowboy operators," citing the deaths of two Australians in Iraq who were working for BLP. "Deaths in Iraq Highlight Dangers Facing Contractors," ABC Radio's *The World Today*, July 16, 2007.

82 Langdon was sentenced to death in 2010 for the killing, but the sentence was commuted to twenty years in prison. He claims he acted in self-defense, but his family nonetheless paid compensation to the relatives of the victim, and they accepted it. It remains unclear how much support the Australian government has provided to Langdon. What is clear is that the lack of media attention paid to the case highlights the absence of transparency in war profiteering.

83 The suicide rate of returned US servicemen and women is extremely high. It is believed that one active-duty soldier commits suicide every day, while disability benefits stemming from the wars in Iraq and Afghanistan are off the chart, into the trillions of dollars. Linda J. Bilmes, "A Conspiracy of Silence," *International Herald Tribune*, July 18, 2012.

84 Various scandals involving contractors in Afghanistan have emerged since 2001. In 2012, male employees of Jorge Scientific were caught on video staggering around drunk and semi-naked, despite the company allegedly having a "zero-tolerance" policy regarding substance abuse. A list of some of the worst contracting debacles has been published by *Mother Jones*. Adam Weinstein, "The All-Time 10 Worst Military Contracting Boondoggles," *Mother Jones*, September 2, 2011, at motherjones. com. For a list of Blackwater misbehavior, see John Cook, "'Gentlemen, We Shot a Judge' and Other Tales of Blackwater, DynCorp, and Triple Canopy's Rampage through Iraq," *Gawker*, December 13, 2011, at gawker.com.

85 Margherita Stancati and Nathan Hodge, "Kabul's Economic Bubble Bursts," *Wall Street Journal*, June 12, 2014.

86 However, the CIA is talking about maintaining covert forces in the country to battle supposed enemies for years to come. Julius Cavendish, "CIA Trains Covert Units of Afghans to Continue the Fight Against Taliban," *Independent*, July 20, 2011; Kate Clark, "War Without Accountability: The CIA, Special Forces and Plans for Afghanistan's Future," Afghanistan Analysts Network, October 2, 2012, at afghanistan-analysts.org.

87 John Sopko, special inspector general for Afghanistan reconstruction, speech at Georgetown University, September 12, 2014.

88 Matthieu Aikins, "Afghanistan's Fiscal Cliff," *Foreign Policy*, October 17, 2012.

89 "Paying Afghanistan's Bills," *New York Times*, October 1, 2014.

90 Esther Zuckerman, "Leaving Afghanistan by 2015 Requires Shipping a Container Every 7 Minutes," Reuters, July 20, 2012.

91 Thomas Ruttig, "Happy Christmas (2014): Will War Be Over?" Afghanistan Analysts Network, May 25, 2012, at afghanistan-analysts.org.

92 Martine van Bijlert and Sari Kouvo, eds, "*Snapshots of Intervention: The Unlearned Lessons of Afghanistan's Decade of Assistance (2001–2011),*" Afghanistan Analysts Network, 2012, at afghanistan-analysts.org.

2   Greece

1 "Indefinite Detention: A Direct Infringement of National, European and International Law," Greek Council for Refugees, July 2014.

2 "EU: Border Agency Exposes Migrants to Abusive Conditions," Human Rights Watch, September 21, 2011.

3 Helen Smith, "Greece to Open New Detention Centres for Illegal Migrants," *Guardian*, March 30, 2012.

4 In 2014 Global Detention Project listed Greek detention sites, at globaldetentionproject.org.

5 Apostolis Fotiadis, "Immigrants Face Indefinite Detention in Greece," Inter Press Service, May 28, 2014, at ipsnews.net.

6 Damian Mac Con Uladh, "Migrants on Hunger Strike at Corinth Detention Centre," EnetEnglish, June 12, 2014, at enetenglish.gr.

7 United Nations High Commissioner for Refugees Office in Greece, June 19, 2014.

8 "Greece: Human Rights Watch Submission to the United Nations Committee against Torture," Human Rights Watch, March 24, 2014.

9 Paul Mason, "Greece Shows What Can Happen When the Young Revolt Against Corrupt Elites," *Guardian*, January 26, 2015.

10 Paul Krugman, "Ending Greece's Nightmare," *New York Times*, January 26, 2015.

11 "World Press Freedom Index 2014," Reporters Without Borders.

12 Paul Mason, "Germany vs Greece Is a Fight to the Death, a Cultural and Economic Clash of Wills," *Guardian*, February 9, 2015.

13 Daniel Trilling, "Kostas Vaxevanis interview," *New Statesman*, April 22, 2013.

14 MSF's "Invisible Suffering" report offers unprecedented details of life inside Greek immigration detention centers. By interviewing detainees, MSF reveals the overcrowding, substandard hygiene, dirty toilets, and shabby bedrooms and bathrooms all causing extreme medical problems. Arbitrary detention leads to severe mental health problems. "Invisible Suffering," MSF, April 1, 2014.

15 Submission of the Greek Council for Refugees to the Committee of Ministers of the Council of Europe in the Case of MSS v. Belgium and Greece, April 2014.

16 Jon Henley, "Greece on the Breadline: 'Potato Movement' Links Shoppers and Farmers," *Guardian*, March 18, 2012.

17 Liz Alderman, "More Children in Greece Are Going Hungry," *New York Times*, April 17, 2013.

18 Alexander Clapp, "Diary," *London Review of Books*, December 4, 2014.

19 Gianluca Mezzofiore, "Golden Dawn Mob Threatens NGO for Treating Migrants in Perama Clinic," *International Business Times*, April 11, 2014.

20 Greg Palast, "Trojan Hearse: Greek Elections and the Euro Leper Colony," January 26, 2015.

21 Dimitris Psarras, "Oath Treason!" *Efimerida ton sintakton*, June 23, 2014.

22 Nick Malkoutzis, "In the Absence of Light, Darkness Grows," *Macropolis*, June 4, 2014.

23 Farrell Dobbs, "The Greek Orthodox Church Openly Supports the Neo Nazi Golden Dawn," *Liverpool Antifascists*, June 24, 2012, at liveraf. wordpress.com.

24 Darren Mara, "Golden Dawn Stops Fundraising Drive in Australia, Refuses to Impose Blanket Ban," *SBS News*, October 4, 2014.

25 John Feffer, "The Collapse of Europe?" *TomDispatch*, January 27, 2015, at tomdispatch.com.

26 "Golden Dawn Seeks 'One-Party State,'" EnetEnglish, June 19, 2014, at enetenglish.gr.

27 Andrew Higgins, "Far-right Fever for a Europe Tied to Russia," *New York Times*, May 20, 2014.

28 Richard Schwartz, "Greek Jews Laud Leftist Win—Despite Chilly Stance on Israel," *Forward*, February 3, 2015.

29 Helena Smith, "Greek Prime Minister Facing Resignation Calls after Aide's Golden Dawn Gaffe," *Guardian*, April 4, 2014.

30 Peter Beaumont and Patrick Kingsley, *Guardian*, October 1, 2014.

31 Belen Fernandez, "Detention in Malta: Europe's Migrant Prison," Al Jazeera English, May 18, 2014.

32 Apostolis Fotiadis, "New Operation Could Hide Major Shift in Europe's Immigration Control Policy," Inter Press Service, September 6, 2014, at ipsnews.net.

33 Apostolis Fotiadis, "Officials Turn Blind Eye to Abuse of Asylum Seekers," Inter Press Service, March 16, 2013, at ipsnews.net.

34 Danai Angeli, "Prolonged Detention of Migrants Is Not Just Inhumane and Illegal, It's Also Futile," Press Project, October 11, 2014, at thepressproject.net.

35 Apostolis Fotiadis, "Europe Sending Armies to Stop Immigrants," Inter Press Service, December 3, 2013, at ipsnews.net.

36 Apostolis Fotiadis and Claudia Ciobanu, "Closing Europe's Borders Becomes Big Business," Inter Press Service, January 9, 2013, at ipsnews. net.

37 Apostolis Fotiadis and Claudia Ciobanu, "People Pay for Research Against Migrants," Inter Press Service, January 11, 2013, at ipsnews.net.

38 Apostolis Fotiadis, "Drones May Track Migrants in EU," Al Jazeera English, November 11, 2010.

39 "Eurodrones Inc.," TNI Peace and Security, February 5, 2014.

40 In an attempt to demonstrate its corporate social responsibility, G4S financially assists the Athens charity Ark of the World, providing support to children and single mothers.

41 Apostolis Fotiadis, "Cecilia Malmstrom and the Fiasco of Detention Centres for Immigrants and Migrants," Press Project, October 20, 2014, at thepressproject.net.

42 "Greece Tops Eurozone Poverty Rate," EnetEnglish, July 24, 2014, at enetenglish.gr.

43 Razmig Keucheyan, "The French Are Right: Tear Up Public Debt—Most of It Is Illegitimate Anyway," *Guardian*, June 10, 2014.

44 Howard Schneider, "An Amazing Mea Culpa from the IMF's Chief Economist on Austerity," *Washington Post*, January 3, 2013.

45 Nikos Konstandaras, "As Greece Goes, So Goes Europe?" *New York Times*, May 28, 2014.

46 Saskia Sassen, "European Economy's Invisible Transformation: Expulsions and Predatory Capitalism," London School of Economics and Political Science, July 3, 2014, at blogs.lse.ac.uk.

47 Harriet Alexander, "Greece's Great Fire Sale," *Telegraph*, April 20, 2013.

48 "Privatization of Athens Water Utility Ruled Unconstitutional," Press Project, May 28, 2014, at thepressproject.net.

49 Niki Kitsantonis, "Greece Wars with Courts over Ways to Slash Budget," *New York Times*, June 12, 2014.

50 Daniel Trilling, "Shock Therapy and the Gold Mine," *New Statesman*, June 18, 2013.

51 "Europe's Failed Course," *New York Times*, February 17, 2012.

52 Joanna Kakissis, "36 hours in Athens," *New York Times*, October 19, 2014.

53 Yiannis Baboulias, "Our Big Fat Greek Privatisation Scandals," Al Jazeera English, June 10, 2014.

54 Helen Smith, "Greece Begins 50 Billion Euro Privatisation Drive," *Guardian*, August 1, 2010.

55 Slavoj Žižek, "Save Us from the Saviours," *London Review of Books*, May 28, 2012.

56 Alexander, "Greece's Fire Sale."

57 Ibid.

58 Katie Allen, "Austerity in Greece Caused More than 500 Male Suicides, Say Researchers," *Guardian*, April 21, 2014.

59 Mark Lowen, "Greek's Million Unpaid Workers," BBC News, December 5, 2013.

60 "Sisa: Cocaine of the Poor," *Vice News*, May 22, 2013, at vice.com.

61 Liz Alderman, "Societal Ills Spike in Crisis-Stricken Greece," *New York Times*, May 22, 2013.

3 Haiti

1 Mark Schuller and Pablo Morales, eds, *Tectonic Shifts* (Sterling, VA: Stylus, 2012).

2 Ibid., p. 2.

3 Ansel Herz and Kim Ives, "Wikileaks Haiti: The Post-Quake 'Gold Rush' for Reconstruction Contracts," *Nation*, June 15, 2011.

4 Deepa Panchang, Beverly Bell, and Tory Field, "Disaster Capitalism: Profiting from Crisis in Post-Earthquake Haiti," *Truthout*, February 16, 2011, at truth-out.org.

5 Herz and Ives, "Wikileaks Haiti."

6 The AshBritt company was accused of questionable practices in the wake of Hurricane Katrina, the CEPR revealing that a "2006 congressional report examining federal contract waste and abuse noted AshBritt used multiple layers of subcontractors, each of whom got paid while passing on the actual work." "Katrina Redux: New Disaster, Same Contractors," CEPR, June 11, 2010, at cepr.net. AshBritt spent tens of thousands of dollars on lobbying after the Haiti earthquake—one of the paid lobbyists was the former chief of staff to Senator John Kerry, who eventually co-sponsored legislation for Haiti relief.

7 Herz and Ives, "Wikileaks Haiti."

8 Peter Hallward, *Damming the Flood: Haiti and the Politics of Containment* (London: Verso, 2010), p. xxiii.

9 Belen Fernandez, "Paramilitarism and the Assault on the Democracy in Haiti," Al Jazeera English, October 4, 2012; Geoff Burt, "From Private Security to Public Good: Regulating the Private Security Industry in Haiti," Centre for International Governance Innovation, June 2012; Jeb Sprague, *Paramilitarism and the Assault on Democracy in Haiti* (New York: Monthly Review, 2012).

10 "Freedom of Press in Haiti: Report Finds Haitian Journalists Face Death Threats, Intimidation, Retaliation and Hindered Access to Information," Institute for Justice and Democracy in Haiti, September 27, 2012.

11 Nathalie Baptiste, "Harkening Back to Dark Days in Haiti," *Foreign Policy in Focus*, March 11, 2014, at fpif.org.

12 One of the key texts on the successful slave revolt in Haiti is C. L. R. James, *The Black Jacobins* (London: Vintage, 1989).

13 Kim Ives, "How the US Resumed Military Aid to Duvalier," *Haïti Liberté*, April 16, 2013, at haiti-liberte.com.

14 Hallward, *Damming the Flood*, p. 15.

15 Ibid.

16 Ibid., p. 227.

17 Amy Goodman, "Uncut Interview with Former Haitian President Jean-Bertrand Aristide upon his Historic Return to Haiti," *Democracy Now!*, March 22, 2011, at democracynow.org.

18 Deborah Sontag, "In Haiti, Global Failures on a Cholera Epidemic," *New York Times*, March 31, 2012.

19 Louise C. Ivers, "A Chance to Right a Wrong in Haiti," *New York Times*, February 22, 2013.

20 Randal C. Archibold and Somini Sengupta, "UN Struggles to Stem Haiti Cholera Epidemic," *New York Times*, April 19, 2014.

21 Joan Arnan, "Voices from the Field: Tackling Haiti's Cholera Epidemic," Médecins Sans Frontières, July 12, 2012, at doctorswithoutborders.org.

22 "Haiti Unprepared in Face of Resurgent Cholera," Médecins Sans Frontières, May 8, 2012, at doctorswithoutborders.org.

23 Richard Knox, "5 Years After Haiti's Earthquake, Where Did the $13.5 Billion Go?" NPR, January 12, 2015, at npr.org.

24 Jonathan M. Katz, "Haiti's Shadow Sanitation System," *New Yorker*, March 12, 2014.

25 Michael Kimmelman, "In Haiti, Battling Disease with Open-Air Clinics," *New York Times*, December 28, 2014.

26 "Haiti in the Shadow of Cholera," *New York Times*, April 23, 2014.

27 Knox, "5 Years After Haiti's Earthquake."

28 Mark Weisbrot, "UN Should Get Rid of Cholera Epidemic that It Brought to Haiti," McClathy-Tribune Information Services, August 9, 2012, available at cepr.net.

29 Justin Podur, *Haiti's New Dictatorship* (London: Pluto, 2012), p. 2.

30 Ibid., p. 7.

31 Lauren Carasik, "The United Nations' Role in Haiti Cholera Outbreak," Al Jazeera English, November 20, 2012.

32 "Haiti: 'Open for Business,'" *Haiti Grassroots Watch*, November 29, 2011, at haitigrassrootswatch.squarespace.com.

33 "Haiti: Open for Business—Part 1," Inter Press Service, December 20, 2011, at ipsnews.net.

34 "Rebuilding Haiti: Open for Business," *Economist*, January 7, 2012. Haiti's subservience towards Washington is clear from the following story about Martelly. In March 2012, he held a press conference to display his eight passports in an effort to prove he was not a US citizen anymore—something which is forbidden by the Haitian constitution. The US ambassador at the time, Kenneth Merten, then stood up and declared in Haitian Creole that the passports proved Martelly's presidency was valid. The fact that it is deemed necessary for a US ambassador to validate the credentials of a supposedly democratically elected leader of a sovereign nation says all you need to know about Haiti's relationship with America.

35 "Haiti's Long Road," *New York Times*, January 1, 2013.

36 Isabel Macdonald and Isabeau Doucet, "The Shelters That Clinton Built," *Nation*, July 11, 2011.

37 Amy Goodman, "Haitian Activist Patrick Elie: 'Haiti Is Controlled by Foreign Governments and Foreign Interests,'" *Democracy Now!*, January 12, 2011, at democracynow.org.

38 Cyanide is often used to loosen gold particles during mining. An accident that occurred in Ghana in 2010, in which cyanide poisoned water supplies and killed fish, and was caused by Haiti's biggest mining-sector investor, Newmont, highlights the dangers. Jacob Kushner, "Haiti's Gold Rush," *Guernica*, August 15, 2012, at guernicamag.com.

39 "Haiti's 'Gold Rush' Promises El Dorado—But for Whom?" Inter Press Service, June 27, 2012, at ipsnews.net.

40 Jane Regan, "Haiti's Rush for Gold Gives Mining Firms a Free Rein Over the Riches," *Guardian*, May 30, 2012.

41 "UN Envoy Says Haiti 'Not Yet'" Open for Business," Associated Press, February 16, 2013.

42 Digicel coincidentally funded the trip of President Michel Martelly to the World Economic Forum's annual meeting in Davos, Switzerland, in 2011.

43 Mark Schuller, "Tectonic Shifts? The Upcoming Donors' Conference for Haiti," *Huffington Post*, March 24, 2010.

44 Randal C. Archibold, "Already Desperate, Haitian Farmers Are Left Hopeless After Storm," *New York Times*, November 17, 2012.

45 Jacob Kushner, "Haitian Farmers Call on US to Stop Subsidising Its Own," *GlobalPost*, April 12, 2012, at globalpost.com.

46 "With Poor Track Records, For-Profit Development Companies Team Up to Fight Reform," CEPR, December 1, 2011, at cepr.net.

47 Jake Johnston, "Is USAID Helping Haiti to Recover or US Contractors to Make Millions?" *Nation*, January 21, 2015.

48 John Norris, "Hired Gun Fight," *Foreign Policy*, July 18, 2012.

49 Deborah Sontag, "Rebuilding in Haiti Lags After Billions in Post-Quake Aid," *New York Times*, December 23, 2012.

50 Jake Johnston, "Blacklisted Contractor Continues Receiving Government Money through Haiti Contracts," *The Hill*, December 2, 2011, at thehill.com.

51 "Private Prison Company Gets Haiti Contract," CEPR, February 19, 2010, at cepr.net.

52 "Contractor Accused of Waste in Katrina Reconstruction Lands USAID Contract in Haiti," CEPR, January 4, 2012, at cepr.net.

53 "Leaked Contract Reveals Inadequate Oversight of Beltway Contractors: Haitian Firms Remain Sidelined," CEPR, November 28, 2011, at cepr.net.

54 Jake Johnston and Alexander Main, *Breaking Open the Black Box: Increasing Aid Transparency and Accountability in Haiti*, CEPR, April 2013, at cepr.net.

55 "GAO Report Suggests That USAID Remains 'More of a Contracting Agency than an Operational Agency," CEPR, November 21, 2011, at cepr.net.

56 The *New York Times* reported in late 2012 that the goals set for Haiti after the earthquake, which were to utilize the billions of dollars pledged, have largely not been delivered. A Spanish development official in Haiti told the paper: "It's not a problem of the availability of money but of the capacity to spend it." This was due to local government failures and the incapacity or unwillingness of foreign donors, subcontractors, and corrupt officials to deliver what was promised. Deborah Sontag, "In Reviving Haiti, Lofty Hopes and Hard Truths," *New York Times*, December 23, 2012.

57 "Without International Help, Haiti Faces a Political Meltdown," *Washington Post*, December 27, 2014.

58 Deborah Sontag, "Earthquake Relief Where Haiti Wasn't Broken," *New York Times*, July 5, 2012.

59 Sontag, "Rebuilding in Haiti."

60 Ibid.

61 Jacqueline Charles, "Building Permanent Housing Remains Haiti's Biggest Challenge Following the 2010 Earthquake," *Miami Herald*, January 11, 2015.

62 "Haiti: 'Open for Business,'" *Haiti Grassroots Watch*.

63 Sontag, "Rebuilding in Haiti."

64 Ibid.

65 The safety of twenty-first-century sweatshops is questionable, and accountability can be lacking. After a devastating factory fire in Bangladesh in 2012 that claimed the lives of over one hundred people, US giant Walmart claimed ignorance of the terrible conditions inside it. Jim Yardley, "Horrific Fire Revealed a Gap in Safety for Global Brands," *New York Times*, December 6, 2012.

66 Sarah Lazare, "Clintons' Pet Project for Privatized 'Aid' to Haiti Stealing Workers' Wages: Report," *Common Dreams*, December 16, 2013, at commondreams.org.

67 "Haiti: Open for Business—Part 2," Inter Press Service, December 20, 2011, at ipsnews.net.

68 Sontag, "Rebuilding in Haiti."

69 "Haiti: 'Open for Business,'" *Haiti Grassroots Watch*.

70 Jacqueline Charles, "New Industrial Park in Northern Haiti Sparks Controversy," *Miami Herald*, June 4, 2012.

71 The documents were obtained by journalist Matt Kennard, formerly of the *Financial Times*.

72 Sontag, "Rebuilding in Haiti."

73 Mary Anastasia O'Grady, "Hillary's Half-Baked Haitian Project," *Wall Street Journal*, January 11, 2015.

74 Randal C. Archibold, "Palace in Haiti, Damaged by Quake, Is Being Razed," *New York Times*, September 13, 2012.

75 Panchang, Bell, and Field, "Disaster Capitalism."

76 Unni Karunakara, "Haiti: Where Aid Failed," *Guardian*, December 28, 2010.

77 Catherine Porter, "In Haiti, building people, not things: Porter," *The Star*, February, 20, 2015.

78 Jonathan Katz, "Three Years After the Quake, How the World Came to Save Haiti and Left Behind a Disaster," *Democracy Now!*, January 11, 2013, at democracynow.org.

79 Michelle Chen, "How Humanitarian Aid Weakened Post-Earthquake Haiti," *Nation*, September 2, 2014.

80 Tate Watkins, "Port-au-Prince's Aid Economy," *Reason*, March 12, 2012.

81 Wyclef Jean, *Purpose: An Immigrant's Story* (New York: It Books, 2012).

82 Deborah Sontag, "In Haiti, Little Can Be Found in a Hip-Hop Artist's Charity," *New York Times*, October 11, 2012.

83 Mark Schuller, "What Wyclef Exposed," *CounterPunch*, October 22, 2012, at counterpunch.org.

84 Laura Zanotti, "Cacophonies of Aid, Failed State Building and NGOs

in Haiti: Setting the Stage for Disaster, Envisioning the Future," *Third World Quarterly* 31: 5 (September 1, 2010).

85 Briquettes, a relatively clean fuel compared with charcoal, are now produced in Haiti and used in many of the country's schools and homes. Patricia Grogg, "Solar Energy and Briquettes Make Headway in Haiti," Inter Press Service, April 4, 2013, at ipsnews.net.

86 Mark Schuller, "The Pretense of Doing Good (While Raising Millions)," *CounterPunch*, March 1–3, 2013, at counterpunch.org.

87 Allie Torgan, "Haitians Living in Fear 'Under the Tent,'" CNN, October 18, 2012.

88 Athena Kolbe and Robert Muggah, "Haiti's Silenced Victims," *New York Times*, December 8, 2012.

89 The Red Cross was the largest recipient of funds for Haiti from American citizens, though its record of transparency around its work was far from satisfactory. For example, it claimed in a 2015 release to have "helped 132,000 Haitians to live in safer conditions" since the 2010 earthquake, but Haiti experts the Center for Economic and Policy Research questioned its accuracy: "It's Been Five Years and All the Money Raised Is Gone: What Did the Red Cross Accomplish in Haiti?" CEPR, January 16, 2015, at cepr.net.

90 There are many community-led initiatives striving to improve society because the government has failed to do so. The NGO Fokal led a project in a Port-au-Prince slum, Martissant, to clean up the garbage there and encourage recycling. The idea was to show citizens that it was their responsibility to keep the area clean. Eventually, the state joined in.

91 This occurred despite there being more than enough locally produced food to provide for the needy.

92 Justin Podur, "Help That Hurts: An Interview with Tim Schwartz about Haiti," *Killing Train*, March 17, 2012, at killingtrain.com. Schwartz has authored an influential book called *Travesty in Haiti* that details how the majority of foreign aid is wasted. "Charity is manipulated to serve political ends," he writes. "Lack of accountability allows the aid to be distorted into something that arguably does more harm than good." Timothy Schwartz, *Travesty in Haiti* (Charleston, SC: BookSurge, 2010), p. 3.

93 Timothy Schwartz, "History of NGOs and Disaster in Haiti," *Salon*, February 9, 2013, at salon.com.

94 David Adams, "Neglected Islanders Resist Plan for Haiti Tourism Revival," Reuters, April 6, 2014.

95 Hallward, *Damming the Flood*, p. 179.

4   *Papua New Guinea*

1 "PNG Govt Acknowledges Major Mines Using Unsafe Waste Disposal," *National*, February 26, 2013.

2 From a report by Ross Garnaut and Rabbie Namaliu. Rowan Callick, "Growth Stymied by Big-Man Rorting," *Australian*, October 12, 2011.

3 Bougainville Land Summit report, 2011.

4 Daniel Jones, *Mekamui News*, February 15, 2013.

5 "Voices of Bougainville: Our Land, Our Future," Jubilee Australia, 2014, at jubileeaustralia.org; Helen Davidson, "Opposition to Bougainville's Panguna Mine 'Higher than Media Suggest,'" *Guardian*, September 15, 2014; "Australian Advisor Revealed to Be Behind Bougainville President's Attacks on Panguna Landowners," *PNG Exposed*, December 15, 2014, at pngexposed.wordpress.com.

6 Dr. Kristian Lasslett, "The Evidence of BCL's Role in the Bougainville Conflict: A Reluctant Response to Axel G. Sturm's Open Letter," *Act Now*, April 26, 2012, at actnowpng.org. A BCL memo from that time seemed to indicate some sympathy from parts of the PNG government towards the BRA and its cause. Eventually, BCL concluded that the PNG government was "divided among itself," and the mine was no longer able to operate functionally. Martyn Namorong, "BCL Memo Reveals Dying Moments of Panguna Mine," *Namorong Report*, September 1, 2011; Kristian Lasslett, "Winning Hearts and Minds: The Bougainville Crisis 1988–1990," in R. Jackson, E. Murphy, and S. Poynting, eds, *Contemporary State Terrorism: Theory and Practice* (London: Routledge, 2010), pp. 141–62.

7 Kristian Lasslett, "State Crime and Resistance in the South Pacific: Uncovering a Denied History," Pluto Press blog, September 1, 2014, at plutopress.wordpress.com. I was asked to endorse Lasslett's 2014 book, *State Crime on the Margins of Empire: Rio Tinto, the War on Bougainville and Resistance to Mining* (London: Pluto, 2014).

8 Kristian Lasslett, "The Greatest Threat to Bougainville Copper's Future Is Its Hidden Past," *Act Now*, April 23, 2012, at actnowpng.org. Namaliu is just one of the past leaders of PNG who have established particularly close relationships with mining companies. He is also friendly with the Australian National University, which regularly hosts him as a speaker. Kristian Lasslett, "From Civil War to the Boardroom," *New Matilda*, March 28, 2013, at newmatilda.com.

9 The entire transcript of the BCL chairman's 1999 testimony before the Australian parliament can be found at parlinfo.aph.gov.au.

10 Kristian Lasslett, "Bougainville: Rio Tinto Faces War Crimes Allegations in Bid to Reopen Mine," *Green Left Weekly*, February 26, 2013, at greenleft.org.au.

11 Kristian Lasslett gave me US court documents from November 2001 that detailed the evidence offered by John Momis against BCL, Rio Tinto, and the PNG government.

12 "Will the Real Anthony Regan Please Stand Up," *PNG Exposed*, March 7, 2013, at pngexposed.wordpress.com.

13 Kristian Lasslett, "AusAid Fuels Bougainville Mining Tensions," *New Matilda*, April 23, 2013, at newmatilda.com.

14 "Australian Academics Paid $500,000 Over Two Years for Mining Work on Bougainville," *PNG Exposed*, April 3, 2014, at pngexposed.wordpress. com.

15 "Bougainville Landowners to Share Mining Rights with Govt," ABC Radio's *PM*, March 7, 2013.

16 "Copper Mine Must Not Be Blocked," *Canberra Times*, August 13, 1969.

17 Anthony Fenson, "Papua New Guinea: Riding the Resource Boom," *Diplomat*, February 5, 2013.

18 "PNG's Constitutional Planning Committee Foresaw the Perils of Large-Scale Mining," *Papua New Guinea Mine Watch*, June 10, 2012.

19 PNG has vast areas of virgin forest. The country has been targeted by the UN's Reducing Emissions from Deforestation and Forest Degradation in Developing Countries policy, which in reality has seen "carbon cowboys" traveling to poor areas of PNG and offering money for the use of land. With a landowner system in place, it is impossible to avoid corruption, and other locals receive little of the money. Ilya Gridneff, "Beware the Climate Cowboy," *New Matilda*, July 14, 2011, at newmatilda.com. In October 2012, the ABC revealed that an Australian logging company, Independent Timbers and Stevedoring, had been involved in the taking of more than two million hectares of PNG land, including pristine forest, away from its traditional owners. Jemima Garrett, "Australians Involved in PNG Land Scandal," *ABC News*, October 14, 2012. In addition, one of the major developments in PNG over the last decade has been the signing of long-term (often ninety-nine-year) leases of customary land to the state, which is then subleased to various corporations for exploitation. Jo Chandler, "PNG's Great Land Grab Sparks Fightback by Traditional Owners," *The Age*, October 14, 2011. In recent years, PNG has become one of the world's largest suppliers of illegally logged tropical timber, thanks to Chinese, American, Canadian, and European contracts and consumer demand.

20 Steve Lewis and Lisa Cornish, "AusAID Investigates Fraud Claims Surrounding Australia Award Education Scholarships," *Adelaide Now*, March 10, 2013.

21 The paper gave a number of examples of companies winning contracts for projects that sounded suspicious, including a $55 million deal for "public service evaluation in PNG." Steve Lewis, "Seven Corporations Rake In $1.81 Billion Dollars from Foreign Aid Program," *Daily Telegraph* (Sydney), January 9, 2012. Bernard Keane published an investigation in 2010 that detailed the major Australian companies making a profit from aid and explained how one of Australia's richest families, the Packers, was involved in the process. Wendy Bacon, "Who Profits from Our Foreign Aid? From Cattle Company to Global Aid," *Crikey*, July 13, 2010, at crikey.com.au.

22 Aviva Imhof, "The Big, Ugly Australian Goes to Ok Tedi," *Multinational Monitor*, March 1996.

23 Jemima Garrett, "Ok Tedi," Radio Australia, January 3, 2013. Since 2001, Ok Tedi has been theoretically fully owned by the people of PNG through a flawed agreement called the Papua New Guinea Sustainable Development Program (PNGSDP). As part of the deal, the PNG government effectively indemnified BHP over the ecological catastrophe the mine had caused, including diseases such as endemic tuberculosis that continue to inflict a huge toll on nearby communities. Jo Chandler, "Up the Fly Without a Paddle," *Global Mail*, December 17, 2012. One example of the skewed priorities of the PNGSDP, revealed in February 2013, was that hundreds of millions of dollars was being invested in constructing a deep-sea port in Western Province that would be principally used by mining companies. Prime Minister Peter O'Neill said in 2013 that PNG, and not a fund managed in Singapore, would control how the PNGSDP money was allocated. He slammed BHP for its attempts to maintain control over the fund and announced that the government would take ownership of the Ok Tedi mine in 2014, although the company would continue to manage it.

24 "Greens Want Crackdown on Australian Miners Overseas," Radio Australia, July 29, 2011.

25 Eric Shek, "Australian Aid to Papua New Guinea: Where Is This Aid Really Going?" *Cross Sections* v (2009).

26 Rowan Callick, "Prospect of Mutual Benefits in Lively Ties with PNG," *Australian*, January 24, 2013.

27 Rowan Callick, "PNG Ripe for Huge Change," *Australian*, October 18, 2013.

28 The Solomon Islands also face rapacious mining interests. Japanese miner Sumitomo threatened to cut foreign aid to the island unless it won rights to exploit a nickel deposit. Joshua Robertson, "Japanese Mining Giant Threatened Aid Cut in Bid to Win Solomon Islands Deal," *Guardian*, December 3, 2014.

29 Daniel Flitton, "The Troubles in PNG Australia Can't Ignore," *The Age*, May 28, 2014.

30 Ryan Dube, "Mining Companies Don't Take into Account the Cost of Community Conflicts, Study Says," *Wall Street Journal*, May 12, 2014.

31 Malum Nalu, "BCL Landowners Slam 'State Ownership' Stance," *Papua New Guinea Mine Watch*, March 2, 2012.

32 Details of these allegations against Daveona can be found at pngexposed. wordpress.com.

33 In June 2012, the Autonomous Bougainville Government approved a motion to create a local oil and gas exploration policy that would "protect the interests of the landowner rights and investors." Canadian resource company Morumbi was one of the first to announce a memorandum of understanding concerning two new areas of Bougainville that it planned to explore.

34 Samuel Kauona, "For Peace in Bougainville," *Green Left Weekly*, November 2, 1994, at greenleft.org.

35 In 2013, Kauona, now the chairman of the Bougainville Resources Owners Representative Council, warned Australia to butt out of Bougainville and not to adopt once again a colonial mindset towards the province.

36 Peterson Tseraha, "Environment Is More Important than Mining for Bougainville," *Papua New Guinea Mine Watch*, September 14, 2011.

37 Julie Bishop, "Why We're Gunning for the Illegal Trade in Weapons," *Australian*, June 2, 2014.

38 "Move to Boost Women MP Numbers in Pacific," AAP, February 4, 2013.

39 "MSF Chief Urges PNG to Act on Sexual Violence," AFP, November 15, 2012.

40 Catherine Wilson, "Papua New Guinea: Women Call the Shots on Mega Copper Mine," Inter Press Service, October 16, 2011, at ipsnews.net.

41 Aloysius Laukai, "Pipiro Wants Rehabilitation Before Decisions on Panguna," *New Dawn*, October 8, 2012. Even Fiji's self-imposed head of state, Prime Minister Commodore Frank Bainimarama, expressed caution, in March 2012, about a proposed Australian mining company, Newcrest, expanding its operations into his country, saying, "I have been to Bougainville and I don't want to see what happened there [occurring]

here in Namosi." He was adamant that the wishes and concerns of local landowners must not be ignored.

42 "Bougainville Landowners Speak Out on Latest Moves with Rio Tinto Mine," Radio Australia, July 19, 2012.

43 Ibid.

44 Malum Nalu, "Rio Tinto Keen to Reopen Panguna Mine," *Papua New Guinea Mine Watch*, May 3, 2012.

45 "Rio Tinto Warned on Environmental Damage on Bougainville," Radio Australia, May 2, 2013, at radioaustralia.net.au.

46 Jemima Garrett, "Bougainville's President Says Rio Tinto Cannot Assume It Will Operate Panguna Mine," *Australian Network News*, May 22, 2014.

47 Blair Price, "Uncertainly over Panguna Is Poison: Sturm," *Papua New Guinea Mine Watch*, March 16, 2012.

48 "Rats Begin Fleeing Sinking BCL Ship," *Papua New Guinea Mine Watch*, May 26, 2014.

49 Peter Korugl, "Rio Tinto, BHP Make Way to Return to PNG," *Post-Courier*, February 13, 2012.

50 Patrick Talu, "PM Welcomes Return of Shell," *Post-Courier*, February 10, 2012. The O'Neill administration is fully committed to the mining industry in PNG but has implemented few environmental safeguards against bad mining practices.

51 "Return of Shell and Other Discredited Companies Queried," *Papua New Guinea Mine Watch*, February 25, 2012.

52 In 2012, Shell, BHP, and other multinationals opposed attempts to strengthen US and EU anti-graft rules so that they would force energy companies to disclose monies paid to governments in the countries where they operated.

53 David Robertson, "Wealth Fund Dumps Rio Tinto Holding over Grasberg," *Australian*, September 10, 2008. Australian academic N. A. J. Taylor has written extensively about this decision in "High-Risk Areas—Red River: The Blacklisting of Rio Tinto," in Cary Krosinksy, Nick Robins, and Stephen Viederman, eds, *Evolutions in Sustainable Investing: Strategies, Funds and Thought Leadership* (London: Wiley, 2011).

54 Indonesia Human Rights Committee, September 27, 2012. The collusion between mining multinationals and the state was made clear when Indonesian police admitted in 2011 that they were on the payroll of the mining company Freeport. Tom Allard, "Police Paid 'Pocket Money' by Giant West Papua Mine," *Sydney Morning Herald*, November 1, 2011.

55 "US Appeals Court Revives Bougainville Challenge Against Rio Tinto," Radio Australia, October 27, 2011, at radioaustralia.net.au.

56 Kristian Lasslett, "How Australia, the US and Britain Helped Block Bougainville's Class Action against Rio Tinto," *PNG Exposed*, December 12, 2014, at pngexposed.wordpress.com.

57 *Unsustainable: The Ugly Truth about Rio Tinto* (IndustriALL Global Union, 2014).

58 "The Documents That Show Our Government Caved In to Corporate Lobbying," Amnesty International UK, April 7, 2014, at amnesty.org.uk.

59 Liam Fox, "PNG Task Force Finds 'Mobocracy' Ruining the Country," ABC Radio's *AM*, May 11, 2012; Hamish McDonald, "Port Moresby in a Storm," *Saturday Paper*, December 13–19, 2014, at thesaturdaypaper.com.au.

60 Philip Dorling, "PNG Exposed as 'Dysfunctional Blob,'" *Sydney Morning Herald*, September 4, 2011.

61 Liam Fox, "Claims Stolen PNG Funds Laundered in Australia," ABC Radio's *AM*, October 10, 2012.

62 Mekere Morauta, "Managing the Boom in Mineral Revenue in Papua New Guinea," *Papua New Guinea Mine Watch*, January 3, 2012.

63 Eoin Blackwell, "PNG to Restructure Major Assets," AAP, April 8, 2013.

64 Joe Kelly, "PNG Can Be a Regional Leader, Says Bob Carr," *Australian*, December 5, 2012.

65 Dan Oakes, "Coalition Accused of Trying to Palm Off Its Diplomatic Image," *Sydney Morning Herald*, August 13, 2010.

66 Rowan Callick, "$300m Pillaged on PNG Graft," *Australian*, April 28, 2010. In 2010, PNG's foreign minister, Sam Abal, complained to Australia that too much aid money was being spent on Australian "consultants." Rowan Callick, "PNG Irked by Fees for Experts," *Australian*, April 23, 2010.

67 Claire Parfitt, "When Aid Is Good for Business," *New Matilda*, December 10, 2012, at newmatilda.com. In December 2012, Australia announced it was subscribing to the Voluntary Principles on Security and High Rights to "provide practical advice to mining, oil and gas companies on managing security while respecting human rights and preventing conflict." BHP and Rio Tinto were already signed up to the initiative. Foreign Minister Bob Carr, press release, December 11, 2012.

68 Stephen Stockwell, "African Women Tour Australian Mines," ABC Rural, November 1, 2012.

69 Martyn Namorong, "AusAID's Neo-Colonisation Agenda Extends to 'Sustainable Mining,'" *Namorong Report*, February 27, 2012.
70 Sylvia Pfeifer, Xan Rice, and Andrew England, "Energy: Trial by Oil," *Financial Times*, January 10, 2013.

5 The United States

1   Michelle Alexander, *The New Jim Crow: Mass Incarceration in the Age of Colorblindness* (New York: New Press, 2012), pp. 6–7.
2   "US: A Nation Behind Bars," Human Rights Watch, May 6, 2014, at hrw.org.
3   Adam Gopnik, "The Caging of America," *New Yorker*, January 30, 2012.
4   Victoria Law, "California Turns to Private Prison to Address Overcrowding and Medical Care," *Truthout*, June 10, 2014, at truth-out.org.
5   Marisa Taylor and Saila Huusko, "Immigrant Women Allege Sexual Abuse at Detention Centre," Al Jazeera America, October 9, 2014.
6   "Privatization of the US prison system, Arrest Records," April 12, 2014, at blog.arrestrecords.com.
7   "Prisons for Profit: A Look at Privatization," ACLU, April 2011.
8   Sarah Lazare, "Skyrocketing Prison Population Devastating US Society: Report," *Common Dreams*, May 2, 2014, at commondreams.org.
9   Justin Jones, "How to Starve the For-Profit Prison Beast," ACLU, April 24, 2014.
10 Charlotte Silver, "US Criminal Justice System: Turning a Profit on Prison Reform?" Al Jazeera English, September 27, 2013.
11 Sam Ali, Luke Visconti, and Barbara Frankel, "The Prison Industrial Complex: Biased, Predatory and Growing," *DiversityInc*, October 11, 2010, at diversityinc.com.
12 Paul Krugman, "Prisons, Privatization and Patronage," *New York Times*, June 21, 2012.
13 Sarah Lazare, "What Won't This Private Prison Corporation Do to Turn a Profit?" *Common Dreams*, February 13, 2014, at commondreams.org.
14 "End Mass Incarceration Now," *New York Times*, May 24, 2014.
15 Glen Ford, "Private Prison Corporations Are Modern Day Slave Traders," Alternet, April 29, 2012, at alternet.org.
16 Sarah Seltzer, "For Profit Company Oversaw Davis Execution," Alternet, September 22, 2011, at alternet.org.

17 Azadeh Shahshahani, "Georgia Teams Up with ICE to Target Latinos," Al-Jazeera America, August 8, 2014.

18 "Profiting from the Poor," Law Office of the South Center for Human Rights, 2008.

19 "Profiting from Probation," Human Rights Watch, 2014, at hrw.org.

20 Sarah Stillman, "Get Out of Jail Inc.," *New Yorker*, June 23, 2014.

21 Cindy Chang, "Louisiana Is the World's Prison Capital," *Times-Picayune*, May 13, 2012.

22 Richard A. Oppel, Jr., "Private Prisons Found to Offer Little in Savings," *New York Times*, May 18, 2011.

23 Renee Lewis, "US Prisons Home to 10 Times More Mentally Ill than State Hospitals," Al Jazeera America, April 8, 2014.

24 Abby Haglage, "US Prisons Becoming De Facto Home of the Mentally Ill," *Daily Beast*, April 10, 2014, at thedailybeast.com.

25 Laura Sullivan, "Shaping State Laws with Little Scrutiny," NPR, October 29, 2010, at npr.org.

26 Laura Sullivan, "Prison Economics Help Drive Arizona Immigration Law," NPR, October 28, 2010, at npr.org.

27 Suevon Lee, "By the Numbers: The US's Growing For-Profit Detention Industry," ProPublica June 20, 2012 at propublica.com.

28 Paul Ashton and Amanda Petteruti, *Gaming the System: How the Political Strategies of Private Prison Companies Promote Ineffective Incarceration Policies* (Washington, DC: Justice Policy Institute, 2011).

29 "Private prison companies want you locked up," Justice Policy Institute, June 22, 2011.

30 Rania Khalek, "The Shocking Ways the Corporate Prison Industry Games the System," Alternet, November 29, 2011, at alternet.org.

31 Lael Henterly, "Gates Foundation Resists Pressure to Pull Private Prison Investment," *Seattle Globalist*, May 8, 2014.

32 Shane Bauer, "The Making of the Warrior Cop," *Mother Jones*, October 23, 2014, at motherjones.com.

33 Shane Bauer, "Solitary in Iran Nearly Broke Me. Then I Went Inside America's Prisons," *Mother Jones*, November/December 2012.

34 Dana Liebelson, "This Is What Happens When We Lock Children in Solitary Confinement," *Mother Jones*, January/February 2015.

35 "The Deportation Dilemma: Reconciling Tough and Humane Enforcement," Migration Policy Institute, April 2014, at migrationpolicy.org.

36 Ginger Thompson and Sarah Cohen, "More Deportations Follow Minor Crimes, Records Show," *New York Times*, April 6, 2014.

37 Ted Robbins, "US Grows an Industrial Complex Along the Border," NPR, September 12, 2012, at npr.org.

38 Steve Fraser and Joshua B. Freeman, "Locking Down an American Workforce," *TomDispatch*, April 19, 2012, at tomdispatch.com.

39 Chris Hedges, "Food Behind Bars Isn't Fit for a Dog," Truthdig, December 22, 2013, at truthdig.com.

40 "Living in the Shadows: Detention Centers Deaths Raise Immigrant Rights Questions," New America Media, February 19, 2014, at newamericamedia.org.

41 Jamie McGee, "CCA Denounces Shareholder Resolution on Re-Entry Programs," *Tennessean*, January 12, 2015.

42 Taylor Woffard, "The Operators of America's Largest Immigration Detention Center Have a History of Inmate Abuse," *Newsweek*, December 20, 2014.

43 Maria Sacchetti and Milton J. Valencia, "Courts Inside Prisons, Far from Public View," *Boston Globe*, December 11, 2012.

44 Aaron Cantu, "How US Private Prisons Are Making Millions by Jailing Migrants in Deplorable Conditions," Alternet, June 11, 2014, at alternet.org.

45 Priscila Mosqueda and Forrest Wilder, "Immigrants in Federal Prisons 'Subjected to Shocking Abuse and Mistreatment,'" *Texas Observer*, June 9, 2014.

46 Wil S. Hylton, "The Shame of America's Family Detention Camps," *New York Times*, February 4, 2015.

47 Zoe Carpenter, "Who Profits from Plans to Lock Up More Immigrant Families? Private Prison Companies," *Nation*, September 30, 2014.

48 "Advocates Slam ICE Plans to Open New Family Detention Facility in Dilley, Texas," Detention Watch Network, press release, November 18, 2014.

49 Dan Beeton, "The Legacy Children of the Honduran Coup," Al Jazeera America, June 28, 2014.

50 "Detention Must Be Paid," *New York Times*, January 20, 2014.

51 "Prisoners of Profit: Immigrants and Detention in Georgia," ACLU Georgia, 2012.

6   *The United Kingdom*

1 James Meek, "Where Will We Live?" *London Review of Books*, January 9, 2014.

2 "Asylum Seekers Put Up in Four-Star Hotels Because of Shortage of Beds in Specialist Hostels," *Daily Mail*, May 17, 2014.

3 George Monbiot, *Captive State: The Corporate Takeover of Britain* (London: Macmillan, 2000), pp 3–4.

4 George Monbiot, "The Gift of Death," *Guardian*, December 11, 2012.

5 Rupert Neate, "Undervaluing Royal Mail Shares Cost Taxpayers 750 Million Pounds in One Day," *Guardian*, April 1, 2014.

6 Guy Bentley, "Lord Myners Report: Here's Why the Royal Mail Sale Wasn't Done on the Cheap," *City AM*, December 18, 2014.

7 Niall Ferguson, "Sales of the Century to Balance the Books," *Daily Beast*, February 21, 2011, at thedailybeast.com.

8 Despite the constant propaganda for privatization, the financial facts challenge the benefits of selling public assets, including the addictive mantra that a crisis should never be wasted. Bob Walker and Betty Con Walker, "Privatisations: Governments Have Distorted Financial Facts," *Dissent*, Autumn/Winter 2010. For example, a report by Australian economist Dr. Nicholas Gruen found that keeping toll roads in public hands benefited the taxpayer much more than if they were sold to or run by the private sector. "Toll Roads Better in Public Hands," ABC Radio's *AM*, November 15, 2010.

9 Mark King, "Wage Inequality Rises Across the UK," *Guardian*, November 7, 2012.

10 Randeep Ramesh, "Increasing Numbers of Working People Live in Poverty, Report Finds," *Guardian*, November 26, 2012.

11 Steve Morris, "Poverty Hits Twice as Many British Households as 30 Years Ago," *Guardian*, June 19, 2014.

12 Aditya Chakrabortty, "Ghost Jobs, Half Lives: How Agency Workers 'Get By' in Britain's Shadow Economy," *Guardian*, January 20, 2015.

13 Interview with Noam Chomsky: "The United States Has Essentially a One-Party System," *Spiegel Online International*, October 10, 2008.

14 Tom Clark, "Poll Shows Doom and Gloom for Decades as Citizens Fear for Living Standards," *Guardian*, April 15, 2013.

15 James Meek, *Private Island: Why Britain Now Belongs to Someone Else* (London: Verso, 2014), p. 14.

16 Ibid., pp. 16, 19.

17 Rupert Neate, "German Executive Pay Overtakes Britain's for the First Time," *Guardian*, January 6, 2015.

18 David Taylor Smith, head of G4S for the UK and Britain, predicted in 2012 that large parts of the British policing service would be privatized by

2017. Matthew Taylor and Alan Travis, "G4S Chief Predicts Mass Police Privatisation," *Guardian*, June 20, 2012.

19 British human rights group Reprieve reported the G4S contract at Guantánamo to police, alleging that the company could be financially liable for profiteering from abuses at the facility. Chris Green, "Exclusive: Activists Report Security Company G4S to Police over Its 'Illegal' Work at Guantánamo Bay," *Independent*, January 12, 2015.

20 In 2013 Labour's shadow justice secretary, Sadiq Khan MP, slammed Serco and G4S, called for extending freedom of information legislation to include the private sector, and argued: "We cannot afford to be so reliant on the same few corporations."

21 Shiar Youssef, "Capita Company Profile," Corporate Watch, 2014, at corporatewatch.org.

22 Felicity Morse, "Anti-Racism Campaigner and Immigration Caseworker Sent 'Go Home' Messages by Home Office," *Independent*, October 17, 2013.

23 Oliver Wright, "'We Need More Wars': Head of Controversial Private Outsourcing Firm Blames Lack of Conflict for Spectacular Collapse in Army Recruitment since It Took Charge," *Independent*, November 21, 2013.

24 The G4S theme song includes lines such as: "G4S! Protecting the world. G4S! So dreams can unfurl."

25 Andrew Hill and Gill Plimmer, "G4S: The Inside Story," *Financial Times*, November 14, 2013.

26 "The Shadow State: A Report about Outsourcing of Public Services," Social Enterprise UK, December 2012, at socialenterprise.org.uk.

27 Larry Elliott, "Britain's Five Richest Families Worth More than Poorest 20%," *Guardian*, March 17, 2014.

28 Paul Krugman, "The Austerity Agenda," *New York Times*, May 31, 2012.

29 Nigel Morris, "The Poorest Pay the Price of Austerity: Workers Face Biggest Fall in Living Standards since Victorian Era," *Independent*, December 9, 2013.

30 Tom McTague, "David Cameron Calls for Capitalism Lessons in Schools to Celebrate Profits in the Classroom," *Mirror*, November 11, 2013.

31 Rajeev Syal and Alan Travis, "Britain's Immigration System in Chaos, MPs' Report Reveals," *Guardian*, October 29, 2014.

32 Randeep Ramesh, "Hundreds of Contracts Signed in 'Biggest Ever Act of NHS Privatisation,'" *Guardian*, October 3, 2012.

33 Charlie Cooper, "NHS Funding Crisis: Boss Warns of 75 Pounds a Night Charge for Hospital Bed," *Independent*, October 7, 2014.

34 Benedict Cooper, "The NHS Privatisation Experiment Is Unravelling Before Our Eyes," *New Statesman*, January 9, 2015.

35 "'People Will Die'—The End of the NHS. Part 1: The Corporate Assault," Media Lens, April 23, 2012, at medialens.org.

36 Charlie Cooper, "International Arms Firm Lockheed Martin in the Frame for One Billion Pound NHS Contract," *Independent*, November 19, 2014.

37 John Pilger, "The Party Game Is Over. Stand and Fight," *New Statesman*, November 4, 2010.

38 Emma de Vita, "'Failure Is Never an Option'—Ruby McGregor-Smith, CEO of Mitie," *Management Today*, July 1, 2014.

39 Clare Sambrook, "Fail and Prosper: How Privatisation Really Works," Open Democracy, March 6, 2014, at opendemocracy.net.

40 Phil Miller, "'Care & Custody': Mitie's Detention Centre Contracts," Corporate Watch, September 1, 2014, at corporatewatch.org.

41 Jamie Doward, "Children 'Kept from Parents' at Centre for Failed Asylum Seekers," *Guardian*, April 27, 2014.

42 "HM Inspector of Prisons Exposes Deputy Prime Minister's Fabrication to have Ended Detention of Children," Medical Justice, October 25, 2012, at medicaljustice.org.uk.

43 Karen McVeigh, "Pregnant Woman at Yarl's Wood Denied Hospital Scan Despite Baby Scare," *Guardian*, October 8, 2010.

44 Simon Cox, "Whistleblower's Concerns over Safety at Yarl's Wood," BBC Radio 4, *File on 4*, June 24, 2014.

45 Mark Townsend, "Serco, the Observer and a Hunt for the Truth about Yarl's Wood Asylum Centre," *Guardian*, May 18, 2014.

46 Karen McVeigh, "Yarl's Wood Detainees 'Paid 50p an Hour,'" *Guardian*, January 3, 2011.

47 Phil Miller, "True Scale of Captive Migrant Labour Revealed," Corporate Watch, August 22, 2014; Phil Miller, "Detained Migrants Slam Low Pay," Corporate Watch, December 22, 2014, both at corporatewatch.org.

48 "Mental Health in Immigration Detention Action Group: Initial Report," Medical Justice, press release, December 17, 2013, at medicaljustice.org.uk.

49 "Detained and Denied: The Clinical Care of Immigration Detainees Living with HIV," Medical Justice, press release, March 22, 2011, at medicaljustice.org.uk.

50 "Expecting Change: The Case for Ending the Detention of Pregnant

Women," Medical Justice, press release, July 23, 2013, at medicaljustice. org.uk.

51 "'The Second Torture': The Immigration Detention of Torture Survivors," Medical Justice, press release, May 22, 2012, at medicaljustice. org.uk.

52 Haroon Siddique, "G4S Ordered to Pay 6,000 Pounds to Elderly Disabled Man over Hospital Handcuffs," *Guardian*, September 25, 2014.

53 Rajeev Syal and Solomon Hughes, "New 'Revolving Door' Row as G4S Hires Ex-Mandarins," *Guardian*, December 26, 2010.

54 Paul Lewis and Matthew Taylor, "G4S Security Firm Was Warned of Lethal Risk to Refused Asylum Seekers," *Guardian*, February 8, 2011.

55 Owen Bowcott, Paul Lewis, and Matthew Taylor, "G4S Security Guards Accused over Restraint of Colombian Deportee," *Guardian*, October 21, 2010; Robert Verkaik, "A Disturbing Insight into G4S's Tactics," *Independent*, October 30, 2010.

56 Robert Booth and Matthew Taylor, "Jimmy Mubenga's Widow Shocked as Security Guards Cleared of Manslaughter," *Guardian*, December 17, 2014.

57 Simon Hattenstone and Eric Allison, "G4S, the Company with No Convictions—But Does It Have Blood on Its Hands?" *Guardian*, December 23, 2014.

58 Avan Judd Stallard, "Welcome to Curtin," *Overland* 214 (Autumn 2014), at overland.org.

59 Frances Webber, "The Jimmy Mubenga Case Exposed a Racist System in Denial," *Guardian*, December 20, 2014.

60 Guy Grandjean, Matthew Taylor, and Paul Lewis, "Deportation Contractor Reliance Faces Litany of Abuse Claims Against Staff," *Guardian*, April 13, 2012.

61 "Outsourcing Abuse: The Use and Misuse of State-Sanctioned Force During the Detention and Removal of Asylum Seekers," Medical Justice, 2008, at medicaljustice.org.uk.

62 Phil Miller, "Majestic Deportations?" Institute of Race Relations, April 10, 2014. "UK: Ill-Trained, Dangerous and Unaccountable, Amnesty Calls for Complete Overhaul of Enforced Removals by Private Security Companies," Amnesty International, press release, July 7, 2011.

63 Robert Verkaik and Chris Green, "Failed Asylum Seekers Are Abused by Private Security Companies, Says Report," *Independent*, July 14, 2008.

64 Amelia Gentleman, "Rising Unemployment Puts Cameron's Work Program in the Spotlight," *Guardian*, February 1, 2012.

65 Ibid.

66 Patrick Butler, "Benefits Sanctions: They're Absurd and Don't Work Very Well, Experts Tell MPs," *Guardian*, January 9, 2015.

67 John Grayson, "Enquiry into Asylum," House of Commons, Home Affairs Committee report, June 17, 2013.

68 Oliver Wright, "Record Number of Prison Deaths 'Due to Cuts and Overcrowding,'" *Independent*, October 31, 2014.

69 "Child Detained for Two Months 'By Mistake' at Mitie Center," Corporate Watch, February 3, 2015, at corporatewatch.org.

70 Miriam Ross, "UK 'Aid' Is Financing a Corporate Scramble for Africa," *Ecologist*, April 3, 2014.

71 Paul Mason, "The Best of Capitalism Is Over for Rich Countries—and for the Poor Ones It Will Be Over by 2060," *Guardian*, July 8, 2014.

72 Russell Brand, "New Era 4 All," December 22, 2014, at russellbrand.com.

7 Australia

1 When I visited Christmas Island, the local publication *The Islander* published a front-page feature on how to navigate around the animals: "A broom or grass rake is ideal for moving crabs from in front of the vehicle." The stapled pages are otherwise filled with information about the cinema club, TV highlights for the week, and "tips for coping with the anniversary of the SIEV 221 boat tragedy."

2 Paige Taylor, "Christmas Island Miners on Indefinite Strike over Pay," *Australian*, November 4, 2011. One of the few Australian journalists pursuing the reality of detention centers is the *Australian*'s Paige Taylor. Her many reports, involving visits to Christmas Island and other detention center sites, offer rare insights into these privatized facilities. When we met in Perth in late 2011, she told me that her editors in Sydney were mostly willing to allow and fund her to investigate these stories, despite the editorial line of the Murdoch-run paper being in support of outsourcing.

3 I have obtained access to the minutes of a Christmas Island Community Reference Group meeting in November 2012, which gathered together senior DIAC managers and a range of Christmas Island officials. The committee admitted that DIAC had left "an enormous footprint … and has simply squeezed the life out of the island and its tourism." At any one time, there are between 500 and 600 FIFO workers on Christmas

Island who are employed by Serco, DIAC, the Australian Federal Police, customs and private medical contractor International Health and Medical Services.

4 An expert in international law at the Australian National University, Jean-Pierre Fonteyne, told the ABC in 2002: "You can't sign a [refugee convention] treaty and then subsequently turn around and decide it won't apply to part of your territory." The prime minister at the time, John Howard, said: "We have good reason for wanting to excise these further islands, and Labor shilly-shallying and ducking and shoving shows that it is weak on border protection."

5 Philip Dorling, "Australians Want Boat Arrivals Treated More Harshly: Poll," *The Age*, January 8, 2014.

6 Inga Ting and Conrad Walters, "Asylum Seekers Languishing in Detention," *Sydney Morning Herald*, May 5, 2014.

7 Fiona Harari, "The Forgotten Isle," *Good Weekend*, August 28, 2014.

8 Oliver Laughland, "Trauma, Segregation, Isolation: Christmas Island, the Tropical Outpost Where Asylum Seekers Are Held against Their Will," *Guardian*, October 13, 2014.

9 Missed in much of the rhetoric around "stopping the boats" was the myopia of the campaign. Although virtually no boats arrived on Australian shores at the time of writing in 2015, countless asylum seekers still died at sea in the Asia-Pacific region and globally. Australia's harsh policy was all about domestic political consumption rather than contributing to a reduction of the ever-growing number of refugees fleeing from conflict. Canberra made deals with Malaysia, Myanmar, Sri Lanka, and other states to "boost immigration and border control," a euphemism for preventing people from fleeing persecution. Ben Doherty, "'Stopping the Boats' a Fiction as Australia Grows Even More Isolationist on Asylum," *Guardian*, December 31, 2014.

10 Ben Doherty, "Senate Gives Scott Morrison Unchecked Control over Asylum Seekers' Lives," *Guardian*, December 5, 2014.

11 Paige Taylor, "Locals Paid $4 an Hour at Nauruan Detention Centre," *Australian*, October 30, 2012. Conditions on Manus Island were revealed in early 2013 to be ugly, with refugees sleeping outside in the searing heat without protection from malaria, and exposed to poor sanitary conditions. Bianca Hall, "Life on Manus Island: Disease, Heat and Suffering," *The Age*, January 5, 2013.

12 Jamie Walker, "ALP Asylum Solution Built to Last," *Australian*, February 2–3, 2013.

13 Sarah Whyte and Michael Gordon, "Sexual Abuse, Rape Threats Alleged by Nauru Asylum Seekers," *Sydney Morning Herald*, September 30, 2014.

14 Georgina Wilkins, "Don't Do It: Plea from Survivor," *The Age*, August 15, 2012.

15 Jo Chandler, "Welcome to Manus, the Island That Has Been Changed Forever by Australian Asylum Seekers," *Guardian*, December 16, 2014.

16 Ben Doherty, "Transfield Immigration Staff Told They Can Be Fired for Using Facebook," *Guardian*, April 7, 2015.

17 Lauren Wilson and Lanai Vasek, "Bowen Confirms Detention Blowout," *Australian*, May 5, 2011.

18 David Marr, "The Indian Ocean Solution: Christmas Island," *Monthly*, September 2009.

19 Peter Mares, "Private Detention Centres Reap Mammoth Profits," ABC Radio's *PM*, November 23, 2000.

20 Susannah Moran, "Detention Contractor Returns Record Profit," *Australian*, May 23, 2012.

21 Michael West, "It Costs More to House a Detainee on Manus Island for a Day than a Night at 5-star Sydney Hotel," *The Age*, June 5, 2014.

22 Sonia Kohlbacher and Paige Taylor, "Deal Signed for Manus Upgrade," *Australian*, September 8, 2014.

23 Ben Butler and Georgia Wilkins, "Big Bills and Tax Havens: The Business of Immigration Detention," *The Age*, February 28, 2014.

24 Nick Evershed, "Mandatory Immigration Detention Is a Billion-Dollar Business—Analysis," *Guardian*, August 25, 2014.

25 Soon after Transfield secured the $1.2 billion contract to run Nauru and Manus Island, the company's head of the legal and risk division, Kate Munnings, told the *Australian* that asylum seekers must be "provided for in a way that's humane and respectful." She then went on to explain that a relative of hers had fled the Nazis, and therefore she understood the need to protect the vulnerable. Abuses continued long after Transfield started running the centers. Steve Waterson, "Detention Centre Boss Vows to Bring a Caring Touch," *Australian*, March 29–30, 2014.

26 Anthony Deceglie, "Security Guard Exposes 'Horrendous' Conditions at Manus Island Detention Centre," *Perth Now*, April 12, 2014.

27 Ben Doherty and Nick Evershed, "Manus Island Asylum Seekers Put in Solitary Confinement at a Rate of Three a Week," *Guardian*, December 12, 2014.

28 Nina Bernstein, "Companies Use Immigration Crackdown to Turn a Profit," *New York Times*, September 28, 2011.

29 Ibid.

30 Amy Wilson-Chapman, "Serco Boss David Campbell Defends 'Secret Group,'" *Perth Now*, October 29, 2011. The media's relationship with Serco can be contradictory. Despite the Murdoch press backing privatized detention, in 2011, Sydney's *Daily Telegraph* described how Campbell lived in a $2.5 million apartment in an expensive part of Sydney. The paper was apparently upset that Serco was getting increasing amounts of money from the federal government for running the detention facilities: "The only boat people Mr Campbell is likely to see at his McMahon's Point pad are the yachtie and motor cruiser set, with eight marina berths exclusively used by residents." But none of these excesses made the paper question the outsourcing that had enabled them. Nick Tabakoff, "Detention Centre Boss David Campbell Lives in Luxury," *Daily Telegraph* (Sydney), May 25, 2011.

31 Antony Loewenstein, Paul Farrell, and Marni Cordell, "Our Contract with Serco: No Audit Requirement for Serco and Serco Hires Untrained Guards," *New Matilda*, November 9, 2011, newmatilda.com. DIAC restrictions on media access to detention centers remains troubling, with the "privacy" of asylum seekers often given as the reason why mainstream reporters, especially those who appear on TV, must have their footage vetted by officials before broadcast. Paige Taylor, "Privacy or Censorship?" *Australian*, January 4, 2012. Journalist Philip Dorling discovered that DIBP's restrictive media access rules were partly based on the draconian restrictions imposed by the US military on journalists visiting Guantánamo Bay. Philip Dorling, "US Prison Inspired Media Rule," *The Age*, March 14, 2012.

32 Leaked documents from NSA whistleblower Edward Snowden proved that this was a common position for the state in a privatized age; investigative journalists were viewed by the British government as a threat that should be monitored by private corporations contracted by the government.

33 Bernstein, "Companies Use Immigration Crackdown to Turn a Profit."

34 Eileen Baldry, "USA Prison Privateers: Neo-Colonists in a Southern Land," in P. Moyle, ed., *Private Prisons and Police: Recent Australian Trends* (Leichhardt, NSW: Pluto Press Australia, 1994).

35 Abdul Karim Hekmat and Ben Doherty, "Resurgent Taliban Targets Afghan Hazara as Australia Sends Them Back," *Guardian*, December 17, 2014.

36 Paul Farrell, "Australia-Run Asylum Detention Centres See Sharp Rise in Serious Incidents," *Guardian*, January 21, 2015.

37 I have changed the names of most sources in this chapter due to the sensitivity of the material and their request for anonymity.

38 Jewel Topsfield, "Detention Shake-Up Follows Scandals," *The Age*, March 2, 2006.

39 Paul Farrell, "Villawood Asylum Seekers in Solitary for More Than 24 Hours at a Time," *Guardian*, September 10, 2014; Paul Farrell, "Ariak's Life in the Annexe: Six Months in Solitary in Immigration Detention," *Guardian*, September 10, 2014.

40 Oliver Laughland, "Immigration Detention Doctors 'Should Consider Boycott,' Says MJA Article," *Guardian*, September 11, 2014.

41 David Marr and Oliver Laughland, "Australia's Detention Regime Sets Out to Make Asylum Seekers Suffer, Says Chief Immigration Psychiatrist," *Guardian*, August 5, 2014.

42 Paul Farrell and Melissa Davey, "Doctor Max Mehta, on US Child Sex Abuse Charge, Worked on Christmas Island," *Guardian*, November 27, 2014.

43 Jason Om, "Leaked Immigration Document Reveals Disagreements with Detention Centre Doctors," ABC News, December 12, 2014.

44 Chris Vedelago, "Government in Fight Over Refugee Injury Claims," *The Age*, July 10, 2014.

45 Michael Gordon and Sara Whyte, "Asylum Staff Hit by Mental Health Crisis," *The Age*, August 21, 2014.

46 Bianca Hall, "Hell on Nauru Revealed," *The Age*, February 25, 2013.

47 A case in which it did happen was when a senior Serco employee was found to have sent a text message to a former detainee that read: "I miss you." Guards inside the Christmas Island center told the *Australian* that it was an open secret that the two had had a "close association." Paige Taylor, "'I Miss You': Serco Guard Sacked over Text to Refugee," *Australian*, September 28, 2011. But it seems that some seriously inappropriate behavior has remained unpunished. In March 2011, several asylum seekers claimed they were threatened with a cattle prod during a move to Christmas Island from Villawood. DIAC rejected the allegation. Natalie O'Brien, "Guard 'Held Cattle Prod,'" *Sun Herald*, March 13, 2011.

48 In November 2010, Amnesty International released a report into Australia's immigration detention system, which noted that even Serco officials had complained to DIAC about the use of tents on Christmas Island for asylum seekers.

49 At the time of writing, Hayatullah was out of detention and living in an Australian mainland community.

50 Paul Farrell, "Journalists Reporting on Asylum Seekers Referred to Police," *Guardian*, January 22, 2015.

51 Australia and New Zealand are two nations enthusiastically embracing privatization. The *Wall Street Journal* breathlessly reported in late 2013 that "privatization sprees" were turning both countries into attractive investment opportunities for global investors. Gillian Tan, "Privatization Raises Billions in Australia, New Zealand," *Wall Street Journal*, November 5, 2013.

52 Australian Human Rights Commission, *Immigration Detention at Curtin: Observations from Visit to Curtin Immigration Detention Centre and Key Concerns Across the Detention Network*, 2011, at humanrights.gov.au.

53 Ibid.

54 Jonathan Swan, "Malcolm Turnbull Denounces 'Vicious Ingratitude' of Biennale Artists after Transfield Withdraws as Sponsor," *The Age*, March 11, 2014.

Conclusion

1 Arundhati Roy, *Capitalism: A Love Story* (London: Haymarket, 2014), p. 96.

2 Nathan K. Lujan, Devin D. Bloom, and L. Cynthia Watson, "A Rumble in the Jungle," *New York Times*, January 17, 2013.

3 Andrea Germanos, "Naomi Klein, 'Anti-Shock Doctrines' Show the Way to Resist," *Common Dreams*, June 6, 2013.

4 Roy, *Capitalism*, p. 33.

5 The mainstream media rarely talks about individuals or groups that challenge capitalism, but there are exceptions. Economist Richard Wolff told *Democracy Now!* in March 2013 that alternatives to capitalism were being tried around the world, including the Mondragon model in Spain. "Capitalism in Crisis: Richard Wolff Urges End to Austerity, New Jobs Program, Democratising Work," *Democracy Now!*, March 25, 2013.

6 "The *Guardian* View on Taming Corporate Power," *Guardian*, December 13, 2014.

7 Universities across the United States have begun far more aggressively to investigate the reality of capitalism in their courses and to assess the damage it can cause. Jennifer Schuessler, "In History Departments, It's Up With Capitalism," *New York Times*, April 6, 2013.

8 Satyajit Das, *Extreme Money: Masters of the Universe and the Cult of Risk* (Upper Saddle River, NJ: FT Press, 2011), p. 21.

9 Matt Taibbi, *The Divide: American Injustice in the Age of the Wealth Gap* (New York: Spiegel & Grau, 2014), p. xx.

10 Ibid., p. 12.

11 Aditya Chakrabortty, "Outsourced and Unaccountable: This Is the Future of Local Government," *Guardian*, December 16, 2014.

12 Noam Chomsky, "The Responsibility of Intellectuals, Redux," *Boston Review*, September/October 2011.

13 Claire Provost and Matt Kennard, "Hamburg at Forefront of Global Drive to Reverse Privatisation of City Services," *Guardian*, November 12, 2014.

14 Rebecca Solnit, *A Paradise Built in Hell: The Extraordinary Communities that Arise in Disaster* (London: Penguin, 2010), p. 9.

Index

Index